Damien Lewis

SAS

BROTHERS IN ARMS

CHURCHILL'S DESPERADOES: BLOOD-AND-GUTS DEFIANCE AT BRITAIN'S DARKEST HOUR

QUERCUS

First published in Great Britain in 2022 by

QUERCUS

Quercus Editions Ltd
Carmelite House
50 Victoria Embankment
London EC4Y 0DZ

An Hachette UK company

A CIP catalogue record for this book is available
from the British Library

HB ISBN 978 1 52941 378 6
TPB ISBN 978 1 52941 381 6
Ebook ISBN 978 1 52941 379 3

Every effort has been made to contact copyright holders. However, the publishers
will be glad to rectify in future editions any inadvertent omissions brought to their attention.

Picture credits (in order of appearance): 1, 5, 8, 10, 16, 20, 21, 22, 23, 24, 25, 27, 29, 38, 44, 45, 46, 51 – Fiona
Ferguson; 2, 3, 37 – Author's collection; 4, 18, 26 – Imperial War Museum; 6, 7, 9, 11, 12, 34, 35, 39, 40, 41,
42, 43, 50 – John O'Neill; 13 – ptsheritage.com/Doug Peacock; 14, 19 – Margaret Duncan; 15, 17 – © National
Museums of Scotland; 28 – Riggio family; 30, 31, 32, 52 – Gary Hull; 33 – Australian War Memorial; 36, 47 –
Bundesarchiv; 48 – Wikimedia; 49 – National Archives

Map artwork by Bill Donohoe

10 9 8 7 6 5 4 3 2 1

Typeset by CC Book Production
Printed and bound in Great Britain by Clays Ltd, Elcograf S.p.A.

Papers used by Quercus are from well-managed forests and other responsible sources.

For Lt. Col. R. B. Mayne DSO,
The Pilgrim

Lament for No. 11 (Scottish) Commando
(Litani River, June 1941, Syria)

Grey, grey was the sea that we came from;
Dawn was our sorrow, dawn of that day;
Wae, wae for the lads on their lanesome
Under the palms in Litani Bay.

Bitter the fight that they faced in that dawning;
Three score ten their colonel amang them
Went to their rest in the lands of the morning;
Waves of Litani Requiem sang them.

Play, play for them wailing pibroch; play
Lament ayont tears in the moorland rain;
Children of bog moor, mountain mist, sea spray
Dry is their dust in the Syrian plain.

George I. A. Duncan MC

SAS Regimental Song
(sung to the tune of Lili Marlene)

There was a song we always used to hear,
Out in the desert, romantic, soft and clear,
Over the ether, came the strain,
That soft refrain, each night again,
To you, Lili Marlene, to you Lili Marlene.

Check you're in position; see your guns are right,
Wait until the convoy comes creeping through the night,
Now you can pull the trigger, son,
And blow the Hun to Kingdom come,
And Lili Marlene's boyfriend will never see Marlene.

Twenty thousand rounds of trace and ball,
Forty thousand rounds of the stuff that makes 'em fall,
Finish your strafing, drive, drive away,
And live to fight another day,
But Lili Marlene's boyfriend will never see Marlene.

Creeping into Fuka, forty planes ahead,
Belching ammunition, and filling them with lead,
A 'flamer' for you, a grave for Fritz,
He's like his planes, all shot to bits,
And Lili Marlene's boyfriend will never see Marlene.

Afrika Korps has sunk into the dust,
Gone are the Stukas, its Panzers lie in rust,
No more we'll hear that haunting strain,
That soft refrain, each night again,
For Lili Marlene's boyfriend will never see Marlene.

Composed by Lieutenant Colonel Blair 'Paddy' Mayne,
DSO and Three Bars, Légion d'Honneur

Contents

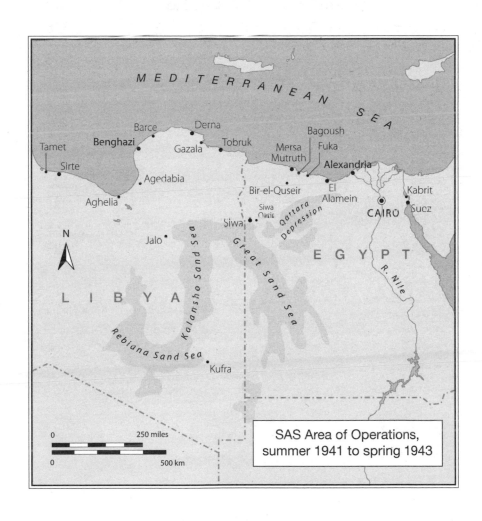

MEDITERRANEAN SEA

Barce • Derna
Benghazi •• Gazala • Tobruk   Bagoush
Tamet •   Mersa   Fuka
• Sirte   Mutruth   Alexandria
        • Agedabia   Bir-el-Quseir   El
Aghelia •   Alamein   Kabrit
    Siwa   Qattara   •
    Oasis   Depression   CAIRO   Suez

Siwa •
Jalo •

N

LIBYA   EGYPT

Kalansho Sand Sea
Great Sand Sea
R. Nile

Rebiana Sand Sea
• Kufra

0   250 miles

0   500 km

SAS Area of Operations,
summer 1941 to spring 1943

Author's Note

There are sadly few survivors from the Second World War operations depicted in these pages. Throughout the period of researching and writing this book I have sought to be in contact with as many as possible, plus surviving family members of those who have passed away. If there are further witnesses to the stories told here who are inclined to come forward, please do get in touch, as I will endeavour to include further recollections of the operations portrayed in this book in future editions.

The time spent by Allied servicemen and women as Special Service volunteers was often traumatic and wreathed in layers of secrecy, and many chose to take their stories to their graves. Memories tend to differ and apparently none more so than those concerning operations behind enemy lines. The written accounts that do exist tend to differ in their detail and timescale, and locations and chronologies are sometimes contradictory. Nevertheless, I have endeavoured to provide an accurate sense of place, timescale and narrative to the story as depicted in these pages.

Where various accounts of a mission appear to be particularly confused, the methodology I have used to reconstruct where, when and how events took place is the 'most likely' scenario. If two or more testimonies or sources point to a particular time or place or sequence of events, I have opted to use that account as most likely.

The above notwithstanding, any mistakes herein are entirely of my own making, and I would be happy to correct any in future editions. Likewise, while I have attempted to locate the copyright holders of the photos, sketches and other images and material used in this book, this has not always been straightforward or easy. Again, I would be happy to correct any mistakes in future editions.

During the period covered in this book the Special Air Service went through various iterations in terms of its official name and identity (L-Detachment, Special Service, SS, Special Raiding Squadron, etc.). These can be confusing, and for ease of reading and comprehension I have tended to stick to the words Special Air Service or SAS to describe the unit portrayed.

To preserve the authenticity of quotations and extracts from primary sources such as diaries, letters, telegrams etc., I have reproduced spelling and grammatical errors as they appear in the original, and mostly without further explanation. Where explanation of specific references in the sources is required, a note is included in square brackets.

The War Chest

Though beloved of Britain's wartime leader, Churchill, this band of elite warriors had never been particularly favoured by the top brass. Accused of forming a private army with distinctly piratical intentions – of being 'cut-throats' and 'raiders of the thug variety' – there were those in power who wanted nothing more than to see them consigned to the dustbin of history. Many among the battle-worn ranks of the SAS realised this, and in the spring of 1945, even as they risked all during the final thrust into Nazi Germany, there were fears that once the war was won, their fortunes were destined to take a drastic downturn.

They were not mistaken. Just a matter of weeks after the final surrender of Germany and Japan, the SAS would be summarily disbanded (apart from a small, top-secret war-criminal-hunting unit, which became known as 'The Secret Hunters'). Of course, all among the ranks of the SAS were volunteers. Upon disbandment, with little fanfare or due process, these men who had served for so long on repeated back-to-back missions behind enemy lines, were returned to their original units. Or, for those who could not face such a fate, they were to be turned loose on Civvy Street to fend for themselves.

A rightfully proud regiment with an unrivalled *esprit de corps*, there were those among the top echelons of the SAS who figured it would be wrong if the short but exalted history of this unit – never mind the sacrifices made by so many, who would never return from blood-drenched foreign fields – were to be forgotten. With that in mind, in mid-April 1945 a column of heavily armed Willys jeeps nosed towards the district of Schneeren, in the north-west of Germany.

Their journey to get there had been long, and fraught with much danger, death and bloodshed . . .

Several days earlier, on 8 April 1945, a long-standing SAS veteran, Lieutenant Johnny Cooper, had been told by his troop commander, Captain Ian Wellsted, to ready their jeeps for a patrol. They were there serving on Operation Archway, as A and D Squadron 1 SAS spearheaded the drive into Germany and the push across the Rhine and Wesser rivers – the culmination of many years at war. There were reports that troops up ahead had run into trouble, where the road cut through a patch of thick, hillocky woodland known as the Grinderwald. Wellsted had been tasked to investigate.

Mounting up their column of jeeps, Wellsted and his men moved cautiously onto the Nienburg–Neustadt road, which ran south-west for a good fifteen miles, enveloped by the dense oak forest and boggy terrain of the Steinhuder Meer, an expanse of impassable terrain crowding in on all sides. This land could hardly have been worse for 'jeeping' operations; driving off-road by stealth was all-but impossible here. The column of eleven Willys jeeps bristled with weaponry – mostly twin-Vickers-K light machineguns, but also the odd .50-calibre Browning, all of which were mounted on pivots. They crept ahead, eyes scanning the thick vegetation for movement or sign of the enemy. Every inch of German territory had been hard and bitterly contested, and this promised to be no different.

Up ahead a British armoured car was halted by the roadside. Wellsted stopped, to check with its commander. The woods to their left-front were thought to be thick with enemy, he warned.

Giving his orders, Wellsted 'led the Troop into battle', some two dozen Vickers-K guns bursting into 'full-throated life', unleashing with a shattering broadside that blazed all down the column of vehicles, until every last gun was blasting away. The wall of vegetation to their left began to 'dance' under the rain of red and white tracer, as it was swept with a storm of rounds. There was not a sniff of answering fire.

Calling the barrage to a halt, Wellsted grabbed his Thompson submachine gun and made for the woods, yelling for all to follow. Bursting through the fringe of trees, he stumbled across a German trooper face-down in a ditch, a *Panzerfaust* – a single-shot German anti-tank weapon – lying beside him. Imagining him to be dead – felled in the Vickers-K onslaught – Wellsted kicked him, only for a trembling individual to rise from the ditch, hands above his head. Leaving him to one of his men, Wellsted dashed further into the woods, spraying the undergrowth with bursts, but even as he did, heavier fire broke out from behind him, plus the roar of *Panzerfausts*.

Amid cries of alarm, Wellsted ordered all to pull out, sensing that they'd stumbled into some kind of ambush. Back on the road Cooper warned him that this was a well-laid trap, as blast after blast of *Panzerfaust* salvoes underscored his words. A first jeep was hit, the vehicle engulfed in a blinding flash and a cloud of roiling smoke. Another crew were blown out of their vehicle by a near-miss. A third jeep's gunner just managed to fell a *Panzerfaust* operator, before he was able to blast them all to hell.

An MG42 opened up, otherwise known as 'Hitler's buzzsaw' due to its fearsome rate of fire, rounds kicking off the road and slamming into vehicles. In a helter-skelter retreat, jeeps began to hurtle back the way they had come, as every weapon available let rip, Wellsted's convoy roaring 'out of the valley of death'. But one jeep, and one of its occupants, failed to get moving. The wrecked vehicle lay where it had been hit, enveloped in thick smoke, the bloody figure of its gunner face down beside it on the tarmac.

The dead man was John 'Taffy' Glyde, a former factory worker who'd long been part of Wellsted's section. Wellsted had got used to Glyde's catchphrase, uttered in his thick Pontypridd accent, whenever an enemy soldier was hit: 'Another one bites the dust.' Sadly, it was Taffy himself who had done so now. As the 1 SAS report would note of the twenty-five-year-old's death: 'German Bazooka [sic] landed about 2 yards from his jeep. His head nearly blown off.'

Wellsted's battered column pulled back to a road intersection. There they halted, as they began to count the cost. Glyde, of course, was dead. Another man was wounded in the upper leg, one other had taken a bullet through the ankle. On balance, they'd got off pretty lightly. They'd also seized two German prisoners. Then someone pointed out that Wellsted himself was hurt. He had blood dripping from his left hand. There was no time to worry about that now. Someone gestured down the road, in the direction from which they had originally come. Distant, grey figures were darting forward, advancing on the British party. In short, there seemed to be enemy before them on the road to Neustadt, and at their rear towards Nienburg.

They were boxed in.

Wellsted ordered a barrage of fire to be unleashed in both directions, as the 'pop-swoosh-bang' of the patrol's 2-inch mortar firing, joined the rip-tear buzz of the Vickers, plus the crack of Bren light machineguns opening up from the ditches that flanked the highway. To one side, a sandy track branched away. It ran south-west and was signposted to 'Schneeren'. Lest anyone might imagine that offered any hope of sanctuary, bursts of heavy fire erupted from that direction. Seconds later a pair of armoured cars hove into view, moving up from Schneeren towards the road. For a moment Wellsted hoped they were friendly, until the nearest opened fire.

A short, sharp duel ensued – the three nearest jeeps letting rip with their .303-inch Vickers-K guns, versus the Germans' 20mm cannons. The armoured cars kept coming, the Vickers rounds ricocheting off their flanks, harmlessly. Finally, they got close enough for those riding in them to start hurling grenades. The first to go down were the two German captives, felled in the crossfire. Then the leading jeep, riddled with fire, was 'shot out from under' its occupants. In the second vehicle, the commander was hit in the thigh. The third jeep was hit, a wounded figure just managing to drag himself beneath it, in a desperate search for cover.

As the Germans closed for the kill, a British armoured car roared into a position from where it could open fire. 'Blam – a shell smashed into the leading German,' Wellsted remarked, of the first strike on the enemy. In short order, some exceptional work by the British gunners, who hailed from 11 Hussars, took care of both enemy targets, the surviving German crew 'tumbling into the low scrub' at the roadside.

Wellsted dashed forward to check on the wounded. The man beneath the rearmost jeep, Trooper Roy Davies, had been shot in the back and was not long for this world, he feared. Even so, Wellsted managed to inject him with a shot of morphine. Davies, an SAS original, had deployed on the unit's first ever mission, the November 1941 North African parachute insertion, codenamed Operation Squatter. Injured during the drop, on which he'd formed part of Irishman Lieutenant Eoin McGonigal's patrol, Davies had been captured and held in various POW camps. In October 1943 he'd managed to escape, rejoining the SAS as soon as possible thereafter.

Before Wellsted was able to do much more for Davies, he was himself hit, for the woods were thick with enemy. The round knocked his legs out from under him and he fell heavily. Badly injured, Wellsted was dragged back towards the road junction by others in his troop. But when they went forward to try to retrieve Davies, Trooper Dougie Ferguson was shot and wounded, and the rest were forced to withdraw. Eventually, Wellsted accepted that it was hopeless to try to rescue any more of the fallen. There was no option but to pull out with whatever vehicles remained.

They were forced to leave behind four comrades. Taffy Glyde had been killed in the initial ambush. Davies would die of his wounds. Ferguson, injured, was captured and likely executed by the enemy in cold blood (to this day his fate remains uncertain). There was also a Trooper James Blakeney, hit in the initial onslaught by the enemy armoured cars, who was also unaccounted for.

Blakeney was another SAS original, who, like Davies, had deployed as part of Lieutenant McGonigal's stick on Operation Squatter. He'd likewise been captured, and had escaped from a POW camp in Italy in the autumn of 1943. Upon hearing of Blakeney's safe return to Britain, 1 SAS's commander, Lieutenant Colonel Blair 'Paddy' Mayne, had made a special point of bringing him back into his regiment; into the SAS family. The SAS's record of Blakeney's death at Schneeren concluded simply: 'Shot through stomach and head.'

Once they had withdrawn from that bullet-scarred road junction, the wounded, including Wellsted, were evacuated to an Advance Dressing Station, where they could be properly treated. As Wellsted was to confess, the battle around Schneeren had represented his single greatest defeat during the war. Four of his men had been killed, five more were seriously wounded, plus a total of four jeeps had been lost, one of which, nicknamed 'Homer', had been captured by the enemy.

In a day or two the padre of 1 SAS, J. Fraser McLuskey, was able to retrieve the bodies of the fallen. They were buried locally after a short and sombre service.

Three weeks later VE Day was declared. The war in Europe was over. A long column of battle-worn jeeps formed up, making their way towards Ostend, in Belgium, to catch a ship bound for

Britain. Wellsted was with them, his wounds having been patched up and bandaged. The spirit of victory was in the air, and the procession was striking to look at, with 'each jeep, battle-scarred and dirty; still flaunting its peculiar individuality'. Some were flying giant swastikas, among an assortment of other symbols of Nazi Germany's demise. All were overloaded with war booty, booze being a favourite. One was piled so high it looked like 'an enormous mobile cat's cradle'. Incredibly, even Homer was there, the SAS jeep captured at Schneeren by the enemy.

Indeed, there was more among that convoy which hailed from Schneeren, than simply the lone liberated jeep. One item in particular would come to have talismanic significance as far as the SAS were concerned. On 12 April 1945, Schneeren and its surroundings had been finally taken, the SAS seizing dozens of prisoners – 'marines attached to the SS' – winkled out of the woods at gunpoint, plus others trying to sneak away dressed as civilians, or even wearing Allied uniforms. Secreted in Schneeren itself – which calls itself the 'place under a thousand oaks' – the SAS discovered a huge, leatherbound volume. Embossed in thick gothic lettering on the cover were the words *CHRONIK der Gemeinde Schneeren, Kreis Neustadt a.Rhge* – Chronicle of the municipality of Schneeren, District of Neustadt in the Rhineland. On its spine was engraved the emblem of Nazi Germany, an eagle with outstretched wings grasping a swastika.

In 1936, the Interior Ministry of the Third Reich had issued an edict that all *Gemeinden* – councils – across Germany should keep such a chronicle, 'in the spirt of our Führer and Chancellor'. One such tome was to be given to each district, to record the history of the municipality 'from its beginnings up to the World War'. There was to be kept a yearly record of all that transpired during the Third Reich, 'in accordance with the wishes of our Führer and Reich Chancellor, Adolf Hitler'. Each *Chronik* was to document district life, from cultural traditions to large political rallies – the kind of things that welded the peoples together as an 'Aryan elite' under the credo of Nazism.

Those war-bitten SAS veterans who had conquered Schneeren decided they would seize the *Chronik*. The battle for that 'place under a thousand oaks' had cost them dear in terms of dead and injured. Even as the conquest of Nazi Germany was in its final, desperate stages, so much blood had been needlessly shed. In return, they were going to steal Schneeren's very identity; its Nazi-era heart and soul. In that spirit, that heavy leather tome – the *Chronik* – was loaded aboard one of the jeeps and whisked away.

Whether those men who took it did so with the intention of using the *Chronik* for its final purpose, remains unclear. Either way, shortly after the SAS was disbanded, in October 1945, the *Chronik* of Schneeren district was eviscerated. The heavy brass studs that held its spine together were removed, the Nazi-era pages taken out, and in their place was assembled a detailed, blow-by-blow account of the SAS at war, from its formation, in the summer of 1941, to disbandment, five years later, and covering all episodes in between. Part official history, part scrapbook, it included scores of official mission reports, orders, strategy documents, maps, photos and biographies of the key players involved, plus a slew of newspaper cuttings from the war years.

Compiling it was a communal effort, but it was Captain Mike Blackman MC (and bar), one of the SAS's intelligence officers, who oversaw the task's completion. Leading the push into Germany, just as he had tended to lead operations ever since the SAS's formation in the summer 1941, Lieutenant Colonel Paddy Mayne had returned to the family home in Northern Ireland, after war's end. The former *Chronik* of Schneeren, now packed full of the most comprehensive and compelling record of the SAS's wartime history, was duly presented to Mayne, after which it was quietly secreted away in the Mayne family home under his personal care.

As all realised, this clandestine record – the SAS's own diary of its Second World War history – was best kept well below the radar for a good long while. If nothing else, this was a unit that had been disbanded and disavowed by many on high, though not by Winston Churchill, of course. Voted out of power in July 1945, Churchill would become the first patron of the SAS Regimental Association, of which David Stirling, the SAS's founder, and Blair Mayne, among others, served as its chief luminaries.

Decades later, long after the tragic death of Mayne, in 1955 – aged just forty, in a car accident – what had become known to the few who were aware of its existence as the 'Paddy Mayne Diary' emerged from the shadows. The SAS had long been resuscitated, for the realities of modern warfare called for a unit such as this, and by then its security was beyond all doubt, its profile firmly established in the public eye. The diary was offered to the SAS Regimental Association by Mayne's younger brother, Douglas. In that way, and renamed the *SAS War Diary*, the precious founding history of this legendary unit was preserved for posterity.

Several years ago I was invited to visit the home of Fiona Ferguson and her husband, Norman. Fiona (née Mayne) is one of Colonel Blair Mayne's nieces, and she had become the keeper of the flame, safeguarding the Mayne family archive and wartime memorabilia long after her uncle had passed away. In her Northern Ireland home I was able to see and to study at first hand not only the gutted skeleton of the original *Chronik*, in all its glory, and what had taken its place, but also Colonel Mayne's war chests, plus the heaps of other wartime mementoes – those that he had brought back to Ireland, after five years of waging war across two continents. Needless to say, they constituted a precious hoard of SAS wartime history.

The original massive pages of the *Chronik* were there, each a sheet of thick, heavy parchment embossed in broad, dark Gothic script, and separated by a thin layer of protective gossamer-like paper lying between. I was shown where Mayne's war chest and the diary had been kept safe, in the dark, labyrinthine cellars and tunnels of the Mayne family's Mount Pleasant home. As I sifted through the contents of the war chest and related materials, I found a treasure trove of wartime letters, official reports, photos (Mayne was a prolific photographer), undeveloped films, plus countless other original artefacts, including some of the material that had been loaded aboard that convoy of jeeps at Schneeren, and which had sailed from Ostend to Britain in May '45.

Simply incredible.

This book is based in part upon that rich trove of materials, generously and freely offered, in the spirit that this story might be written. To tell it has been a privilege and an honour.

Damien Lewis
Dorset, June 2022

CHAPTER ONE

The Cauldron

The ghostly silhouette of HMS *Glenroy* glided through the darkness, on all sides a chill and dank mist blanketing the surface of the sea. On her deck, some five hundred men from one of the finest fighting units in the entire British Army readied themselves for battle. As they loaded up with assault equipment, weaponry, ammo, grenades, communications kit, plus rations and water, they hoped and prayed that this time it really was for real – for their present mission had been plagued by dither, indecision and cancellations.

Sadly, those tendencies – an inability to deploy and to utilise this intensively trained, iron-willed unit – had dogged its every step, ever since formation almost a year earlier, in Scotland, when scores of men had stepped forward to answer Winston Churchill's call for volunteers for 'Special Service', undertaking hazardous duties. Much that they had hungered to pit themselves against a seemingly omnipotent enemy, months of on-again-off-again abortive missions had followed, interspersed with mind-numbing garrison duties.

The present undertaking – Operation Exporter – was supposedly the moment all had been longing for: their much-anticipated baptism of fire. But twenty-four hours earlier the *Glenroy* had steered this very course and cleaved these very waters, the slab-sided converted merchant ship, grey hull streaked with black,

1

creeping ever closer to enemy shores. Forming part of a carefully timed, multi-layered June 1941 assault – the first combined operation undertaken by the Allies in the Second World War, one utilising sea, land and air forces – those aboard the *Glenroy* were to form the spearhead, supposedly taking their adversaries by complete surprise. Striking well behind the lines in a series of lightning thrusts designed to seize vital targets – key bridges, roads and gun-emplacements – they would enable the main force, advancing overland, to surge forwards, unmenaced and unhindered.

That, at least, was the plan.

It hadn't quite worked out that way.

The men of the superlative – some would argue, incomparable – No. 11 (Scottish) Commando had wound themselves up to a fever pitch, only to face the bitter disappointment of a last-minute cancellation. Already, they had boarded the Assault Landing Crafts (ALCs), when the naval officer in command of the *Glenroy* had judged that the seas were just too rough to risk making an approach, fearing that the assault boats would get swamped and the commandos drowned en masse. Recalled to the mothership, that eleventh hour let-down had been a bitter pill to swallow.

There were more reasons to want to get off the *Glenroy* than simply a burning desire for action. Originally a cargo vessel of the Glen Line sailing between Britain and the Far East, she had been converted for wartime duties by having her holds partitioned into rough-and-ready billets, and her decks fitted out with an array of guns, plus cranes and derricks to lower landing craft into the sea. But the bulky fittings and weighty cargo made the *Glenroy* top-heavy, with the result that she rolled horribly in even a slight swell, with sickening consequences for those billeted in the makeshift quarters below.

Yet instead of speeding their way towards an enemy coastline shrouded in darkness, the assault force had been thwarted. The commandos had reboarded the *Glenroy* amid pitching seas, after which she had turned away from the shoreline and ploughed her ungainly passage back to Cyprus, the base from which they had originally set sail. Upon arrival, the cancellation order had itself been promptly rescinded, and the *Glenroy* was turned right around again, with instructions that the men of No. 11 Commando were to be landed, no ifs or buts, and come hell or high water.

Those twenty-four-hours of dither and the resulting loss of surprise – the forewarning of the enemy, for the *Glenroy* had been spotted in the faint light of early morning – would have near-catastrophic consequences. Only a fraction of the hundreds of warriors crammed aboard the ship would be fortunate enough to escape death, injury or captivity in the hours to come. In a paroxysm of bitter combat and close-quarter fighting, this iconic unit would face a bloody and bruising baptism of fire. But all of that lay some hours in the future. Right now, at 0300 on 9 June 1941, these elite warriors wanted nothing more than to slip into the night and to hit the enemy like a whirlwind.

For many aboard the *Glenroy*, the reality of the coming battles would be forever seared into their minds. One, Captain George Ian Alastair Duncan, would never speak to his family of his wartime experiences. But he would write haunting, nerve-jangling verse, as he struggled to capture the hell and the shock of hitting the shoreline neck-deep in water (amidst the rush and confusion no one had thought to properly check the beaches for depth and gradient); of the churning, violent surf which had soaked everything in seawater, putting every single one of the commandos' radios out of action, rendering all means of communications impossible; of the horror of making landfall facing ranks of gaping gun-barrels manned by an enemy who knew they were coming:

3

Thud, thud of engines –
Swish of bow wave – Black night . . .
Long, steely grey landing craft inrushing . . .
Silence,
Save for tight breathing . . .
Swoosh-crump.
Forward-run-stumble-stagger . . .
Smack-Crack-Smack-Crack-trt-tat-tat –
Men falling – bare sand –
Men falling – falling . . .

One of the first to step into the *Glenroy*'s landing craft that 9 June morning – leading from the front, as always – was an iconic figure, distinguished by an intense physicality combined with a seeming preternatural calm. Standing six-feet-two-inches tall and built like the powerful rugby player that he was, Lieutenant Robert Blair Mayne was blessed with a shock of sandy hair above laughing, slightly mocking grey-blue eyes. Though he was only twenty-six years old, Mayne was a comparative veteran in No. 11 Commando, for the average age of the officers was just twenty-one. Working as a qualified solicitor before the war, he'd earned a towering reputation as a world-class sportsman – he was the 1936 Irish Universities heavyweight boxing champion, and a rugby player of international acclaim. Selected multiple times for both the Irish team and the British Lions, his 'quiet, almost ruthless efficiency' on the field, combined with his ability to play on through injury had won him high praise.

By contrast to the field of sports, his initial forays into the British military had earned a cutting, withering rebuke. In 1938, with the clouds of war gathering, Mayne had volunteered for the Officer Training Corps at Queen's University, Belfast, where he'd studied law. But he simply couldn't abide drill and mindless square-bashing, and in short order the Queen's training

4

officer had concluded that he was 'unpromising material for a combat regiment, undisciplined, unruly and generally unreliable'. Fortunately, the founder of No. 11 Commando had seen something quite different in Mayne's spirited, somewhat irregular approach to soldiering. Indeed, those very 'unruly' qualities – recast as self-possession, independence and initiative – were just the kind of things valued in the commandos, Churchill's much-vaunted 'butcher and bolt' raiders.

Oddly perhaps, for a figure with such a tough reputation on the sporting field and in the boxing ring, Mayne was rarely to be seen without a book close to hand, more often than not a collection of works by his favourite poets – James Elroy Flecker, Omar Khayyam and Siegfried Sassoon. Indeed, he'd been something of a shy child, his head forever stuck in novels. As his physique had matured he'd earned the reputation at school of being a gentle giant. For sure, Mayne was a complex, multi-faceted character. And no matter his sporting prowess, as with so many aboard the *Glenroy*, today was to be his first taste of combat, leading his men into the teeth of battle and fearful that many would not live to see another dawn.

This would be Mayne's baptism of fire. His testing.

As a natural marksman of great physical prowess – Mayne liked to wield a Bren light machinegun from the shoulder, as if it were a rifle – he had been appointed the weapons instructor of No. 11 Commando. He shared that duty with another young recruit and crack shot, who likewise was commanding a troop of heavily laden commandos that June morning. Fellow Irishman Lieutenant Eoin (pronounced 'Ian') McGonigal was dark-haired, dark-eyed, strikingly handsome, whippet-fit and fleet of foot. Though he was six years Mayne's junior, they had struck up a close friendship, one forged in and around the rugby fields of Belfast, at Queen's University's various bars, and absolutely irrevocably when they had decided to volunteer for No. 11 Commando, hungering for action.

5

On paper, their camaraderie appeared all the more remarkable in that McGonigal was a southern Irish Catholic, and Mayne was a Northern Irish Protestant. But frankly, neither man put much store in niggling sectarianism, especially when there was a war to be fought, and particularly when that war was going so very badly for Great Britain, then the only world power still standing against the fire and vitriol and the blitzkrieg emanating from Berlin. On many levels the two friends were strikingly different – 'like chalk and cheese', as a fellow soldier would remark. But what united them was their fierce, fiery, rebellious spirit, and their determination to fight the Nazi onslaught, no matter the odds.

McGonigal had the charm of the southern Irish and his taste in ladies was more for blondes, while Mayne favoured the raven-headed look. McGonigal's foremost sporting talents lay in both rugby and cricket, while Mayne dominated the rugby field. A teller of 'tall tales' and blessed with the gift of the gab, McGonigal's garrulousness contrasted sharply with Mayne's quieter, contemplative, still-waters-run-deep mien. Despite being considerably younger, McGonigal 'was far more eloquent', remarked Sergeant Joe Welch, a future elite forces comrade, 'whereas Paddy was more like Ares, the Greek God of War. It was a dangerous combination. Eoin could talk them into all sorts of trouble, and Paddy could get them out of it. A perfect friendship.'

There was one other compelling element that fused the two Irishmen together. McGonigal knew how to handle Mayne in his cups. Known as a soft-spoken and courteous figure when not on the field of battle – or sports – Mayne's chief weakness was drink. Realising this, McGonigal was perfectly prepared to take no prisoners. While training on the Island of Arran with No. 11 Commando, the two men had shared a billet at Lamlash, a village on the island's eastern shore. It was a wild existence on a wild part of Scotland's west coast, the relentless training distinguished by punishing route marches no matter what the weather – driving rain and sleet mostly seeming the norm – topped off by regular plunges off the Lamlash pier in full kit at night, to swim back to shore.

Mayne and McGonigal alighted upon a novel means to kindle a fire and to warm frozen limbs and to dry sodden clothes, after a pier-dunking: 'The coal is in very large lumps,' Mayne would write, in a letter home. 'To split it we just fire a revolver shot into it; it cracks it wonderfully.'

Likewise, on the occasion when Mayne had been drinking and threatened to get out of hand, McGonigal would simply turn a pistol on him. 'I'll shoot you, Blair,' he would threaten. Being the commando's weapons officers, there was never a shortage of live ammunition lying around their digs, nor youthful high spirits for that matter, and the walls of Landour, the private house in which they were billeted, had ended up peppered with bullet holes.

In short, No. 11 Commando's two weapons officers exuded a wild martial spirit and a sense of devil-may-care invincibility that made those under their command – their 'Jocks', as the ranks were known – keen to follow them into the heart of battle. There was another stand-out quality that united the two Irishmen. The *esprit de corps* of No. 11 (Scottish) Commando was defined by the saying: 'Look after your Jocks.' Few had a stronger sense of care or devotion to those under their command than McGonigal and Mayne, and it hadn't gone unnoticed by their men. Yet neither man had actually proven himself in combat, and especially when the odds were very much stacked against them, as they were today.

A third figure within No. 11 Commando had attained a similar steely reputation, but upon first appearance he seemed an unlikely candidate for the archetypal warrior. Lieutenant William 'Bill' Fraser had a strikingly boyish face, protruding ears and doleful eyes, atop a tall, skinny frame that made him resemble a bag of skin and bones. Hence his nickname 'Skin Fraser'. Hailing from Aberdeen, Fraser came from a long line of forebears who had served with the Gordon Highlanders. Enlisting in that regiment aged nineteen, Fraser was the first in his family to be commissioned as an officer. He differed from McGonigal and Mayne in that his was no wealthy lineage, one peopled by senior lawyers and businessmen, and decorated British military figures. Fraser was not from the 'officer class' as he saw it, which made him something of a misfit, especially in the officer's mess.

But Fraser had earned his spurs the hard way, being one of the most battle-experienced men then aboard the *Glenroy*. In June 1940, aged just twenty-three, he'd served with the 1st Battalion the Gordon Highlanders in the spirited and bloody defence of France. Ending up at the port of Saint-Valery-en-Caux, they had been tasked to hold the line so that the massed ranks of British, French and Allied troops could be evacuated from the beaches. Wounded in action during those bitter and dark days, Fraser was one of the few from the 1st Battalion to be spirited back to Britain. Surrounded, outgunned and with ammunition, food and water all-but exhausted, the remainder of the battalion had been forced to surrender, along with the bulk of the 51st (Highland) Division.

General Johannes Erwin Rommel had taken the Division's surrender – the German commander who later would earn the nickname 'The Desert Fox', as the focus of the war pivoted to North Africa. It was in North Africa that Fraser would finally get his chance to avenge his vanquished comrades, and with a dash and daring that belied his somewhat shy and retiring air. But in June 1940 he'd found himself back in Britain, nursing his injuries and an overwhelming sense of defeat. There was only one way the Scotsman saw fit to respond. He had volunteered for Special Service, and that August 1940 was accepted into No. 11 Commando's ranks. Just a year after that humiliating defeat in France, Fraser – strikingly quiet, a deep thinker – would be leading a troop of Jocks into battle on this dark June morning, charging down the enemy guns.

Once all were crammed into the flat-bottomed, box-sided landing craft, one by one the ALCs were swung wide of the *Glenroy* and lowered towards the waves. As the ten diminutive vessels turned eastwards and headed for the dark shoreline, the flotilla split into three distinct units – Forces X, Y and Z – each of which was charged to hit a particular stretch of coastline and to seize a specific set of targets. What lay before these elite warriors was daunting. The enemy had vowed to resist to 'the last man and the last shell', and they had the means to do so, boasting ranks of armoured cars, swift-firing field guns, plus mortars and reinforced machinegun nests overlooking the beaches.

The ungainly ALCs ploughed through the dark seas, the slap of the swell resounding against their high sides, the salt tang of spray sharp in the men's nostrils. Those aboard felt rather than heard the dull, rhythmic thud of the silenced engines reverberating through the hulls. They were acutely aware that for this, No. 11 Commando's first ever foray into action, the enemy held all the aces. The about-turn of the *Glenroy* had led to inevitable delays, which meant they were motoring towards the beaches at a far later hour than originally intended. To their backs a full moon was fast sinking into the glimmering sea, silhouetting their approach. To their front, the sun would rise directly into their eyes.

At the thirty-minutes-to-landfall mark, the order was given: 'Issue the rum.' Ranged upon wooden benches that ran along either side of the ALCs, shadowy figures accepted their ration in a tense, nervy silence. A little Dutch courage was very welcome, but it was far from enough to settle the stomachs of even the hardiest. During the long months of relentless training, their commander, Lieutenant Colonel Richard 'Dick' Pedder, had impressed upon his men the need to strike with deadly force and to do so by total surprise, so discomfiting and overwhelming the enemy. But as these elite warriors hugged the shelter of the ALCs' mixed hardwood

9

and lightly armoured sides, they knew that their present mission had been compromised from the very outset.

With faces and exposed skin blackened with burnt cork, they sat in silence, emotions veering between spikes of excitement at the thought of the coming action, and the dread of what might await them on the beaches. Lightly equipped and kitted out to strike with maximum aggression and speed, they wore khaki shirts and shorts, rope-soled boots, and steel helmets camouflaged with sacking. Armed with knives, pistols, rifles-with-bayonets and grenades, the heaviest firepower most carried was the tommy gun – the 1918-vintage Thompson submachine gun, known as the 'Trench Broom', for it was originally invented to clear First World War trenches. Once the ALCs' ramps slammed down and they hit the beaches, speed was going to be of the essence. The longer it took to find cover, the more likely they were to take casualties.

At the ten-minutes-to-landing mark the 'Standby' order was whispered along the lines. *Soon now.* The tension and nervous excitement was jacked up to another level. But beneath the nerves, there was also a certain confidence that pulsed back and forth. Utterly ruthless in his selection and unforgiving in his training, there was no finer commander than Colonel Pedder, and no better-prepared force than theirs. Indeed, some of their sister units were in the habit of taking the micky out of No. 11 Commando's punishing, altogether spartan regime. The likes of No. 7 Commando – 'under-trained . . . no discipline' – and No. 8 (Guards) Commando – 'the good-time Charlies' – accused their rivals, No. 11 (Scottish) Commando, of being over-trained and over-strict.

Pedder was unrepentant. Charged to shape his command as he saw fit, from the outset he'd seized upon Churchill's exhortations to form units capable of striking deep in enemy territory, leaving 'a trail of German corpses behind'. In the first week of June 1940, even as the flotillas of ships plucked the British and Allied troops off the French beaches, so Churchill had warned that on no account would Britain resort to the same defensive strategy that had led to crushing defeat in France. Rather, he demanded the formation of 'specially trained troops of the hunter class', to strike wherever the enemy was vulnerable, delivering 'a reign of terror first of all of a "butcher and bolt"' kind, seeking to 'kill and capture the Hun garrison . . . and then away.' Pedder was of an exactly similar mind: attack was by far the best form of defence.

Churchill's butcher-and-bolt directive had been inspired by the musings of one of the most remarkable, yet little-heralded figures of the war. Brigadier Dudley Wrangel Clarke had grown up in South Africa, where he'd witnessed at first hand how fast-moving bands of Boer Commandos – irregular, horse-mounted, guerrilla-type fighters – had launched audacious hit-and-run attacks against the British military, in the Boer War. 'Guerrilla warfare was always in fact the answer . . . in the face of a vaster though ponderous military machine,' Clarke would declare, 'and that seemed to me precisely the position in which the British Army found itself in June 1940.'

In the immediate aftermath of defeat in France, Clarke had sketched out his back-of-an-envelope plan for a British commando, men 'operating by night, fighting alone or in small groups, killing quickly and silently, using independent initiative and thinking'. Clarke had got it into Churchill's hands and secured his enthusiastic backing, after which he'd been charged to do whatever was necessary. Of course, there was no training manual for founding such units, for nothing like this had ever been tried before by the British military. As a consequence, commanders were given exceptional leeway to shape their units as they saw fit, and there was a flood of eager recruits.

Lieutenant Colonel Pedder understood instinctively that at the heart of any such outfit lay camaraderie and *esprit de corps*. As with those crouched in the ALCs, the individual soldier would fight tooth-and-nail for his mates on his shoulder, his fellow recruits. Those bonds – unbroken unto death – would be forged first and foremost in training. Pedder realised that all who volunteered were taking a step into the unknown. That took a certain kind of mindset, and it was exactly that kind of individual – driven, adventuresome, embodied with initiative and self-belief – that he sought.

Pedder's philosophy was typified by the infamous 'route march' from Galashiels, where they had raised the original cadre of recruits, to the Isle of Arran, a hundred-odd miles away. For days men had tramped westwards on blistered feet, sleeping in hedges and washing in rivers, and eating mostly what they could beg, scavenge and steal. At the vanguard went pipers from the Cameron Highlanders, with Pedder stepping out, scrutinising and measuring up all. As if the march alone weren't challenge enough, he had arranged for a convoy of British Army trucks to chug along companionably. As he made clear, at any time any individual was free to break ranks and retire to the comparative warmth and comfort of the vehicles. Only, none who choose to do so would ever reach Arran. Though they might not know it, taking the easy road would lead to summary rejection and being returned to one's unit (RTU'd), no second chances.

No matter where a recruit hailed from, Pedder made it clear all were honorary Scotsmen, once accepted into his commando. The headwear he adopted for No. 11 Commando – the Black Hackle – was not only highly distinctive, it sent a powerful message: these were men who 'had a quarrel with someone'. Those who wore the Black Hackle did not shy away from trouble. At the same time Pedder prized mental dexterity and quickness as much as physical toughness. The kind of individual he sought was 'quick in thought and quick on his feet' and could think outside of the box. Equally, his unit was a meritocracy, within which every man would be counted upon to execute a mission, even if all around him were killed or captured. Pedder maintained that under his command the only discipline to be relied upon was self-discipline.

In January 1941, towards the end of six months of intensive training, Pedder granted his men one week's leave. They returned to discover that he had set them a final exercise. They were to 'raid' an RAF aerodrome, treating it as if it were a hostile airbase packed with enemy warplanes. With the leftfield mindset to the fore, a pair of commandos were chosen with suitably feminine-like physiques, each being dressed as a young and lissome woman. As the 'ladies' paraded before the RAF base gates, so distracting the guards, the main body of raiders cut their way through the wire, stole across to the officer's mess and hurled a volley of Mills bombs – the ubiquitous pineapple-shaped grenades – through doors and windows. Fortunately for the RAF officers, the grenades were unprimed, but the message was crystal clear: through subterfuge, speed and surprise, they were to leave a trail of destruction and bloody mayhem in their wake.

Pedder's credo was not without its risks. From the outset, the wholly irregular and 'ungentlemanly' ethos of the commandos proved unpopular with Britain's top brass. As Pedder well appreciated, he drew to his command men who walked on the borderline of what was acceptable behaviour, if not of sanity itself. Gifted warrior and leader of men though he was, 'Paddy' Mayne was not always one for civilised niceties. That New Year's past he had gone on a serious bender. A fresh recruit, Lieutenant Gerald Bryan, an expert mountaineer, had joined Mayne and McGonigal in their Arran billet. He was out on guard duty, but had called into the Landour house shortly after midnight, to wish Mayne a happy New Year. He'd found the Irishman severely the worse for wear and an altercation had ensued. It ended with Mayne punching the far smaller man into one wall. It was only when Mayne went to fetch some water that Bryan managed to slip away, 'pursued by Paddy firing at me with his Colt .45'.

By the time Bryan and McGonigal mustered the courage to return to their digs, it was New Year's morning. They found Mayne alone in the house, largely sober, with all the windows shot out, and surrounded by 'thirty-six small bottles of cherry brandy, one side of beef, one leg of lamb and two loaves of bread'. They posed the obvious question: 'Blair, where the hell did you get all this stuff? Get up that track and hide the lot!' It turned out that some-time in the night Mayne had raided the Brigade headquarters, stealing all the food and drink he could lay his hands on. They'd just managed to hide it all and patch up the windows, by the time the local police arrived to investigate.

The other thing that had struck Bryan most powerfully was how Mayne had no recollection of their fisticuffs the previous evening. He'd eyed the smaller man's swollen, bruised face with real concern.

'Who hit you?' Mayne had demanded. 'Just you tell me and I'll sort the bugger out.'

That fist fight, the shooting out of the Landour windows, and above all the outrageous theft of food and drink was quickly hushed up. But a while later Pedder had cornered Mayne at the bar. Single-minded, tough and uncompromising, the chief of No. 11 Commando was not universally liked, and especially by those in high command, for he epitomised all they abhorred. But over time Mayne and Pedder had struck up a certain camaraderie, sharing the mutual respect of single-minded, maverick-spirited warriors. Over the months of training they had developed a friendship; a closeness even.

'By the way,' Pedder announced, eyeing Mayne pointedly, 'I know who broke into Brigade HQ on New Year's Eve and stole the drink.'

Mayne fixed his commander with a deadpan look, but with just the twinkle of a grin. 'Och, do tell,' he countered, in his soft, lilting, Ulster brogue, 'because it was a great mystery at the time.'

14

For a beat or two Pedder held Mayne's gaze, but decided no more would be said about the matter. Even so, the message had been sent. The commander of No. 11 Commando would brook no further shenanigans of that order of magnitude. The last thing he needed was any of his prize officers being investigated by the police, and the adverse scrutiny that might bring, and especially since his commando was poised to board the Glen ships and sail south.

That was a voyage that would end with No. 11 Commando securing the pivotal role in Operation Exporter. Pedder would choose a password by which his men would be able to identify each other in the coming darkness of the landings, one replete with the wild and unyielding commando spirit: 'Arran'.

The symbolism was crystal clear, and it would prove entirely fitting.

CHAPTER TWO

Sand and Steel

At shortly after 0400 hours the deafening thump of the foremost bow-ramp crashing into the surf announced the moment was upon them. Before the figures crowded aboard the leading ALC stretched a dark mass of seething water, with little sign of any land. The men knew this didn't look right, but it was now that their training kicked in, figures piling off the bows. The first to do so plummeted downwards, disappearing completely, bodies and then helmeted heads getting sucked into the hungry sea. Somehow, the landing craft had dropped them well short, and in treacherously deep water.

It was now that, perhaps unintentionally, the trainee jumps from Lamlash pier really would pay dividends. Though shocked, soaked and laden with heavy and bulky kit, all had faced such conditions before. One by one, figures kicked for the surface, intent on swimming their way to shore. Those still on the ALC could not delay. The ramp was firmly down, the boat was shipping water, and hesitation was inviting death. They piled after those already gone, throwing themselves into the sea and striking out for land, desperate for boots to make contact and to get some kind of a foothold.

Though a superlative sportsman, the one discipline Mayne most definitely did not enjoy was swimming. While he'd never shied away from a pier jump, his loathing of that element of their training was well known to all. He had written home about the Lamlash leaps and the freezing, night-dark swims, describing them as 'A Madhouse'. He was far from alone in abhorring them, but not a single man among the commando baulked or stalled on this dark June morning.

As the lead ALC went into reverse, seeking the comparative safety of the open sea, so a first human chain was formed, men, ammo and weapons being ferried towards the beaches. But as figures neared the shore, so the guns opened up, long bursts of machinegun fire raking through the surf. It was still too dark for the enemy to see and to aim accurately, so their procedure seemed to be to blanket sand and shallows with bullets. The lead warriors of No. 11 Commando did their best to return fire, but precious few could do so. The dousing in seawater where the surf churned itself into a mucky brown stew, meant weapons had got jammed with mud and grit, and refused to fire. A first figure collapsed bloodily into the sand. As eighteen-year-old Bren-gunner George Dove had tried to take cover and get his weapon working, a round had struck his helmet, the bullet ricocheting off and cutting through the flesh of his backside. Though injured, miraculously Dove was still alive. He finished cleaning his weapon and opened fire.

To left and right along the bullet-whipped shoreline, other figures stumbled and faltered in the darkness. Corporal Robert McKay believed he'd found a patch of decent cover, and was preparing to advance, when he too was hit; as was Private Ben Hurst. Neither would make it off the beaches. But it was to the far south of the landings that the ALCs of Force X had disgorged their men into the deadliest inferno of all. Commanded by Major Geoffrey Keyes – eldest son of the First World War hero and admiral of the fleet, Sir Roger Keyes, 1st Baron Keyes – Force X had been charged to seize the foremost objective, the all-important stone-built Qasimiya Bridge, which forded the Litani River. Just to the south of there, troops of the 21st Australian Infantry Brigade were waiting for the signal, poised to surge forward and take the enemy by storm.

But during the twenty-four-hour delay in getting No. 11 Commando to shore, the enemy had decided to blow the Qasimiya Bridge, and it was already down. Keyes' force was supposed to land to the north of the Litani River, so they could hit its defenders squarely from behind. Yet by the creeping light of dawn they realised they had somehow been set down on the wrong – southerly – side. It was little short of calamitous. Advancing through the Australian positions, Keyes and his men faced a full-frontal assault across open water, and over terrain menaced by 75mm field guns, mortars, snipers and heavy machineguns. As they tried to press ahead, dragging a handful of boats that the Australians had loaned them, with which they intended to ford the river, they came under a murderous barrage.

In a series of unbelievably courageous bounds, Keyes and his men tried to push on, and to launch their boats, but each time they were driven back. 'Can get no further, as open ground,' Keyes would record, bleakly, in his diary. Pinned down by highly accurate fire on the southern bank of the Litani, Force X found itself being torn to shreds. Captain George Duncan – a two-year veteran of the Highland Light Infantry, the Black Watch – was one of Keyes' deputies. He'd volunteered for the commandos, for he hungered to 'defeat a great evil, and to preserve the way of life he, and millions of others, cherished', his daughter, Margaret, would write. Captain Duncan was now embroiled in the shocking realities of war, as his poem, *The Litani River Battle*, would reflect:

Men falling, falling –
Thump-roll-lie-still –
Hit in the head –
Shrill screaming –
Jack knifed and writhing.
A stomach burst. Cough bubbling.
Shrapnel pierced chest . . .
Men crawling, cursing, sweating, dragging,
To the river.

Despite the unfolding carnage, as Keyes – and Captain Duncan – were painfully aware, they had to press on. They were here at the personal behest of Churchill, who would stress to parliament how the 'military and strategic significance' of Operation Exporter was of 'the very highest point'. Britain's wartime leader had been incensed to discover the perfidy being perpetrated by Vichy France, the southern sector of the French nation, which, following the fall of France was ruled by Marshal Phillipe Pétain's Vichy government. Pétain was allowing the German and Italian air forces to use bases in the French-controlled territory of Syria and the Lebanon, from where to attack British forces across the Middle East and North Africa. It was one thing to allow the Luftwaffe to fly sorties against Britain and her interests from occupied France – there was precious little the French could do about that. It was quite another to allow the Axis powers to do so across Vichy-controlled lands, including France's overseas colonies.

While Britain had weathered the summer 1940 Battle of Britain, against all odds, and subsequently the Blitz, elsewhere the war was plagued by calamity on all fronts. Across North Africa, the Balkans, in Greece and in Crete, wherever Britain's forces had come up against the German enemy they had been thwarted. If the foothold seized by the Luftwaffe here in the eastern Mediterranean was allowed to take hold, the ramifications for Egypt, and Britain's vital supply lines via the Suez Canal, were grim. Hence the need for Operation Exporter, in which a combined force led by the 7th Australian Division would advance north from British-held territory, sweeping along the Mediterranean coast towards the key cities of Damascus and Beirut.

Few believed Exporter would be any kind of a pushover. Vichy France's military chief in the region, General Henri Dentz, had some 45,000 troops under his command, including members of the French Foreign Legion. Ranged against them were some 20,000 Australian, Indian, British and Free French forces – those Frenchmen who had vowed to remain loyal to the Allied cause. The enemy were expected to contest every inch of territory, which made No. 11 Commando's mission all the more vital. Hence Keyes urging his men forward, into the dirt-dry sandscape of the southern bank of the Litani River. But no matter how courageously – some might argue suicidally, bearing in mind the fast-strengthening dawn light – Keyes and his men tried to reach the river, and to launch their assault boats, they were cut down in their droves.

Two thousand yards to the north of there, Mayne had likewise managed to get his men to shore, but under withering fire. Serving as part of Lieutenant Colonel Pedder's Y Force, consisting of 150 men spread across three ALCs, they had been targeted by the enemy's machineguns even as the assault boats had powered towards the beaches. With the craft slamming their ramps down just as soon as they hit the first sandbar, Mayne and Pedder had leapt into deep, dark water. To left and right they could not have had better men on their shoulders, for on the one side Bill Fraser urged his men forward, while on the other Lieutenant Gerald Bryan – Mayne and McGonigal's Lamlash room-mate – did the same. McGonigal himself was with the third landing party – Force Z – charged to hit the beach another thousand yards north.

One of the men in 7 Troop – Mayne's command – fell almost instantly, shot dead even as he struck out for land. But it was as they reached the open, exposed stretch of beach that the real horror unfolded. From the high ground lying directly inland the enemy rained down salvoes of mortars, plus heavy machinegun fire, as blasted shrapnel churned up sand and sea into a hellish maelstrom. It was 0420 hours, so mercifully a blanket of pre-dawn gloom still enveloped all. It was only thanks to that, that Mayne, Fraser and Pedder were able to make the nearest cover with most of their men still alive. There, they paused to catch their breath, and to try to make radio contact with Keyes' force, but all they would receive was an echoing void of silence.

As matters transpired, one of Keyes' radios had got a bullet through it, and the other was also out of action. Soaked – doused in sea-water – Pedder's radio sets were in little better shape. With no way of knowing if the southern force had managed to cross the Litani River, or if the men of the 7th Australian Division were surging north as planned, lesser hearts might have baulked, for without the Australians advancing to relieve them, the few hundred lightly armed commandos stood barely any chance. But Pedder, typically, gave short shrift to such concerns. They were here with a mission to execute, and they were the very best that Britain had to offer. Now was not the time for fateful indecision, and these were not men to turn aside.

'I raced madly up the beach and threw myself into the cover provided by a sand dune . . .' Lieutenant Bryan would recall of the landing. 'Away to the right we could hear the rattle of a machinegun and the overhead whine of bullets . . . Colonel Pedder was shouting at us to push on as quickly as possible. Soon, the ditch that I was in became too narrow and there was nothing for it but to climb out into the open. The ground was flat with no cover. The machine-guns were now firing fairly continuously . . . I shouted, "A Section No. 1 Troop," which represented my command. Before long we were in pretty good formation . . .'

It was 0500 and fully light by the time Bryan's section scuttled

21

into the low hills. Pretty quickly they found themselves pinned down by sniper fire. Joined by one of his corporals, Bryan was just deliberating on the best course of action, when that man was shot through the left eye and killed. As Bryan scrambled for cover, he realised that just twenty-five yards from where the dead corporal lay, a French 75mm field gun had opened fire. Leaping to his feet, he hurled a volley of grenades, silencing that gun. Once Bryan and his men had seized it, they went about cutting the field wires which linked the enemy's headquarters, positioned on a hill above them, to their heavy guns and mortars. That barracks-cum-HQ was now the focus of Pedder's – and Bryan's – attentions. If they could take that, they could cut the head off the snake and dominate the high ground.

Having seized that first, and then a second, field gun – 'it was rather bloody,' Bryan recalled – he did the only thing that seemed sensible. He and his men heaved the 75mm weapon around, so that the barrel faced the enemy. Bryan, like many in his section, hailed from the Royal Artillery, and knew exactly what to do. They opened fire. 'The result was amazing,' he recalled. 'There was one hell of an explosion in the other gun site and the gun was flung up into the air like a toy.' Taking aim on a second enemy position, they fired once more. 'There was a pause. Where the devil had the shell gone? Then there was a flash and a puff of smoke in the dome of a chapel about half a mile up the hillside. A thick Scottish voice said, "That'll make the buggers pray!"'

Three more 75mm guns, plus a clutch of mortar and machinegun pits were silenced by Bryan's gunnery skills, and by 0700 hours Pedder had declared the barracks-cum-HQ was theirs. He ordered twenty-two-year-old Private Jack Adams to haul down the French flag, to signal to his fellow commandos that the key objective had been taken, though not without significant casualties. Indeed, later that day Adams would be one of the many killed in action. Mayne, likewise, was in the thick of it, although with the signature luck of the Irish that would come to define his war, his section would suffer some of the lightest losses of all.

Skirting around a pair of machinegun posts, Mayne pressed inland, with Bill Fraser and his men in support. Set a thousand yards back from the shoreline, a twisting road sliced through the dun-coloured hills. This was the planned line of march of the 21st Australian Infantry Brigade, for it linked up with their intended crossing point over the Litani River. Holding it was key, and at 0520 Mayne's force took possession of a chief stretch of that road. Whatever nerves Mayne may have initially felt, they were long gone now. He was laser focused, and hell-bent on doing 'a good piece of work . . . behind the French lines'.

A few hundred yards further along the road he spied a group of vehicles, plus men, firing northwards, so in the direction of McGonigal and Force Z's landing beach. They were too far away to identify, and could just as easily be friendly, as enemy forces. It was now that Mayne's calm, hunter instinct kicked in. He'd lost two men already. It was time for decisive action. Spying 'quite a lot of cover – kind of a hayfield – I crawled up to thirty yards or so & I heard them talking French,' Mayne would later write, in a letter to his younger brother, Douglas (they were the last of seven siblings). Mayne's official reports would prove famously terse and understated. Of this, his earliest action, he would simply state that he took twenty-five prisoners, after Colonel Pedder's troop scared them stiff and they surrendered. The reality, as he would relate to his brother, was far different.

Just as soon as he'd heard those figures speaking French, Mayne inched closer, moving through the thick cover of the corn, before unleashing what would become his trademark instant aggression and force. He 'started whaling grenades at them', as his men opened fire. The fight was fierce, but short-lived, as bullets and shrapnel cut through the corn. Shocked at the speed and surprise of the assault, the enemy proved not to have the stomach for it.

23

'After about five minutes up went a white flag,' Mayne wrote. More interesting than the few dozen prisoners they'd seized were the pair of machineguns, plus the mortar. It was 'a nice bag to start with', Mayne remarked, especially as 'they had been firing at McGonigal's crowd who had landed further north'.

With no sign of the expected Australian troops, Mayne was unsure what to do next. He had two injured men, one of whom, his second-in-command, Lieutenant Robert McCunn, had been shot through the shoulder. McCunn needed medical attention, so Mayne dispatched him towards the Australian lines, with one man serving as escort. Having seized a large section of the road, he sent a runner to let Pedder know, and seeking an update on the state of play. But with a confused and fast-moving battle raging around the enemy barracks, Mayne's runner was unable to get through. None the wiser as to the bigger picture scenario, Mayne decided to continue to their objective, which was to link up with Keyes' force and to secure the road from end to end.

Needing to move swiftly and primed for instant action, Mayne abandoned the prisoners they'd taken; they were disarmed and turned loose. Swinging south, he led his section at a fast march, remaining totally oblivious to Keyes' horrific predicament – that they'd landed on the wrong bank of the Litani, and were pinned down and trapped. With the injured and dead that his section had suffered, Mayne was now down to 'around 15 men', so about half his original number. Luckily, Fraser's section was moving in tandem with Mayne's, seeking to link up with Keyes force and the Australians.

As they flitted across the dry, sparsely vegetated hills, keeping well off the road, Mayne could sense that something just wasn't right. It was far too quiet, and as far as the eye could see it was utterly deserted of friendly forces. His letter to his brother takes up the story. 'It got hilly and hard going & Frenchies all over the place.' Stumbling across isolated groups of enemy, Mayne and

Fraser began rounding up prisoners once more. Finally, some hours after they had first hit the beaches, Mayne's force reached the ridgeline overlooking the Litani River and what remained of the Qasmiya Bridge. Emerging from hiding and waving a make-shift white flag – the agreed signal for friendly forces – they were met by a ferocious barrage of fire, as the Australians on the southern river bank let rip.

'0800, pinned down with Bren fire from Australians on other side of river,' Mayne would write, in his official report. 'No notice taken of white flag.'

Hurriedly, they crawled back into cover. It was becoming increasingly obvious that Operation Exporter had floundered. Somehow, it looked as if Mayne and Fraser's sections were pretty much alone and cut off, and worse still, taking fire from all sides. Mayne figured the only suitable response was to go on the offensive, for someone had to break the stalemate. First, he made sure his men 'concentrated all prisoners', who would be taken with them at gunpoint. Turning east along the ridgeline, they began to climb, eventually stumbling upon a well-worn path. Taking point, Mayne crept ahead, sensing danger.

The first sign of trouble was a few mules – pack animals – milling about beside the path. Skirting around them, Mayne edged forwards, his sixth sense working overtime. He stole up to a corner, only to spy 'about 30 of these fellows sitting 20 yards away. I was around first, with my revolver, and the sergeant had a T-gun [Tommy gun].' The surprise on the faces of the enemy was absolute. Mayne 'called on them to "Jettez vers a la planche," but they seemed a bit slow in the uptake.' It was perhaps not surprising, for in his bastardised French, Mayne had issued a jumbled warning to 'Throw to the plank.' (*Jetez-vous à terre* would be 'throw your-selves to the ground'.) But the menacing gun muzzles should have more than compensated for the garbled order.

As it was, 'one of them lifted a rifle and I am afraid that he had not even time to be sorry . . .' Mayne's instant and deadly reaction – shooting dead the first enemy fighter who showed the slightest sign of resistance – drove the message home: he and his men might be outnumbered, but they were no less deadly for it. The remaining enemy troops chose to surrender rather than fight, Mayne and his men seizing a 'sort of H.Q. place' that was full of 'typewriters, ammunition, revolvers, bombs and – more to the point – beer and food'. Having been on the go for several hours, Mayne and his men fell upon the supplies with a vengeance.

As they were tucking in, there was the trilling of a telephone. 'We didn't answer it,' Mayne remarked. Instead, moving stealthily, they traced the phone-line to the source of the call. There they hit the jackpot, stumbling upon a veritable armoury – '4 machine-guns, light machineguns, 2 mortars and 40 more prisoners'. All were seized in a swift and decisive firefight. Mayne had still 'only lost 2 men', he wrote to his brother, adding, with his signature wry humour, 'Sounds like a German communique.' But this was no propaganda. By now his small force had rounded up several dozen prisoners, and so much weaponry that they were obliged to make the *captives* carry the bulk of it.

'We were rather tired,' Mayne explained, 'so the prisoner laddies kindly carried our booty and equipment.'

With so many POWs in tow and laden down with so much captured weaponry, they needed to get back to friendly lines. The question was, how on earth were they to do so? Bill Fraser's section, operating close by, were in the same dire situation. Having come up against a sizeable force of French cavalry, Fraser and his small band of commandos had killed several, and taken thirty captives. But upon making for the Litani River with their prisoners, they'd come under not only Bren fire from the Australians, but also a ferocious barrage from their artillery. It was hardly the welcome they were hoping for.

Upon formation in the summer of 1940, No. 11 (Scottish) Commando had adopted the age-old, iconic, stirring sound of 'Scotland the Brave' – the unofficial Scottish anthem – as their regimental march. But in recent months one of the unit's pipers, Jimmy Lawson, had composed lines to a new version – 'The 11th (Scottish) Commando March'. He'd wanted to name the new verses after Colonel Pedder, but Pedder was having none of it: No. 11 Commando was certainly not about one man, no matter the role he had played in shaping it.

The first lines of the new song heralded the 11th's peculiarly Celtic brotherhood – Scots to Irish.

> From a' the crack regiments cam oor men
> The pick of the Heilands and Lowlands and a'.
> And stout-hearted Irish frae mountain and bog
> And stout-hearted Irish frae mountain and bog . . .
> And noo we're awa, lads, to meet the foe
> And noo we're awa, lads, to meet the foe . . .

But as death stalked the Litani Hills, it would prove no respecter of nationality, creed or clan.

It was around mid-morning by now, and both Fraser and Mayne's sections faced the same dire predicament. With no safe route back to friendly lines, and burdened with scores of captives, they were isolated in terrain that was crawling with the enemy. True to Pedder's inspiration for No. 11 (Scottish) Commando, they resolved to carry on fighting. What else were they supposed to do?

Fraser spotted a force of enemy gunners, using their French 75mm cannons to rain down high explosives on their adversaries, situated just a few hundred yards across the steep, dry-sided ravine through which flowed the Litani. Realising he and his men were nicely sited to the rear of those guns, Fraser launched a lightning assault, charging down from the ridge and taking the enemy gunners by complete surprise. In the ensuing close-quarters melee, he and his men overran three gun positions, but in the process Fraser was hit. Miraculously, the bullet struck the chin strap of his helmet, jerking his head violently backwards, but ricocheted off, leaving Fraser largely unharmed.

Still, the impact had rendered him light-headed and reeling. Once the worst of the firefight was over, and the surviving enemy had been rounded up, Fraser tried to take stock. Confused and disorientated, he realised he was suffering from concussion. Reluctantly, he was forced to hand over command to his deputy, Sergeant John 'Jack' Cheyne, a fellow Gordon Highlander. At least with Cheyne, Fraser knew his men were in fine hands. A former farm worker, Cheyne had enlisted in the Gordons in 1932, aged eighteen, which made him one of the oldest in No. 11 Commando, being all of twenty-seven years of age.

With long experience, loyal to a fault and the ultimate professional, Cheyne would earn the following praise from Fraser for his performance that day: 'Jack behaved with extreme coolness under fire and repeatedly went alone into the woods to search for snipers.' Fraser would also praise his skill in keeping the unit together – *bidand,* abiding and steadfast, to use the Gordon Highlanders' own motto. But in the confusion of the fast-moving battle, and while dealing with his concussion, Fraser lost contact with Mayne's group. Increasingly fragmented, the men of No. 11 Commando were being scattered ever more thinly across the war-torn Litani Hills.

Sensing the critical nature of their situation, and knowing they were running short of water, food and ammunition – not to mention options – Mayne was determined to get his unit back to friendly lines. Pushing further east along the ridge, he decided to risk turning southwards once again, to approach the Litani River for a second try. This time, not only was their appearance met by murderously accurate fire, but one of Mayne's men was hit and killed. It was a bitter outcome to have one of his own shot dead by their own side. It looked as if there was no way back across the lines. Mayne and his men – plus Fraser and his force – appeared trapped.

Yet in truth their trials were as nothing, when compared to how the rest of the commando was faring.

CHAPTER THREE

Scotland the Brave

It was well into the morning of 10 June, some twenty-four hours after they had first hit the beaches, when Mayne was able to finally lead his men – plus a column of some seventy-odd POWs, laden with captured weaponry – across the Litani River. '0430 Crossed pontoon bridge and marched down to Australian camp,' he recorded, in his official report. 'Prisoners escorted to Tyre.' Adjacent to where the Qasimiya Bridge had been blown, the Australians had managed to construct a 'pontoon bridge' – a crossing suspended on floats. Tyre is a coastal city in the far south of the Lebanon – one of the first to fall to the advancing Allied forces – so it was as good a place as any to corral the POWs.

Mayne's entire report on the part his section played in the Litani River operation runs to some ten lines of incredibly sparse, staccato prose. While it is signed-off with the words 'Lt. R. B. Mayne, R.U.R. [Royal Ulster Rifles, his parent unit]', he didn't in fact write it. If anything, it was dictated by Mayne to one of his fellow officers, and the entire document reads as if getting any words at all out of him was akin to pulling teeth. In retrospect, it is hardly surprising, for upon reaching friendly lines Mayne began to discover just how dark the fates had proven for No. 11 (Scottish) Commando on that fateful day.

Of those sections dropped behind enemy lines, Mayne's was

the first and only one to return, so far, testament to his gift of leadership and the keenness of his men to follow him, regardless of whether death beckoned. Indeed, Mayne had proved himself possessed of an unrivalled ability to inspire confidence in those under his command, a sense – a heartfelt belief – that somehow, under his stewardship, all would come right in the end. As the padre who would serve with Mayne later in the war would remark, 'The gift of leadership and the ability to inspire complete devotion and loyalty were his to an exceptional degree.'

This was something Mayne had proved most powerfully in the hours just gone, but the foundations had been laid during commando training. In a December 1940 letter to his mother, entitled 'Sunday Night, Machrie Bay', Mayne had waxed lyrical about the trials and tribulations they'd experienced on Arran, during a seventeen-mile route march in atrocious conditions, from Lamlash west to Machrie Bay: 'the final shower lasted for thirteen miles, and there was a regular gale blowing off the sea into our faces. I walked through a river the other night and I don't think it was any wetter!'

True to No. 11 Commando's credo, they had moved light and fast. 'We were carrying nothing except some food, we would not demean ourselves by carrying blankets.' They'd reached route's end, a tiny hamlet of eight or nine houses, at which point Mayne went from door to door, 'to find somewhere for my twenty-five men to dry their clothes'. In doing so he came across 'one old lady [who] reminded me of you', Mayne wrote. A door was opened by a young mother. She looked worried, as the wild and bedraggled stranger towered over her. But once Mayne had explained who he was and his purpose – 'that we intended sleeping out and wondered if she could get some clothes dried' – she countered: 'You'll not stop outside as long as I have a bed in my house.'

After a hurried discussion with her daughters, she told Mayne she could accommodate six. 'To cut a long story short,' he had concluded in his letter, 'I am sitting in borrowed pyjamas and an overcoat made for a much smaller man than myself, so much so that when one of my lads saw me he said, "Let Burton dress you!"' That was the then slogan of the well-known Burtons high street menswear store. What jumps off the pages of Mayne's letter is his care for and camaraderie with those in his charge – 'my lads' – and in turn, their residing affection for their commander.

During the past twenty-four hours' fighting, he had lost a considerable number of those young soldiers that he treasured – dead, injured or missing in action. That was never easy, and Mayne would become famed for making a point of writing to the kin of those of his own who were killed, wounded or captured in battle. Worryingly, of his second-in-command, Lieutenant McCunn, who'd been shot in the shoulder, there was still no sign. But in exchange for the losses they'd suffered, Mayne and his men had seized a vast haul of prisoners and weaponry, and accounted for many of the enemy in battle.

Yet of the other sections – of Fraser's, McGonigal's and even of Colonel Pedder's force – there was zero news. Bereft of any radio contact, there was little chance of receiving any, unless other parties made it through the lines. Here on the southern bank of the Litani, one other thing became painfully clear to Mayne – the decimation of Major Keyes' section, Force X. Incredibly, Keyes had succeeded in getting his men across the Litani River, and in turning the enemy's guns against them, but the price had been heavy in courage, death and blood.

Of Force X's 150-odd men, just fourteen had managed to fight their way over the river. 'Not all of the rest were casualties, but a lot of them were,' Gunner James Gornall remarked of their struggle to ford those bloody waters. Keyes' assault had been executed in the full glare of daylight and it had left a bitter taste in the mouths of many. 'He had no artillery support. He hadn't recce'd any of the area. He knew nothing of the south bank of the river. And yet he made a frontal attack.'

As one Australian observer reported, Keyes' advance 'had been met with a murderous hail of steel and H.E. [High Explosive] from French 75s, mortars and heavy machineguns. Their dead literally littered the beach.' In short, Force X's assault had been a hugely heroic gesture, but the cost had been immense. Captain Duncan, who had himself survived the hell of that terrible river crossing, rounded off his poem 'The Litani River Battle' with these dark and haunting lines commemorating the fallen:

> Alone
> Unconscious of battle
> They pass;
> Flitting, flickering thoughts
> Surge and recede –
> All time, all loved ones
> Filing – filing to death.

The first concrete news of the missing sections of No. 11 Commando that June morning would come from none other than Bill Fraser. As the first blush of dawn lit the skies to the east, illuminating an angry and smoke-enshrouded sky, so Fraser finally made it across the Litani. To the north, the RAF had bombed a series of coastal petrol refineries and other key targets, causing a pall of thick oily fumes to billow along the shoreline. Under its screen, Bill Fraser had led what remained of his men to safety. Or rather, Sergeant Cheyne had, for Fraser was still groggy from concussion.

After losing contact with Mayne, Fraser had turned north, managing to link up with Force Z, the unit tasked to seize the furthermost objective, the Kafr Badda Bridge, which lay a good three kilometres beyond the Litani. As with so many of No. 11 Commando, Force Z had been dropped on the wrong beach, right beneath the enemy's guns, and in deep water, which put their radios out of action from the outset. Even so, with McGonigal front and centre of the action, they had seized their objective in a blistering assault, taking hundreds of enemy prisoners. But as the morning wore on and the 21st Australian Infantry Brigade had failed to materialise, the enemy had counter-attacked, using columns of armoured cars, aircraft and even French warships steaming off the coast.

At dusk, after a series of ferocious battles often fought at close-quarters, Force Z had split up in an effort to reach friendly lines. Fraser's party had stolen south through the hills, in the process of which they had run into the injured Lieutenant McCunn, Mayne's second-in-command. Taking McCunn, and the man charged to care for him, under their wing, at 0330 hours they'd reached the north bank of the Litani. Under cover of darkness, Cheyne, together with a fellow sergeant, Nicol, had swum across the fast-flowing river, towing a line behind them. Once a heavier rope had been pulled over and made secure, Fraser and his men were able to ford the treacherous waters, though their haul of prisoners had to be left behind – boots and trousers removed, just to scupper any chances of them creating trouble.

Fraser brought with him a first-hand account of the battle for the Kafr Badda Bridge, which at any number of points had descended into a horrific bloodbath, with scores of French prisoners caught in a withering hail of crossfire. The last Fraser had seen of McGonigal's section, or any of the others for that matter, was as they split up and started to make their way towards friendly lines. In short, there was still no sign of McGonigal or his men, and little news of Colonel Pedder or any of his commandos.

It was then that a lone, bedraggled figure emerged from the sea to the west of the Litani, bringing with him the most extraordinary tale of derring-do, coupled with the most worrying news. Lance Corporal Robert 'Bob' Tait had just executed one of the most incredible escapes of the war. He'd fallen in with a party of commandos moving south from the Kafr Badda Bridge, taking to the beach in an attempt to skirt around enemy positions. Under the leadership of Captain George More – Z Force's overall commander – and with McGonigal and around twenty troops in their number, all had gone well until they'd reached a double fence of barbed wire. Even as they'd tried to cut their way through it, the darkness was torn asunder by a pair of heavy machineguns, plus a 75mm field gun, opening fire on them from no more than forty yards away.

Within minutes three men lay dead, cut down in a hail of bullets and shrapnel, and three more lay wounded. In an act of extraordinary heroism, Lieutenant Geoffrey Parnacott, one of More's deputies, had broken cover to try to throw grenades, but had been shot in the head and killed. Realising that any further resistance was futile, the survivors had no option but to surrender. Yet one among them, Bob Tait, felt there was still just a chance of making a getaway. Slipping into the darkness, he stole down the beach and crept into the sea. From there, he had struck out for deeper water, before turning south and swimming for three thousand yards or so, until he was able to crawl out onto the southern bank of the Litani.

Rightly, Tait's coolness under fire would be praised in the after-action reports of several of No. 11 Commando's surviving officers. It wasn't simply his audacious escape that won acclaim. Earlier, pretty much single-handedly, Tait had taken out an enemy armoured car, using the cumbersome and archaic Boys anti-tank rifle – more commonly known as the 'elephant gun' due to its massive size – and driven off six more, as the enemy had attempted to retake the Kafr Badda Bridge. During Tait's fighting retreat, it had become clear that the enemy had retaken the high ground, including the barracks, which Colonel Pedder had earlier made his headquarters. This did not bode well for the fortunes of No. 11 Commando's chief, or for those under his command.

In short, Tait's surprise appearance that grim June morning did little to assuage the worries of Mayne, Fraser or their fellows. At that moment, well over a hundred of No. 11 Commando's officers and men were missing in action, fate unknown, including the unit's founder and iconic leader, Colonel Pedder, and Mayne's best friend in all the world, Eoin McGonigal. To Mayne, it was inconceivable that McGonigal – plus Pedder – might have perished in and among the battle-scarred Litani Hills. Mayne's closeness to McGonigal went far deeper than simply a love of sport, of Ireland and of elite soldiering.

It ran to the roots of shared kinship, clan, homeland and family.

Robert Blair Mayne was one of seven siblings – Mary (Molly), Thomas, Barbara, William, Frances, Robert and Douglas. But even in the Mayne family tree his name is recorded simply as 'Blair', and that was how he was known by friends, family and colleagues. It was a name with a special resonance. He had been christened after his mother's cousin, Robert Blair, who had served with the Border Regiment in France, being killed by a sniper's bullet in 1916. The year before, Robert Blair had been awarded the Distinguished Service Order (DSO), for rescuing wounded comrades 'without regard for his own safety' and 'while coming under heavy and sustained fire'. The words of his namesake's citation would echo uncannily down the ages, almost as if Blair Mayne's fate somehow had been preordained.

While the Mayne family could trace a lineage stretching back several generations living in and around the Ards Peninsula, the tongue of land forming the east coast of County Down's Strangford Lough, Blair Mayne's great-grandmother was actually one Frances O'Neill, hailing from the ancient O'Neill clan, one of the oldest documented families in Europe. The O'Neills trace their roots back to A D 360. More to the point, their ancestors had migrated to the Nether Clan de Boy region of Antrim, and then to County

Down in the early fourteenth century, meaning that their Irish roots reached back some seven centuries.

Mayne's father, William, was a successful businessman and property owner, and his mother, Margaret, was the daughter of a wealthy linen merchant. The family home, Mount Pleasant, was a distinguished looking Georgian house set in forty acres of woodland overlooking the town of Newtownards. As a young boy Mayne had a warm, big-sisterly relationship with Barbara and Frances, Molly having married and moved away. With a father and older brothers who excelled at sports, he showed real aptitude at ball games, and proved a fine marksman with a .22 (small bore) rifle. Fly-fishing, hunting and deer-stalking in the surrounding countryside were favourite childhood pastimes.

Their Mount Pleasant home was a singularly musical, convivial place, and the young Blair showed an early love of Irish folk songs, particularly those of Percy French, the singer, poet and writer whose work was often distinguished by comic, ribald and irreverent - deliciously rebellious – lyrics. There was one shadow that cast a pall over Mayne's early life: the death of his hard-drinking, hard-fighting, wild-at-heart eldest brother, Tom. It was said to have been a shooting accident. It might well have been suicide. At school the young Blair proved somewhat withdrawn, shy and 'bookish', being drawn to poetry, music and writing. Aged ten, his school report showed his highest mark being in English – 87 per cent - with Algebra a close second, at 81 per cent. 'Works well. General form work good,' concluded his headmaster.

It was chiefly on the sports field that Mayne would overcome his reserve, and his true leadership qualities would begin to shine through. At Regent House Grammar School, in Newtownards, his love of rugby came to the fore, and at the age of eighteen he was chosen to captain the local Ards Rugby Club First XV. This was unprecedented in a team of far older, more experienced and grizzled players. Team photos from the time show Mayne as a fresh-faced teenager seated among bearded and balding veterans. But he proved to have the maturity and self-awareness to captain the team without displaying arrogance or any sense of his young ego getting in the way. Indeed, Ards Rugby Club reports from the time note how Mayne's 'enthusiasm and thoroughness made him an ideal leader'.

Likewise, the McGonigal clan was rooted in a similar milieu. They too hailed from a peninsula, in their case Donegal, which forms the rugged north-west coast of Ireland, reaching out into the Atlantic. It was a setting that defined the family – wild, independent, untamed. The earliest McGonigals counted smugglers ('gentleman farmers'), bootleggers, priests, soldiers – and latterly lawyers – among their ranks. With parts of the clan emigrating to Belfast, marriages across the religious divide were common – Catholic McGonigals marrying into Presbyterian families and somehow making it work. They were fiercely proud of their Irishness, while remaining resolutely non-partisan, and cherishing their ability to straddle the sectarian divide.

In terms of martial tradition, few McGonigals had evidenced any hesitation in joining the British military. Eoin's first cousin, Harold McGonigal, raised as a Catholic on Ireland's west coast, had served with the Leinster Regiment in the First World War, winning the Military Cross (MC) for bravery. Another first cousin, Robert McGonigal, had served with the Royal Garrison Artillery, earning his first MC in 1916, during the battle of St Eloi, in the Ypres Salient, when a mortar shell fell into his trench and failed to explode, Robert picking it up and hurling it back at the enemy. His second MC (bar) was earned two years later, when his position was surrounded, yet he kept his guns firing, until, though badly wounded in one leg, he managed to lead his men to safety.

It was Ambrose McGonigal, Eoin's older brother, who had pioneered the pair's warrior spirit. Adventurous, unconventional individuals, Ambrose and Eoin used to joke that for the Irish especially, rules were made to be broken. Indeed, one of the brother's aunts, Carmen, would end up serving as a driver for Winston Churchill during the war, and she would be awarded an OBE for her service. But she would return it 'in disgust' in 1965, when all The Beatles were awarded MBEs. This was the first time such an honour had been bestowed upon 'pop stars', previously being reserved almost exclusively for military veterans, and the fighter in Carmen did not approve.

In time, Eoin proved the wilder, more mischievous of the brothers, yet he managed to get away with almost anything due to his quick humour and charm. Their father was a judge, their mother the daughter of an Irish whiskey magnate. While the family home lay on the Malone Road, an upmarket area of Belfast, the brothers were sent away to boarding school in the south – first to Dominicans, in Dublin, run by a Catholic religious order. They'd hated it, and made several dramatic escape attempts. From there they were sent to Clongowes Wood College, in County Kildare, a Catholic boarding school known as 'the Eton of Ireland'. There they had thrived. The brothers were appointed 'leaders' of the school debating society, and Eoin was praised for being 'very good at repartee', his prize-winning speeches typically combining 'humour and reason'.

Eoin earned a reputation as being a fast, decisive and aggressive sportsman. Captaining school and county cricket teams, he was praised for having 'steadiness, and the patience to wait for bad balls ... He has a quick eye, good hands and an abundance of courage.' Studying law prior to the outbreak of the war, the McGonigal brothers shared a strong idealistic streak and a rigorous sense of duty. Just days after Nazi Germany's invasion of Poland in September 1939, they had signed up as officer trainees with the Royal Ulster Rifles (RUR), and that brought them directly into the orbit of Blair Mayne.

The Royal Ulster Rifles epitomised the McGonigal clan's

outlook – it recruited from both north and south of the border, welcoming both Protestants and Catholics. Its motto – *quis seperabit*; 'who shall separate us' – spoke volumes. Recruits made a point of sticking together, regardless of religion or creed, and were in the habit of singing each other's sectarian fighting songs.

While Mayne would be nicknamed 'Paddy' during the war – all Irishmen seemed to automatically earn that moniker – to Eoin and Ambrose he was always known simply as 'Blair'. Outside of the barracks, their friendship blossomed over pints of Guinness in the local Adair Arms Hotel, and reliving tales of sporting glories new and old. Of course, Mayne – three years older than Ambrose, six years senior to Eoin – had already lived the life of sporting legend. He recognised the McGonigal brothers as kindred spirits, and when not immersed in training duties the three friends spent their leave visiting each other's homes.

The RUR barracks was a former granary, situated in the green and leafy park-cum-parade and sporting ground, The Mall, in the town of Armagh. There, they'd shared stone-cold, bare rooms, sleeping in bedding rolls on canvas-framed camp beds. The regiment boasted a fine rugby team, including 'a number of top class players, among whom were the brothers Eoin and Ambrose McGonigal', but none more so than 'the legendary Blair (Paddy) Mayne'. At the officer's bar, regular bouts of 'mess rugby' were fuelled by copious quantities of Guinness and Irish whiskey. During one such evening, the stocky figure of the unit's Commanding Officer (CO), Victor Crowley, was at the heart of the melee. Then, a 'tall, lean, dark figure' loomed behind the CO, and brought a heavy silver tray down on his head, using both hands to deliver maximum force.

The blow was dealt by Ambrose McGonigal, and the burly Crowley sank to his knees. But 'tough guy that he was, he got up again almost immediately.' By then, Ambrose had disappeared. He was discovered outside, completely passed out. It turned out that

40

one of the company's batmen had drugged the trainee officer, 'to keep him from any further trouble'. He was carried to the sleeping quarters, where his friends undressed him, put him in his pyjamas and got him safely to bed. The CO never did discover who or what had hit him, and in any case all was deemed fair in love and war . . . and mess rugby.

During his time with the RUR, Eoin had nurtured a love of writing. This was one of the quiet passions he shared with Blair Mayne, for both cherished a dream of one day becoming writers. Eoin penned short stories with a dramatic, rebellious, romantic bent. In one, the village beauty spurns the offer of marriage and an easy life from a respectable local man, choosing instead to run off with a one-legged, wild-eyed, crude-spoken seaman, who whisks her away with the 'promise of impassioned argument and adventure'. In another, entitled 'The Escape', Eoin's main protagonist discovers that his wife, a former cabaret dancer, is having a wild love affair with a dashing, Casanova-type character named . . . Mayne.

In the spring of 1940, the 2nd Battalion Cameronians (Scottish Rifles) had sought officer recruits from the RUR to join their ranks. Eoin McGonigal and Blair Mayne had volunteered right away. Ambrose, sadly, could not, for he had broken his leg while riding a motorcycle during training. The two volunteers had been with the RUR for months, and the motive behind their move was a thirst for action. Shortly after getting attached to the Cameronians – their parent regiment was still officially the RUR – they volunteered in turn for No. 11 Scottish Commando. It was 8 August 1940, and at the time they were the only two Irish officers to have joined its ranks. It was fully ten months before they would get to see the action they had so craved.

It would culminate in the decimation of No. 11 Commando, the unit which they held so dear.

CHAPTER FOUR

The Fallen

It was not until mid-morning on 10 June that Mayne would receive a hint of any positive news. As the Australian-led forces pushed north of the Litani River, their armoured cars and scout vehicles to the fore, enemy commanders saw the writing on the wall. In a bitter irony, those French soldiers who had opened fire on More and McGonigal's makeshift section, taking the surrender of those who had survived, would in turn offer their surrender to their captives. On the morning of 10 June, Captain More accepted it, and around 1100 hours he was able to lead what remained of his unit across the Litani River, to rejoin the rump of No. 11 Commando.

In spite of the joy at their reappearance, the news they brought was utterly stark. Over and above their own heavy losses, it was Colonel Pedder's Force Y that had suffered the worst casualties of all. One of the few survivors from Pedder's unit was the Regimental Sergeant Major (RSM), Lewis Tevendale, who likewise had been captured by the enemy, and released once the Australian advance got under way. Having commandeered a car and evacuated the wounded to the nearest field hospital, Tevendale had made his way back to friendly lines. It was from him that Mayne would hear the most shattering news of all.

By 0900 hours the previous morning, Colonel Pedder had realised how tenuous was their hold on the enemy barracks-cum-HQ.

They were surrounded on three sides, the enemy launching a series of ferocious counter-attacks, using machineguns and highly accurate sniper fire to harass his forces. As Pedder's men dashed this way and that, setting up Bren positions to repulse the enemy, they began taking casualties. One of the first to fall was twenty-three-year-old Lieutenant Alistair Coode, shot in the chest and killed outright. As reports came in thick and fast of others hit and wounded, Pedder gave the order to withdraw, using the deep gully via which they had seized the barracks, and aiming to move south towards the Litani River.

Leading from the front, Pedder spearheaded the dash for that ravine, but even as he did a cry went up: 'Tevendale! Farmiloe! I'm shot!' The call was to his RSM, plus his second-in-command, Captain Robin Farmiloe, both of whom had been racing for the cover themselves. Tevendale was the first to reach Pedder. 'I dashed across to him,' he would report, 'and found that he had been shot through the back and chest and died immediately.' Of course, the loss of No. 11 Commando's iconic founder was a devastating blow, but at that moment there was little time to grieve. Captain Farmiloe was forced to assume command, and he ordered the surviving men to take cover and return fire.

Meanwhile, Lieutenant Bryan – Mayne and McGonigal's Lamlash room-mate – was unaware that Pedder had been killed. He dashed across the bullet-torn terrain, in an effort to report to their CO. As he approached, he heard a voice yelling out: 'The Colonel's hit.' In a shouted conversation, Bryan learned the terrible news that Pedder was dead. There was nothing for it but to try to rejoin those forces gathered in the gully, and from there to make a stand. As Bryan ordered his men to make a run for it, the first to his feet, a figure who'd suffered one flesh wound already, was cut down.

Moments later Bryan himself felt a 'tremendous bang', and tumbled over. He'd actually been shot in the leg and was bleeding

43

profusely and in immense pain. As he swallowed a morphine pill, he realised that even the slightest movement drew accurate enemy fire, and that his only chance of survival was to lie perfectly still. In the nearby gully, matters were little better. Captain Robin Farmiloe, known as 'Bambino' – 'Little Boy we nicknamed you, Body and spirit of a happy lad,' as Captain Duncan would write of him – was shot by a sniper in the right temple, and killed instantly.

Finding Farmiloe's body, RSM Tevendale was forced to assume command himself. Gathering up a rump of survivors, he retreated to a knoll of high ground, from where they would resist for an incredible further seven hours, 'inflicting heavy casualties' on their adversaries. But eventually – all out of bullets and bombs, not to mention water and food – Tevendale and his men were forced to surrender. They were taken to a makeshift POW muster point, which doubled as a medical station. There, they discovered the badly wounded Lieutenant Bryan, among others. Shortly, a French doctor would be forced to amputate Bryan's leg, using a guillotine, in an effort to save his life.

Of course, for Mayne, Fraser, McGonigal and the other survivors, learning of the loss of Colonel Pedder was the bitterest blow of all. That, along with the death of so many of their fellow officers, meant that No. 11 Commando had been effectively decapitated. More to the point, of the 456 men who had deployed from the commando, it would transpire that over 130 had been killed or grievously wounded, and scores more had suffered injuries. Was this something from which No. 11 Commando could ever recover? Could they reshape, reform and resuscitate their iconic unit? Who could tell.

As the weary survivors withdrew from the field of battle, all they did know for sure was that they had paid a terrible price for the Litani River landings. As Mayne wrote to his brother Douglas, in what was effectively a requiem for No. 11 Commando, 'it was not the same once the CO got written off . . . I think the commandos are finished out here.'

Those would prove darkly prophetic words.

On 14 June 1941 the survivors of the Litani River operation sailed back to Cyprus. Upon arrival, they learned that their exploits were being hailed as those of true heroes who had pulled off a historic victory. 'It was a complete Military success,' declared an official British Army briefing, of their mission. Lieutenant Colonel Robert 'Bob' Laycock, the commanding officer of the Middle East Commando – the umbrella unit for Nos. 7, 8 and 11 Commandos – praised their courageous and outstanding performance. General Archibald Wavell, then the overall commander of British forces in the Middle East, commended their standout success, 'although at the cost of somewhat heavy casualties'.

In London, in due course, Churchill would herald 'a daring raid by No. 11 Commando, which was landed from the sea behind enemy lines. In this devoted stroke the Commando lost its leader, Colonel Pedder, who was killed with four of his officers . . .' Britain's wartime leader noted that the commando's heroic deeds had cost them dear, the unit losing 'over a quarter of its strength'.

Rightly, there were to be a slew of decorations, including MCs for Lieutenant Bryan (who had survived his injuries and the amputation of his leg) for Major Keyes and Captain More. Lieutenant Eric Garland, the first of Keyes' men to make it across the Litani River, was awarded a bar to his existing MC. RSM Tevendale received the Distinguished Conduct Medal, and so too did Bob Tait, the miracle escapee. Mayne himself was mentioned in dispatches.

There was no decoration, even posthumously, for Colonel Pedder.

Yet despite the shower of accolades, there was seen as being little future for all three commandos in the Middle East, or anywhere else for that matter. Nos. 7 and 8 Commandos were already facing disbandment, and all signs were that No. 11 would suffer the same fate. Following a string of defeats at the hands of General Erwin Rommel's Afrika Korps, Britain's senior commanders in the Middle East were desperate for reinforcements to fill gaps in their frontline positions. Those three commandos were seen as offering rich and easy pickings. In short, the writing was well and truly on the wall.

For Mayne, and others, this was the bitterest pill to swallow. Despite the sterling performance of their unit, and the bloody sacrifices of recent days, they were to face the final cut. The brotherhood was finished. Anger, disappointment and disillusionment seethed, as these highly trained warriors nursed their wounds, grieved for the fallen and wondered what the future might hold. It all came to a head one evening in their officer's mess on Cyprus. Accounts differ, but one thing is for certain: Mayne ended up running Major Keyes out of there on the end of a bayonet.

After Colonel Pedder's death, command had fallen by default to Keyes. Mayne had come to dislike Keyes, and especially in view of the near-suicidal sacrifices that had resulted from his orders at the Litani River. The feeling was mutual, and particularly following Mayne's bayonet-charge. Mayne and McGonigal had been playing chess at the time, and it was Mayne's ability to go from flash to bang in the blink of an eye that had convinced Keyes he was 'a loose cannon . . . who couldn't control his temper'. A disciplinary investigation – a blood-letting – followed, in which Keyes would write of Mayne, in his diary: 'Produced Paddy before Div Commander, and he is rocketed . . .'

In spite of receiving that 'rocketing' – a verbal dressing down – Mayne's disquiet festered. What was really eating him – plus all the men of his section – was the killing of their dog. During the long weeks of tiresome garrison duties they had performed on Cyprus – betwixt the Arran training and their Litani River baptism of fire – they had found and adopted a stray. Mayne was a die-hard lover of animals. He'd been brought up that way, at the Mount Pleasant family home. Rare was the childhood photos that didn't feature an animal, whether cat, dog or chicken, alongside Mayne and his siblings. His own dog, a collie-St Bernard cross, would wait for him to come home, if ever he went out without him.

But during Mayne and his men's absence fighting and dying in the Litani Hills, one of No. 11 Commando's officers had seen fit to shoot their dog, which he'd disparaged as a tiresome stray.

Tiresome stray it was not. It was the adopted mascot of Mayne's section. Upon returning to Cyprus, they had discovered the dog's demise, and Mayne and his men were not happy. A few nights after the Keyes-bayonetting incident, the alleged dog-killer, Major Bevil Charles Alan Napier – like Keyes, a fellow high-born officer – was set upon by a 'huge unknown assailant' as he was returning from the mess to his tent. In the ensuing ruckus, Napier was soundly thrashed. Though he could not say for sure that his attacker had been Mayne, he reported as much to Keyes, who would note in his diary: 'Charles got beaten up . . . Paddy suspected, and Charles sure of it; but no proof.'

Regardless of the lack of proof, Keyes ensured that Mayne took the rap, and on 23 June 1941 he was formally RTU'd – returned to his unit. With trite and easy prejudice, Keyes would conclude of the incident: 'Very sorry to lose him, as he did awfully well in battle . . . He is however, an extremely truculent Irishman . . .' Mayne had neither denied nor accepted responsibility for the Napier drubbing. Any number of his men were incensed at the loss of their dog. Any one of them could have administered the tent-side thrashing. Either way, Mayne took the fall and was sent on his way.

With Mayne gone, Colonel Pedder killed, and so many more injured, or dead and buried, Eoin McGonigal was similarly racked by disquiet, and especially since the Commando itself faced dissolution. While he continued writing his short stories, the light-hearted romantic and rebellious adventure tales were replaced by 'markedly colder stories of murder and extortion', featuring a 'series of particularly callous and unnecessary' killings, as his grand-nephew, Patric McGonigal, would describe them. Through their pages ran one unifying theme – the thirst for revenge, and the need to satiate a burning sense of payback.

Shortly after the Litani River mission, Eoin wrote to his brother Ambrose. Though constrained by the censors in terms of what he could say, his letter is replete with disillusion and resentment. 'As you probably saw from the papers, the Scottish Commando has been blooded, and blooded was the only word for it. The McGonigal carcass is still undamaged, I'm glad to say; but I do not suppose we are allowed to say anything more . . .' Most shocking, in terms of McGonigal's volte-face, is the stark warning with which he signs off the letter – 'for goodness sake don't volunteer for this Commando business . . . certainly this job has not panned out as we were led to hope it will.'

As matters transpired, Mayne would get waylaid on his route back to the British Isles to be RTU'd. He fell ill with malaria and was admitted to the 19th General Hospital, in Alexandria, Egypt. In spite of his being assailed by burning high temperatures and nausea, things could have been worse and for several reasons. First, as Mayne wrestled with his malarial fevers and delirium, so the wheel of fate in London was turning, and this time it would augur well for commando-style operations.

That July, Churchill met with Brigadier Laycock, and he was incensed upon learning the fate of the Middle East Commando. On 23 July 1941 he duly issued an order to his Chiefs of Staff, and a stern reprimand: 'I wish the Commandos in the Middle East to be reconstituted as soon as possible . . . Laycock should be appointed the DCO [Director of Combined Operations] . . . The ME Command have indeed maltreated and thrown away this valuable force.' At least Britain's prime minister could be relied upon to see sense.

Secondly, during his hospitalisation Mayne had plenty of time to think and to plan. He'd learned that a new, volunteers-only outfit was being raised, the No. 204 Military Mission to China, the aim of which was to raise and train a Chinese guerrilla army to fight the Japanese. Anticipating Japan's joining the Axis in the not too distant future, Churchill had decreed that Britain would need to send 'well-equipped experts in this form of warfare' to train the Chinese.

Churchill charged Brigadier Laycock to form what was to be a top-secret unit, for of course Britain and Japan were not yet formally at war. Laycock sought recruits, both officers and men, who were to commence their mission at the British military's Bush Warfare School in Burma. To Mayne, this seemed right up his street. He put his name forward, while giving the nod to McGonigal that he should do the same. In volunteering for the China mission, Mayne was very much pushing on an open door. After learning of his Litani River exploits, Laycock held him in the very highest regard. After all, leading from the front Mayne had seized his objective, captured the largest number of prisoners and brought them back to friendly lines laden with weaponry.

As far as Laycock was concerned, Mayne embodied all the qualities of a commando leader, displaying ingenuity of thought and action, the ability to operate with speed, aggression and surprise, and to adapt his orders to fast-moving situations. Laycock requested a report from Mayne, summarising his actions at Litani River. But with Mayne hospitalised, it was left to Captain Moore to interview several of the men of Mayne's unit, to document exactly what they had achieved. Regardless of the 'cloud' that Mayne was under – RTU'd, malaria-racked – when he volunteered for the No. 204 Military Mission to China, he was doing exactly what Laycock had hoped he would.

As a bonus for Mayne, in that Alexandria hospital he met a pretty Irish nurse, who seemed to make it her special duty to nurture this feverish, war-worn and beguiling young officer who had fallen under her care. Jane Kenny was a thirty-one-year-old Nursing Sister from Longford, a town lying well to the south of the border. She'd been drawn to Mayne's Irishness, and especially once he loaned her his copy of the *Works of Percy French*, for she was as homesick as anyone. Mayne asked her to write to his big sister, Barbara, to let her know how he was faring. Now, Mayne was as fine a letter-writer as any. None better, one could argue. He didn't need any Irish nurse to pen his missives for him. But as a means to woo Jane Kenny, it was a subtle and endearing come-on.

Mayne was known to be especially shy with women. As a sixteen-year-old, with typical teenage angst, he'd bemoaned in his diary about not being able to compose a decent love letter. His overtures to Jane Kenny seemed to have proven far more effective. In due course she did indeed write to his sister, opening with the line: 'I'm sure you will be surprised to get a letter from somebody you never heard of – so I must introduce myself.' After doing just that, she explained that when she had told Mayne 'how well he looked', he'd asked her to 'write and tell my sisters', because 'I know they worry about me . . .'

Of Mayne's lending her the Percy French book, she pointed out how 'any little bit of Ireland out here is welcome.' And she closed with this: 'I must say au revoir now – and don't worry about your brother (sorry, I don't know his Christian name, all Irishmen out here are called Paddy), he is very fit and I needn't tell you is doing a grand job of work – I'm sure you must all be very proud of him.'

Jane Kenny and 'Paddy' Mayne would meet again during the war, and long after the latter had been discharged from hospital.

But for now, as he lay there wrestling with malaria and its debilitating fevers, Mayne realised how much he missed his Irish friends. He wrote to his sister Barbara – 'Babs' – lamenting how,

'I haven't seen McGonigal for over a month now ... As well as McGonigal, there was another Belfast boy in our unit. Gerald Bryan was his name, lived somewhere on the Malone Road. He unfortunately got wounded in the foot and is, I think, a prisoner of war.' Once he had recovered from having his leg amputated, Lieutenant Bryan would get released from captivity. He would be awarded the MC for his exceptional bravery at the Litani River, and would go on to serve with the Special Operations Executive (SOE) – Churchill's 'Ministry for Ungentlemanly Warfare' – for the remainder of the war.

Much that Mayne might miss his wounded and dead comrades, as he tossed and turned on a hospital mattress that was often sopping wet with sweat, what he hungered for most was vengeance. Vengeance for those dear friends – those brothers-in-arms – whose life blood had drained into the dry dust and dirt of the Litani Hills. There were so many to be avenged, and what made matters worse was that they had fallen fighting enemies who should have been allies; adversaries who should have been true and constant friends.

It was Nazi Germany's brute aggression – the blitzkrieg unleashed upon Western Europe and the lightning seizure of France – that had turned long-lived ally against ally, forcing the showdown in the Litani Hills, and all the horror and carnage that had followed. In June 1940 Churchill had reached out to the French Government, seeking to convince them to stay true to the tried and trusted alliance that had proved so enduring during the First World War, and no matter the Nazi onslaught. But Pétain had rejected Churchill's overtures, declaring that Britain was doomed. If France continued to stand with her, it would be 'a fusion with a corpse', Pétain had pronounced in a damning riposte.

Well, as Mayne appreciated – and as the actions of No. 11 Commando had so powerfully shown – a pulse still beat in the heart of that corpse. There was life in the mother country yet. The

British Isles might be down and out, but their peoples remained far from vanquished.

In short, there was everything to fight for, if only Mayne could find the means to wage war.

CHAPTER FIVE

In the Beginning

The signboard looked decidedly forlorn and incongruous in the half-light, sat as it was amid a flat, desolate, wind-blasted sand-scape: 'STIRLING'S REST CAMP'.

To its rear lay a somewhat slapdash military encampment shrouded in pre-dawn murk. Its makeshift appearance was hardly surprising, for the men of this small, barely formed unit had been forced to steal everything in sight – every tent, guy rope, camp bed, chair and table; even the piano and the knives and forks in the mess – so loath was Middle East Headquarters (MEHQ) to properly supply and outfit these 'roguish upstarts'. In fact, the first order issued by the visionary founder of this unit was for his few dozen recruits to pilfer all they might need, which typified the kind of lateral thinking that would come to distinguish their operations. In all that they did, they would be challenged to think the unthinkable and to do the unexpected.

Right now, the unthinkable and the unexpected had manifested itself in the fearsome-looking figure who was charging across a bodged-up 'sports field', rugby ball clutched firmly in one of his massive, size-eleven hands. Dust billowed and spurted around the melee of players, as the fortunes of the game ebbed and flowed, but today's match seemed markedly different. Word had done the rounds that the new recruit was a seasoned Ireland and British Lions rugby international, and while some had refused to believe it, his performance was starting to convince them otherwise. For all his muscled bulk and his spade-like hands, he seemed remarkably fast, nimble and light on his feet.

In reality, the daily routine here at Stirling's Rest Camp wasn't particularly restful. Each morning before sunrise, when the surrounding desert was still noticeably cool and crisp, the recruits donned navy-blue PT shorts and set out on either a punishing route-march, a desert run, or for a game of rugby, the chief aim of which was to 'knock each other about a bit'. If the rumours about their newest player were anything like accurate, there should be knocking about aplenty in store, and for all, regardless of rank or stature. Word was that Lieutenant Blair 'Paddy' Mayne had 'smacked' his last Commanding Officer, flooring him in a particularly heated argument.

Captain David Stirling, the Rest Camp's CO, was said to have had to resort to quite unprecedented measures to secure Mayne as one of his officer-recruits. Supposedly gaoled for assaulting an officer, Mayne was rumoured to have been facing a court-martial when Stirling bailed him out of trouble. In fact, the truth about Mayne's recruitment was somewhat more prosaic. Far from being imprisoned, he was still recuperating from malaria when Stirling paid him a visit, and he stood accused of nothing more serious than executing a messroom bayonet charge against Major Keyes, followed by an alleged drubbing of Major Napier, which had earned him an RTU from a commando unit that was in any case being disbanded.

In the ghostly light thrown off by the storm lanterns that served to mark the rough outlines of the pitch, the players had to keep moving simply in order to keep warm. It lent the match an added sense of pace and urgency. As the game ebbed and flowed, the knot of players flitting between the pools of illumination thrown off by the lanterns, they thundered from light to shadow and into light again, their cries ringing out through the pre-dawn stillness.

Supposedly all about instilling fitness and robustness, that was all quickly forgotten, for the only thing that mattered was the winning.

'Ouch!' rang out a startled cry, as one of Mayne's ham-sized fists ripped the ball away from an opposing player, after which he darted away with the prize, eyes flashing.

The bruising contact embodied in the anarchic pastime of 'bush rugby' – this up-close rough-and-tumble on a wholly unforgiving dirt pitch – conveyed a certain inner-confidence on these men; a sense that they could break all the rules, take the hardest of knocks, shrug them off and keep going. They would need to master that kind of mindset for what was to come. It also helped to forge a formidable team spirit – a sense that they were all in this together and that nothing much was to be taken too personally. As they got to know each other's strengths, weaknesses and foibles, the bonds between men – the camaraderie essential to such a unit – were deepened and strengthened.

As that morning's match progressed, Mayne proved himself to be noticeably vocal and animated. It was as if he had truly come alive. By contrast, those who'd had contact with him prior to this morning's knock-about had been struck by his still and quiet nature, which almost seemed to verge upon the brooding at times. When he did speak he generally volunteered few words, issued in a quiet, lilting Irish brogue. It was almost as if he did not have the words to waste, as if they were a peculiarly precious commodity.

True to character, at half-time Mayne's on-pitch volubility seemed to evaporate. From somewhere he produced a battered paperback and a cigarette, and he settled down to read and to smoke in silence. 'Enigmatic' was the thought that crossed many of the men's minds. That, and potentially dangerous. And a damn fine player on the rugby field. After that first match there were few who doubted his international sporting credentials, and especially since there were a handful of men present at Stirling's Rest Camp who knew of Mayne's prowess only too well.

Among Stirling's earliest recruits was Eoin McGonigal – the youngest officer then present – who had seemingly overcome his reticence for volunteering for any further 'commando business' in the name of wreaking bloody vengeance. Likewise, Bob Tait was there, a matter of weeks after executing his miracle escape, swimming across enemy lines. So too was the tough, bony frame of Bill Fraser – Skin Fraser – and his rock-hard-reliable deputy Jack Cheyne, who had taken command during the Litani River battle, when that lucky bullet had grazed Fraser's chin, but had left him largely unharmed. They knew the Mayne legend intimately, rugby exploits to the fore.

During the 1938 Lions tour – the apex of Mayne's sporting achievements – the epithet repeatedly used by the South African sports reporters, who were never ones to offer easy acclaim, was 'outstanding'. A press critic hailing from the legendary South African Morkel rugby-playing clan had declared of Mayne: 'He is the finest all-round forward I have ever seen and is magnificently built for the part. In staying power he has to be seen to be believed.' Fellow Irishman and Lions captain on the tour, Sammy Walker, hailed Mayne as being 'out on his own in strength, pugnacity and general usefulness'.

In the third and final Test against South Africa, at Cape Town's famous Newlands Stadium – slogan: 'We never lose at Newlands' – there were eight Irishmen, Mayne included, in the starting line-up. At the end of the match the crowd lifted the visiting captain, Walker, and his teammates high on their shoulders, for the Lions had confounded all expectations, winning the match 21 points to 16. Mayne himself was acclaimed as being 'outstanding in the open and magnificent in defence'.

'He was the roughest and strongest man I have ever known,' said Jammie Clinch, a renowned Irish forward, who confessed privately that Mayne was the only man he ever feared on the pitch. 'Off the field he was quiet, soft spoken and self-effacing,' Sammy Walker said of Mayne, 'but in the heat of the match he could be frightening. He never lost his temper but was cool and calculating on the field in everything he did.' As he was on the field of sports, so he would prove to be at war.

In a sense that had made it all the more impressive when Mayne had returned home, having been showered with international accolades, seemingly unchanged. To all appearances he was the same unassuming, intensely loyal individual as always. At a dinner held in his honour, at his old club, Ards RFC, they hailed this constancy: 'Loyalty of his magnitude was not common.' Presenting Mayne with a gold watch, inscribed *Ards RFC. Presented to R. B. Mayne, member of British Touring Team in South Africa, 1938*, they told him they hoped that this small token of 'affection and esteem from his old Club would perhaps come nearer to his heart than all the others he had received'.

In reply, Mayne gave a 'most humorous speech' – one met by deafening cheers and catcalls – in which he assured all present that he would treasure their precious gift as long as he lived, for his games with Ards were as memorable as any. He went on to regale his audience with stories of some of the club's more colourful players, one of whom was reputed to wear a leather belt onto the field, so he could tow the rest of the pack behind him, and another of whom ran with 'knees going up and down like pistons', and with his free arm 'smashing his way through all the opposition'.

Before heading home from the Lions tour, Mayne had perpetrated one act of singularly wild eccentricity, which epitomised how he was born to break the rules, and to do so with irrepressible high spirits, at least before the darkness of war and death came down. It was an incident that encapsulated his propensity to turn night into day, and to toss convention on its head. He had attended

57

a dance with his teammates, dressed in all their black-tie finery, but had clearly got bored. In the early hours he'd gone for a stroll and simply disappeared. He did not reappear until mid-morning, when he'd stepped into the hotel in which all were staying, a dead springbok slung across his shoulders, and his dress suit looking somewhat the worse for wear.

Heading for the room of fellow player Jimmy Unwin, he'd dumped the carcass on the sleeping man's bed, declaring as he did so, 'Fresh meat!' (Unwin had been complaining of a lack of meat on the tour.) As Unwin seemed markedly unimpressed, Mayne had carried the buck out of a window, climbed onto a ledge and proceeded to hang it outside of the bedroom of the South African team's coach, together with a note reading 'FRESH MEAT'. Apparently, he'd met a group of locals at a streetside coffee stall, accepted their invitation to go hunting on a farm some distance away, borrowed a rifle and shot the buck. The best bit was, Mayne did not see his behaviour as particularly odd or unusual. He had the 'full measure of Irish wit and imagination', a news article in the *Johannesburg Star* would declare of the incident, once a reporter got wind of it.

A photo of Mayne from around this time shows him in the Mount Pleasant grounds, a tall, fit, confident young man with sparkling eyes, one of his favourite nieces, Margaret, aged around nine, perched atop his shoulders. He'd written to her from South Africa, declaring enthusiastically: 'You would certainly enjoy yourself out here, there are hundreds of animals, stags, antelopes, elephants – in fact everything that runs on four legs. And in the towns . . . I've seen coal-black women walking up the streets with happy looking babies strapped on their backs, and a load of washing balanced on their heads, it is really wonderful the way they can balance things . . . just walk along chattering away.'

He described seeing a 'snake-charmer, an old, old man with a white beard and a turban wound around his head, he played on his pipe and the snake weaved and danced to and fro. He was also a wonderful conjurer. I watched him very closely and I couldn't see how on earth he did his tricks. They seemed like black magic.' Mayne's fascination with trickery, sleight of hand and deception – the 'black arts' as he called it – would serve him well for what was coming, when the men of Stirling's Rest Camp would need to execute the unthinkable and the unexpected, deep behind enemy lines.

Back then, in the summer and autumn of 1938 – three years prior to his being 'blooded' in the war – Mayne was intent on nothing more than some light-hearted, avuncular teasing. He signed off his letter to his niece thus: 'By the way, Maggie my girl, I am printing this [the letter was written out in capitals] in order that you can read it yourself and if I hear of you getting your Daddy to read it to you, there will be a big row and I will tie your ears together when I come home.'

Yet by the time Mayne had reached Stirling's Rest Camp, in early September 1941, something had changed. As with McGonigal, a shadow had fallen over his sunnier disposition, darkening it noticeably. The horror and the loss and the subsequent let-downs – the perceived betrayal – following the Litani River battle, blighted the mood and the minds of many. The loss of over 130 fellow warriors to whom they had been so close, and the wider litany of wartime defeats in the face of a supposedly invincible enemy, quickened the hunger for payback, not to mention the appetite for risk and for blood.

In accepting Stirling's invitation to his Rest Camp, Mayne had decided against accepting Laycock's guerrilla warfare invitation – joining the No. 204 Military Mission to China. There is little doubt that Mayne had had his heart set on it, for he'd written to his brother Douglas, stating: 'I have put my name down for another move to the East. I think I should get it.' But certainly, David Stirling could be highly convincing when he set his mind to it. Stirling had the gift of being able to make whoever he was speaking to believe that he was offering him – or her – the world, and that he could deliver it.

Mayne and Stirling knew each other passably well, for whereas Mayne had served in No. 11 Commando, Stirling had volunteered for No. 8 (Guards) Commando, more commonly known as 'the Blue Bloods'. As well as counting Stirling, the scion of a well-connected Scottish landowning and military family, within its ranks, No. 8 boasted Winston Churchill's son, Randolph, as one of its officers. Stirling's nickname in the military was 'the Great Sloth', and he'd earned it by spending as much time drinking and gambling as he had in any kind of serious commando training. The fact that he had convinced a disillusioned Mayne – plus McGonigal, Fraser, Tait, Cheyne and others – to join his fledgling enterprise, reflected his powers of persuasion; his ability to make whoever he was talking to feel like a million dollars.

Mayne was just a few months older than Stirling, but he'd seen bruising action in the Litani Hills, whereas Stirling had yet to fire a shot in anger. At first, Mayne had regarded the offer to join his Rest Camp with undisguised scepticism. Why should he throw his lot in with this inexperienced, high-born officer and his seemingly far-fetched plans? Mayne grilled Stirling mercilessly as to his intentions, demanding proof that this wasn't simply another 'hare-brained paper scheme'; a case of out of the frying pan into the fire.

'What are the prospects of fighting?' Mayne had demanded, for of course that was all he hungered for just then.

Stirling had fixed him with a steady eye. 'None,' he had answered, levelly, 'except against the enemy.'

There had been a moment's silence, as Stirling had let the words sink in. Mayne's propensity for fisticuffs was well known, especially against his own side. Stirling went on to ask Mayne to guarantee that *he* would be one senior officer that would not be subjected to a drubbing, which seemed to do the trick.

Mayne cracked a smile. 'All right. I'm with you.'

The deal was done.

In time, Mayne and Stirling would forge a close bond – one of friendship, as well as that of fellow warriors. Stirling would liken Mayne to Harry Percy, known as 'Hotspur', the famed English knight of old who earned his iconic nickname from the Scots, due to his brave and fearless actions in battle and his speed of attack. As with the real-life Hotspur, Mayne was 'quick-tempered, audacious, vigorous in action,' Stirling would remark, 'but not one who took kindly to being thwarted, frustrated or crossed in any way.'

While Mayne did refrain from giving Stirling any kind of a drubbing, he was not averse to testing the man's loyalty and his steel. At one point he would subject the Great Sloth to his very own 'test of courage'. Mayne asked Stirling to stand very upright, rising to all of his six-feet-six inches, and with his arms clamped firmly by his sides. He was then to allow himself fall backwards, and Mayne would catch him with one hand, just before he hit the ground. Of course, Stirling didn't want to do it, and for obvious reasons. But Mayne insisted. It was to show that he could be trusted and that Stirling should 'never betray him'.

In the Special Air Service's own War Diary – for, of course, that was the unit that Mayne had agreed to sign up to – there are what amount to official photos of Stirling and Mayne, in the opening pages. Both show bearded, desert-worn individuals dressed in a motley collection of gear. Stirling's is entitled '"Phantom" Major' – the nickname he would earn even among his foremost enemies, the Afrika Korps. Mayne's is entitled 'Desert Rat'. Rat he may have been, but he was one with a set of iron-hard principles, among the foremost of which was being a champion of the underdog.

At one stage during the 1938 Lions tour, Mayne had discovered a group of black convicts working on constructing a new stand, at Johannesburg's Ellis Park stadium. Chained, they slept beneath the scaffolding. Mayne and a favourite teammate of his, the Welsh hooker Bill 'Bunner' Travers, went to investigate. Falling into conversation, they asked the convicts just what they might have done to be so treated. One explained he'd been caught 'stealing chickens, for which he got seven years'. Mayne and Travers nicknamed their new acquaintance 'Rooster'. Returning that night with bolt cutters and sets of clothing, they had proceeded to set the prisoners free.

In the SAS War Diary – a record 'devoid of glamour or romance . . . a history of British soldiers who preferred to fight in a technique all of their own' – Stirling's powers of persuasion are lauded. 'It was said of him he could "argue the hind leg off a full Colonel at least".' He certainly worked his magic on Mayne, whose recruitment is described thus: 'Chafing under too many cancelled operations, his restlessness drove him . . . to throw in his lot with Stirling's band of desert raiders. This was work which appealed to him. Reckless he may have seemed, but . . . he brought a firm conviction that to take unreasonable risks was to invite disaster. That conviction he never lost.'

Stirling's pitch had appealed to many others with equally hard-earned reputations. Among No. 11 Commando's disaffected ranks he had discovered fertile recruiting grounds. (There were half-a-dozen courts-martial pending at the time of the commando's demise, a sure sign of how greatly discipline and *esprit de corps* had fallen apart.) In fact, almost all of Stirling's sixty-seven originals would be culled from Nos. 7, 8 and 11 Commandos. Fortuitously, those highly trained and driven soldiers would make perfect candidates for what the SAS's founder had in mind. He was to take a crack outfit – the Middle East Commando – and transform it into the elite of the elites.

Yet right then, in early September 1941, Stirling's SAS was little more than a sketchy idea on paper. There was much work to be done, if he was to get everything ready for their very first operation in a little under three months' time. The Commander-in Chief of Middle East Command, General Sir Claude Auchinleck, was planning a winter offensive, Operation Crusader, which was designed to reverse the enemy's fortunes, driving Rommel's Afrika Korps back across the desert, over lands they had only recently conquered. The SAS was to be deployed in support of Crusader, striking deep behind enemy lines. The scheduled start date was the night of 17/18 November 1941, leaving Stirling precious little time to prepare.

But that was what he had signed up to, and he and his men had better be ready.

CHAPTER SIX

Brothers in Arms

Stirling and Mayne were not so very far apart from each other, in terms of background, upbringing and outlook. The main differences lay in what each had achieved in life during their first twenty-something years.

Stirling was born into a well-to-do Scots-Catholic clan, which had inhabited Keir House, a grand, sprawling country residence in Perthshire, central Scotland, for little short of five centuries. His father was an MP and his maternal grandfather was the 16th Baron Lovat. One of six children, at war's outbreak he had two brothers serving in the Scots Guards. One, Hugh, his junior by four years, had sadly fallen victim to the struggle. On 20 April 1941, Lieutenant Hugh Stirling had been shot while on a desert patrol. Listed as 'Missing and Wounded', his body was never found. He had fallen near El Alamein, Egypt, a place that would come to have iconic significance during the war.

Passionate about the archetypal Scottish pursuits – shooting, deer-stalking, mountaineering – the Stirlings were known for their enthusiasm for life and their sociability. But David, the middle child, had proved something of an errant son. Sent to Ampleforth – a Catholic boarding school run by Benedictine monks – he'd done relatively well, but by the time he went to Cambridge University he'd lost interest in his studies, spending too much time at the horses, gambling. Seeming rudderless in life, he'd moved to Paris, where he was determined to make it as an artist, but he'd never quite managed it. He'd dabbled in a spot of ranching in the USA, before setting upon a suitably ambitious life venture, aiming to become the first person to scale Mount Everest.

But all such aspirations were cut short when war broke out, which promptly ended his dreams of conquering the world's highest peak. He'd headed home from the USA, joining up with the Scots Guards. Like Mayne, he'd demonstrated an instinctive dislike of drill and mindless military routine. During officer training at Sandhurst, he was assessed as being 'irresponsible and unremarkable', and was criticised for disobeying orders and spending too much time partying. He'd volunteered for the commandos, hoping to see action as one of 'Churchill's cut-throats', as Lord Haw Haw, the traitor who broadcast propaganda from Nazi Germany, would call them, and which was exactly what Stirling hoped they would become.

It hadn't quite worked out that way, for a string of abortive missions had followed. With the Middle East Commando facing disbandment, a disheartened Stirling had cast around for something useful to do. He certainly didn't believe that the concept of Special Service – the commandos – had no future in North Africa. To his mind, the nature of the terrain – a thin strip of cultivated Mediterranean coastline, with a vast expanse of sun-blasted, waterless and deeply inhospitable desert and mountains lying to the south – had to lend itself to guerrilla-style warfare. The problem with the commandos had been their means of insertion – they were chiefly an amphibious force, trained for the kind of seaborne landings of the Litani River ilk. Their raiding units had been too large and too hard to conceal, with the result that they had failed to achieve the all-important element of surprise.

Stirling had put his mind to thinking if there mightn't be another way. His family were influential. They had friends in high places. That would play a key role in the summer of 1941, as he conceived of his Big Idea – the SAS. At its inception, of course, the unit existed only on paper and in Stirling's head, and it had no name. That June, he'd managed to get his hands on a few dozen parachutes. Teaming up with Lieutenant John Steel 'Jock' Lewes, of the Welsh Guards, another commando veteran, and with Brigadier Laycock's blessing, they'd decided to give parachuting a try. If that means of insertion could be mastered, surely they could drop anywhere along the hundreds of miles of Rommel's supply lines, stealing in from the desert to cause havoc and mayhem.

There were six wannabe parachutists – Lewes and Stirling included – who took to the skies over Egypt one morning in late June 1941. They were riding in an RAF Vickers Valentia, an ageing biplane of 1934 vintage more commonly used for transport and mail-delivery duties. On that first flight the Valentia disgorged nothing more exciting that a makeshift dummy cobbled together from 'sandbags and tent poles'. The parachute seemed to open just fine, but the tent poles were smashed upon impact. Next up, it was the human dummy's turns. They had been advised to 'dive out as though going into water'.

All seemed to be proceeding just fine, before the first of the jumpers 'was surprised to see Lt. Stirling pass me in the air ...' He was going like a rocket and hurt himself upon landing, having 'injured his spine and also lost his sight for about an hour'. Stirling had managed to snag the canopy of his parachute on the Valentia's angular, box-like tail, tearing it badly – hence his precipitous rate of descent. Hospitalised, he faced a long recovery, and it was three weeks before he could even begin to walk again. However, his enthusiasm for parachuting remained undimmed. The others had completed their jumps largely unscathed. To his mind, there was everything to play for.

In hospital, Stirling had ample time to reflect. It was there that he came up with the idea to form a unit intended to 'harass

66

the enemy to the very last', realising that 'in the wide space of the Desert, adventurous men, resourcefully led, could play merry hell with the enemy . . .' In his mind, the ideal number for such raiding parties was around six, the size of the stick that had taken their leap of faith from the Valentia. They needed to operate with complete autonomy, hitting enemy airbases, arms and fuel dumps, plus any other targets of opportunity. And of course, surprise would be key. Dropping in from the skies, he wasn't entirely sure how they would get out again, but very possibly the Long Range Desert Group (LRDG) could retrieve them. Formed in July 1940, the vehicle-borne LRDG were desert navigation and survival specialists, charged to gather intelligence on the enemy deep inside hostile territory.

Having sounded out his idea with Lewes and others, and got a qualified thumbs-up, the next major challenge was to get it passed by MEHQ. Despite Churchill's recent edict that the commandos should rise again in the Middle East, Stirling feared that his idea would prove deeply unpopular. It would be seen as radical and revolutionary heresy, especially the suggestion that small bands of raiders should roam free across the desert, with little if any reference to high command. That kind of independence of action and free-thinking initiative was anathema to those in authority, whom Stirling would later characterise – with ample justification – as being 'fossilised shits'.

In his future fights with MEHQ, he would variously deride the middle ranks as 'freemasons of mediocrity', 'unfailingly obstructive and uncooperative' and 'astonishingly tiresome'. If he followed the proper chain of command, Stirling knew he would get nowhere. There is a tale – very likely apocryphal – of him breaking out of hospital and somehow breaking into the MEHQ building while on crutches, before busting his way into a senior commander's office, in order to present his plan in person. The truth is almost certainly far more mundane. Using the Stirling family influence – his brother, Bill, was based in Cairo, and via his secret service and military work was famously well connected – David Stirling got his written proposal into one or two senior commanders' hands, which eventually won him an audience with General Auchinleck himself.

Fortuitously, in 'The Auk' as he was universally known, Stirling found an enthusiastic ear. Auchinleck was in the midst of planning Operation Crusader. With Britain rocked by defeats on all fronts, Churchill was desperate for a victory in North Africa, if for no other reason than to shore up the morale of the British people. Equally, General Auchinleck had arrived in North Africa like a much-needed breath of fresh air, making it his mission to slash through the bureaucracy and red tape of MEHQ. He'd put a rocket under the slothful staff officers, demanding they work, like him, around the clock, making the men under their command the absolute number one priority.

For Auchinleck, the concept presented by Stirling, though quite unprecedented in terms of conventional military thinking, held out one great promise: at the risk of a few good men, it had the potential to strike a telling blow. If Stirling could do as he claimed and hit Rommel's airbases, that could have a real impact, for the Luftwaffe's fleets of warplanes were a fearsome menace in the clear blue skies of North Africa. Not only did the enemy have air-superiority right then, but in their Messerschmitt Me 109 they boasted a fighter aircraft that had the edge over any comparable British warplane.

Towards the end of June 1941, Stirling's paper proposal got the formal stamp of approval. In it, he argued persuasively that 'the destruction of 50 aircraft or units of transport was more easily accomplished by ... five men, than a force of 200.' To help sell the idea he proposed that 'The Unit', as it was then called, would deploy just before the planned Crusader offensive. On 'D minus 2' – so forty-eight hours before the opening shots were fired – five raiding parties would drop by parachute, to attack the 'five main forward Fighter and Bomber Enemy landing grounds'. They were to be inserted in the open desert, on a night with little moonlight, 'thus preserving surprise to the utmost'.

As each of the five parties would carry some sixty demolition charges, hundreds of enemy warplanes could be destroyed. It was little wonder that General Auchinleck was sold on the idea. At the risk of no more than sixty men – five sticks of around a dozen each – and very little war materiel, Stirling held out the promise of obliterating the lion's share of the enemy's warplanes. If the raiders could get in unseen, there was every reason for them to succeed. As with British forces, the enemy tended to feel invulnerable in their bases set hundreds of miles from hostile lines. There was little sense of any threat emanating from the open desert, where no living thing thrived.

Recognising this was Stirling's genius.

Churchill's July '41 edict to restart commando-style operations in North Africa was also starting to bite. MEHQ was forced to act. The rump of No. 11 Commando landed a similarly audacious mission as to what Stirling was proposing, if somewhat less strategically refined. In Operation Flipper, Major Keyes was to lead a party of twenty-five men, landing from the sea to attack Rommel's headquarters. The aim was simple: it was to kill or capture the German general. Flipper was slated for the evening of 17 November 1941, to coincide with the SAS's inaugural raids. Keyes, though excited, had reservations. In a letter to his parents he wrote of how it was 'dirty work at the crossroads with a vengeance, on the old original conception of the Commandos'.

Having secured the Auk's blessing, Stirling sat down with Brigadier Laycock to flesh out his plans, and to suss out who he might recruit for his fledgling unit. Laycock agreed that Jock Lewes was key, but so too were McGonigal, Bill Fraser and Mayne, fresh from their Litani heroics. Stirling suggested an old friend of his from Ampleforth days, Charles Bonington (the father of the future mountaineer, Chris Bonington), to complete the officer contingent. As to the 'other ranks', as Laycock pointed out, the remainder of the Middle East Commando were kicking around, just hungering for something to get their teeth into. Stirling was sure to find ample recruits there.

Stirling had few illusions as to the kind of men he sought. In one of his earliest plans, entitled 'L-Detachment, S.A.S. Brigade/ Aims and Men', he declared that 'An undisciplined TOUGH is no good, however tough he may be.' He stressed how he sought those who exhibited 'courage, fitness and determination in the highest degree', but equally 'discipline, skill, intelligence, and training'. Later, he would remark on what he termed his 'band of vagabonds', that 'they weren't really controllable. They were har-nessable [sic] . . . The object was to give them the same purpose and once they were harnessed to that proposition, then they . . . policed themselves, so to speak.'

Stirling referred to his fledgling unit as 'L-Detachment, S.A.S. Brigade' for very good reasons. Having overseen the formation of the commandos, Brigadier Dudley Clarke had been dispatched to North Africa, with deception firmly in mind. That February, the first ever airborne raid by British forces had been launched. In Operation Colossus, a team of thirty-six parachutists, christened No. 11 Special Air Service Brigade, had dropped deep into Italy's Apennine Mountains, tasked to blow up the Tragino Aqueduct, which piped fresh drinking water to millions of Italians. The aque-duct's water supply was critical to the smooth running of Italy's main ports, from where men and materiel were being shipped to North Africa. Destroy it, and those ports would be paralysed.

An audacious mission conceived by the Special Operations Executive, the Colossus raiders had succeeded against all odds (although all were subsequently captured and/or executed). Equally, as Clarke noted, the very idea that British parachutists might strike deep inside their territory had struck fear into the Italians. His deception operations in North Africa were designed to play on those fears. Clarke ensured that dummy parachutists were dropped at points where the enemy were bound to see them, and that mock-up gliders were positioned in the desert where enemy reconnaissance flights were sure to capture photographs of them.

Clarke and Stirling had struck up a friendship. When Stirling shared his idea for a behind-the-lines airborne raiding unit, Clarke spotted an immediate opportunity. If Stirling would christen his new force the 'Special Air Service', he would inherit the Operation Colossus mantle and lend real substance to Clarke's deceptions. As Stirling noted, 'Dudley Clarke welcomed the creation of a flesh and blood parachute unit, which greatly assisted him in his game with the enemy.' To further that deception, naming it 'L-Detachment' would suggest that there were also Detachments A–K in existence, so further pumping up the fearsome trickery. To 'humour' Clarke, Stirling agreed.

At the same time, the real purpose and function of the SAS remained top secret. When reports of the unit's existence did finally make it into the newspapers – much later in the war – their deception role would be to the fore. In a February 1945 article, entitled 'Confusion Is Their Business,' the *Reader's Digest* would hail the 'incredibles who create havoc behind the German lines . . . Britain's phantom army and its most irregular regulars'.

Stirling's Rest Camp – the base at which to train his 'irregular regulars' – was situated at Kabrit, in the aptly named Bitter Lakes region of Egypt. Lying on a headland jutting into the western reaches of the Bitter Lake – a stretch of water so salty as to be undrinkable – they had pitched their purloined camp almost on the very shoreline. Hewn from the nearby desert was a large air-base, RAF Kabrit, from where Stirling intended his men to begin their airborne training, while on the opposite side of their modest encampment lay HMS *Saunders*, a Royal Navy base (the Great and Little Bitter Lakes are linked to the Suez Canal, and thus to both the Mediterranean to the north and the Red Sea to the south).

Despite the strategic sighting of the Rest Camp, it was a god-forsaken wasteland of a setting; 'a wind like Emery Paper scoured the Great Bitter Lake', making it 'very unpleasant'. Spending any extended length of time there was a recipe for homesickness. Not long after his arrival, Eoin McGonigal would write to his brother Ambrose, exclaiming, 'This is a bloody repeat bloody part of the world. The Adair Arms and a thick glass of Guinness and heavy rain outside haunt every moment of the day.'

But in a sense, this desolate, alien setting was only as it should be, for where they were heading – the heart of the Sahara desert – promised to be far worse; infinitely more remote, wind-and-sun blasted, otherworldly, and life-threatening. The task before them was to prepare for the inhospitable, the untried and the unknown, and they had better be ready.

On 4 September 1941, barely a week after arrival at their new camp, Stirling paraded his recruits, telling them exactly what he expected. While discipline was to be strict, it was to be self-discipline, so there would be no saluting senior officers every time they crossed each other's path, and no ritual cleaning of weaponry and kit for parade ground inspections. Self-motivation, modesty at all times, and absolutely no bragging were key, plus 'one hundred per cent devotion to having a crack at "the Hun"'.

Stirling appointed Jock Lewes as the unit's training officer. Lewes – nicknamed 'the Wizard', due to the magical way he had with explosives – had led the 'Tobruk Four', a group of like-minded individuals who had taken to embarking on freelance raiding operations outside the perimeter of Tobruk, the British-held port-fortress in North Africa, at that time under siege by the enemy. Operating stealthily at night, the Tobruk Four had snatched unsuspecting prisoners – often, while blind-sided and relieving themselves – spreading terror and mayhem. They did so with such panache that Lewes noted in his diary: 'No wonder the enemy fear us.' Eventually, they'd managed to get themselves ensnared in a minefield. With dawn fast approaching, Lewes had calmly led his four comrades across, feeling out the mines all the way, and even as the enemy had opened up on them with sniper fire.

As a bonus to his own recruitment, Lewes had persuaded his fellows in the Tobruk Four – Jim 'Gentleman' Almonds, James Blakeney, Bob Lilley and American Pat Riley; all of who would be hailed as 'pure gold-dust' by a fellow SAS recruit – to join him at Kabrit. Lewes was a man who expected the very best from all, just as he drove himself to the limits and beyond. Realising they faced long periods moving on foot in arguably the world's most inhospitable terrain, he instigated a merciless training regime, during which he perfected the SAS's all-important credo of water-discipline. When not engaged in bouts of desert rugby, he set a schedule of punishing route-marches, gradually cutting down the available water to just one bottle per man per day.

Lewes stressed that while the desert should be respected, it was not to be feared. He explained how it was essential never to run or to flee, for once you did your mind stopped thinking clearly. He explained how it made sense to operate during the hours of darkness; to own the furtive night; before sunrise, and the blistering heat that came with it. Silent movement and night-attacks were essential skills to learn, for they would aim to strike like beasts from the black pit of hell. At first, they practised during the day, wearing blindfolds, crawling about and touching objects, to familiarise themselves. They learned to recognise sounds, even without being able to see the source. Above all else, they were taught that the secret to night operations was confidence – learning to feel utterly at home in the darkness.

Lewes challenged his recruits to march for thirty miles during the night, after which they were to lie-up all day, bodies covered in hessian sacking – serving both as shade, and as DIY camouflage – and charged to save their precious water until the cool of the evening. During the route-marches, they were warned that if they had to take a sip, it was chiefly to be used to rinse out the mouth, and to be spat back into the bottle. It was never to be gulped and never to be shared with a friend, for that kind of behaviour could make you more unpopular than you ever thought possible.

While not quartering the surrounding desert on route marches, Lewes taught the recruits how to blow up all and sundry, including railway tracks and locomotives. He brought in an officer from Egyptian Railways – the national rail company – to better show them how to do so. It was best to target a curved stretch of track, the Egyptian Railways officer explained, for not only would that very likely derail the train, it was far harder to replace curved sections of rails. There was an awful lot to learn at Stirling's Rest Camp, and not much time in which to do so. Everyone had to help take the strain.

As Stirling's youngest officer, in a sense Eoin McGonigal had a great deal to prove, but he was no less valued for it. The founder of the SAS recognised that the twenty-year-old Irishman was 'a huge character of a guy', prizing his leadership skills, his strong ideals and his artistic – imaginative – bent. Here at Kabrit, McGonigal landed a similar role to that which he'd had on Arran, being appointed the SAS's weapons officer, plus also its night operations specialist. They would have to familiarise themselves with all kinds of arms, for they would need to travel light, and be ready to scavenge weapons, ammo and explosives off the enemy.

Bill Fraser was appointed Stirling's desert navigation and languages specialist, for he argued it was crucial that his men should learn at least the basics of the enemy's lingo. That way, they would be able to yell orders and spread verbal confusion, when infiltrating targets. As for Mayne, he took the only obvious roles that

Stirling could foresee for a man of his nature: physical training (PT) and camp discipline. In spite of his run-in with Keyes, and his alleged thrashing of Napier, Stirling saw fit to saddle the big Irishman with keeping his band of trainee 'vagabonds' in line. He would do so in no uncertain terms, and in typical Paddy Mayne fashion.

Any malefactor was paraded before Lieutenant Mayne, and his infraction read out. If he accepted he was 'guilty as charged', he was led to a makeshift boxing ring, where he was expected to stand as many rounds as possible against none other than the Irish Universities former heavyweight boxing champion. After the 'punishment' was duly administered, all was promptly forgotten. But if the offender managed to proffer up some kind of defence, he might be spared. Typically, for a man who'd been something of a practical joker in his youth, the more 'utterly implausible, absurd or humorous' the excuse, the more likely that Mayne would deem no punishment was necessary.

The headmaster at Mayne's secondary school, Regent House, a Mr John Rodgers – 'affectionately known as the "Wee Boss"' – was extremely house-proud, and he had assigned a section of the grounds as each form's responsibility. Mayne's class had landed a particularly fancy flower bed. Within two weeks, a huge patch of dock leaves had somehow sprung forth, right at the heart of the finest blooms. The Wee Boss wasn't happy, but he never did discover who was responsible. Most suspected it was the young Blair Mayne, for he had a wry and wicked sense of humour. At school he was known as the 'benign big fellow', but within whom lurked 'the heart of a lion'.

One Kabrit trainee was paraded before Mayne, accused of being late back to camp after an evening out. In his defence, the accused argued that he'd been returning in good time, but had paused to light a cigarette. The desert wind had proved too strong, so he'd been forced to turn his back, in order to light it. When he'd set off once more, he'd gone a good distance before realising he'd forgotten to turn around again, thus ending up back where he'd started. One patch of desert did look pretty much like any other! An amused Mayne knew it was complete bunkum, of course, but the offender was let off, for he'd demonstrated imagination, quick-thinking and not a small degree of wit.

But mostly, there was no 'pissing about' allowed at Kabrit. Neither Mayne, Stirling nor Lewes – the three most senior officers – showed much clemency, and any repeat offenders were promptly RTU'd. The qualities Mayne most abhorred were bigotry, conceit and gratuitous crudity. Modest to a fault, he would write approvingly of one individual – 'I like good manners in people.' In his own diary, Mayne had described how he had found some of the more excessive sporting accolades heaped upon his person embarrassing. About those characters took against, he would conclude of one, 'insufferable . . . appears to consider himself most important'; of another, 'a bore, considers himself important'. For sure, any such big-mouths in Kabrit were destined for the boxing ring.

As the weeks flashed past, those recruits who had stood the test of training began to appreciate what a truly exceptional outfit they had joined. No one had ever operated – fought – like this before. It took the original commando credo to a whole new level. In early October, McGonigal would write to his brother Ambrose, proclaiming that 'This unit I am in now is first class. I have never had better men under me, all mad keen to get a crack at Jerry or the Italians. They've all been well "blooded" and are fairly howling for more.' Reflecting the transformational effect of the rigours of SAS training, he concluded, 'am in very rude health . . . Doing night marches through the desert of 30 miles and P.T. every morning . . . just now I feel very virtuous.'

But time was pressing, and Operation Squatter – the SAS's inaugural mission – was fast approaching. Above all else, the key element to learn now was parachuting. Without mastering that, they were going nowhere. It was Jim Almonds – nicknamed 'Gentleman', due to his thoughtful, contemplative, unfailingly polite nature – who was tasked with masterminding that side of things. Sergeant Almonds was very good with his hands. In his youth, he and a pal had built a DIY aeroplane, using scavenged wood and fabric, with an old motorbike engine to power it, and fashioning a two bladed propeller lovingly by hand. At Kabrit, Almonds reassembled a small-gauge railway line that had fallen into disuse, running trolleys down it from which the trainees would leap, simulating landing at speed under a parachute. They also tried jumping from moving vehicles, but the injury rate proved too prohibitive.

From those modest beginnings, Almonds constructed jump-towers of ever-increasing height, to add realism. Finally, the day came to make their first exit from a real live aeroplane. All that could be made available by the hard-pressed RAF was a lone and ageing Bristol Bombay, a slow and outdated transport aircraft that doubled as a bomber. While it was pretty much a museum piece by the autumn of 1941, it would have to do. Stirling's men cut a hole in the floor of the fuselage, and on 16 October they made their first leaps. Two No. 11 Commando veterans were some of the first through the hole – Ken Warburton, followed by Joe Duffy. Duffy hesitated for just an instant, sensing all was not as it should be, before both men plummeted to their deaths.

Mayne, who hated parachuting from the outset, was on the drop zone at the time. To him, throwing oneself out of aeroplanes was as bad as the Lamlash pier leaps. He heard Duffy and Warburton screaming as they fell. They were discovered on their backs, side by side, as if awaiting burial. Duffy's parachute was found to be half-out of its pack. He'd 'tried to pull it out but couldn't twist round to get it'. The reasons for the tragedy were simple: their 'static lines' had failed. These were lengths of cord which hooked the parachute to a cable within the aircraft, so as to pull it free

77

moments after the man had jumped. Both snap-links attaching line to cable had broken.

Stirling was absent from Kabrit at the time, engaged in yet more tussles with MEHQ in Cairo. Upon hearing what had transpired, he signalled that all should assemble the following morning to jump. Lewes paraded the men, and told them of Stirling's order, with the caveat that anyone who preferred not to was free to leave – to be RTU'd. No one baulked, but it proved a horribly sleepless night. In keeping with the SAS's founding ethos – that officers led from the front – Lewes was the first off the Bombay the following morning. He was followed by Pat Riley – one of the Tobruk Four – with Stirling himself not far down the order, for he had hurried back from Cairo to take part in the jump.

This was truly make-or-break – the most vital drop in the history of the SAS. The entire body of trainees made that morning's jump, leaping from 1,000 feet in five back-to-back lifts. One man, Private Bob Bennett, temporarily blacked out – most likely as a result of bashing his head on the far side of the hole in the Bombay's floor, a common-enough occurrence – but once he had regained consciousness, he played his mouth organ the whole way down. Otherwise, all went well. Further training, including night jumps followed, as they geared up for Operation Squatter itself.

One other thing resulted from those parachuting deaths, and the aftermath. David Stirling's standing with his men had been irredeemably heightened. Before then, he'd been viewed by many as a distant, aloof figure, who spent most of his time in Cairo dealing with higher command. He'd found it hard to shake off the image of being an inveterate Blue Blood, and a stalwart of Cairo's Silver Circle Club – infamous high-living gamblers and drinkers. But his insistence on returning to Kabrit following the fatalities, to join the jump, had impressed all. There was no doubt about it, Stirling was one of them, cut from the same cloth.

With their parachute training complete, Operation Squatter was pretty much a go. The plan remained largely as Stirling had originally pitched it to General Auchinleck, when seeking his blessing for the formation of the SAS: five patrols would parachute from five Bombays, deep behind the lines, aiming to hit five key enemy airbases. By early November 1941, all seemed set, apart from one final detail.

First, they were going to raid an RAF airfield, blowing its Vickers Wellingtons, Valentias and Bristol Bombays to smithereens.

CHAPTER SEVEN

A Monstrous Scheme

An inveterate gambler, Stirling had been unable to resist proposing the wager.

A somewhat stuffy RAF group captain had visited their Kabrit base to watch a demo parachute jump. Having observed the Bombay circling overhead, the string of tiny white mushrooms flowering in the air beneath it and drifting gently to earth, he'd seemed somewhat impressed. It was Stirling's insistence that his men could steal onto the German or Italian desert airbases and cause untold mayhem that seemed to have got his goat.

'I hope the enemy is as careless as you mention,' he'd told Stirling, making a barbed reference to their adversaries' alleged lack of the most basic security measures. No raiding party would be able to get onto an RAF airbase, of that he was certain.

A red rag to a bull, Stirling had issued the obvious challenge – a bet that his men could sneak onto Heliopolis, Cairo's main RAF airbase, any night they chose. 'It will be all right,' he'd added, provocatively. 'We'll leave labels on the planes instead of bombs.'

To quicken the group captain's sense of the odds being stacked very much in his favour, Stirling added that he was happy for a warning to be issued to RAF Heliopolis to expect an attack sometime in the next few days. Needled, the group captain accepted Stirling's challenge. They agreed £10 as the wager, which is the equivalent of £350 today, so no trifling amount.

On 23 October 1941 the raiders set out for Heliopolis on foot, with Mayne's patrol taking point. The target lay over a hundred miles due east, so a similar distance to that which the No. 11 Commando recruits had covered on the route march from Galashiels to Arran, though the climate and terrain here would prove infinitely more challenging. The way ahead lay across flat expanses of windswept, arid desert devoid of all life, apart from the ever-present swarms of flies. Prior to departure, Eoin McGonigal wrote to Ambrose, his letter reflecting the elation he felt, plus the stomach-knotting tension, as they prepared to embark upon this dummy raid.

> We are starting this evening a monstrous scheme across the desert Marching up to 100 miles, lying up during the day, sweating, thirsty, overloaded . . . I have just been making out a list of what I will carry: It is: 2 water bottles, 2 pairs of socks, 1 pair of shorts, 1 shirt, 1 blanket, 2 books, cigarettes, flask (very full), chocolate . . . When I start packing the ruck-sack, the total weight will be 100lbs and McGonigal will discard blankets, books, shorts right left and centre. Moral . . . desert marching is not meant for Irishmen!

Despite the faux peevish tone of the letter, the sense of excitement and anticipation was palpable – and this for simply a dress-rehearsal.

They set out after sundown, forming up in separate patrols, mimicking the five sticks that would deploy on Operation Squatter. Despite restricting their movement to the cool night hours, the marchers were soon parched with thirst, which made even exchanging the odd few words painful. Knowing the RAF would be quartering the skies, come sunrise they lay up under hessian sacking, hiding in the shadows of rocky escarpments. At dusk they set off once more. Moving under 'cloudless skies that burned . . . during the day and froze them during the night', increasingly they were plagued by heat exhaustion and hallucinations.

By day three, even as they were nearing the airstrip, Bob Bennett – the mouth organ-playing parachutist – remarked on how all he could see in his mind's eye was a tap of cool gushing water. Bennett was on Mayne's patrol, and in time the two were to become inseparable; brother raiders. Before the war, Bennett, who hailed from Oxford, seemed to have lived for nothing more than the university 'rags' – wild street parties, during which the city's vast student population was set loose, causing mostly harmless chaos and mayhem. Bennett loved it. Mixing with the students, it was time for payback on the 'coppers'; by the end of the night he would have a fabulous 'haul of Bobbys' caps'.

The 'coppers' didn't stand a chance of grabbing Bennett among that riotous student crowd. When not kicking policemen 'up the backside', or causing similar bedlam, the easygoing Bennett would have his head stuck in a book. Like McGonigal and Mayne, he'd carry at least one in his backpack, even on the most testing of missions. At one point during their long march to RAF Heliopolis, Bennett witnessed another of Mayne's men getting his due come-uppance. He'd been 'whingeing the whole day', Bennett observed, and finally Mayne had had enough. They were camped out on a high desert outcrop known as the 'Big Flea'. Mayne lifted the offender up with one hand, and held him over the drop.

'Another word out of you and that's your lot!' he growled.

That was the end of his, or anyone else's griping.

By midnight on the fourth day they'd reached the perimeter of the target airbase, apparently undetected. Working independently, the patrols had cut their way through the wire, flitted past the tented quarters and the hangars, making for the shadowy ranks of British warplanes. Within minutes all had been tagged with a sticker declaring 'BOMB'. Not a man among them was detected, and the patrols hadn't even caught sight of each other. Even so, several of the aircraft had been stickered multiple times.

At dawn the raid was discovered. The commander of RAF Heliopolis admitted that as his air patrols had failed to spot any parties in the open desert, he'd presumed the raiders were coming by road, concentrating his guards that way. Stirling and his men made their way to a nearby barracks to celebrate. Upon reaching it, with their four-day's growth and their dishevelled, unwashed appearance, plus their Italian haversacks – they were far superior to the British Army-issue packs – they were mistaken for being Italian POWs. Having first made sure to properly slake their thirst, they'd made their true identities known, at which point the barracks commander had arranged for transport to ferry them back to Kabrit.

Once the success of the raid was communicated to the RAF group captain, he duly paid up the £10 wager, writing to Stirling to promise that 'steps would be taken to remedy the defence system' at Heliopolis. Some sixty aircraft had been 'destroyed' at that RAF airbase, similar to the number of enemy warplanes shot down in one afternoon's combat during the Battle of Britain. It was some achievement, if only it could be replicated in the field for real.

During the exercise, only one man had failed to make the cut. Exhausted from the route march, he'd fallen out and was RTU'd. For the remainder, this was as good as it got – proof, as near as dammit, that they could accomplish the real thing in the field. As Jock Lewes would proclaim at the time, 'We are a team and we are friends and we are soldiers. David [Stirling] and I are willing to back them [the SAS] against any unit in the Middle East, friend or foe. We have shown what we can do in training: soon, please God, we shall show what training can do in battle.'

Stirling figured one final flourish was in order, before embarking upon Operation Squatter. His fledgling unit needed a distinctive motto and insignia, to encapsulate all that they held dear. He set his men the challenge. It was Corporal Bob Tait, the Litani River veteran who'd executed the epic seaborne escape, who came up with the winning design. Its exact inspiration seems lost to time, but it is either the flaming sword of Damocles, or King Arthur's Excalibur, and not a 'winged dagger' as popular myth has come to suggest. The wording for the SAS motto – Who Dares Wins – was coined by Stirling himself, after various other suggestions – 'Seek And Destroy', 'Strike And Destroy', 'We Descend To Avenge' – were rejected. A set of iconic parachutist's wings were added to the package, the entire assemblage being made up by John Jones and Co., an English hatter's company based in Cairo.

Predictably, when MEHQ found out about the unit's entirely unofficial set of insignia, there was an attempt to ban it, amid accusations of Stirling forming a 'private army'. Working on the tried and tested adage of 'ask forgiveness, not permission', Stirling set upon a cunning means to win approval. A few days before the launch date for Operation Squatter, he asked General Auchinleck to visit Kabrit, to see what his men could do. Making sure to stand at his side, sandy beret and insignia firmly atop his six-foot-six frame, when the general went to salute his troops, Stirling turned to face him, which meant that Auchinleck had effectively saluted the SAS's insignia.

Under British military law, that one act legitimised it all.

Upon spying the distinctive flaming sword design, the Auk had realised how he had been duped. 'Good heavens, Stirling, what's that you have on?' he'd demanded.

'Our operational wings, sir.'

'Well, well, and very nice too . . .' Choosing to see the funny side of the affair, he'd ended up complimenting Stirling on a remarkable show of verve and initiative.

On 10 November 1941 Stirling received his final orders for Operation Squatter. Marked 'Secret & Personal', they outlined how a force of

54 men would raid 'both aerodromes at TMIMI ... GAZALA No. 1 and GAZALA No. 2 ... destroying as many aircraft as possible'. There were two airbases at Tmimi and three around Gazala, hence the need for five raiding parties. With some 300 enemy warplanes spread across the aerodromes, the orders listed the types of aircraft they should expect: 'GERMAN – ME 109 E & F, ME 110, HE 111 ... ITALIAN – G 50, MACCHI 200 ...' The priority of targets was made crystal clear: 'The destruction of fighter aircraft is of greater importance than bombers and GERMAN aircraft of more importance than ITALIAN.'

As Stirling had originally surmised, the retrieval of his raiding parties once the job was done was to be effected by the LRDG. 'Recognition signals between your force and the LRDG patrol will be arranged between you,' concluded the orders. Formed in July 1940, the LRDG was chiefly a desert reconnaissance force then consisting of some hundred men, riding in 1.5 tonne open-topped Chevrolet trucks, a US-made two-wheel-drive vehicle that was relatively light and fast, and surprisingly handy off-road. They needed to be, for the North African desert was far from uniform, consisting of flat gravel plain (*serir*), rocky plateau (*hammada*), steep-sided dry watercourse (*wadi*), treacherous salt marsh (*schott*) and vast dune sea (*erg*). The SAS would be in the very best of hands, for the LRDG were in Stirling's view the 'supreme professionals of the desert'.

A rendezvous was set in the open desert, at a point where all patrols would converge, following the raids. One member of Stirling's unit was to be 'loaned' to the LRDG, to help guide the raiders in, though he was at best a reluctant recruit. Bill Fraser had managed to injure his arm during a parachute jump, and was deemed unfit for the coming raids. One other man was also to be left behind. In recent weeks, Jim Almonds had discovered that his infant son, John, was critically ill. There were concerns that he might not even survive. Stirling had told Almonds to remain at

Kabrit, in case there was 'any news that comes' – in other words, in case his son's condition worsened.

Almonds had noticed kindness from other quarters, too, not just from his CO. While he couldn't be sure that Mayne knew about his son's illness, nothing else seemed to explain why the Irishman was 'particularly solicitous' at this juncture. He'd approached Almonds, as the SAS's self-confessed 'bogus engineer' was working on a design for a new piece of training kit. 'Here,' Mayne had ventured, as he'd held out a set of draftsman's instruments in a neat box, 'this might prove very handy.' The gesture had not been lost on Almonds, who'd been driven sick with worry in recent days.

On 15 November, the day before heading out to the RAF airbase from where they were scheduled to depart, Stirling turned twenty-six years of age. In lieu of a birthday celebration, he gathered his men at Kabrit for a final pep talk. Having revealed the basic plan for Operation Squatter, there were enthusiastic murmurs of approval. There were very few, if any, soldiers in the British Army who would ever get the chance that they had, Stirling declared. 'With luck, we'll polish off Rommel's entire fighter force.' That pronouncement brought wild whistles and heartfelt cheers from all sides.

Riding that wave of enthusiasm and excitement, the fifty-four SAS, plus their CO, flew west the 300-odd miles to Bagoush Airbase, in north-west Egypt, putting them within striking distance of the targets, which lay some 300 miles to the west of there again. Upon reaching Bagoush, Stirling handed out their sealed orders, which detailed exactly what was expected of each of his men. The RAF made it clear that they had prepared a splendid feast, one fit for condemned men, for they feared that theirs was a suicide mission. They had never been asked to cast out a 'human cargo' into thin air deep behind the lines, and few believed that any of the parachutists would be returning.

86

The SAS were given the run of the officer's mess, a sumptuous meal being followed by a bottle of beer for each man, plus books, games and a wireless set to listen to. 'It was just like having whatever you wished, before going to the gallows,' remarked Bob Bennett. Getting well into the spirit of things, they proceeded to break into the booze store, raiding the base commander's personal stash. They were duly cornered and accused of doing just that, but by then all were 'ingloriously drunk' and beyond any meaningful censure.

Nursing sore heads, they were paraded before Jock Lewes early the following morning, who tore into them verbally. This was no way to prepare for such a critical mission, he admonished. The only responses were ranks of empty stares and a stony silence. At the same time Lewes couldn't help a hint of stubborn pride creeping into his voice. Finally, he burst out laughing, exclaiming that the hungover soldiers ranged before him were either 'habitual criminals' or a group of 'congenital idiots!'

As matters transpired, far more worrying things were afoot than a spot of opportunistic pilfering, or the need to shake off a slew of stubborn hangovers. It was the morning of 16 November 1941, and the weather forecast had just been radioed through. It was alarming, to put it mildly. The Met Office was tracking a storm that was predicted to break over the target area, with winds of 30–35 knots (as much as 65 mph). Heavy rain and swirling sandstorms – *khamsin* – were also forecast, which meant visibility could be down to near-zero. That kind of weather was unprecedented and utterly unexpected.

Stirling gathered his officers. Already, they could feel a breeze stiffening around the base, presaging the coming storm. Normally, winds of anything over 15 knots would render parachute drops untenable. Messages from MEHQ advised cancelling the raids, for all the obvious reasons, but the final decision was left up to Stirling and his men. They were acutely aware that if their teams were stood down, they would get no second chance, for everything

87

had been timed down to the last minute, to coincide seamlessly with Operation Crusader.

Stirling canvassed the views of those present. In light of their experiences with the commandos – the repeated delays and the aborted missions – they were loath to cancel. As all were acutely aware, they were an unproven, fledgling unit with enemies in high places. If they aborted, that could be used as an excuse to disband the SAS before they'd even got started. Jock Lewes pointed out that 'conditions are never perfect', and to cancel risked spending 'the duration on our backsides'. Stirling concurred. Others disagreed. As the debate raged back and forth, Mayne and McGonigal remained unconvinced, although on balance they figured they had little choice but to proceed.

Accounts differ as to what exactly was said at this juncture. There were dissenting voices. Sergeant Kenneth 'Joe' Welch was a parachute jump instructor (PJI) who'd been sent out from England to assist with airborne training at Kabrit, and to help get everything ship-shape for Squatter. As he pointed out, if the wind speeds were anything like those forecast, the Bombays shouldn't even fly, let alone anyone attempt to jump. In such conditions, 'chutes were likely to collapse and men would die. As Welch made his arguments, some seemed to be swayed, agreeing that maybe it was too risky. The debate became extremely heated, and Welch was forced to declare that they may as well jump without parachutes, for at least that way they would die clean and quick.

Eventually, it was the SAS's discipline officer, Mayne, who stepped in. He insisted that everyone should be allowed to air their view. This was potentially a life-or-death decision, and all needed to be free to speak plainly, with no fear of reprisals. Having heard Welch out, Lewes had reservations. Stirling was adamant that the mission should proceed. He made the telling point that General Auchinleck had put his faith in the SAS, on the promise that they would strike in the hours before Crusader and deliver a telling blow. Now was the moment to repay the belief that he had shown in them. Mayne argued that all might still be well, as long as they pulled together as one team.

Finally, in keeping with the founding spirit of the unit, they decreed that the final decision should rest with the men. By a quirk of fate, the wind had dropped, which may have swayed the vote. Either way, after hearing a summary of the situation from Lewes, and after Stirling had added a few words, a show of hands was asked for. These were men who had been selected for their free-thinking, independently minded, risk-taking attitude. They had to be willing to break the rules if need be, and to exercise their powers of judgement under pressure.

They did so now. All were of the one mind: this was a job that had to be done, no matter the risks. Maybe they were right to press ahead. Maybe the gale would blow itself out. After all, the wind had dropped noticeably. Or maybe, this was the calm before the storm . . . Either way the decision had been made.

There was one last unpalatable matter to be aired, which assumed a somewhat portentous significance, in light of the worries over the forecast storms. If anyone became injured or otherwise incapacitated, and was unable to continue with the mission, they were to be left behind – either to face death or capture, or to await rescue if at all possible. Achieving their objectives had to take the absolute overriding priority.

In light of that, Mayne and McGonigal reached a private agreement between themselves. If either failed to make the rendezvous with the LRDG, the other would hold off writing to his family for at least a month, to allow whoever was missing time to make it back. If the worst happened, they figured they could sit tight and await the arrival of an LRDG patrol, to pluck them out of the desert. Apart from the possibility of becoming a POW, they didn't so much as mention the worst – that death might await.

*

By early evening that 16 November, the wind seemed to have died to little more than a whisper. Conditions at Bagoush were recorded as 'clear and still'. It looked as if the 'green-for-go' decision had been the right one. Fifty-five men geared up for the jump. They wore standard-issue shirts and shorts, with webbing thrown over the top, in which was stuffed an 'entrenching tool' (a small, foldable shovel). Each man also carried a backpack bulging with grenades, emergency rations (dates, cheese, biscuits, chocolate, boiled sweets) and water bottles. Over the entire lot they pulled a pair of dull green mechanic's overalls, to try to ensure that none of the kit would get ensnared in their parachute rigging during the drop.

Most also packed smokes. Stirling carried a case of his favourite Cuban cigars. McGonigal was rarely without his 'lucky' solid silver cigarette case. A gift from his grandparents, it was engraved with his initials, reminding him of home. It went with him everywhere, combat missions included. Or at least, normally it did. For whatever reason – weight, space, superstition – McGonigal opted not to take it with him on the coming mission, one on which they would arguably need all the luck in the world to get in and out alive.

The bulk of their heavy equipment – Tommy guns, explosives, detonators, spare ammo and grenades, blankets, plus extra water and rations – was packed into special drop-containers, which were to be heaved out alongside the jumpers, each floating to earth under its own expanse of parachute silk.

One by one, the five patrols formed up and boarded the waiting Bombays. Even as they did so, the breeze began to stiffen, the ageing airframes creaking and swaying in the gusts. It was ominous. Figures found themselves mouthing silent prayers, as they prepared to take to the darkening skies. The flight plan for 216 Squadron RAF, the unit operating the Bombays, was for the five aircraft to take off at around ten-minute intervals. First to go would be Stirling's, followed by McGonigal and Lewes's patrols – those targeting the airfields around Gazala. The Tmimi raiders would follow after, with Bonington's patrol leading and Mayne's being the tail-end Charlie.

Stirling's stick of eight took to the skies at 1930 hours, just as a dark, moonless sky began to spit rain. The final flight carrying Mayne and his stick of ten raiders suffered a last-minute hitch, meaning it didn't get airborne until 2020 hours. Those long minutes of heart-stopping delay would have untold consequences. Though Mayne and his men couldn't know it, that would turn out to be a rare stroke of good fortune in what would otherwise prove to be a night plagued by bad luck and trouble, and bitter tragedy.

After flying north over the sea, the first Bombay shadowed the coastline heading west, before turning inland towards the drop zones. But as it did, the nearest land was lost from view, being subsumed by a boiling cloud of desert dust and sand. As the wind strengthened and the aircrew searched desperately for navigational markers, so the first searchlights lanced up from below and the ferocious pounding of the anti-aircraft guns began. Streams of burning tracer groped skywards, the pilot throwing his ponderous aircraft into the kind of evasive manoeuvres that were the best he could muster. Slow and cumbersome at the best of times, the Bombays were flying into the kind of storm in which they would struggle to make even the barest of headway.

As the lumbering airframes were thrown this way and that, pieces of kit broke free and crashed about, adding to the deafening noise. With the enemy gunners finding their mark, spears of fiery tracer punched through the aircrafts' undersides, one shell embedding itself beneath a parachutist's seat, but miraculously failing to explode. Diving in a desperate effort to gain speed, the lead Bombay shot out the far side of the barrage of coastal flak and limped onwards into the beckoning night. But while the cacophony of shell bursts and the punching beat of tracer fire were now behind them, the very night itself had begun to howl, as if it were some kind of enraged and feral beast.

So it was that the leading aircraft were sucked into the heart of one of the worst storms ever known, at least in that part of the world. Stirling's Bombay limped on, doggedly, the aircrew searching for a drop-zone that was never going to be visible amid such terrible conditions. But if anything, those coming behind were in even worse shape. In desperation, Bombay number four, flown by Flight Sergeant Charlie West, dropped down to little more than two hundred feet, in an effort to get a visual fix on some kind of identifiable landmark. At that altitude, it was begging to get hit.

Sure enough, just as soon as the aircraft broke through the thick mass of cloud mixed with rain and wind-whipped sand, the enemy guns spat fire. The slow-moving warplane was struck almost immediately, shrapnel tearing through the instruments in the cockpit and punching into the port engine. With the Bombay barely airworthy, Flight Sergeant West told Bonington that he was turning back. He pressed east for fifty minutes, before dropping his aircraft down onto a flat stretch of desert, in what he assumed was friendly territory. But it turned out that his compass had been struck by a burst of shrapnel, with the result that they had been flying around in circles.

West was determined to get airborne again, and to use the last of their remaining fuel to press onwards towards friendly lines. Turning into the howling wind, he managed to nurse the Bombay off the dirt, clawing into the tempestuous skies once more. Whatever fate might hold in store for them now, Bonington and his men knew for sure that their role in Squatter was over. They had flown in here determined to strike a powerful blow against the enemy, and hellbent on vengeance.

But right now, this was all about desperate escape and brute survival.

CHAPTER EIGHT

Baptism of Fire

The raging tempest that hit on the night of 17 November 1941 would pass into regimental legend. It pounced out of the ink-black sky like a rampaging beast, deafening claps of thunder roiling across the heavens, and blinding flashes ripping apart the darkness, as jagged streaks of lightning speared earthwards to sizzle and crackle among the wet sand. War reporters writing at the time would hail it as 'the most spectacular thunderstorm within local memory' and the 'worst storm in forty years'.

By a quirk of fate the last aircraft – carrying Mayne and his men – would hit that beast of a storm just as it was starting to lose the worst of its power and its rage. Even so, Bob Bennett, a master of understatement, and a future stalwart of Mayne's patrols, sensed that the 'wind was getting up', which left all feeling 'not at all thrilled'. It was freezing cold in the Bombay's bare metal fuselage, and eerily tense, as flashes from exploding flak pulsed through the darkness. Battling gusts all the way, it had taken two-and-a-half hours for the aircraft to near its target, which, as Bennett pointed out felt like a lifetime.

In his official report on Squatter, Mayne would record them reaching the drop zone (DZ) at 2230 hours amid winds of around '20–25 miles per hour', and scudding over desert that was 'studded with thorny bushes'. Though the windspeed had dropped to less than half of that forecast, these were still hellish conditions in which to attempt to jump. Regardless, as Bennett recalled, he had 'never seen a party leave a plane so quickly'. But even as those ten men hurled themselves into the darkness, they could have little conception of the calamity that had befallen their fellow patrols.

Mayne plummeted into the void, spying what seemed to be a series of sharp flashes on the ground far below. At first he figured it had to be enemy fire, and that they were dropping into a firefight. But as it turned out, it was their containers exploding on impact, for in the fierce winds their parachutes had failed to open. Buffeted by sharp gusts, the stick of parachutists were thrown around the sky, before hitting the unforgiving terrain going like the clappers. Landing hard, they were dragged along the stony surface and over thorn scrub. Scattered far across the desert, ten lonely warriors found themselves battling against the storm, and fighting for their very lives.

A badly grazed Bennett managed to struggle to his feet, but moments later a gust knocked him down again, catching his 'chute and dragging him at speed across the dirt. Finally, he was able to punch the release catch on his parachute harness and roll out of it, at the same time grabbing the expanse of silk before it could be torn away in the darkness. He struggled to his feet, gazing all around. Not another soul was to be seen in any direction. In that dark and storm-lashed night, it struck him that he might have been the only man to have made it down alive. It would be pointless shouting or blowing the whistles that each man carried, for the wind was utterly defeating.

Unfastening his mini-spade, he managed to scrape a hole in the hard earth and bundle his 'chute into it. That done, he resolved to quarter the desert on foot, moving in concentric circles from the point at which he had come to a stop. Doing that, it was fully thirty minutes before he spied another living soul. At first Bennett was 'naturally dubious' as to the man's identity, for obvious reasons – they were deep inside enemy territory. But it turned out to be a fellow patrol member. With his stocky boxer's physique, sandy moustache and unruly brown hair, the figure was unmistakable – it was the irascible, combative, rebellious, self-confessed brawler, Albert Reginald 'Reg' Seekings.

If anything, Seekings – a No. 7 Commando veteran, who was wont to describe himself as a 'rough tough so-and-so' – had suffered an even worse landing that Bennett. Trapped in his 'chute and unable to shake himself free, he'd been dragged across the desert at 'a hell of a lick'. Unable to stop himself, he was convinced that he'd had it – that he would be battered to death. Flipped onto his stomach by a powerful gust, it had rammed him head-first into a thorn bush. As the blood streamed down his face, Seekings' temper had spiked. In a wild, seething rage he'd finally managed to find the strength to struggle out of his harness. But as Bennett could see, Seekings' skin had been ripped off his hands and arms and his face was 'a hell of a mess'.

It took far longer for the rest of the patrol to gather, and most were in a similar state; a few, sadly, far worse. The nightmare of the landings had been exacerbated by two unforeseen factors – the weather apart. First, as they had been dragged along sand had got into the release-catches, clogging them up. Secondly, their entrenching tools – the mini-shovels – had got entangled in parachute rigging, so that even when a man had managed to punch himself free, the spade remained snagged, and the murderous hell-ride had continued. Most had come to a stop only when they'd become impaled upon a firmly rooted thorn bush, the impact halting them in their tracks.

One figure, Sergeant 'Honest' Dave Kershaw, had been struggling with his 'chute, tugging first on one side and then the other as he tried to 'spill the air out of the canopy'. Despairing, he'd felt his skin getting ripped off, sand burning into his open wounds. Realising he was in 'a shocking state', it was only when he collided with a boulder that he finally came to a crashing standstill. Tall, with a lean, dark, almost piratical look, Kershaw had earned the 'Honest' nickname largely as a micky-take. He was a veteran of the Spanish Civil War, in which he'd joined the International Brigade battling against General Franco's fascist forces. Though he'd been on the losing side, he'd lost none of his idealism – hence the 'Honest' nickname. He'd volunteered for the SAS with a hunger to fight Nazism, and was firmly on the side of the angels.

Thankfully, their patrol commander, Mayne, had made it down apparently unscathed, though it would turn out that he had broken a toe upon landing. He was also hurt in other ways, too, but concealing the considerable pain he was in, he got his men straight to work, sending them out to locate the all-important para-containers. Unless some of those had survived the drop and could be found, the mission was a non-starter, for they were packed full of explosives and detonators, not to mention the bulk of their water.

Two of his men could offer no help in the search. They had been injured so badly they were unable to move. One, Lance Corporal Doug Arnold, had sprained both of his ankles. The other, Private Douglas Keith, had hurt – possibly broken – his leg.

Despite the extensive search, only four para-containers were found, of the sixteen that had been dropped. From those they retrieved two Tommy guns, sixteen explosive charges, a dozen water bottles, food rations for four men, plus four blankets. They might be dangerously low on water, food and other essentials, but at least they had a half-decent stock of detonators and charges, plus they had their grenades. While recognising that they were 'lacerated and bruised . . . and wet and numb with cold', Mayne was struck by how all had dealt with the nightmare landing 'extremely well' and 'remained cheerful'.

They had the means to hit their target.

They remained undeterred.

The mission was on.

It was 0245 on 17 November when Mayne and his men prepared to set out for Tmimi airbase. Or rather, eight of them did. As all knew full well, the two casualties would not be joining them. As Mayne recorded in his official report on Operation Squatter, 'I left the injured men there . . .' He advised Arnold and Keith to stay put for the night, in the hope that they might strengthen and rally. Come sunrise they should scavenge what they could from any containers lying about, and make for the rendezvous with the LRDG, if they were able to move. Mayne figured it was no more than fifteen miles south of there.

If they couldn't get going under their own steam, Mayne would see what might be done, once the mission was accomplished. In the SAS War Diary, Bennett recorded the parting of the ways thus: 'Three bottles of water were handed to the injured . . . together with a few rations. We shook hands with them, wished them luck, and set out to find our objective.'

As with so many of the SAS originals, Douglas Keith was another Gordon Highlander and No. 11 Commando veteran, and also a survivor of the Litani River operation. He'd volunteered for the SAS on 28 August 1941, the day upon which the unit was officially founded. In the few short months since then he'd earned a sterling reputation, being praised in an official report for marching '40 miles across the desert in stockinged feet with a 75lb load, rather than fall out after boots gave way.'

To be forced to abandon Keith and Arnold to their fate must have been utterly soul-destroying, especially for soldiers who had trodden a very similar road, shoulder to shoulder, to war. But a burning hunger drove Mayne and his men on, and in the early hours of 17 November 1941 there was everything to play for. They simply could not afford to fail.

Mayne led his remaining force on a compass bearing of 360 degrees, so heading due north, for around three hours. If they had been dropped at the correct DZ, this should take them to within striking distance of the target – Tmimi airbase. But amid the conditions in which the pilot had been forced to fly, it would be little short of a miracle if they had been released anywhere near their intended objective. As Kershaw, the Spanish civil war veteran, recalled, they hoped to return via the DZ to retrieve their injured comrades, en route to their rendezvous with the LRDG. If they could find Keith and Arnold, they'd move heaven and earth to get them married up with the rescue vehicles.

When, by Mayne's estimation, they were five miles short of the airbase, he called a halt. They took cover in a deep wadi – a dry riverbed that cut through the desert landscape – aiming to execute a full reconnaissance at first light. No one slept. The nervous energy and tension ensured all were absolutely wired. They chain-smoked, and chatted in whispers 'until dawn broke'. First light revealed the most unbelievable sight: Tmimi Airbase was situated no more than four miles to the north of their place of hiding. Even better, as they stole forward to take a closer look, they counted seventeen Messerschmitt Me 109s – the choicest of all targets – ranged across the runway.

Other than a patrol of enemy armour with some motorcycle escorts, and a lone tented encampment, there was nothing lying between their hideout and the target to impede any attack. Mayne issued his orders. They would lie up in the shadows of the wadi all day. Come sunset, they'd move forward under cover of darkness, each man armed with two explosive charges, while Mayne and one of his sergeants carried the Tommy guns. They had sixteen 'bombs', so were only one short to deal with all of the Me 109s; with the grenades they were carrying they should be able to account for the last.

One curious – potentially worrying – factor had struck Mayne, as they carried out their recce. As far as he could tell, there was no sign of Lieutenant Bonington or his patrol, those who had flown on the Bombay directly ahead of his own. The Squatter plan of attack had called for the two SAS patrols to link up and operate in tandem, so launching a pincer movement on Tmimi – one striking from the eastern side and the other from the west. But as far as he could tell, Bonington and his party were nowhere to be seen. There was nothing they could do about it. They had to keep hidden, ride out the hours of daylight, and strike hard come nightfall.

Just prior to dusk – so some thirty minutes before they intended to break cover – it started to rain. Like the previous night's storm, this was no half-hearted affair. As Bob Bennett reported, 'It rained as I have never seen it before; clouds burst by the score.' With the downpour intensifying, Mayne and his men dashed about trying to shield their most precious kit under their meagre blankets. Then there came an ominous roaring from the depths of the wadi. Channelling the downpour, what had previously been a dry ravine was transformed into a raging torrent. Scrambling for higher ground, the raiders salvaged what they could, and with 'constant wringing out of the blankets and the occasional sip of the old "rum stakes" [most carried a small hip flask] . . . managed to survive'.

But the rain kept coming. The muddy-brown, churning water thundered ever more powerfully through the guts of the wadi, carrying all before it – tree-branches, boulders and other assorted debris. Some of their kit was swept away, and almost everything was soaked. The downpour proved so intense that it cut out the light, bringing nightfall early. As darkness crept in, Mayne decided to try out one or two of their spare timers and fuses. With sinking spirits, he realised the rain had ruined them. None seemed to work. The soaking had 'rendered them useless'. After all they had endured, it was the cruellest blow.

Still, they refused to give up. If they could last out the night, surely the weather would return to more typical desert conditions come dawn. In which case, maybe they could dry out the fuses? Maybe they could still have a crack at those Me 109s? Plus they had their grenades. One of those lobbed into a Messerschmitt's cockpit would surely do the warplane no end of harm. In that hope, eight men huddled beneath four shared blankets and tried to catch some sleep, as the long night of the 17/18 November dragged on.

Dawn brought a slight improvement, but it remained overcast and chill. The fuses still refused to function. More to the point, the wadi – now an angry, turbulent torrent – lay between them and Tmimi airbase. They faced the prospect of having to ford it, if they were to try to mount an attack. Few believed it was remotely possible.

They would be swept to their doom.

With great reluctance, Mayne made the decision that all had been dreading: he was calling off the attack. Frustration, disappointment and anger were at fever pitch: they were so near and yet so far. But neither Mayne nor his men could let that get the better of them. They still had to get out of there.

Come nightfall on the 18th they set off, aiming to retrace their steps. Even as they moved out, Mayne was noticeably silent and grim-faced, his jaw clamped shut. Some suspected that it was anger that was driving him. Rage at their failure. In truth, it was a single-minded focus, as he was gripped by a determination to lead his men to safety so that they would live to fight another day.

Even so, the trek proved to be a gruelling, cheerless slog through a waterlogged landscape, with little food or shelter to sustain them. As they stumbled across what they believed was their original DZ, they fought to stay alert and to search for Keith and Arnold, but there was no sign of either of their injured comrades anywhere. Sergeant 'Honest' Dave Kershaw quartered the night with aching eyes, but eventually he was forced to admit that 'either we had misjudged the distance' or Keith and Arnold had 'decided to wander off', fearing that no help was coming. It was a double blow. Not only had they failed in their attack, but they had lost two of their men in the process.

The torrential downpour had transformed the landscape. Shallow lakes, raging rivers and treacherous mudflats had appeared where there were none before. Maybe as a result of that, Mayne and his men had actually missed the DZ. Keith and Arnold were where they had been left, some forty-eight hours earlier. Though neither of the injured men could know it yet, their comrades had 'walked past us in the darkness' and pressed on towards the rendezvous.

The SAS were accustomed to the vagaries of British winters. Many had trained on places like Arran, or other, equally inhospitable parts of the British Isles. Even so, none had ever experienced the kind of mind numbing cold that assailed them now, as they stumbled through what had once been a typical desert landscape. At times they were up to their waists in water. At others, they were forced to ford wadis in wild spate. It was impossible to put any of this into words. Whenever a figure tried to open his mouth to speak, all that came out was a bony clacking sound, as teeth chattered uncontrollably.

One thing several of the men noticed about their commander, as he steered them through the dark expanse of that storm-lashed desert: the tougher the situation seemed to become, the calmer Mayne seemed to get. It was almost as if he thrived on the knife-edge danger and uncertainty that this kind of mission entailed. It inspired enormous confidence in those that he led, even amid such conditions, for it seemed impossible when commanded by such a figure that any real harm could come to any of them. It was a magical characteristic; a talismanic quality which would come to define Mayne's war.

It was just after midnight on 20 November when Mayne's patrol finally made the rendezvous with their rescue party. The men of the LRDG were camped up in a patch of thick bush. Despite their parlous state, Mayne and his men delayed making contact for several hours, and for good reason. They had spotted a mysterious light and the smoke of a fire. Unsure if it was friendly, or perhaps an enemy outpost, they had lain in hiding and watched for a good while before being certain that this was indeed the LRDG encampment.

This would prove a bittersweet reunion. The joy of their arrival was very quickly tempered by the realisation that only one other Squatter patrol had reached there, and even that was sadly depleted. A few hours earlier, Jock Lewes had led a frozen column of men into the rendezvous, to be greeted with hot mugs of tea laced with rum, and cans of bully (corned) beef. Once Mayne and his men had likewise thawed out and sated their ravenous hunger, they swopped news with the other SAS men. It was grim indeed.

If anything, Lewes and his team had leapt into even worse conditions than had Mayne's stick, for the wind was fiercer when they had jumped. Lewes had gone first. His men were under strict instructions to remain at the point where they landed, and he would find them. He intended to trek along the compass bearing of the Bombay's flight path, collecting all of his patrol – 'rolling up the stick', as they called it. But of course, they were scattered far and wide. When finally all had gathered among the injured, one man, Jack Cheyne, was in serious trouble. The Litani River veteran – Bill Fraser's seasoned deputy – had broken his back upon landing. They'd had no option but to leave Cheyne 'with a bottle or water and a revolver', but with precious little hope.

Lewes and his remaining men had pressed north towards their objective, the airbase at Gazala. They had never even got close. Dropped a way to the south of their intended DZ, by the time the heavens opened and they were knee-deep in water, they were still many miles from their target. As with Mayne, Lewes was forced to abort and head for the rendezvous. In the coming hours, even Lewes's legendary stamina had faltered. Frozen stiff, soaked to

In April 1945, in a fierce and bloody battle during the closing days of WWII, a column of SAS jeeps took the town Schneeren, in northwest Germany. There they discovered a massive leather tome, the *CHRONIK* – Hitler's gift to the townsfolk; a record of life under the glorious Third Reich. The SAS filched it, removed the pages (*right top*), and replaced them with what became known as the 'Paddy Mayne/SAS War Diary'. For decades it was kept in the home of Lt-Col. Robert Blair Mayne DSO, the longstanding SAS wartime commander, so safeguarding the SAS's wartime history for posterity, along with Mayne's war chests (*right bottom*), full of a trove of documents, photos, letters, trophies and memorabilia.

In the summer of 1941, then-Captain David Stirling (*left*) founded the Special Air Service in the North African desert. One of his most sought-after recruits was then Lieutenant Robert Blair Mayne (*right*), known as 'Blair' or 'Paddy' to all. As one fellow officer observed, Stirling and Mayne were a 'powerful combination of courage, endurance, bare-faced impertinence . . . terrifying in their effect'.

Baby Blair Mayne (*above left*) in pram with one of the family's chickens, and with sister Barbara looking on. One of seven siblings, the family's Northern Ireland home was full of music, poetry and Irish spirit, plus pets galore. Mayne (*above right*) with sister Francie, and little brother, Douggie, to whom he would write graphic accounts of the war years.

Mayne (*above left*), with niece Margaret, who he'd nickname 'Funnyface' in the letters he would write her from the war, revealing a softer side to the warrior rarely seen by his men. He was named after Captain Robert Blair (*above right*), who won the Distinguished Service Order (DSO) in 1915, for rescuing wounded comrades 'under heavy and sustained fire.'

● A springbok for the captain' — with the compliments of Blair Mayne.

By his early twenties Mayne was a sportsman of international renown, excelling at both boxing and rugby. He played for the Irish rugby team, and toured South Africa in 1938 (*above left*) with the British and Irish Lions, during which he was acclaimed as 'outstanding.' His leftfield mindset was also to the fore: as the team were short of fresh meat, he famously took a break from a formal function, went hunting in his dinner jacket and bagged a springbok for the pot, as pictured in a newspaper cartoon (*above right*).

With the drums of war beating, Mayne signed up for officer training, but he didn't take easily to mindless drill and discipline. He was assessed as being 'unpromising material for a combat regiment, undisciplined, unruly and generally unreliable.'

In June 1940, at Britain's darkest hour, Winston Churchill called for 10,000 volunteers for Special Service, charged to deliver 'a reign of terror', to 'kill and capture the Hun garrison . . . and then away.' Mayne and his fellows answered the call, signing up with No. 11 (Scottish) Commando, a unit whose superlative legacy would underpin the SAS.

No. 11 Commando's founder, Lieutenant-Colonel Richard 'Dick' Pedder (*above left*), sought recruits who were physically tough, but also 'quick in mind' and who could think on their feet. He found them in Lieutenant Gerald Bryan (*above right*), Mayne (*below left*) and Mayne's closest friend in the war, Lieutenant Eoin McGonigal (*below right*), who hailed from south of the Irish border. The three shared digs on Arran, where Pedder began his merciless training regime, forging an unbreakable bond unto death.

The men trained relentlessly to serve as Churchill's 'butcher and bolt' raiders, striking by speed and surprise. That spirit was captured admirably by fellow No. 11 Commando recruit, Captain George Duncan, in his war poetry, plus the cartoon, 'GEORGE GOING ASHORE' (*below*). But their bloody baptism of fire would sin against all the Commando's founding precepts. That mission would decimate their unit, sending many who survived into the arms of the Special Air Service, then being founded in the desert.

David Stirling wanted 'Paddy' Mayne – war-bitten, after his Commando exploits – as a founder SAS recruit. But Mayne was under something of a cloud. His dog, the mascot of his troop, had been shot by a fellow officer, and Mayne and his men had taken fitting revenge: 'Charles got beaten up . . . Paddy suspected.' Regardless, Stirling got Mayne, making him the SAS's PT and discipline officer. Mayne instigated 'bush rugby' for fitness, plus a few bouts in the boxing ring for anyone who stepped out of line.

At the SAS's Kabrit, Egypt base – known ironically as 'Stirling's Rest Camp' – training was relentless. Under Eoin McGonigal, their Weapon's Officer, recruits had to learn to use all types of arms and explosives, the enemy's as well as their own. Most challenging was the parachute training, which involved jumping through a hole cut in the floor of an obsolete Bristol Bombay Aircraft. Terrifying and more than once . . . lethal.

Mostly quietly spoken and modest to a fault, Mayne proved at his most sociable – and dangerous – when drinking, here shown seated at the table, third from left, with tie. The SAS mess was peopled by a cast of the wild and eccentric. The high-born Stirling set the tone, with Lieutenant Bill Fraser (*right*), another No. 11 Commando veteran and future deputy to Mayne coming a close second, resplendent in Scottish kilt, and with his dog, Withers, a dachshund, dressed in a Royal Navy coatee (a smart tunic), at his side.

In November 1941 the SAS departed on their inaugural mission, Operation Squatter, a raid on enemy airbases deep behind the lines in the North African desert. This was make or break for a unit that was far from popular with high command. Sadly, a once-in-a-lifetime storm, complete with ferocious winds and torrential rains, turned the airdrop into a disaster.

the skin and exhausted, he had had no option but to hand over command to the patrol sergeant, the indomitable Charles George Gibson 'Pat' Riley. Pat Riley – known as 'Rat Piley' to his mates – was a hard-as-nails amateur boxer, who had the physique and stamina to give even Mayne a run for his money. More to the point, he seemed 'oblivious to the conditions' and unstoppable.

Born in Wisconsin, in the American Midwest, as a young child Riley had moved to what was then known as Cumberland, in the north of England. The Irish-American had grown up working in the local granite quarry alongside his father and grandfather. He seemed as tough as the rock they had hewn. Riley had kept Lewes and his men moving, even when all the bones in their bodies were numb to the marrow, allowing only intermittent rest, and only when they found a patch of high and relatively dry ground.

Lewes and his men were indebted to Riley for getting them to the rendezvous. Without him, they doubted if they would have made it. But as for Jack Cheyne, few held out even a shred of hope for his survival. Worse still, they had detected not the slightest sign of either Stirling's patrol or that of Eoin McGonigal. The three forces were supposed to have linked up, to coordinate their assault on the Gazala airbases. But just as Mayne had failed to find any sign of Bonington's stick, so Lewes and his men had seen nothing of the others.

A little later that morning, movement was spotted a way off in the desert. The LRDG had left two lighted storm lanterns on a high point, around a mile from their place of hiding. The 'pre-arranged signal' to indicate that some of the SAS had arrived was a lantern being lifted, and 'swung from side to side'. That kind of movement was spotted, and an acknowledgement flashed back. A while later, two figures emerged from the darkness. One was the unmistakable form of Stirling, his tall, lanky frame appearing stark in the starlight. The other was his patrol sergeant, Bob Tait, the Litani River miracle escapee.

Once the two arrivals had been brought in and thawed out a little, they shared their grim tale. Riding in the lead aircraft, they had leapt into winds gusting over 35 mph. All had made 'very bad landings', as Tait later recounted, and were scattered over a wide area. Worse still, the raging, howling wind was thick with sand, and it was impossible to see anything, and hard even to breathe. Stumbling about, flashing torches, they eventually found each other, but one man had simply vanished. The missing individual, twenty-one-year-old Stanley 'Stan' Bolland, hailed from Liverpool and was a No. 8 (Guards) Commando veteran. The others could only presume that he had been killed upon landing and his body dragged away on the wind, for they had searched far and wide.

All were nursing injuries. Stirling himself had hit the dirt with such force that he had blacked out. Tait had sprained an ankle. Most of their containers were missing. Even so, they had pressed north towards Gazala, hoping that McGonigal and Bonington's patrols had fared better, and to link up for the attack. They had found no one. Eventually, as the weather worsened, Stirling decided they should split up. He and Tait would press on, in the hope of salvaging something of value from their mission. The other six, under the command of Sergeant Major Yates, would head for the rendezvous. They were little better than walking wounded, as all were nursing sprains and fractures.

Stirling and Tait had found themselves struggling north when 'a terrific electric storm broke with hail and rain. We were unable to see more than a few yards in front and within fifteen minutes the whole area was under water.' Eventually, Stirling had been forced to do as Mayne and Lewes had, and he turned back. He and Tait had been guided into the rendezvous in the early hours of 20 November, after an epic trek of around 70 miles, executed in murderous conditions. At one point they'd spied the rest of their patrol, some distance ahead and moving in the right direction.

They'd lost contact, but had fully expected them to be there ahead of them. Their whereabouts remained a complete mystery.

In an otherwise confused and confounding situation, one thing was clear. The only team to have got anywhere near achieving their objective was Mayne's – that was unless McGonigal or Bonington's patrols had somehow managed to press home their attacks. But if they had, where were they now? Stirling managed to convince the LRDG patrol commander, Captain John 'Jake' Easonsmith, to remain at the rendezvous for far longer than the agreed cut-off point, in the hope that the missing men might materialise.

In truth, Easonsmith had needed little persuading. As with all in his unit, he felt the loss of the missing men almost as powerfully as their SAS comrades – so many young lives potentially snuffed out in the blighted desert sands. At all of thirty-two years of age, Easonsmith was comparatively the old man of the desert. A wine merchant before the war, he was a leading light in the LRDG's behind-the-lines reconnaissance operations, at times launching the occasional off-the-cuff ambush, if they stumbled across an enemy patrol. Easonsmith typified the huge professionalism and quiet determination of the LRDG, a unit that was unrivalled for its mastery of the desert.

The former Commander-in-Chief of Middle East forces, General Archibald Wavell – Auchinleck's predecessor – had written of the LRDG: 'In conditions of indescribable hardship these patrols constantly scoured the desert, shooting up convoys, destroying petrol dumps and generally harassing Italian desert garrisons.' He added, with great admiration, 'For obvious reasons patrols were unable to use recognised tracks and have found their own ways over sand, seas, uncharted desert, outcrops of rock and other difficulties previously considered . . . to be totally impassable.'

Around midday on the 20th, Easonsmith decided they had no option but to move out. Thirty miles to the south, Bill Fraser would be waiting with a column of trucks, at the northern end of the Wadi El Mra, a location that offered decent cover. They needed the provisions and the space that Fraser's convoy offered, for both room and supplies with the LRDG were limited. They could not afford to miss that rendezvous. Leaving a stash of provisions where they were – 12 gallons of water, plus two 4-gallon tins of dried dates – they loaded up their vehicles and, with heartfelt reluctance, set out.

Even so, neither Easonmith, nor the twenty-two SAS that his patrol now carried, with Bill Fraser being included, were ready to give up the search. The following day they sent out vehicles to comb an eight-mile front, quartering the desert in the hope of locating the lost patrols. There was no sign of anyone anywhere. 'No incidents, no results,' was all Esonsmith was able to report. The fate of the missing remained a mystery. As far as anyone could tell, they had been swallowed by the desert and scattered to the four corners by the storm.

For those two dozen survivors who boarded Fraser's truck convoy, it was hard to imagine how the mood could have been any darker. Assailed by abject failure and loss on all sides, few held out much hope for their absent comrades. Few rated their chances of survival as a unit, either. The SAS was on life support. Once MEHQ discovered all that had transpired, they would be sure to use it as an excuse to snuff them out for good. As the trucks turned southwards and set a course for distant Kabrit, they feared that their days were numbered. A mission designed truly to put the SAS on the map would instead result in its demise.

So many of these men had come here seeking vengeance. Mayne – for the fallen of the dirt-dry Syrian hills; for Colonel Pedder, Captain Farmiloe and those countless others who had not returned. And now, quite possibly – though he absolutely refused to countenance it – for the loss of dozens of his SAS brothers in arms; first and foremost his dear friend, Eoin McGonigal. Bill Fraser – likewise for the Litani fallen, but now very possibly also for Sergeant Jack Cheyne, his rock-solid second-in-command, the man he had heaped with praise for leading their patrol across the Litani River to safety, evidencing 'extreme coolness under fire'.

Instead of finding vengeance they were leaving the desert, twenty-two bruised and battered survivors – truly, the vanquished.

CHAPTER NINE

Do or Die

Jalo was as good a place as any in which to hide.

The remote oasis would be the launch-pad; the place from where they would venture forth 'into the desert to finish the mission', do or die. They would be doing so in the strictest secrecy. No one knew they were here, apart from the LRDG, plus a few other maverick military figures. Or so Stirling fervently hoped. If they were found, tracked down, nailed by MEHQ, then they would almost certainly be stopped. Dead in their tracks. The SAS would be finished; stillborn; the disaster of Operation Squatter killing them off before they had even got to fire a shot in anger.

At Jalo – an island of green set in a sea of rolling sand dunes – they could lie low, lick their wounds, rearm and re-bomb. At least, that was the plan. Recently seized off the Royal Italian Army unit that had garrisoned this fortress-oasis, it was chock-full of abandoned supplies and weaponry. War-fighting kit to scavenge; an arsenal for vengeance. In that manner the SAS had managed to get their hands on a fleet of Lancia 3Ro Militare heavy trucks, their makeshift wheels for what was coming. But they still could not afford to mourn. Not here. Not yet. Not when they didn't know the fate of the missing. Not when confusion, rumour, raw fear and gut instinct were all they had to go on.

They had arrived here on 7 December 1941, so barely two weeks after they had pulled out of their ill-fated desert mission, to make their way back to friendly lines. During that journey, insult had been added to the injury of their recent disasters, when an Italian Savoia-Marchetti SM.79 Sparviero (sparrowhawk) – a distinctive medium bomber, with three engines, one set in the snub nose, and the fuselage's signature hunchbacked profile – had buzzed their convoy. They had been 'seen and machine-gunned', but the LRDG had returned a storm of fire, using their vehicle-mounted weaponry. In no time the Italian pilot had 'cleared off', only to fetch a friend. Shortly, a German Heinkel He 111 had pounced, 'bombing and machine gunning' – but all had fallen wide of the mark.

Other than that, Captain Easonsmith had reported their journey as a 'trouble-free run'. Even so, those air attacks had been enraging, for those were the very kind of warplanes that the SAS had been sent in to find and to kill. By the time they'd reach Jalo, those attacks had attained an even darker significance, due to a snippet of intelligence that had filtered through. British code-breakers had intercepted a radio message, sent from the base commander at Gazala Aerodrome to Afrika Korps headquarters.

It read: 'Reference the sabotage detachment of the Lay Force [sic] from the shot down Bombay . . . five [sic] further Bombays . . . operated . . . count on the probability that further sabotage detachments were dropped.' By Lay Force it would mean Layforce, the informal name given to the Middle East Commando, after its CO, Brigadier Laycock. The message had to signify that someone had been captured, and very likely in or around Gazala, and after their flight had been 'shot down'. That somebody had clearly talked, and hence the enemy warplanes flying search patrols.

But did that mean an entire planeload of SAS raiders had fallen into enemy hands? Of the two missing patrols, it was McGonigal's that had been slated to hit Gazala – alongside those of Stirling and Lewes – so did it mean that McGonigal and his men had been taken prisoner? There was just no way of knowing. Either way, the survivors of Operation Squatter had bigger issues to wrestle with right then – chiefly, the continued existence of their unit. To admit defeat would be to invite disaster. What they needed was a success; proof that the SAS could deliver; that despite Squatter, the concept still held good.

Matters were made infinitely worse in that all was going disastrously in North Africa for the Allies. Operation Crusader had failed. A week into the Eighth Army's offensive, rapid early gains had been reversed, as Rommel launched a daring counter-attack, sweeping around the British flank. A week later, British forces were in retreat, and the Afrika Korps had managed to push across the border into Egypt itself. Heads had rolled in high places. On Auchinleck's insistence, General Alan Cunningham, chief of the Eighth Army, had been removed. General Neil Ritchie was appointed in his place, charged to hold the line come what may.

In addition, the one great hope to put an end to the march of Rommel, the so-called Desert Fox, had imploded. Operation Flipper, Major Keyes' assassination mission, had failed spectacularly. Keyes and his commandos had got ashore successfully, and, battling the same torrential storms that had assailed Stirling's men, they had made it to what was believed to be Rommel's headquarters. But the German commander was most certainly not there. In the firefight that had ensued, Keyes himself had been shot dead and all but two of his men were killed or captured. It had been yet another courageous commando raid that had promised everything but delivered precious little.

In short, all of the special service raids scheduled to coincide with Operation Crusader had been standout failures. They had also proven costly in terms of the price paid in lives, for by far the majority of the raiders had failed to return. But with its strategic location, Jalo offered Stirling the best chance of turning those fortunes around. Set 250 miles south of the Mediterranean coast, the oasis was also a similar distance behind Rommel's new frontline. It was a remote British outpost, lying slap-bang in the German general's backyard.

Due north of the Beau Geste-like oasis lay a string of Axis aerodromes, dotted along the coast – so, well within striking distance. But this was going to be it: the SAS would get no further chances. They needed to strike firm and swift and hard, and to bring back tangible results – ideally, an airbase littered with burned-out and wrecked enemy warplanes.

En route from the desert to Jalo, they had passed by Kabrit, taking the long way around. They had done so to retrieve any useful kit for what was coming. Stirling, Mayne and Lewes had settled upon two key takeaways from Squatter, to give them cause for hope. The first was the record of Mayne's patrol. They, of course, had made it to their target. Had it not been for the failure to properly waterproof their explosives, they would have attacked. As Mayne himself concluded in his post-mission report: 'I am certain that given normal or even moderate weather our operation would have been entirely successful.'

The second was the lesson learned from their encounter with the LRDG. Even as Stirling had made his pre-dawn entry to the desert rendezvous, his mind was working overtime: what had they got so wrong, he wondered. And what could they do better next time, that's if there was a next time? As if by a miracle, he'd run into a man who would seem to have the answers. Lieutenant David Lloyd Owen was Jake Easonsmith's deputy on that patrol. He would go on to command the LRDG, after Easonsmith was killed late in 1943. But for now, he was fascinated by those who had made it out of that desert hell-storm *on foot*, and by two figures in particular.

The first was Blair Mayne, who was a 'most gentle and kind person', Lloyd Owen would write, blessed with all the qualities of a great leader. Mayne had an 'aggressive and ingenious brain, which was always seeking new ways to harry the enemy' and was the kind of individual who would never ask anyone to do anything he hadn't first done himself. Even so, Lloyd Owen would have 'hated to have found myself on the wrong side of Paddy Mayne . . . As a fighter he was unsurpassed, for his very presence in the full flood of his wrath was enough to unnerve the strongest . . . He had all the colour, dash and attraction of a great buccaneer.'

The second was David Stirling, who Lloyd Owen recognised as being so similar to Mayne, yet so very different. Stirling had many of Mayne's qualities – 'his aggressive outlook, his courage, his quite remarkable powers of leadership' – and both men demonstrated a powerful 'disregard and contempt for authority'. Stirling was blessed with having 'ideas of genius . . . He also had a power over men that I had never seen before.' But Stirling's wild flights of fancy – he produced more ideas in a week, than a dozen men might in an entire military campaign – needed to be brought down to earth, and that was where Mayne came in.

Stirling had flashes of brilliance; Mayne made them happen. Stirling was more cerebral and theoretical; Mayne was all innate emotion and animal gut instinct.

In a sense, Lloyd Owen's own brilliance was to recognise what the two SAS leaders, combined, offered. In his view it was providence that had brought them together, for they constituted 'the most powerful combination of courage, endurance, bare-faced impertinence, initiative and leadership . . . their combined personalities were almost terrifying in their effect.'

Drawn to them, Lloyd Owen had his own dash of genius to offer. When Stirling had mentioned the hazards of parachuting, and how that had really let them down, Lloyd Owen made what to him was the obvious suggestion. 'I don't see why you don't let us take you there,' he'd ventured. If the SAS rode with an LRDG patrol, they could drop them close to their target, and pick them up again afterwards.

'Can you guarantee to get us anywhere without being seen on the way?' Stirling queried.

'Yes, very nearly.' There was always the chance of a spot of trouble en route, Lloyd Owen explained, but he was pretty certain that 'we'll get away with it.'

From the seeds of that chance meeting had grown the plan to launch a raid, or set of raids, mounted from Jalo, and with the LRDG acting as the SAS's makeshift taxi service.

At some stage before leaving the desert rendezvous, having waited for the missing who never showed, Captain Easonsmith had taken a photo of those SAS who remained – a ragged, battered, grim-faced, bearded band of brigands, bowed but not broken. Not quite. But Mayne in particular appears distracted, down-hearted and disengaged. He stands in the background of that thin and desert-weary line, head turned half-away, gaze empty. Mayne enjoyed a powerful, gut-felt, visceral connection to those he commanded. To his friends. Losing them tortured him, and he was unable to hide how hard this had hit.

During their stop-over at Kabrit the disaster of Operation Squatter had – perhaps inescapably – come home with a vengeance. This was the place where they had forged their unbreakable camaraderie – in dust-bruising pre-dawn rugger matches, in wild leaps of faith from Jim Almonds' para-training towers, and during their epic, throat-parching night-marches. It was from there that they had launched their triumphant raid on RAF Heliopolis, the runaway success of which had promised so much. But it was here that they now encountered tents full of the photos of loved ones, the half-read paperbacks, plus the letters that might never be opened, for all the obvious, horribly tragic reasons.

'From their appearance on arrival back in camp, the last ten days in the desert must have been hell,' Gentleman Jim Almonds recorded in his diary, regarding those who had returned. He, of course, had not been on Squatter. He'd been ordered to stay behind, due to his son being ill. Of the missing he wrote: 'In our tent, the beds remain empty and their personal effects lie strewn where they left them. I do not have the heart to alter things. I still cannot give them up for lost . . . What happened to that plane, no one knows. Was it shot down? Anyway, I will keep the hope for another month.'

Reports had filtered in that one of the Bombays – Flight No. 4 – had failed to return at all. As a result, Lieutenant Bonington and all of his stick were to be listed as missing in action, as were the flight crew. But as for Eoin McGonigal and his patrol, it was as if they had vanished into thin air. There is a photo in the SAS War Diary taken at Kabrit, shortly after Operation Squatter. It is captioned: 'Paddy Mayne – injured after Operation Number One.' It shows a dejected Mayne, heavily bandaged, his eyes downcast, avoiding the camera, his expression gaunt-faced and haunted.

The unit's future padre, Fraser McLuskey, would write of Mayne, 'He had a natural sensitivity . . . with the men he commanded. If they were in trouble . . . if they suffered from a raid, he would suffer with them. Although he was so good and big and strong and apparently fearless, he wasn't unfeeling – certainly not . . . More than that, he was both loved and trusted by them in a unique degree.' Mayne, as with so many who had returned, was troubled. In return for such mind-numbing losses, they had scored not a single hit against the enemy. There was a heavy score to be settled, and it made every sense to hurry away from Kabrit and all the bitter, harrowing memories.

Those few days at Stirling's Rest Camp proved nightmarish; funereal. 'The camp was so silent without the men – those who had survived just sat and waited for news,' Sergeant Joe Welch, their parachute jump instructor (PJI), remarked. Mayne seemed especially dispirited, refusing to accept 'that any of those classed as missing were dead. Paddy could not let his great friend Eoin go, and because he could not let him go, he could not let any of them go. Paddy was of the view that they were just "lost" until proven otherwise.'

With Eoin missing, there was one letter that Mayne was dreading having to write – to McGonigal's family. Brooding, he pulled Joe Welch to one side, revealing how deeply the whole thing had got to him. In a rare moment of candour, Mayne confessed to Welch that 'unlike himself, Eoin was not shy in front of women – he had the charm of the Irish and had a lady at home,' and someone was going to have to say something to her. Visibly upset, Mayne made it clear to Welch that he blamed himself for the loss of so many. In the months to come, he would speak often about Eoin McGonigal, 'guessing he was probably a POW somewhere far away from the desert, living the life of Riley . . . spinning some yarn to his guards about being Hitler's long lost brother'. Or something.

There was one other unsettling development at Kabrit. British Pathé, the newsreel company, had produced a two-minute film in which they, the SAS, featured. Entitled *British Paratroops in the Middle East*, it had been shot three days before their departure for Operation Squatter. It was screening at the nearby RAF airbase, and some went to watch. Intended as morale-boosting propaganda, 'images of smiling, hopeful men flashed across the screen'. For those who had returned, it was a heart-rending reminder of missing friends. Of course, the SAS name had been coined as part of Brigadier Clarke's wider deception in North Africa and the newsreel helped to further that deceit. But it did little to lift the survivors' spirits.

On 5 December, two days before departing for Jalo, Mayne raised a toast to his missing friend. It was the day of Eoin's twenty-first birthday. Having spent time with his family at their home on Belfast's Malone Road, Mayne knew how heavily the news would lie upon his parents, but he would have to find the words to write. Finally, he decided he would pen a letter to Ambrose. It was triggered in part by a snippet of intelligence that seemed to offer a glimmer of hope. An intercepted radio message made mention of a raid around Gazala, in which a German patrol had been wiped out and a large dump of weapons destroyed.

The timing was right, as was the location. There was also mention of one 'enemy' parachutist being killed, but no reference to any of the others making up McGonigal's patrol. Still, a buzz of excitement pulsed around Kabrit. Maybe, just maybe, one of their patrols had hit home. As McGonigal was the SAS's weapons officer, maybe he had foreseen the issues that had plagued the other patrols – the waterlogging of the fuses? At Kabrit, McGonigal's chief stalking ground had been the ranges, and it was there that Jock Lewes, the Wizard, had tested out his various explosive concoctions, settling at last upon one designed specifically to incinerate enemy aircraft, the aptly named 'Lewes Bomb'.

Those charges that the patrols had carried had all been Lewes bombs. A cunning mixture, it consisted of a pound of plastic explosive (PE), kneaded together with a quarter-pound of thermite – a highly inflammable metal powder – plus a good dash of diesel oil. The great advantage of the Wizard's invention was its light weight combined with destructive power, especially when placed close to an aircraft's fuel supply. The blast caused by the PE would punch through the fuel tank, whereupon the burning thermite–diesel mix would serve to ignite it, rendering the target into a raging inferno.

Tests at Kabrit had more than proven its efficacy. When combined with a timer-fuse, the Lewes Bomb was perfect for the kind of sabotage missions the SAS intended. But its one unforeseen weakness had been the fuse's vulnerability to water. In the North African desert, no one – least of all the Wizard – had considered that to be an issue. But maybe McGonigal had. Maybe he and his patrol had somehow safeguarded their fuses, waited out the weather, and attacked when conditions allowed. To have done so would have meant missing the planned rendezvous. They would have been forced to try to escape on foot, heading for friendly lines. Or they would have had to reconcile themselves to being captured. But cither way, it offered a spark of hope.

Mayne wrote to Ambrose, explaining that they had been on a mission into the desert, but that 'Eoin has not yet come back.' Attributing the intercepted enemy message as referring to Eoin's patrol, he explained that 'one of his party had been killed, but that they had wiped out a large party of Germans . . . If I get any more news I shall write . . . but I am certain that barring bad luck it will be from your brother you will be hearing next. I have not written to your family as I would not like to worry them unduly.'

Among Eoin McGonigal's possessions at Kabrit, Mayne discovered his lucky silver cigarette case. For whatever reason, Eoin had optcd not to take it with him on Operation Squatter. It had gone with him on the Litani River mission, and Lord knew how torturous those landings in neck-deep water and onto bullet-torn beaches had proven. Regardless, Eoin had refused to be parted from that talisman of good fortune. But on Squatter, he had decided to leave it behind. Mayne did not know what to make of it.

Either way, it had now become an agonising waiting game.

And in the vacuum of any news, Mayne vowed revenge.

CHAPTER TEN

Vengeance

The plan was to launch a three-pronged attack, utilising almost all of those who had weathered Operation Squatter. On 8 December, barely twenty-four hours after having got there, the first party would depart from Jalo, combining Stirling and Mayne plus ten others in a potent force that promised much. Their target, Sirte Airbase, lay 350 miles north-west, bang on the Mediterranean coastline. They had selected it for a very specific reason: it was reported to be one of the largest and busiest of enemy aerodromes. They were going for gold.

Two days later, Jock Lewes would lead a smaller force to hit Agheila Airbase, the nearest to Jalo as the crow flies, this being their insurance policy. If Stirling and Mayne should fail, by rights Lewes should be able to strike home, for his target was close, being no more than 150 miles away. The staggered start was designed to enable simultaneous attacks, so that the enemy would not be forewarned. Both parties were scheduled to strike on the night of 14/15 December 1941, when, as a bonus, there would be practically no moon.

A third party, under Bill Fraser, would set out on 21 December, to hit Agedabia Airbase, which lay 200 miles due north of Jalo. This was a belt-and-braces approach. Should the two preceding raiding parties somehow falter, Fraser's was the fallback operation. In terms of getting the SAS teams to and from their targets,

118

Easonsmith and Lloyd Owen had come good, for all were scheduled to be ferried across the desert riding with LRDG patrols. For the longest, most challenging of the journeys, west-north-west to Sirte, the LRDG would use their top navigator, Mike Sadler, in an effort to guide the raiders to their target without fail.

Shortly after dawn on the eighth, Stirling and Mayne's party set off. The seven Chevrolet trucks were loaded to the gunwales, with a dozen SAS perched atop groaning heaps of cargo. The LRDG's Chevys were painted a distinctly unwarlike rose pink and light green, but apparently this was the camouflage scheme that had proven to best blend in with the kind of terrain they were heading into. Piled high in the trucks were jerrycans of petrol, water, weaponry and ammo, spare tyres and tubes, blankets, camouflage netting, food rations, cooking gear and all the other necessities for waging this kind of highly mobile, clandestine warfare.

As the column of vehicles disappeared into the vast spread of the early morning desert, the raiders carried the ghosts of the fallen and the missing with them.

Riding in the lead vehicle, Willis Michael 'Mike' Sadler had already earned a reputation as being one of the most capable of desert navigators. In fact, his ability to steer a route across hundreds of miles of seemingly mind-bogglingly indistinguishable terrain was legendary. Hailing from Gloucestershire, Sadler had been working on a ranch in Rhodesia (today's Zimbabwe) when war was declared. Right away he'd volunteered to fight, finding his way into the LRDG after falling into conversation with some of its members in a Cairo bar. On his very first outing, he'd become fascinated with the craft of desert navigation, which was executed by a combination of standard compass work, the use of a sun compass, plus regular celestial observations.

Fittingly, Sadler went on to be trained by a former seaman – for steering a course across an 'empty' expanse of desert had much in common with ocean navigation. Some 3.6 million square miles in area, the Sahara desert – *as-sahra al-kubra*; the Great Desert in Arabic – is almost the same size as Europe. Like any ocean, it is incredibly sparsely populated, and as with anyone shipwrecked at sea, being lost in the desert was no recipe for survival. Mostly a process of mathematical calculations, combined with rigorous observation and record-keeping, there was also an intangible, instinctive art to desert navigation – a gut feeling – with which Sadler would prove to be uncannily blessed.

As Sadler steered the convoy of vehicles away from Jalo, so the dawn chill burned away, and by mid-morning the travellers were peeling off layers in an effort to enjoy any cooling breeze. Sadler pulled over at midday, to make his noon position check, using a sextant to take a reading of the sun, which should give him a fairly accurate fix. That would be cross-checked with his ongoing 'dead-reckoning' – a set of scribbles noting direction travelled times speed, which in turn equalled distance covered. One of the chief challenges of such navigation was the dearth of any detailed maps or charts. So much of North Africa, bar the fertile coastal strip, remained unexplored and uncharted.

Sadler's navigation break doubled as a lunch stop. The LRDG managed to carry far more appetising rations than most of the regular army, being fond of Irish stews (mixed meat and vege-tables), Rhodesian biltong (salted, spiced, dried meat) and New Zealand canned steaks. Indeed, its cuisine reflected the nation-alities who crewed its vehicles, for there were scores of New Zealanders, Rhodesians and Irish Guards veterans making up its ranks. Sadler aimed to cover around a hundred miles per day, but progress was never easy to predict. By contrast to the common-place view of the Sahara as a vast expanse of unrelenting sand, it is in truth a hugely varied terrain. Moving on billiard-table like *serir* – flat gravel plains – the Chevys could race along at a steady clip, but when crossing *hammada* – jumbled rocky plateaus – or *erg* – the vast dune seas – they were forced to slow to a crawl.

At sunset, the column of vehicles pulled to a standstill. This far out into the desert there was little chance of being seen by the enemy, so no need to travel during the night hours. For whatever reason, Rommel had not thought to form a similar kind of a unit to the LRDG, and the Luftwaffe tended to stick to the coastal strip. That was where the war was to be fought, and it was also where a downed pilot might stand at least a chance of survival. If a warplane failed over the sunblasted wasteland that stretched south, and any of the aircrew managed to bail out, their chances of escape were painfully small – hence both the enemy and the RAF avoiding the open desert like the plague.

Sadler checked his position again, this time taking a reading from the stars. All around his fellow patrol members were busy, for the evening ritual was under way. The patrol mechanics worked on the Chevys, while the gunners cleaned the vehicle-mounted weapons, and others patched up tubes and tyres. There were bound to be punctures. The signaller tuned into headquarters for the daily 'sitrep' – situation report. Tonight, there was nothing much that was new. No fresh intelligence had been received, and the frontlines seemed fairly static.

Stirling and Mayne warmed themselves at a blazing fire, as they pored over their maps. While the navigation was strictly Sadler's affair, they were keen to keep up and to learn. This far out into the wastes, kindling a blaze was standard procedure, for as soon as the sun went down the heat dissipated and the desert nights were bitterly cold. On the rare chance that their fire might be spotted, any observer was likely to conclude that it was a group of Bedouin – the nomads who wandered the desert – making camp for the night. Indeed, the LRDG would often spy distant fires, denoting such Bedouin encampments.

Once their various duties were done, all were drawn to the blaze. A ring of figures – unwashed, with tousled hair and heavy growths of stubble – warmed their hands, as they stared into the dancing flames. The chat ebbed back and forth, companionably. At moments such as these, the Sahara embodied a strange, almost uncanny contrast. As all knew full well, a few hundred miles to the north a bitter and bloody struggle was under way, as two armies of over a quarter of a million souls sought to grind each other into dust and oblivion. Yet here, all was wrapped in infinite silence and peace.

So the journey continued, with only a snapped steering rod to impede their steady progress, and the punctures, which seemed as regular as clockwork. When Sadler called a halt on the evening of the third day and checked his navigation, he was pleased to announce that they were no more than seventy miles short of their target. If their luck held, they should reach Sirte the following evening, forty-eight hours ahead of schedule, leaving plenty of time for reconnaissance. Compared to the dark and murderous journey that had been their previous insertion into the desert, this had been a pleasure.

However, all that was about to change.

As they moved off the following morning the going worsened. The column of vehicles began to crawl over broken, rocky terrain, moving at only 7 mph. At midday, Sadler was searching for some cover in which to call a lunch and navigation check, when the cry went up: an aircraft was in-bound. Clearly, their column had been spotted, for the unidentified warplane was making straight for them. No one doubted it was hostile, for Allied aircraft had no business operating this far west. It was identified as an Italian air force Caproni Ca.309 Ghibli (desert wind), a sleek, dual-purpose reconnaissance and ground-attack aircraft.

Each of the Chevys sported a Lewis light machinegun, mounted on a pivot. The command was given and all seven barked fire. A barrage of bullets rent the air, as the pilot tried to press home his attack, releasing a pair of bombs. Both missed, and the Ghibli sped away. It was unarmoured and only lightly armed – those two bombs were all it carried – but the real danger was that it had found their patrol. The LRDG gunners chased it with fire, in the hope of bringing it down, and before it might radio in their position to base. But shortly, it had sped over the horizon and was gone.

They had to expect more to follow. The only patch of cover thereabouts was an expanse of sparse scrub, set two miles back. They retraced their steps, the Chevys jolting and smashing their way over the rough ground, before pulling in among the bushes. No more than a few feet tall, they were too low to cover the vehicles, but with camouflage nets thrown over, to break up the Chevys' profiles, it should present a confusing patchwork of light and shade. The dry, thorny scrub stretched for hundreds of yards in all directions, so they would just have to hope they would be lost among its expanse.

They heard the incoming warplanes before they saw them. The silhouettes of three bombers powered low out of the skies, the aircrew scouring the terrain below. They flew in formation right across the patrol's hiding place, speeding onwards until it seemed as if the Chevys and their passengers had been overlooked. But then the warplanes' engine notes changed, the pilots executed an about turn, and one by one they swooped down to attack. The whine of the engines was subsumed in a roar, the guns opening up and long bursts of cannon fire began to tear up the desert. As the shadows of the hunters flashed overhead, those lying beneath the scrub could see the bombs tumbling out of the wing racks and plummeting towards earth.

A series of deafening explosions rent the air, as blasted rock and debris sliced through the scrub. For fifteen long minutes the trio of enemy aircraft quartered the skies, pounding the terrain with bullets and bombs. It was clear that the pilots didn't know exactly where their prey was hiding, so were determined to blanket the bush in a whirlwind of blasted shrapnel and burning lead. To the hunted, it seemed impossible that they wouldn't take casualties, but when at last the warplanes had exhausted their munitions and turned for home, it turned out that no man or vehicle had been hit.

According to the LRDG veterans, this was a regular-enough occurrence, yet it never failed to strike them as miraculous when they emerged unscathed. As Mayne rolled over to watch the bombers fade into the distant heat-haze, he was acutely aware that a dozen young German or Italian pilots had just set about them with absolute determination, aiming to kill them all and tear their trucks to shreds. This was the nature of the total war that was being waged here, and he was in it 'up to the hilt' and to the death. Today, they were the hunted. But in forty-eight hours, God willing, the tables would be turned.

With the skies clear of aircraft, they got moving again. An hour prior to dusk, Sadler reckoned they were just a few dozen miles short of Sirte. They decided to press on into the darkness, with the intention of getting the SAS into the Jebel – the thickly vegetated escarpment that ran along the coastline, situated just a few miles inland and overlooking the coastal plain. The rocky bluffs and deep wadis of the Jebel would offer fine cover. From that vantage point, Stirling and Mayne would be able to observe the target airfield and be in a perfect position to attack.

A little before nightfall, there was another cry of alarm. A second Ghibli had been spotted. This time, the pilot chose to hold off making any form of attack. Keeping well out of range of their guns, he shadowed the convoy's progress, until the light had failed completely. It was too late for the enemy to make any kind of a follow-up attack, but the pilot was sure to have radioed in their presence, not to mention their line of march. Showing no lights, the Chevys nosed ahead, seeking to hide, but shortly one of them got stuck in a patch of soft sand.

The column halted so they could help free the bogged vehicle – digging it out, using the shovels they carried; 'unsticking', as the men called it. One by one the drivers killed their engines. But no sooner had the last of the Chevys gone quiet than they detected distant yells. An engine fired up, revved, and there were further shouts, before they heard a vehicle pulling away and gathering speed. By the sound of things it was an enemy convoy, and it had to be moving on some kind of a decent surface, and most likely a highway.

'The coast road,' remarked Sadler, in exasperation. 'We must be almost upon it . . . Damn these maps.'

All along the coastal plain there ran a surfaced road, which served as Rommel's key supply line. It was the route to ferry war materiel from the coastal ports to the frontline troops.

They gathered for a hurried chat, SAS and LRDG. If the pilot of the Ghibli had radioed in their position, the enemy were bound to send out search parties. As Stirling made clear, they could not afford to mess up, not this time. Everything depended on the success of their present mission. Fearful of putting 'all our eggs in one basket' – Sirte – he suggested they divide forces. He would take one party, and attempt to execute the original plan of attack, hitting Sirte airbase. Meanwhile, Mayne would take a second group and press on towards Tamet, a town set thirty miles further west, which was believed to have a brand new airfield somewhere thereabouts.

At Tamet, Mayne should 'still have the advantage of surprise', Stirling pointed out. 'If one of us fails, the other may still be lucky.'

The LRDG would split their convoy in two to ferry each party to and from their points of attack. They'd aim to strike at 2300 hours the following night, so neither group of raiders would spoil the chances of the other. As what little moon there was wouldn't show until an hour after midnight, they should get both raids done and dusted under the cloak of darkness. So it was agreed.

As Sadler reckoned that Stirling's party was no more than three miles short of Sirte, it made sense to leave them where they were, so that they could press ahead stealthily on foot. Meanwhile, the Chevys would get moving, making as much noise as possible, so as to convince the enemy that all had moved on. That agreed, Stirling and his half-a-dozen raiders slipped away into the darkness, uttering a faint cry to Mayne and his party, wishing them all the best and good luck.

Mayne was left with the rump of his stalwarts, five men including the redoubtable Reg Seekings and a Private Hawkins. Mayne had developed something of a love-hate relationship with Hawkins. While he was a fine operator, especially with a Tommy gun, he was also something of a foul-mouthed renegade, and Mayne couldn't abide his gratuitous cussing. (He would eventually RTU Hawkins as unsuitable material for the SAS.) But for the coming business, a man like Hawkins might well prove useful.

Having 'unstuck' the bogged vehicle, the convoy got under way. To reach Tamet required Sadler to navigate them down from the high rocky scarp, using the only possible route, a steep-sided crevasse. There was no track. The guts of the canyon proved boulder strewn and perilous. Sadler did his best to steer a path around the largest rocks, as the wheels slipped and spun over a friable, treacherous surface of loose scree. The noise was deafening.

Somehow, via his incredible sixth sense, Sadler got them all down in one piece. By first light they were holed up in a wadi, four miles short of their new target, Tamet airfield. With sunrise, SAS and LRDG alike crawled under hessian sacking and into the deepest shade, remaining motionless, alternately dozing, pecking at food, and smoking in an effort to calm the nerves.

Come dusk, Mayne and his men executed a recce on foot. The sight that met their eyes, once they had stolen to within view of the airbase, was almost too good to be true. Flights of enemy aircraft kept swooping into the Tamet airstrip, touching down like 'crows in a cornfield'. They were buzzing in from the east, so from the direction of Sirte. It looked as if the German and Italian commanders, fearful that Sirte was about to be attacked, had evacuated the airbase completely. The presence of the LRDG convoy must have spooked them mightily, with the result that all aircraft were now concentrated at the one airstrip – Mayne's target.

With nightfall, Mayne handed out the Lewes bombs. He and his men would travel light and fast. He asked the LRDG to drop them a mile to the north of the airstrip, which seemed to offer the best avenue of attack. It was 2200 hours by the time they parted company with the trucks and slipped into the darkness. It was an ideal night for a mission such as this, Mayne noted: 'No moon, and pleasantly cool for walking.' Buzzing with nervous energy they pressed on, a snake of men moving stealthily on foot, making for a point in the night sky just to the right of the North Star, so a fraction east of due north.

After a few minutes the desert terrain came to an abrupt end. They'd hit a road. They flitted across it, acutely aware that they were 'neither expected, nor invited', but that they had surprise on their side. Mayne felt his pulse quicken. 'Keyed-up, tense, nervous', he was convinced that, this time, nothing could stop them. The first sign of the enemy were two military-style huts, set in a shallow scoop in the landscape. The sounds of sleeping came from within. Mayne had no doubt that these were enemy soldiers at rest.

He was acutely aware that this might be the only target they might reach tonight. The faint whiff of aviation fuel on the night air was the only suggestion that they were getting anywhere like close to the airstrip itself. Right now, they had to take whatever came to hand, for who knew what else they might encounter. All that mattered was scoring some kind of a victory, so as to prove that they had what it takes.

Stealthily, he and his men set their first Lewes bombs. Just as they had finished doing so, they heard voices. Italians. Some kind of patrol was approaching. At Mayne's signal he and his men melted into the darkness. Of course, they still had little idea what route to take to the heart of the target. But Mayne's instinct told him the approaching patrol would lead them to the airfield. Slipping in behind the enemy, they followed at a distance. After pressing on a good way, the figures turned off towards a building that resembled a Nissen hut – a long, low, steel structure, like a half-cylinder set on its side, with an entrance in either end. As the door opened and closed, light spilled from the blacked-out interior, as did the sound of laughter and raucous singing.

Ten months earlier, when serving with No. 11 Commando, Mayne had carried out that trial raid on the RAF airbase in Scotland. The chief target had been the officer's mess, for they'd realised that killing pilots was just as effective as taking out enemy aircraft. Arguably more so. On average it took eighteen months to two years to train a fighter pilot, less than a third of that time to manufacture a Me 109. Pilots were in precious short supply, on both sides of the war. Back in the January of that year they had dressed two of their commando brethren as women, to distract the guards, while the remainder stole up to the officer's mess and hurled grenades through the windows, much to Colonel Pedder's satisfaction.

Here, with this Nissen hut, there were no windows. But there was a door.

Mayne gave the order to his men. Half his party were to busy themselves planting bombs around the structure, while he would take Seeking and Hawkins and head for the entrance. Ghost-like, Mayne and his two fellows crept across to the doorway, the same one as had been used by the enemy. With weapons at the ready – Mayne and Seekings grasping Colt .45 (M 1911) pistols, Hawkins brandishing a Thompson submachine gun – the tall Irishman raised a boot and kicked open the door. No doubt, this was a most unusual way to enter the German/Italian officer's mess at Tamet Airbase, and a roomful of faces turned and stared.

After a week crossing the desert the three figures framed in the doorway made 'a peculiar and frightening sight', confessed Mayne, 'bearded and with long, unkempt hair'. For what seemed like an age the two parties – SAS raiders, German and Italian airmen – 'just stood there looking at each other in complete silence'. A fire burned and crackled in the midst of the room; hands of cards were frozen mid-play, as were glasses of beer.

It was Mayne who broke the quiet. 'Good evening, gentlemen.'

A young German officer made a move and Mayne opened fire.

As the officer fell, he knocked a heap of glasses from a table and they smashed onto the floor. Mayne spun and fired again, this time hitting a figure standing no more than six feet away. When training recruits, he would remark of this kind of close quarter combat: 'When you burst into a hut full of enemy soldiers, shoot the first person who makes a move, hostile or otherwise. His brain has recovered from the shock from seeing you there with a gun. He has started to think and is therefore dangerous. You must then shoot the person nearest to you, because he is in the best position to cause you embarrassment. Then you deal with the rest as you think fit.'

In that spirit, at Mayne's side the Tommy gun spat fire. Again and again, Hawkins raked the room with bursts, as bloodcurdling screams and gasps rent the air. With the place littered with dead and dying, Mayne ordered a withdrawal, but not before shooting out the lights, and hurling a volley of grenades to add to the chaos and confusion. One of Mayne's stated aims had been to cause a sense of 'insecurity and anxiety among the Axis'. No doubt they had done that and so much more. The odd burst of return fire erupted from the building, but no one seemed keen to venture forth to take the fight to these terrifying raiders of the night.

Back in June 1940, Churchill had charged his Special Service volunteers to leave a 'trail of German corpses' in their wake; to 'kill and capture the Hun garrison . . . and then away'.

That was exactly what Mayne and his men had done.

It was begun.

CHAPTER ELEVEN

Butcher and Bolt

In his official report on the Tamet Airbase raid, Mayne would describe the officer's mess building as being 'attacked by submachine gun and pistol fire, bombs being placed around it. There appeared to be roughly 30 inhabitants . . . The guards were slack and when alarmed, wasted many rounds in misdirected fire.' That was exactly what transpired now.

In no time, the place erupted into a hive of activity, as furious blasts of gunfire seared through the night. But oddly, none of it seemed to be targeting Mayne and his men. Instead, the Tamet guard force appeared to be firing on 'fixed lines' – unleashing long bursts of tracer along static trajectories, most of which either seared along the perimeters of the airbase at just a few feet above ground level, or speared skywards into the empty heavens. Spectacular and noisy it certainly was. It might deter a raiding party lurking outside of the base perimeter, or those intent on an air attack. But it offered little disincentive to a small, stealthy force that was moving on foot and already in their midst.

Momentarily, Mayne and his men went to ground. Slipping away – vaulting over the enemy's fixed lines of fire wherever necessary – they gathered in a patch of deep shadow for a 'confab'. Some argued that with the Tamet guard force well and truly on the alert, now was the time to bug out. They'd hit and hit hard – now was the moment to run. Others countered that was exactly what the enemy would be expecting; the last place they'd ever think to look for the mystery raiding party was at the heart of the airbase, especially after an attack like the one they had just executed.

Mayne listened to all views. Or at least he *appeared* to. But if he was ever in any doubt as to their next move, Seekings for one didn't believe it was for more than a brief moment. The sky was lightening imperceptibly, as the moon – a 'waning crescent'; the barest sliver of ethereal silver – rose in the sky. Light with which to seek and destroy. As the gunfire died down to the odd, desultory burst, Mayne announced that they would press home their attack. They would search out the landing strip and those ranks of enemy warplanes.

Reasoning that the airstrip had to lie beyond where they had first struck, Mayne led his men in a crouching scurry, giving the dark and bullet-riddled hulk of the Nissen hut a wide berth. The first target they stumbled across wasn't a warplane, but it was still a real beauty – a dump of 40-gallon drums of aviation fuel, roped over by camouflage netting. A second dump was beside it, the entrance to which lay down a flight of steps. It turned out to be stuffed full of aircraft munitions. On Mayne's orders, they sowed both with enough Lewes bombs to incinerate the lot – those charges in the fuel dump set right in the centre, from where the blast would flash outwards, in a raging firestorm; each of those in the munitions store attached to the nose cone of a 500-pound bomb, with the cap unscrewed, so as to expose the detonators.

Their delayed fuses – 'timer pencils', as they were called, due to their distinctive shape – had better work, for no one wanted to be anywhere thereabouts when that little lot went bang. The timers worked on the principle of acid eating through a copper wire, which once severed released a spring, triggering the detonation. The thicker the wire, the longer the fuse would take to blow.

The acid was activated by crushing a glass vial. The timer pencils weren't always accurate to the very minute, but with luck they should leave Mayne and his men enough time to do what they intended and to slip away.

They pressed on, coming across a line of telegraph poles. Communications were a secondary target, but still well worth hitting. A string of bombs was threaded along the poles. Next, someone practically stumbled over a concrete bollard. Surely it had to mark the border of the landing strip? Mayne paused. Getting down on his haunches, he signalled for the others to do likewise. Like that, they executed a 360-degree sweep of the horizon. By the faint light of the moon, a silhouette was visible not so very far away. It had the distinctive high, angular, boxy profile of a Fiat CR.42 Falco (Falcon), the much-reviled Italian Air Force bi-plane.

As the men of the LRDG had been at pains to point out, they hated and feared that aircraft more than just about any other enemy warplane. The reasons why were simple. The relatively slow-flying but highly manoeuvrable CR.42 was able to take exceptional punishment and still remain airborne, meaning there was little chance of shooting one down, still less of hiding from its predations. It had the ability to loiter in the skies, turning on a sixpence to quarter the ground below, before raking its prey with bullets and bombs. In short, it was loathed and detested like no other.

As their eyes adjusted to the light, Mayne and his men spied further shadowy outlines, tracing a line of warplanes ranged around the edge of the landing strip in a rough semi-circle. Each was separated from the next by just a few dozen yards. As well as further CR.42s, there were also the distinctive gull-like outlines of Junkers JU 87 'Stuka' dive-bombers, plus the prize of all prizes – the predatory, powerful forms of Me 109s. 'They looked beautiful,' Mayne remarked of this moment. 'Low, sleek, deadly in the air, but strangely impotent now.'

There was little time to waste. The fuses on the Lewes bombs already set were running down to detonation time. Working quickly, each of his men began placing their charges, making sure that they were planted near the fuel tanks – invariably where the cockpit met the wing. As Mayne flitted from one shadowy form to another, he couldn't believe how quiet the airbase had become. Apart from the odd distant noise, or the hint of movement off to the periphery, there wasn't the slightest sign that anyone might have rumbled what he and his men were up to. In fact, they were left remarkably undisturbed, as they moved from one warplane to another, silently placing their Lewes bombs.

Then Mayne spotted something unusual. There was a distinctive reddish light emanating from the cockpit of a nearby CR.42. For a moment, he figured it had to be a pilot sat at his controls having a cigarette break. Moving silently through the darkness – owning the night, just as they'd trained to do so rigorously, back at Kabrit – he clambered onto the rear of the Falco, inched forward and peered into the cockpit. There was no pilot inside. Instead, whoever had last been in the cockpit had simply forgotten to turn off the aircraft's control panel and instruments, hence the soft glow.

Acting on impulse, Mayne reached in, took a firm hold of the instrument panel and, 'with the titanic strength he displayed in such berserk moods, tore the dashboard out with his bare hands.' Having ripped out that first cockpit panel, it struck Mayne this wasn't such a bad idea. He was all out of Lewes bombs. They'd been too generous with the earlier targets. Indicating to the others what he'd done – his DIY sabotage – he signalled they should do likewise, for all were short of bombs. Amazingly, as Mayne would report, 'Ten aircraft were damaged by having the instrument panel destroyed,' in addition to the fourteen that had been garlanded with Lewes bombs.

Reg Seekings was himself no fading violet. A champion boxer before the war – 'The more he fought, the more he wanted to fight' – he would remark of Mayne's spur-of-the-moment sabotage, in amazement: 'I saw him rip the instrument panel out with his bare hands. How he did it I shall never know.' Of those ten enemy warplanes that had their cockpits eviscerated, rumour would have it that Mayne accounted for the lion's share.

They were almost done when Mayne spied three more aircraft, parked where the airstrip ended and the cliffs ran down to the sea. Flitting past a rank of huts – a swift check proved them to be empty – they made a dash for that final trio. Upon arrival, Mayne and Seekings clambered up and set about the cockpits. Muscles straining, Seekings tried to emulate what his commander had done earlier, but he simply couldn't shift the panel. Instead, he took his Colt and repeatedly drove the butt into the instruments, smashing them asunder.

As he went to jump down, Seekings' lanyard – a length of cord with a clasp at one end, used for keeping a compass or whistle handy – snagged in the cockpit, and he was left hanging. 'I was helpless, until Paddy freed me.' In fact, they would all be rendered far worse than 'helpless' if they didn't get a move on. In the adrenaline-fuelled tension and excitement of the moment, they'd lost track of time, but no one doubted that the first of the Lewes bombs was poised to blow.

When he'd first joined the SAS, Seekings – a former farm labourer hailing from East Anglia – had been more than a little suspicious of Mayne. He'd viewed their wayward, 'scruffy' Irish commander as being something of a misfit in the British Army. To Seekings' way of thinking, 'Nothing fitted.' Mayne had 'a hell of a temper, especially when drinking. Didn't mix. We used to say with his ginger beard, he looked like Jesus Christ.' Since then, they'd soldiered together on Operation Squatter, a mission on which Mayne alone of the patrol commanders had come close to success. And now, as long as the Lewes bombs did their work, there would be tonight's feast of death and destruction to add to the tally.

Seekings' reservations were starting to vanish, which was exactly what Mayne and his men needed to do right now. Moving like wraiths they hurried away from the airstrip and into the beckoning embrace of the night.

'We hadn't gone far, possibly a quarter of a mile, when there was an explosion,' Mayne would write. The first to go up were the guard huts and the officer's mess, but then came the big one – the fuel and ammo dumps. 'A terrific sheet of flame shot upwards, lighting the area. Feeling slightly naked in the light, we turned and got down in the sand . . . It was magnificent and terribly satisfying to watch the petrol dump ablaze.' The triggering of that towering inferno was followed by a series of further blasts, which seemed to trace the outline of the landing strip, as, one by one the warplanes started to blow.

'There would be an explosion, a flash . . . then a steady fire,' Mayne would write of this moment. Unable to move for fear of being etched in the blazing light, he pulled out some cigarettes and a flask of rum, as he and his men took a breather. The gunfire that had followed the attack on the officer's mess had gradually died to nothing. Now, all hell had let loose again. As anti-aircraft guns laced the sky above Tamet with a blinding latticework of tracer, so the shore batteries launched powerful salvoes out to sea. Spying imaginary shadows moving around the airbase, those manning the perimeter defences also opened up, threading fiery bursts across the terrain at just above ground level.

As matters transpired, the Tamet garrison commander had radioed in an alert about a supposed 'amphibious landing' taking place, warning that unless reinforcements were urgently dispatched they would not be able to hold out. In a sense it was hardly surprising, for Mayne and his raiders had wreaked widespread and unmitigated carnage, blowing up two guard huts, shooting up the officer's mess, dynamiting the fuel and ammo dumps, severing communications and sabotaging some two dozen warplanes. That half-a-dozen men could have wreaked such havoc was almost unthinkable.

Eventually, the blinding glare from the fire around the petrol and bomb dumps started to fade into a dull red glow, a thick pall of oily smoke blanketing the scene. Mayne signalled it was time to move out. They pushed south as rapidly as they could, for he was worried they might miss their rendezvous with the LRDG. He'd asked them to flash a torch every three minutes from 0200 hours onwards, to help guide them in. Just as he was losing hope, someone spied a light blinking on and off, rhythmically, a little to their front.

Minutes later they reached the column of distinctive vehicles, to be met with a heroes' welcome. Clambering aboard, they settled among the piles of supplies and, as the adrenaline started to drain from their system and the exhaustion set in, they left it to Sadler to get them on their way. East lay their rendezvous with Stirling, and east of there again stretched the long drive home. Before sun-up, they needed to find a place of hiding, somewhere to conceal their presence from the enemy warplanes that would come hot on their trail.

The link-up with Stirling went without a hitch. With Sirte airfield having been evacuated, due to all the reports of a British patrol being thereabouts, he and his men had been forced to watch as their targets had flown away. But likewise, the carnage wrought by Mayne and his raiding party had been clearly visible, as first the fuel dump blaze and then the repeated flashes of exploding warplanes had lit the horizon a dark and angry orange. Stirling had luxuriated in the light show and all that it signified.

Finally, the SAS had delivered.

Promises, long cherished, had been kept.

The intensive rigours of SAS training had proved their worth.

The ghosts of Operation Squatter could finally be laid to rest – or at least for some they could.

Thanks to the courage, cunning and daring of a somewhat wild and unconventional Irishman, Stirling's Big Idea had been proved beyond all doubt. Their detractors – those who sniped and carped from the sidelines – could put Tamet in their pipes and smoke it.

There was one other standout quality about Mayne that struck Stirling, and any number of the others, on that momentous night. While all around were lauding his extraordinary achievements, Mayne himself remained oddly, strangely reticent. His modesty was striking. It almost seemed to border upon a self-conscious sense of disquiet, as if he couldn't bear all the attention and praise. As if, with his shy, self-effacing smile he shunned the limelight. Of course, to most, this only served to enlarge his stature still further. That enduring modesty was to become a signature characteristic of Mayne throughout the war.

In a way, it was epitomised by the CR.42 control panel that he had cradled in one of his arms, as they'd made their getaway. Most would want to show it off, and lord-knows any man who could rip something like that free with his bare hands had earned the bragging rights. Mayne seemed to want to do nothing of the sort. At one point, Seekings spotted an odd glow on one of the LRDG vehicles – it was Mayne's purloined dashboard, tucked well away. The compass and various other instruments were still intact, and were strongly luminous. Even the CR.42's clock was still ticking. Seekings did his best to point it out to all and sundry. There – that was Paddy's famous control panel!

Mayne's response to the notoriety was typical. Upon their return to their Jalo base, he would unscrew the compass from the CR.42's dash and present it to Gentleman Jim Almonds, the young father struggling with the pain of almost losing his infant son to illness. Mayne explained the gift away by asking Almonds if perhaps there might be a way he could fit it to one of their purloined Lancia trucks, to aid their desert navigation as they sought to cross hundreds of miles of uncharted wastes. Of course, in doing so he managed to deflect the attention away from himself and onto Almonds, the SAS's self-confessed 'bogus engineer'.

Somehow, amid the height of the Tamet Airbase bloodletting, Mayne had also managed to filch a second souvenir. Perhaps in McGonigal's name, he had grabbed a handful of cutlery from out of the bloody carnage of the officer's mess. Each of the knives, forks and spoons was stamped with the Luftwaffe's coat of arms – an eagle with wings outstretched, clutching in its talons a Nazi swastika – plus the German words for 'Flight Barracks Administration', and the initials 'G K & F 39'. That indicated that the manufacturer was Gebrüder Kugel & Fink, of Westphalia, a province in western Germany. The '39' signified the year of manufacture – 1939, the year war was declared.

There was further good news for the SAS as they gathered at Jalo oasis. Almonds had formed part of Jock Lewes's raiding party, and while they had failed to hit Agheila Airbase – they'd found it deserted of targets – they had executed a daring assault on Rommel's main highway. Turning onto the coastal road and riding in their former Italian military Lancia trucks, they'd sped merrily along making like the enemy. In that fashion they'd zipped past several dozen German and Italian military vehicles, before reaching a vast truck stop at Mersa Brega. There, via a combination of bluff, daring and chutzpah, they had laced the ranks of enemy transport with Lewes bombs, after which they had shot the place all to hell, in a 'hectic scrap fought at about thirty yards' range.

But it was Bill Fraser's raid that would truly seal the fate of the SAS and in the most positive way imaginable. His raid on Agedabia had yielded the greatest haul of all. During the infiltration to the airbase, Fraser and his four-man party – Sergeant Bob Tait, the great escapee, had replaced the missing Jock Cheyne as Fraser's deputy – camped up in a patch of desert. But come dawn, they'd discovered they were surrounded by German troops, who were busy digging in. They'd sat tight, held their nerve, and slipped away that night, aiming to launch their attack under cover of darkness.

If anything, Fraser's mission reports were even more terse than Mayne's. His read: 'Walked into drome and destroyed 37 planes without opposition . . . may have been more, as planes were closely packed.' The truth about the attack on Agedabia was infinitely more dramatic and action-packed. As with Mayne's raid on Tamet, it had been distinguished by raw courage and daring. At one stage, the first of the series of Lewes bombs they'd planted had detonated, tearing apart the darkness, and in the light of the explosions Fraser and his men had spotted a second rank of Me 109s, which were as yet untouched. Even though they had been busy 'bugging out' – executing the 'run' stage of a classic hit-and-run attack – they had turned right around and laced those eight prize warplanes with charges.

Wreaking such havoc would have had special significance for Fraser. He'd seen his parent unit, the 1st Battalion the Gordon Highlanders, suffer the hell of defeat and ruin in France. More to the point, he and others had been subjected to horrific attacks by enemy dive-bombers. As they'd fought a desperate defensive action in June 1940, they'd found themselves on roads clogged with refugees, witnessing the terrible realities of such attacks. Men, women and children were shot and bombed relentlessly, the Luftwaffe leaving 'silent, limp, doll-like bodies', the survivors yelling enraged insults at the departing pilots, 'sales Boches'. They'd heard the screams of Stukas, and seen ambulances targeted.

Those rescued from the Dunkirk beaches had gone on to keep tallies of enemy warplanes shot down by the RAF during the Battle of Britain; each was a heartfelt victory. Every enemy aircraft destroyed, every enemy pilot killed, evened up the score a little.

Even so, as more details of Mayne's Tamet mess shoot-up emerged, he would get sniped at from some quarters.

Stirling maintained that he criticised Mayne at the time for his 'over-callous execution in cold blood of the enemy'. Writing about the Tamet raid, he would remark that while Mayne was incredibly successful, he'd taken 'ruthlessness to the point of callousness'. Hindsight is a fine thing. At this point in the war, mid-December 1941, Britain stood alone in the fight. Assailed by defeat on all fronts, this was one of the nation's darkest hours. The stakes could not have been higher, and Britain had her back to the wall, plus the very survival of the SAS hung in the balance.

Equally, Mayne's Tamet attack was hardly without precedent – a precedent cleared to the very highest levels of government and of command. The avowed aim of Operation Flipper, Major Keyes' November 1941 commando raid, had been to assassinate General Rommel. There had been some fluff and flannel in the mission orders about capturing him, but the impracticalities of that were legion. Keyes and his men were to surround his headquarters and shoot the hell out of those inside, first and foremost the German general. Of course, Flipper had had a compelling strategic aim. Rommel had masterminded a series of German victories in North Africa. If they cut the head off the snake, presumably that would render the Afrika Korps significantly less potent.

But so too had Mayne's Tamet mess attack. In one fell swoop it had – potentially – taken out several dozen key targets, those pilots who flew the German and Italian warplanes. (As Mayne himself reported of the mess attack, modesty to the fore: 'Damage inflicted unknown.') That, added to the two dozen aircraft destroyed, represented a serious blow to the enemy's air power in North Africa. It had also put the SAS firmly on the map, proving that Stirling's ideas had teeth and could yield results.

Bloody and brutal it may have been, but at the time it was also absolutely necessary.

As Almonds would note in his diary, about Mayne's Tamet exploits, and without a hint of censure: 'succeeded in destroying

24 enemy aircraft, beside the bomb dumps, petrol dumps etc and shot the staff, pilots etc in the Officer's quarters – no prisoners taken.' In due course, Mayne would be awarded the Distinguished Service Order (DSO) for executing the raid on Tamet. As well as making mention of Mayne's 'courage and leadership', and his 'skill and devotion to duty', the citation for the DSO praised the fact that he 'led this raid in person and himself destroyed and killed many of the enemy'.

At Tamet, Mayne had done exactly what was expected of him. This was war, and in the winter of 1941/42, as Britain fought for her very survival, and that of the free world, it would prove bloody and brutal in the extreme.

In a sense, what made this all the more extraordinary was just who had executed those attacks. As a newspaper reporter would write, of these earliest SAS missions: 'these men to whom one of the most dangerous jobs in the war is just routine now – capture means certain death – are drawn from ordinary walks of life. Before the war one was a shop assistant, another a bank clerk, a third a plumber, a fourth a carpenter. There is a . . . school-master . . . and an ice-cream maker. They were just rookies when they started.'

Indeed, Mayne – the former solicitor – was 'a man possessed', and in truth he had only just begun.

CHAPTER TWELVE

Paddy's Own

Fraser and Mayne, the two No. 11 Commando Litani River veterans, had come up trumps. Three, if Bob Tait was included. In fact, of Fraser's five-man patrol, all bar one had been No. 11 Commando originals. Had Eoin McGonigal still been soldiering in the SAS ranks, there was every chance he would have likewise hit home. But as far as anyone knew, McGonigal had disappeared off the face of the earth, along with his entire patrol. There was no news about their fortunes. Not a clue as to what might have happened.

At around this time Mayne would send a Christmas card to his niece Margaret, whom he had given the teasing nickname 'Funnyface'. It revealed little sense of the demons that were driving him. Showing a jolly Santa riding on a galloping camel, a British Army tin hat perched atop his head, Mayne gave his address as 'Special Air Service Bde [Brigade], M.E.F. (Middle East Force).' The card read: 'Christmas Greetings, From Blair ... Thanks awfully for your letter. I hope you ... have a very pleasant Xmas.' But in truth, there would be precious little time for Mayne, Stirling or any of their men to have a 'very pleasant Christmas', or at least not in the traditional sense of the phrase.

There was work to be done.

Bill Fraser had made it back to Jalo on 23 December 1941, just as Stirling, Mayne and Lewes were poised to set forth again ...

with raiding in mind. Working on the premise that they should do the utterly unexpected – surprise was everything, argued Stirling, for with it you could 'get away with murder' – he and Mayne were heading out to hit Sirte and Tamet Airbases all over again. Arguing that the enemy would never expect a follow-up attack might strike in the same place so quickly, they aimed to repeat the successes of recent days – during which some sixty German and Italian warplanes had been destroyed, not to mention the numbers of enemy pilots killed and wounded. As a bonus, they hoped that striking at around Christmas would be doubly unanticipated.

That evening, the four SAS commanders gathered, both to celebrate their successes and to wish each other farewell. Stirling and Mayne were setting out the following morning, as was Jock Lewes, who aimed to have a crack at Nofilia Aerodrome, after his recent disappointments at Agheila. Fraser, fresh from his spectacularly successful raid, seemed most concerned that he'd actually had to leave two aircraft untouched, for he and his men had run out of Lewes bombs. But as a bonus, credible reports had placed General Rommel himself in Agedabia on the night of their attack, so presumably the commander of the Afrika Korps would have had one hell of 'a headache' when he woke to learn of Fraser and his team's handiwork.

But it very possibly signified something far more momentous, as well.

At Agedabia, Rommel would have had a ringside seat to the aftermath of an SAS raid – an airbase's entire complement of warplanes, bar two, being left as smoking, gutted ruins. Already, the SAS commanders knew that some of their men had been captured on Operation Squatter. They knew that they had revealed at least some details of their operations to their captors. Various signals intercepts suggested that the enemy remained convinced that the elusive raiders were striking from the sea; that the distance overland was just too great, and the terrain too impossible. But for how much longer would that misapprehension hold good? How much did senior enemy commanders really understand about the SAS's aims, objectives and modus operandi? They just didn't know. But one thing was for certain: if they were to continue their recent run of success, they would need to stay one step ahead of the enemy.

Over dinner – washed down with lashings of hot lime juice laced with rum, the Jalo special – seemingly on the spur of the moment, Stirling invited Fraser to ride along with Jock Lewes on his coming raid. There was an enemy airbase at 'Marble Arch' – the Arco dei Fileni, Italian leader Mussolini's massive and garish monument to Italy's colonial power – which was not so far from Lewes's intended target. If Fraser was not too tired, Stirling suggested, he might like to have a go at that. This was vintage Stirling. Never one to bark orders, he simply used his powers of charm and suggestion to convince whoever he was talking to of the wisdom of his words.

Fraser agreed, of course, even though he and his men had just arrived back from an utterly gruelling and exhausting mission.

At first light on 24 December 1941 – Christmas Eve – the raiding parties set forth from Jalo, intent on executing their not-so-festive missions. Riding in the lead vehicle of Mayne and Stirling's convoy was the rock-solid figure of Mike Sadler, once again tasked with finding a route through to Tamet and Sirte, only this time charting a different line of approach. It seemed like a wise precaution. Sadler's key challenge in plotting his new route was the mapping, or rather the lack of it. Large tracts of the desert remained terra incognita – uncharted and unknown.

Most of the maps available to Sadler were of Italian origin, this being Italian Libya territory, known as 'Cyrenaica' at the time. They left a great deal to be desired. The Italian cartographers could be relied upon to get the Mediterranean in the right place, but not a great deal more. Often, key navigational features – wadis, ravines, rocky outcrops – were simply not marked. Roads and desert tracks – the ancient trans-Saharan trade routes plied by camel trains – were delineated miles from where they actually lay. The RAF were busy photographing vast tracts of the desert, to draw up accurate, detailed mapping, but that was very much a work in progress.

This time, the convoy's journey west went with barely a hitch, and with little sign of any hostile aircraft. It looked as if the timing – over the Christmas break – was perfect. Even so, precautions were taken. Upon arrival at each of their desert lie-ups, figures would retrace the line of the convoy's tyre-tracks, using clumps of camel thorn to sweep them away, so their route was less easy to track from the air. A cast-iron friendship, laced with not a little competitive spirit, was developing between the LRDG and the SAS. The former had nicknamed the latter 'The Parashites' – hints of 'parasites', mixed with 'shite' parachutists, for all the obvious reasons. The SAS had in turn nicknamed their LRDG brethren the 'Desert Taxi Company,' and the 'Libyan Desert Taxi Service,' as delicious ripostes.

There were some among the LRDG who hankered after a bit of what the SAS were up to – hitting the enemy where it hurt. In due course some would jump ship. The LRDG's reconnaissance remit, though crucial, could prove repetitive and frankly dull. Their chief mission was known as 'road watch', which did exactly what it says on the tin. Hiding out on the Jebel – the rocky escarpment overlooking the coastal road – LRDG patrols were charged to keep a 24/7 watch on Rommel's chief supply route, making note of all the vehicles that passed. The intelligence so gleaned was spirited back to MEHQ and on to London, where it was praised as being absolutely vital for the war effort. It was, but not in a way that the LRDG were ever fully to appreciate.

In truth, the key function of road watch was to verify the holiest of holies, as far as the Allies were concerned – the Enigma secret. Covered by the highest level of security classification possible – Ultra – the work of Britain's Bletchley Park in breaking the German military codes was known to only the chosen few: the prime minister and a handful of top generals and intelligence figures. Since the spring of 1940, specialists at Bletchley had been intercepting and decoding the Reich's most sensitive messages. This extraordinary breakthrough afforded Allied commanders 'the unique experience of knowing not only the precise composition, strength and location of the enemy's forces, but also . . . exactly what he intended to do'.

German signals were decoded upon the Enigma machine, an electromechanical encryption device that resembled an oversized typewriter. An extraordinary piece of technology, Enigma relied upon a series of wheels, rotors and drums, coupled with electronic circuitry, to churn out an endless stream of unique ciphers. Messages were said to be utterly unbreakable, or so the Germans and their allies thought. But at Bletchley Park a team of cryptologists, mathematical wizards and linguists had worked feverishly to break the Enigma codes, with incredible results.

It was in North Africa that those efforts had first started to be undermined. Badgering Berlin for greater resources to prosecute his war, General Rommel was sending deliberately pessimistic reports regarding his strengths. He put forward his worst case, gambling that it would win him more men and materiel. In doing so the German general unwittingly confounded the Bletchley cryptologists. They knew his true strengths, which made them wonder if they had somehow got their code-breaking wrong? Or was the enemy feeding them a diet of subtle misinformation? Was Ultra somehow being used against them? In short, had the Germans rumbled the ENIGMA secret and turned it to their own ends?

The answer to such vital questions lay in road watch. Its chief objective was to verify Bletchley's work. If the actual numbers moving on the main highway could be married up with Bletchley's intercepts, then the code-breakers could be relieved of their gnawing fears. That was what the LRDG were there to provide: *verification*. Of course, they knew nothing of Enigma, Ultra, or Bletchley Park. It was not until long after the war that this top-secret role was finally revealed. It was hardly surprising that some in the Desert Taxi Company hankered after the kind of action and adventure they saw the Parashites engaged in.

The convoy of six Chevys made good progress, moving across a desert landscape that appeared beguilingly serene. It was almost possible to imagine that all was at peace with the world. For two days and two nights their desert sojourn remained undisturbed. Late in the evening of the third day the convoy approached Tamet, Sadler having steered them to the most distant airbase first, to vary their route of approach. There was zero sign that their presence had been detected, and it was here that the two forces would split up. Three trucks would ferry Mayne and his men the half-dozen miles onwards to Tamet airbase, while Stirling's party would swing east, riding in the other half of the convoy, aiming to hit Sirte, some twenty-five miles distant.

The plan was to strike in just a few hours' time, so shortly after midnight on 27/28 December, which meant that Stirling's party, in particular, needed to get a move on. With that in mind, they opted to head for the main coastal highway, which should speed them to their target. The only other possible route lay across broken, difficult country, plagued by stretches of vast, rolling dunes. Having spent two hours carrying out vital vehicle and weapons maintenance, it was 2300 hours by the time the convoys got moving. Time was running.

Sadler steered Stirling's party across the jumbled, nerve-shredding terrain, before announcing that the highway lay just a few hundred yards to their front. They killed their lights, and nosed ahead at a dead slow, preparing to pull onto the main road, acting like any other German or Italian patrol. But almost immediately they realised something wasn't right. There was a low, throaty rumble that reverberated through the still desert air, and the very earth itself seemed to be trembling. Crawling ahead, they spotted the most unexpected and unwelcome of sights: right now, on this night sandwiched between Christmas and New Year, Rommel was moving what looked like an entire armoured division east towards the frontlines.

A fleet of giant transporters thundered past, each laden with the shadowy form of a German tank. That was followed by a squadron of armoured cars, some towing field guns. After that came more heavy armour, any number of the Panzers moving under their own steam, their tracks emitting an ear-splitting clatter as they clawed along the highway throwing up clouds of choking dust. Some two hundred miles east lay Rommel's frontline positions, which was where all of this heavy war materiel had to be heading. The massive column continued to grind past for two hours or more, for all of which time the watchers had little choice but to remain hidden. If they tried making for Sirte off-road, they stood little chance of getting there by first light.

Long before the last of the armoured vehicles had thundered past, the horizon to the west flashed an angry red and orange, as a series of conflagrations erupted one after the other . . . in the direction of Tamet. 'Paddy's lit another bonfire,' one of Stirling's men whispered. It did indeed appear that way. But all they could do was remain in hiding, as they watched Rommel's mighty parade of armour file past. It looked as if this mission was going to be a vexing repeat of their previous attempt – Mayne striking gold at Tamet, while Stirling's party were going to be left frustrated and thwarted at Sirte.

At 0330 hours the roadway finally fell silent. SAS and LRDG mounted up the Chevys and swung east onto the now-deserted highway. It didn't stay like that for long. A mile or so later, the speeding convoy of three vehicles zipped past the first shadowy forms – a squadron of German armoured cars parked up by the roadside. Ahead lay more vehicles, plus the tented camps for the soldiers, stretching a good distance into the darkness. Hands gripped weapons ever more firmly, as they motored on. All it would take was for one sentry to challenge them, or for one driver to flick on his headlights, and the game would be up.

In their thin-skinned, unarmoured Chevys, they wouldn't stand a chance in a full-on firefight. Their only option would be to let rip with every weapon they had, as they tried to speed for the open desert and safety. 'Motored down road for 9 Kilos through German Armoured Division parked on side of road,' Stirling would write, in his official report on 'OPERATION NUMBER FOUR (A)', as it became known. 'FOUR (B)' was Mayne's raid, which to all appearances had proved wildly successful.

Two miles short of Sirte Airbase, which straddled the highway, Sadler pulled to a halt. To their front and rear lay more armoured cars and tanks, which meant that the tiny British raiding force was sandwiched between the enemy. It was 0400 and less than two hours of darkness remained. With a few hurried words of farewell, and having agreed a password so each party could identify the other, Stirling led his four raiders into the darkness. Keeping well away from the road, they pressed ahead until the sound of boots on gravel brought them to a halt. Before them lay a barbed wire perimeter, quartered by patrols. Worse still, the outer side of the fencing appeared to be sown with mines.

This was a very different set of defences from that which they had encountered just a few weeks earlier, on their first – abortive – visit. No doubt Mayne's inaugural raid on Tamet had triggered the erection of these kind of barriers – a 'new perimeter' with 'sentries patrolling', as Stirling would report it. Reasoning that they did not have the time to feel their away across the minefield and to cut their way through the wire, Stirling led his men back towards the road. Maybe that would offer a less troublesome route of attack. But the highway turned out to be barred by a substantial roadblock, and as Stirling tried to lead his men through, they were 'challenged from several points'.

Withdrawing stealthily, Stirling tried to work out what was best. At least an hour had passed since their little convoy had pulled onto the highway. He had been warned that the LRDG could not wait past 0530 hours, and even that was cutting it fine – for it would leave precious little time to head for the open desert and to find a place to hide. With that deadline fast approaching, Stirling made the difficult decision to abandon the attack.

As they retraced their steps towards their convoy, Stirling hoped that maybe they could execute a swift series of drive-by shootings, before vanishing, so as to salvage something from their venture. Dashing ahead, he arrived at the first LRDG truck having forgotten to give the password. A sharp click cut the night stillness. It brought Stirling to an abrupt halt, as he spied a white face with the muzzle of a rifle pointing right at him.

'It's me,' he hissed. 'No luck.'

'You've had more luck than you know, sir,' the guard replied, in a strangled whisper.

It turned out that the sentry had pulled his trigger, as no password had been given, but by a rare oversight had forgotten to ratchet a bullet into the breech of his weapon. There was no time to dwell upon that now. Once he'd outlined his proposal, Stirling's drive-by shoot-'em-up plan was embraced by the men of the Desert Taxi Company. Although they were strictly speaking a reconnaissance and ferry service, they realised that now was their chance to get a slice of the action. With the sky already lightening, they decided to target soft-skinned vehicles only, for no one fancied taking on a column of Panzers.

One mile down the road they came across the first opportunity – a dozen supply trucks ranged along the roadside, with their crews bedded down in tents to one side. The three Chevys pulled up just beyond, as Stirling and his men crept back and laced the length of the convoy with Lewes bombs. It was now 0450, and there was little time left to engage upon the stealthy craft of planting such charges. Instead, as they raced west towards their rendezvous with Mayne's party, they decided to throw caution to the wind and let rip, all guns blazing.

They made a crazed, piratical sight, as bearded and wild-eyed figures braced themselves in the Chevys' rears, those not manning the vehicle-mounted machine-guns wielding Tommy guns and hurling grenades. First target was a tented camp, which stretched before them into the grey pre-dawn stillness. A storm of bullets erupted from the Chevys, tearing through the canvas sides, before the speeding convoy came upon a second rank of lorries. More of the same was unleashed on those, as grey-uniformed figures dashed out of their tents in panic, only to discover that their trucks had burst into flames.

For twenty-five minutes the hell-ride continued, the convoy tearing through two more tented camps, before unleashing a final volley of grenades on a tank transporter. At that point, with the sun practically up, the vehicles bumped off the road and raced for the safety of the desert. Their big fear now was that the enemy would dispatch an armoured car patrol to chase after them, but none seemed to materialise. The lack of any kind of pursuit was confounding. They could only presume that the German forces, well-disciplined and fully aware of their orders, were under strict instructions to proceed to the frontline, and that no one possessed the authority to determine otherwise.

In any case, the three Chevys made their desert rendezvous unhindered, having somehow got away with their utterly audacious, spur-of-the-moment highway shoot-'em-up. It was 0700 by the time they pulled to a halt. Mayne and his force were already there.

Sure enough, for the second time in just over a month, his patrol had wrought havoc and ruin at Tamet Airbase, which henceforth would become known as 'Paddy's Own'. There they'd discovered twenty-seven warplanes ranged around the airstrip, which constituted a brand new squadron just flown in from Europe. They'd threaded the lot with Lewes bombs, plus the fuel and ammo dumps for good measure. Set with half-hour fuses, typically the first had detonated early.

The initial blast came twenty-two minutes after the charge had been set. Mayne and his men were just completing their handiwork, and were caught in the act by the blinding flash of the explosions. A cry rang out from an Italian guard: 'Avanti! Avanti!' – 'step forwards', or 'show yourself'. Recalling his language lessons at Kabrit, Mayne had yelled back a one word response: 'Freund!' But either his Irish brogue wasn't quite Germanic enough, or he'd got his rendering of 'friend' a little off. Either way, the sentry called for reinforcements, and an 'encircling cordon' of enemy troops was thrown around Mayne and his men.

When stealing onto the airbase, Mayne had noted groups of sentries, set at thirty-yard intervals around the perimeter. Now, they converged onto his tiny force and opened fire. 'That was rather a mistake for them,' Mayne would later write to his sister Frances, 'as I don't like being fired at.' Leading from the front and hurling volleys of grenades, he moved with lightning speed to break out of the trap. At his side, Bob Bennett did likewise. Even as that series of grenade blasts tore apart the night, scattering the enemy, Mayne and his party made a dash for safety.

As at Sirte, the defences at Tamet had been stiffened, with a stout perimeter fence erected. Mayne led his men in a dash for the exit – the hole they had earlier cut through the wire – as wild bursts of gunfire broke out behind them, and further blasts from exploding warplanes ripped across the airstrip. All of Mayne's party made it back to the rendezvous unharmed, and with twenty-seven more enemy aircraft to their credit. That took the grand total for Mayne and his patrol to well over fifty, in under two months of operations. It was some achievement; a fine record with which to wish themselves a slightly belated happy Christmas.

Having exchanged news concerning their raids, there was a good deal of merciless ribbing of Stirling, who yet again had failed to strike at Sirte, or to bag even the one warplane. He took it in the spirit it was intended, remarking that he most certainly did need to pull his socks up, accepting that the 'competition is too hot'. With those sentiments – must do better next time – to the fore, the weary men of the Parashites and the Desert Taxi Company crawled into whatever cover they could find, to wait out the daylight hours. Come sundown, they would be heading back to Jalo.

That night, once they'd put a safe distance between themselves and the enemy, they set camp and had a late Christmas celebration. The LRDG had thought to pack 'plenty of beer and pudding' with which to do so. To add to the festive cheer, they'd managed to shoot a brace of gazelles – a small species of antelope – not exactly Christmas turkey, but fresh meat for the pot all the same. As they ate and drank their fill, Bob Bennett recalled a curious remark of Mayne's, even as they'd made their escape from Tamet airbase, and as the final explosions had torn apart the night.

He'd fixed Bennett with a look. 'What am I doing here messing about on such low pay?' he'd demanded, quietly. 'I could earn much more working for the Germans . . .'

Bennett didn't know quite what to say. Mayne had 'this twist about him', he would remark, which some certainly found unsettling. As Bennett would discover, that kind of comment was vintage Mayne.

Mayne's mind worked in curious ways. He was truly engineered to think the unthinkable. He had a leftfield way of seeing things, a reverse-logic way of looking at the world. It meant that nothing was beyond consideration. When writing to his nine-year-old niece

Margaret – Funnyface – from the Lions tour, he'd signed off by telling her, 'make that mother of yours help with the washing . . . Tell Corden not to hurt Douglas too much.' Most uncles might be expected to urge their nieces to *help* with chores at home, not vice versa. Plus, Douglas was Mayne's twenty-something brother, whereas Corden was Margaret's little brother, less than half Douglas's age.

Mayne's unconventional mindset made him unpredictable, and few understood that side of him – just as Bennett had been thrown by his 'working-for-the-Germans' remark. Of course, Mayne was absolutely right. What Rommel wouldn't have given – wouldn't have paid – to get his hands on a senior commander of these confounding, ghostly desert raiders; better still, to turn him and to learn all of the desert raiders' secrets. Giving voice to such a thought didn't mean that Mayne was entertaining it. It just meant that he could see things from all conceivable angles, including the most unexpected.

Back at Tamet Airbase – attacked and comprehensively gutted for a second time in as many months – a post-mortem was under way. Italian engineers studied the means and route of the phantom raider's strike. They discovered the LRDG's tyre tracks, but they stopped short a good mile from the airbase. From that they deduced that Mayne and his party had made their final approach on foot. They studied the wreckage of the warplanes, working out that the charges must have been lobbed onto the target aircraft, and lodged on the 'wing root, on which they were simply rested'. It was all very simple and basic, and utterly devastating.

Needless to say, means would need to be found to counter such audacious and daring raids. In order to do so, the Italian and German commanders needed to know more. They needed to discover just who the raiders were, where they came from, how many there were, the make of vehicles they were using, their routes of ingress, the kind of arms they carried and the type of explosives they were using. They needed to discover how on earth this mystery force navigated and weathered the open wastes of the desert – if that was indeed the way they came. And they needed the means to gather that intelligence, in order to develop ways to counter the threat.

As Rommel was starting to appreciate, while the main body of the British military had paid scant attention to the demands of fast-moving, flexible, mechanised warfare and the need for close liaison between a commander and his troops, there appeared to be one glaring anomaly. The big exception was 'the British reconnaissance units, whose training was first class'. Rommel didn't yet know their actual identity, but he held these mobile recce and raiding forces in high esteem.

A means would need to be found to defeat them.

Stirling, Mayne and their raiding party returned to Jalo oasis on New Year's Eve, but any celebrations they may have had in mind were to be cut short. The news there was unexpectedly grim. Jock Lewes's raid on Nofilia had gone disastrously wrong. They'd made it onto the airstrip and set bombs on two warplanes, but then a heavy enemy force had appeared and driven them off. Reunited with their LRDG patrol, the convoy of five trucks had headed for Marble Arch to collect Bill Fraser and his men. Only one had made it. Set upon from the air, four of the Chevys had been shot to shreds, and the sole remaining vehicle had only been made serviceable by scavenging parts from the wrecks of the others.

Far worse, Jock Lewes, the SAS's iconic co-founder, its training officer and explosives wizard, had fallen victim to that air attack. In his report on their tragic loss, Sergeant Almonds would write: 'Spotted by aircraft and subjected to a very intense strafing and bombed from 10 a.m. till 4 p.m. Lt. Lewes killed, four trucks destroyed and another damaged.' Being the next most senior SAS rank, Almonds had been forced to take over command, and it was largely due to his skill and determination that the rest of the patrol had managed to make it back to Jalo in their one surviving, battle-scarred vehicle. Almonds would be awarded the Military Medal (MM) for his actions on that mission.

Lewes's death would prove a huge blow to the fledgling SAS. Almonds would write of it in his diary, in moving terms: 'I thought of Jock, one of the bravest men I have ever met, an officer and a gentleman, lying out in the desert barely covered in sand. No one will ever stop by his grave or pay homage to a brave heart that has ceased to beat. Not even a stone marks the spot.' With the loss of Lewes, plus McGonigal and Bonington before him, Almonds and others wondered who was left who might take over the training role in the SAS. They'd need to be battle-hardened, and the only officer left with that kind of skillset was Mayne.

As if that were not enough, the one surviving vehicle of Lewes's patrol had failed to collect Bill Fraser and his men. It had reached the Marble Arch rendezvous, only to find there was no sign of them anywhere. There had been no further hint of them from any quarter: no enemy signals intercepts, nor even the slightest snippet of intelligence. In short, there was no trace of Fraser, the seasoned SAS commander, plus his redoubtable deputy, Bob Tait, along with the three other men of their patrol. They appeared to have been swallowed up by the desert, just as comprehensively as had Eoin McGonigal and his patrol.

With Lewes dead, plus Fraser, McGonigal and Bonington missing, the SAS had lost all of its officers, bar Stirling and Mayne. Its ranks below officer level were also woefully depleted. While they may have transformed Operation Squatter's dark failure into the stand-out successes scored at Tamet and elsewhere, they had paid a heavy price. From the original SAS (L-Detachment) complement of sixty, there were around sixteen remaining, all told.

Mayne lived by the age-old adage of Sun Tzu, the ancient

Chinese warrior-philosopher, and the author of the timeless treatise *The Art of War*: 'Treat your men as you would your own beloved sons. And they will follow you into the deepest valley.' As all were starting to appreciate, when the chips were down, 'Paddy would be in it too – there with the men he loved, where the going was toughest, and the danger greatest. Paddy did more than send others – he went himself, too.' He'd done everything he could to ensure that on his raids, all had come out alive.

But so many others had fallen, or were missing, and Mayne could not be there to safeguard all.

CHAPTER THIRTEEN

The Wake

As the new year of 1942 dawned, there were reasons for hope. The twenty-one-strong SAS – at least, before Fraser's patrol had gone missing – had accounted for well over a hundred enemy aircraft destroyed, across three airbases. That score had been confirmed absolutely by reconnaissance flights, so it could not be gainsaid. It was a truly exceptional achievement – a tally to rival that of the entire RAF in North Africa during a similar period. Stirling, as the unit's visionary founder, and Mayne, as its chief big hitter, were decorated accordingly, both being awarded the DSO. There were also medals for Reg Seekings, Bob Tait and a handful of other key figures in the raids.

Even as Stirling, Mayne, Fraser and Lewes's patrols had been away deep behind enemy lines, so the Japanese military had carried out its own clandestine mission, executed with the maximum of subterfuge and surprise. Apart from the differences in scale, the other chief contrast embodied in the December 1941 attack on the US naval base at Pearl Harbor, was that the Imperial Japanese Navy Air Service had struck at a nation with which it was not even at war.

Duplicitous in the extreme, the surprise strike had unfolded over the dawn skies of Hawaii, on a day that American President Roosevelt declared would 'live in infamy'. Over the course of that fateful morning, nineteen US warships were sunk or damaged, some 300 warplanes destroyed and there were over 3,400 American casualties. On the Japanese side, as few as sixty-five men had been killed or captured. The following day, America and Britain had declared war on Japan, and three days later Germany and Italy had declared war on the USA, which reciprocated.

America's entry into the war boded well for Britain and her allies, and while there was little obvious sign of it on the ground – the Afrika Korps was battling hard for every inch of ground – privately, Rommel himself was unsettled. The German general wasn't simply an astoundingly talented commander, he was also a gifted writer and would keep a detailed diary of the war years. He noted that in declaring war on America, Germany would face the entirety of America's industrial might, which would focus on churning out war materiel. 'It was many times greater than ours.'

While Rommel feared that America's entry into the war risked upsetting the fortunes of Nazi Germany, that only quickened his hunger for a rapid and decisive victory in North Africa. He believed it was within his grasp. While his arch-opponent, General Auchinleck, had made some gains of recent, the German commander was convinced they would prove transient. The Auk was one of the few British generals respected by Rommel, who praised his shrewd-ness, his quick thinking and his 'noteworthy courage'. Even so, the counter-strikes that he was planning would turn the tables, of that he felt certain. He was simply awaiting the moment to attack.

As with so many great military leaders, Rommel had his flaws. He was 'boyish', immature and prone to intolerance. He had little time for contrary views and a temper that was famously explosive. But he nursed no hatred, and not a little respect, for his adver-sary. The key operational tenets that he had adopted in North Africa – speed, flexibility, audacity, surprise – were a winning combination. His methods were designed to strike at both the physical and mental wellbeing of his adversaries. They had proved highly effective.

Rommel's grasp on the concept of blitzkrieg – lightning war: super-mobile operations combining fast-moving armour, motorised forces and air power – was masterful. So was his understanding of the need not only to punch deep beyond the enemy's frontline positions, but also deep into the enemy commanders' psyche. By understanding his opponent's psychology, Rommel was able to use that against them; he could conjure up the least expected moves in order to profoundly unsettle his adversaries.

By striking with speed and surprise, and by doing the unexpected, Rommel aimed to paralyse his enemy. For that to be possible, he needed that rare thing – to keep a cool head in the midst of the chaos and churn of battle, when all around were losing theirs. He needed to be able to remain focused and to calculate the pros and cons and the risks of each move, and often in the blink of an eye. He also needed a powerful creative imagination to envisage what the enemy least would expect and how best to achieve it. With his strong artistic temperament, Rommel often sketched out his ideas and battle plans in intricate detail.

It was no surprise that Rommel had earned the respect of the rank and file of the British military, who spoke of 'the Rommel Legend'. Equally, he was worshipped by those he commanded, and hated by staff officers – the 'layers of fossilised shit', as Stirling would refer to them. On so many levels, the renowned German general and the rag-tag band of desert raiders who struck deep behind his lines, had much in common. Increasingly, their fortunes would fatefully converge. It was perhaps inevitable that the SAS would come to Rommel's attention as their raids bit deep, for they were adopting his way of thinking, his philosophy of war, and developing it still further to use it against him.

But right then, in the earliest days of January 1942, they would have little chance of striking any blows whatsoever unless they engaged in a major refit, rearmament and, crucially, a recruitment drive. Hence their emergence from hiding in Jalo, to return to their base at Kabrit. Fearing that Fraser and his men had suffered the same fate as Jock Lewes and so many others, Stirling headed directly for Cairo, intent on launching a charm offensive. There, he had a meeting with General Auchinleck, who was genuinely impressed with all that the SAS had achieved, and gave the green light for the unit to recruit back to its original strength.

Others at MEHQ proved less sanguine or supportive. Even as Stirling was seeking the Auk's blessing, so there were those manoeuvring to clip the SAS's wings. One, a brigadier, had penned a memo on Christmas Day addressed to the Deputy Chief of the General Staff, the third most senior figure in the British military, complaining: 'Some unit commanders, such as STIRLING, want to be absolutely independent . . . Our experience in the past has proved this very unsatisfactory.' The reply he received concurred: 'I agree. It is of course quite wrong to have a number of little private armies . . .'

For now, Auchinleck's support shielded Stirling from the worst, lending the SAS a blanket of protection. But the naysayers were determined not to be silenced. These were the same British officers that Rommel criticised in his diary. Hidebound, convention-obsessed and lacking in originality of thought, they despised those who could think and act outside the norm – a norm that was governed solely by what had gone before. They burdened the otherwise excellent British military with cumbersome, outmoded ideas, so what was a fearsome fighting force was effectively ham-strung. They constrained it with the 'conservatism of the British officer', as Rommel put it. On that level Rommel and Stirling – and indeed Mayne – would have seen very much eye to eye.

During his meeting with Auchinleck, Stirling had outlined what he next had in mind. He wished to strike especially deep and hard, not to mention unexpectedly. Rommel had started to utilise a new port, at Buerat, which lay well beyond Sirte and Tamet, the location of the SAS's most distant raids. To Stirling's mind, if they could successfully destroy so many enemy warplanes, why not the same with Rommel's ships? He planned to slip into Buerat harbour and sink Rommel's supply vessels, especially his tankers, at anchor. Deprived of fuel, the German general's Panzers and warplanes would be immobilised, so striking at the very heart of what blitzkrieg entailed.

Upon hearing of Stirling's plan, Auchinleck could hardly conceal his surprise. After the signal successes scored against the enemy's airbases, it might have made sense to attempt more of the same. But Stirling's unconventional mindset and its grand flights of fancy were in many ways his greatest assets, ones that the canny and enterprising Auchinleck did his best to nurture. Even so, breaking into a closely guarded harbour far behind the lines to sink a fleet of enemy ships did have a distinctly suicidal ring to it.

When might he be prepared to launch such an attack, the Auk queried? By the middle of January, Stirling replied, so in around two week's time. By the piercing look in Auchinleck's eye, it was clear that he knew the SAS commander must have been planning this raid long before seeking any kind of a blessing, in order to be ready so swiftly. But that was what you got with Stirling and his ilk. It was like riding the dragon – unpredictable, violent and decidedly dangerous, but likewise guaranteed to confound and unsettle the enemy.

Auchinleck gave his quiet assent, before walking Stirling to the door of his office. He paused, and took the tall SAS commander by the elbow. 'By the way, Stirling, from now on you have the rank of major.' Just like that, on the spot, Stirling had been promoted. And Mayne, his only other surviving officer, was to be appointed a captain, the Auk decreed.

So began a frenetic whirl of activity in Cairo, as Stirling sought recruits, kit, supplies and weaponry – for the attack on Buerat would require a very different set of equipment and skillsets from their standard desert-raiding missions. First and foremost, Stirling needed boats and those skilled in their silent operation, moving at night into the heart of an enemy fortress to sow death and devastation.

Returning to the water – the commandos had been chiefly a sea-borne raiding force – was no spur-of-the-moment flight of fancy. A month earlier, Stirling had penned a recruitment plan entitled 'L-Detachment, S.A.S. Brigade. Aims and Men'. In it he'd outlined how the SAS would 'not function as an ordinary parachute battalion . . . Parachuting will be only one of the methods this unit will employ . . . Very often a truck or a boat, or the human foot will be a better method . . .' So impressed was Stirling by the Desert Taxi Company, he believed the LRDG could carry them practically anywhere. With the Buerat raid, the key difference was that they would also have a fleet of boats in tow. Luckily, the kind he had in mind were eminently portable, for they would need to weather several hundred miles of punishing desert terrain.

As Stirling set about finding all that he might need in Cairo, Mayne was holding the fort in Kabrit. There had been several serious drinking sessions in the Rest Camp bar, complete with its purloined piano, for of course there were absent friends and the fallen to mourn, and this was the first real chance any of them had had to do so. But as they awaited the influx of new recruits, Mayne also reverted to his role of PT and discipline officer. No amount of carousing or wakes for the dead would excuse lateness or sloppiness early the following morning, when there were desert runs, bush rugby or other training tasks to undertake.

With Lewes, Fraser, Bonington and McGonigal gone, it all fell to Mayne now. And no one was immune from his laser-eyed scrutiny. One freezing night Mayne's stalwart raider, Bob Bennett, was standing sentry with two of his mates. It seemed the height of insanity to be guarding a camp set so far from the frontlines, which was, of course, exactly the kind of mindset that had made the SAS's own raids so successful, for the enemy tended to think the same way. Never mind the irony of the moment, the three friends let that idea get the better of them, deciding to turn in for the night, and banking on the officers being dead to the world.

All of a sudden, a deafening voice tore them out of their slumber: 'Guard! Turn out!'

Leaping from their bunks, they flailed about for their clothes and weapons in the darkness, but nothing was where it should be. Again, the voice bellowed through the tent's thin canvas sides.

'Hurry up, you lazy louts! Get a move on!' There was no mistaking those distinctive tones.

Cringing with embarrassment, Bennett and his fellows slunk out of their tent in their underclothes, as the night chill cut deep. By the dull glint of the moon they spied their clothes and weapons lying in a heap, presumably where Mayne had dumped them, after he had moved through their tent as silently as a wraith. For thirty minutes he beasted Bennett and his two friends, forcing them to do punishing PT drills, but in a way they were happy in their exertion. At least it kept them warm, and with Mayne they knew this was as far as it would go. There would be no official charge sheets, and no indelible stain on their records.

Rough-and-ready justice delivered on the spot was Mayne's way. On another night, he discovered a Kabrit guard drunk on duty, and pretty close to comatose. Having doused the offender in a bucket of icy water, Mayne cracked him on the jaw just as soon as he came round, and left him to complete the rest of his watch, or else. But of course, for many the drinking was a way to drown out the sorrows. The shock of recent losses and of the missing cast a long shadow. Mayne seemed especially restless, driven and edgy, and especially when pacing Stirling's Rest Camp with no immediate means to hit back at the authors of so many slights and hurts – the enemy.

As LRDG commander David Lloyd Owen had noted of Mayne,

Stirling and some of the others, they were blessed with minds that could never 'lie idle, for they lived on their nerves and their reserves of energy'. Their successes spurred them to 'further endeavours and failure merely reinforced their determination'. Lloyd Owen had ended up wondering if their thoughts ever strayed 'beyond the war', for they were so focused on their intention that 'the enemy must be harried everywhere'.

Of course, the loss of so many had sharpened the appetite to do just that – to harry the enemy at every turn. But first, with Eoin McGonigal in particular, Mayne felt he had to grasp the nettle and send news home. Seated at his desk in his tent, he penned the letters he had long been dreading. He struggled to find the right words to tell a worried mother what had happened to her son in distant, war-torn lands, when even Mayne himself did not know. 'I still believe that the odds are he is a prisoner,' he wrote. 'I wish I knew.'

Brooding over the dark mystery of the vanishing of an entire SAS patrol, one commanded by his closest friend, he wrote to his sister Barbara: 'I haven't heard anything yet of McGonigal. But his people may have, apparently they are advised by the Red Cross first.' Under international protocols, which held good even in times of war, the Red Cross were supposed to be given access to POWs on both sides of a conflict, in part so they could inform their families of their status. It was just possible that McGonigal's parents would have heard something.

In the War Office's casualty reports, McGonigal and his men had simply been listed as 'missing'. Showing how heavily this played on Mayne's mind, he would write to Margaret McGonigal, Eoin's mother, the tone reflecting how close he felt to their family as a whole. His sentiments read like a confession; an unburdening: 'I need not tell you how much I miss Eoin, it would have been impossible to have lived with a person of his character for nearly two years without getting to like and admire him tremendously.

Also, although I am several years older than Eoin I depended on him greatly when I had any serious decisions to make.'

The loss of Eoin wasn't simply a private blow for Mayne, he stressed. Its ramifications were being felt far more widely. 'More important now than the personal loss which I feel, it is the loss which the Unit had suffered. Eoin worked very hard here and was entirely responsible for all the Weapons Training and much of the night training, and we would not have been nearly as successful as we have had it not been for him. The men too liked and admired him tremendously . . .'

The not-knowing was eating away at Mayne. In a letter to his sister Frances, he confessed how he was 'getting very tired of this country, especially since Eoin landed a loser, it was alright when there was someone you could talk to about home . . .' Adding to all the frustration was the mystery surrounding the fate of Bill Fraser and his patrol – more outstanding warriors with whom Mayne's comradeship stretched back to the earliest days of No. 11 Commando. It was only in his letters to Funnyface – his niece Margaret – that he seemed to find a lighter tone, allowing his left-field mindset to shine through.

A nasty *khamsin* – sandstorm – had descended upon Kabrit. 'We had fried sand for breakfast, grilled sand for lunch and cooked sand for dinner,' he wrote to her. 'I slept with one hand holding onto the tent pole last night . . . I must go for my grilled sand. I see my camel is waiting to take me over. Thank your ma for her letters. Your writing is much better than hers, spelling much the same – both atrocious. Love Blair.'

His niece wrote back, telling her uncle all about how a Miss McDermott had a new kitten, which was apparently fond of water. Mayne replied: 'Dear Funnyface, You are an awfully stupid person thinking that kitten of Miss McDermott is an ordinary cat – no cats like water. It must be a catfish, what you want to do is get a large bowl, fill it up to the top with water and put the catfish in . . .

166

the catfish is probably a very good swimmer. Get Douggie to help you next time he is on leave.' Douggie was his younger brother, of course.

By the second week of January 1942 Stirling was back at Kabrit. Among the clutch of new recruits, he had persuaded 11 Commando veteran and standout Litani River warrior, Captain George Duncan, to join him. Duncan, of course, had formed part of Major Keyes' force, those who had carried out their near-suicidal frontal assault on the Litani River positions. Very fortunate to have survived unscathed – in body, if not in mind – Duncan's poems had captured the hell of the moment:

> Men falling, falling –
> Thump-roll-lie-still,
> Hit in the head –
> Shrill screaming . . .

Strictly speaking, Duncan – along with fellow No. 11 Commando veteran, Corporal Edward Barr – were 'on loan' to the SAS, for their parent unit was the Special Boat Section (SBS), a spin-off outfit that aimed to do what the SAS did in the desert, only operating on water.

Even as No. 11 Commando had imploded, Duncan had volunteered for the SBS. His period of 'loan' to the Parashites would turn out to be a long one, and in verse he would capture the essence of the SAS's trans-Saharan exploits, just as he had the Litani River landings. With their shared history of unit and combat, Duncan would also develop a close affection for Mayne, 'an air ace, in the sense that he destroyed more aircraft, albeit on the ground, than any Allied airman . . . a legendary figure, famous for his daring undercover raids.' While Duncan would refuse to talk to his family about any of his own experiences post-war, about Mayne he would wax lyrical, making sure to tell his children all that he knew.

Duncan and Barr brought with them the chief tools of their trade – vital, for what Stirling had in mind at Buerat. This consisted chiefly of a stash of limpet mines – specialist explosive charges that had been developed in the opening months of the war by a top-secret boffin unit, known as Military Intelligence (Research) (MI-R). Consisting of a limpet-shaped magnetic charge approximately the size of a large saucepan, each was packed with some 2 kilograms of explosives. Using a five-foot-long fixing pole, the charge could be clamped to a ship's hull well below the waterline, so that when the timer fuse detonated, it blasted a hole guaranteeing a devastating inrush of water.

To reach their Buerat targets, Duncan and Barr also brought their 'folbots', foldable frame-and-fabric canoes codenamed 'Cockles', which would also need to weather the long desert journey. Out on the Bitter Lakes the new arrivals got busy, teaching their SAS brethren the ropes for this new form of warcraft – paddling silently and unseen at night into the heart of an enemy war fleet, to attach their 'depth charges' to the choicest targets, before slipping away and vanishing into the darkness.

Along with the fresh recruits and the new kit, Stirling also brought news for Mayne. It would prove most unexpected, and it would trigger the first, and most significant, falling out between the two senior SAS commanders. Stirling had decided that Mayne, as the only combat-experienced officer remaining, was to formally take over as the unit's Training Officer. Of course, he'd been performing that role during Stirling's absence, recognising that no one else could easily fill the gulf left by the loss of Lewes, McGonigal and Fraser. But Stirling's decision would require Mayne to remain at Kabrit, even as the old faithfuls set forth on the coming raids.

Stirling was taking with him a sixteen-man patrol, which boasted many of Mayne's stalwarts – Bob Bennett, Reg Seekings,

Pat Riley and Honest Dave Kershaw among them. Unsurprisingly, it rankled. Of course, Stirling could have opted to stay and take on the training role himself. While he didn't have a great deal of battle experience, his recent drive-by shoot-'em-up with the LRDG meant he'd fired shots, and set bombs, in anger. But there was a part of Stirling that worried that Mayne – the natural-born warrior and the outstanding commander of men – was starting to overshadow his own position. While Stirling was the unit's official commanding officer, he feared that Mayne was 'emerging as the natural leader'. He also worried that he was 'growing apart from the men he commanded', as they fell under Mayne's spell.

More to the point, Stirling had yet to bag a single enemy warplane, whereas Mayne already boasted several score. The competition between them was undeniably fierce, and by flying solo – without Mayne – Stirling hoped to even up the score a little. He might even eclipse Mayne's tally, for sinking warships had to top blowing-up enemy aircraft. Stirling's decision would deprive Mayne of what he hungered for most – the red heat of battle.

As recent weeks had proved, Mayne was a raider without compare, especially when it came to hitting his targets and getting his men out alive.

No one else came close.

CHAPTER FOURTEEN

Back from The Dead

If there was a desert mirage to eclipse all others, this had to be it – the vision of a British Army truck pulling up at Stirling's Rest Camp, to allow the distinctive figure of Lieutenant Bill Fraser, plus Sergeant Bob Tait and three others to clamber down . . . Surely, this could not be for real? The five men had been missing for the best part of a month. As with the others listed as 'missing in action', all had presumed that Fraser and his party were gone for good. Irredeemably vanished.

Stirling's raiding party had departed Kabrit on 11 January 1942, heading first for Jalo and onwards from there, courtesy of the LRDG, towards distant Buerat. They were long gone by the time the ghosts of 'OPERATION NUMBER FIVE (B)' melted out of the desert heat-haze. If this was no mirage, then somehow, unbelievably, Fraser and his party had returned from the burning maw of the Sahara and the predations of the enemy, escaping from deep behind hostile lines. In truth, their escape story would turn out to be far more fantastic than any kind of a Saharan mirage could ever hope to be.

Having executed what constituted one of the most epic and death-defying escape and evasions of the war, their return to Kabrit had been further delayed by the need to impart some choice intelligence to MEHQ. As Fraser would report, phlegm and under-statement to the fore: 'arriving AGEDABIA just as big push was going in . . . were able to give very valuable information. Returned to KABRIT . . .' In other words, prior to executing a shattering and nerve-shredding getaway from deep inside enemy territory, Fraser and party had hoovered up some crucial intelligence, which they'd passed on to Eighth Army high command, before making a beeline for Stirling's Rest Camp.

It was 30 December 1941 when Fraser and his men had made it to their original objective, the airbase at Marble Arch, only to discover it devoid of targets. Not a warplane was in sight, and it didn't appear to be a very active base in any case. Chalking it down to experience, they'd headed for their rendezvous with the LRDG. But ominously, they'd spied a squadron of enemy warplanes attacking a distant target, plus thick columns of oily black smoke. That was the moment when their desert taxi service had got strafed and bombed, and Jock Lewes was killed. Oblivious to all of that, they'd waited for several days at the rendezvous, but no vehicles had come. With their water and food all-but exhausted, they were forced to set out for friendly lines on foot.

Moving through the desert, parallel to but a little inland from the main coastal highway, they'd faced a 200-mile trek to the nearest friendly positions – that was if the Eighth Army was still located where they'd last known it to be. Over the ensuing days they'd been trapped within a living nightmare of dehydration and hunger. During their hellish 'death march east', and dying of thirst, they'd finally made it to the shores of the Great Salt Lakes, a series of brackish waterholes which pockmark the otherwise arid terrain, being throwbacks to ancient times when this land flowed with water and was fertile. Though knowing the lakes to be heavily saline and poisonous, they were driven mad by thirst, and so they'd fallen to their knees and tried to drink, with horrendous effects.

Guts twisting, they'd vomited into the hot sands. Still, Fraser had tried to salvage something from having made it to those beguiling, benighted shores. Taking shelter in some nearby caves, he'd kindled a fire and bodged together a Heath Robinson-esque apparatus in an effort to distil the water of the Great Salt Lakes, so as to make it potable. The results proved nauseating and only barely drinkable. Two others on his patrol, Sergeant Bob Tait and Corporal John 'Jack' Byrne, volunteered to head for the nearest section of road, aiming to hijack a truck. They were utterly desperate and had little left to lose.

As with Fraser and Tait, Byrne was a battle-hardened soldier and an SAS original. He'd served on Jock Lewes's patrol for Operation Squatter, after which he'd become one of Bill Fraser's regulars. A fellow veteran of the 1st Battalion the Gordon Highlanders, Byrne had only escaped from the June 1940 hell of Saint-Valery-en-Caux due to his injuries. As with Fraser, Byrne had fought with suicidal ferocity in defence of the evacuation beaches, being injured first by shrapnel, and then again during savage hand-to-hand combat with a German soldier. Wounded in the right hip by a bayonet thrust, he'd been left for dead. Incredibly, he was discovered in a state of semi-consciousness by some French villagers. Realising the injured British soldier was still alive, they'd rushed him to the beachhead. From there he was whisked onto a waiting ship, even as his fellow Gordon Highlanders were urged: 'Every hour you are able to delay the enemy will help ensure the safety of the army.'

Back in Britain, Byrne had volunteered for No. 11 Commando and fought alongside the Litani River heroes, before volunteering for the SAS. Tait and Byrne had opted to take one other member of the patrol with them, as back-up – although as a pair they were fearsome enough to tackle most adversaries. Sure enough, they'd done exactly as they had intended, holding up a truck at gunpoint, after which they'd returned with their prize – a pair of German prisoners lugging a heavy jerrycan of fresh water, filched from their vehicle. But when they'd tried to turn the two prisoners loose, they'd proved so terrified of the open desert that they'd refused to leave.

Having shared around that life-giving water, Fraser made the decision that they should press on. Once they'd persuaded their prisoners that by following a certain star in the night sky they were sure to find the coast road and hence their truck, the five fugitives set off east once more. They'd gone on to weather a full-on sandstorm, to loot an army lorry crammed with terrified Italian cooks, to hijack two more vehicles, one of which they'd driven into a salt marsh in an effort to escape, survived stumbling into a mass grave full of the Eighth Army's dead, before slipping through the German lines under fire, and finally making contact with a British armoured-car patrol of the King's Dragoon Guards.

Theirs was one of the outstanding survival epics of the war in North Africa. Fraser, the SAS's second biggest hitter after Mayne, would be awarded a Military Cross for his role in it, the citation for which praised his unstinting spirit and leadership, which kept his men going and bolstered their morale. But the bitter memories of that epic sojourn would haunt the escapees for months to come. At times they'd resorted to 'eating lizards, berries and snails', so desperately famished had they been. For weeks after that death-defying getaway, neither Fraser, nor any among his patrol could bear the smell of cooking. If they caught the scent of food, they simply had to eat, gorging themselves.

The return of Fraser and his men was absolutely a highpoint; truly, they were back from the dead. It held out more than a glimmer of hope for the others – maybe even for McGonigal and his patrol. But even so, Mayne nursed a 'smouldering resentment' at being left behind in Kabrit. As he'd argued to Stirling at the time, surely there were experienced sergeants and corporals who were more than capable of taking on the training role. While Mayne had promised to do his best, he'd made it clear that he hadn't joined the SAS to languish in Kabrit. Much more of this and Stirling would very likely find him gone. He'd RTU himself and seek another means to fight.

When Stirling had first recruited Mayne for the SAS, the latter had demanded: 'What are the prospects of fighting?' Clearly, there were none, if he was to be locked away at Kabrit and kept busy training. During the weeks that Stirling and his sixteen-strong raiding force were away, the resentment simmered. In the dying days of January 1942, and in an effort to get his mind off things, Mayne reconnected with Sister Jane Kenny, the Irish nurse that he'd first encountered during his malaria-ridden sojourn at the Alexandria hospital in the summer of 1941.

News was breaking about Mayne winning the DSO, which came on the back of his international acclaim as a sportsman. It made headlines as far away as South Africa: 'It takes a good man to win the D.S.O. as a junior officer, and that is exactly what Blair Mayne is [At the time the DSO was normally reserved for the ranks of major and above] . . . it takes outstanding courage and devotion to duty to earn it. Blair Mayne has all the characteristics of a fearless soldier.' The article went on to praise his prowess on the rugby field, plus his sheer stamina and ability to take knocks. It also made a telling comparison to another famous sporting figure turned wartime hero, Bobby Kershaw, who'd 'swooped down under heavy fire at Diredawa, to save his friend, Captain Frost. It was thought he would get the V.C. but he received the D.S.O.'

Robert 'Bobby' Kershaw was a fighter pilot flying Hurricanes with the South African Air Force (SAAF). On a sortie over Italian airfields in East Africa, his Squadron Leader, John Frost, had been hit and forced to make an emergency landing on an enemy airfield. Seeing him go down, Kershaw had taken his Hurricane in to land, after which he'd discarded his parachute to enable Frost to join him in the cramped cockpit, the squadron leader perched on his lap. Like that, they had somehow managed to take to the skies again and return to their base. Unsurprisingly, Kershaw's rescue mission proved a sensation, a postage stamp being minted displaying his likeness, that summer of 1942.

With his self-effacing nature, Mayne wasn't in it for the glory or the medals. Typifying this, he'd written to his sister Frances about his promotion, announcing, 'I am becoming a captain. I am rather sorry, as I was fond of my two pips.' But the glamour and acclaim surrounding his DSO wasn't lost on Jane Kenny. The Irish nursing sister made a point of telling Mayne 'how well he looked', making sure that she 'congratulated him on winning the DSO'. With the two opposing armies facing off against each other, and dead-locked, she'd found her hospital posting 'very slack' after having had a 'heavy time just before Xmas'. Complaining of how there was 'little else to do in this godforsaken country', and decrying the so-called 'glamours of Egypt' as being illusory, Mayne's visits were most welcome.

While Mayne was known to be shy in the ways of love, he was generally relaxed in female company. He'd been brought up in a large, rumbustious family with three big sisters to look out for him, and his letters alone reveal their closeness. When Jane Kenny had nursed him back to health, six months earlier, he'd wooed her with the loan of a copy of his Percy French book. It had worked wonders, Jane writing of how 'any little bit of Ireland out here is welcome.' Now, she confessed that she hadn't had time to finish reading it before Mayne had gone away – on his posting to the SAS, of course. Mayne reassured her he had a spare copy, so she could 'borrow it again' and for as long as she had need.

By the time of Stirling's return to Kabrit, the animosity between the SAS commanding officer and his deputy broke out into open warfare. Some versions of this falling out depict a 'disgruntled' Mayne stewing in his tent, neglecting his duties, drinking heavily and basically having 'thrown in his hand'. *Thrown in his hand.*

To put it mildly, this seems unlikely. If nothing else, Mayne's burning hunger to fight and his sheer professionalism – drilled into him since the earliest days at No. 11 Commando – would militate against it. So too would contemporaneous accounts.

Mayne might well have enjoyed a skinful at the Kabrit bar of an evening, but so did almost everyone based at Stirling's Rest Camp. More to the point, and as Bob Bennett remarked, the sessions would end punctually when the SAS captain checked his watch and announced: 'Call me sir. It is now Reveille.' In other words, once the night's carousing was over there was work to be done, and Mayne expected all to revert to the rigorous standards that had been his touchstone since his earliest No. 11 Commando days. His mantra was train hard, party hard, fight hard. Always, and arguably since his earliest triumphs on the field of sports.

Going out partying all night, and breaking off to bag a springbok in his black tie and tails – fresh meat for the team – hadn't altered one jot Mayne's dedication and rigour on that 1938 Lions tour. The team had faced a victorious South African side fresh from defeating the All Blacks in New Zealand. The Lions had played twenty-four matches, and Mayne had featured in all bar four. While the bruising physicality combined with the hard South African ground had disabled many of his fellow players, Mayne alone of the forwards had remained injury-free. Likewise, the sheer aggressiveness of play had fazed many. Not Mayne. The more fearsome the competition, the more he had risen to the challenge. After the Lions tour, Mayne had run out with an Ireland side at Twickenham, in February 1939, beating England in front of a capacity crowd, and via a display of power and grit by the forwards in which Mayne was singled out for praise.

Stirling's early February return from Buerat ended with him and Mayne being at each other's throats. Perhaps not physically, but verbally, as a bruising shouting match ensued in Mayne's tent. Yet curiously, in the bitter clash and the frank airing of views – both could be fiercely outspoken when the need arose – the two SAS commanders reached a new understanding, one that would see them through to the end of the war as comrades in arms. Both were tortured by their recent losses – Stirling, chiefly that of Jock Lewes, Mayne, by that of Eoin McGonigal. Stirling and Lewes went way back, for both had served in No. 8 (Guards) Commando, also known as 'The House Of Lords', due to the number of titled aristocrats within its ranks. Stirling had been devastated by Lewes's death and especially the fact that his body had been left in a shallow grave in the open desert.

More to the point, Stirling had felt utterly lost once Lewes was gone, for who would train and inspire the fresh recruits? The only option had seemed to be Mayne – the one other officer with a similar standing and reputation among the rank and file. But he recognised now that to try to saddle such a superlative warrior and leader of men with rear-echelon duties was wrong. It had been a dreadful mistake, he confessed, being a singular waste of Mayne's talents. For his part, Mayne recognised that Stirling had been struggling to hold together a battle-torn, casualty-worn unit, in extremis. After losing Lewes and, it had seemed, Fraser, the SAS had been stretched wafer thin. Once again, it had been on life-support. Needs must.

Mayne and Stirling opened a bottle of whisky to drown their troubles, enjoying a heart-to-heart. For the first time Stirling realised what a deeply rooted friendship Mayne and McGonigal had enjoyed, and what the long months and the lack of closure must have meant for Mayne, immured as he was in his pain. Stirling was convinced that the reports they'd received in December of a mystery party of parachutists attacking Gazala airbase had to refer to McGonigal and his patrol. He shared with Mayne a conviction that of all the Operation Squatter parties, it was only the young

Irishman's that had hit home, which made their mysterious disappearance all the more disquieting.

Stirling and Mayne also bonded over a further shared source of angst. Both were frustrated artists. Mayne nurtured the desire to be a writer, after the likes of the Irish novelist and poet James Joyce. It was the chief thing that he wanted from life, and their shared love or writing had been one of Mayne's deepest bonds with McGonigal. As for Stirling, he hungered to be an artist. Neither would ever fulfil his dream. Stirling's was mostly dead and buried, entombed within the 'bitter disappointment' of Paris, where he'd spent months complete with black beret and bohemian residence on the trendy Rive Gauche – Left Bank – of the Seine, producing artworks that had left his tutor singularly unimpressed. As for Mayne, his desire to be a writer was dying a slow but steady death, amid the blood and the horror and the dark losses of the war. It killed creativity, as it was killing off his closest friends.

Over whisky, Stirling shared with Mayne news of the fortunes of 'OPERATION NUMBER SIX', his raid on Buerat. That helped smooth things over still further. Though all had very much *not* gone to plan, on many levels the mission had achieved its objectives admirably. In its execution Stirling had exhibited what was very possibly his strongest trait as a commander – his ability to think on his feet and to act on the fly, changing the plan of attack as the circumstances demanded. The Buerat raid was a case of snatching victory from what were seemingly the jaws of defeat.

At first, all had gone swimmingly, as the LRDG had whisked the SAS patrol west through the stunning desert landscape. There was something of an ocean-like majesty to their progress, as Captain Duncan's poem, *The Great Sand Sea*, illustrates so evocatively, especially with the SBS captain being more accustomed to seaborne operations.

The western sky was bright with red, green and gold,
And as the sun sank down, each wave-like fold
Filled with blue shadows, and the crests were won
By the invading shafts of the setting sun.
Over these crests eternal silence lies;
And in the troughs beneath the burning skies
Silence that seems to move, to rise and fall
Wave upon wave of soundlessness, no call
Of bird, nor hum of insect flight,
To cross the blue path of approaching night.

But eventually, the convoy of vehicles emerged from the Great Sand Sea – an area as large as Ireland containing nothing but towering dunes   edging into tougher, more jolting and exposed terrain. It was there that they had been spotted and strafed by enemy warplanes. Worse still, when the vehicle carrying the folbot had hit a vast, crater-like pothole, the fragile craft had been 'smashed beyond repair'. In one fell swoop their means of getting into Buerat harbour and in among the target ships was no more.

Regardless, they had pressed on, only to be hit with another crushing blow. They'd reached their objective apparently unde-tected, only for a recce of the harbour to reveal 'the total absence of any tanker ships'. At this juncture, a lesser man than Stirling might have called the whole thing off. Undaunted, he refined the plan of attack. Duncan and Barr, deprived of their canoe, would go in on foot to attack the radio mast that stood as a sentinel on the high ground overlooking the harbour. Stirling meanwhile would lead the remainder into Buerat, to see what targets of opportunity they might discover.

Slipping in among the darkened warehouses that lined the har-bourside, Stirling split his force into groups – one led by himself, another by Sergeant Pat Riley. They were to sow the place with bombs, hitting whatever they encountered. Working stealthily, they'd targeted buildings stuffed full of food dumps, crates of machinery and workshops. At one point, two of Stirling's patrols almost shot each other up, so stealthily were they operating. When all the obvious targets seemed to have been covered, Stirling ordered a withdrawal, but even as they stole away into the darkness, Reg Seekings drew his attention to an intriguing sight. Not so far away there was what appeared to be a vehicle park, and they could just make out the blocky silhouettes of trucks.

Moving closer, they'd realised these were fuel tankers. Six columns of three trucks each, and every vehicle full to the brim with some 4,000 gallons of fuel, and just waiting for the order to head to the frontline. Stirling determined they would never get there. Working swiftly, the entire lot were garlanded with Lewes bombs, plus a second convoy of a dozen general supply trucks. As a final parting gesture, Riley managed to stuff his one remaining charge up the barrel of an anti-aircraft gun, even as the crew were fast asleep beside it.

Captain Duncan and his fellow SBS man, Corporal Barr, had also struck home, getting their charges rigged around the radio mast. From their vantage point they had a ringside seat for Stirling's light show. As the first Lewes bombs had gone up, the blasts in the wharf-side warehouses were rapidly eclipsed by what had followed – the fuel trucks detonating; 'all exploded in spectacular style, followed shortly by the destroying of the radio mast . . .' That was left a tangled ruin of twisted cables and shattered steel.

During their withdrawal from a burning Buerat, the LRDG convoy had been ambushed by ground forces, but had blasted its way through, Stirling bringing every man on his patrol out alive. 'Eighteen petrol bowsers, four food dumps and wireless masts destroyed . . .' Stirling would report of the mission; 'ran into ambush on way back but no casualties.' There would be a slew of decorations for the Buerat raid, including an MM for Archie

Gibson, the LRDG driver whose lightning reflexes were credited with getting the convoy out unscathed, plus a Distinguished Conduct Medal (DCM) for John 'Johnny' Cooper, like Stirling a No. 8 Commando veteran, whose work with the Chevy's Vickers-K machinegun had helped blast them through.

Even so, the whirlwind of the last few months had driven Stirling to the limit, and his health was suffering. Unlike Mayne, he wasn't naturally made for the harsh rigours of operating deep behind the lines, or for the hardships of the desert. Pushing himself relentlessly, he had taken to wearing dark glasses, for he was suffering from solar conjunctivitis, caused by a combination of dust blowing into the eyes and the harsh glare of the desert sun. His body was also beset with desert sores. Weeks spent in the burning heat and sand without washing, and with precious little to drink, tended to do that to a man. The difference with Stirling was that the sores dogged him, refusing to heal.

In a sense, it made Stirling's stubborn, warrior spirit all the more admirable, for this kind of soldiering did not come easily to him. Neither did an easy camaraderie with the men under his command. Likewise, Stirling found Mayne's contradictory, multifaceted nature hard to fathom. On the one hand, Mayne had an almost spiritual love for and devotion to those he led into war, combined with a striking compassion and gentleness in everyday life. As Alec Borrie, one of Mayne's future raiders, would remark of the SAS commander: 'If you were having a rough time, he'd make sure to check how you were getting on, to have a few quiet words . . . He'd make sure you were alright.' On the other hand, Mayne had a capacity to flip to extreme violence in the blink of an eyelid, which was the one thing that made him so dangerous, and so capable, in war. Stirling was 'haunted' by the enigma of Mayne: his instinctive, intuitive feel for battle, coupled with an innate care for those he led into the teeth of death.

In Mayne's place as Training Officer, Stirling appointed the

Irish-American, Pat Riley, the only one who could come close to holding his own against Mayne in the boxing ring. To seal his appointment, Riley was promoted to Sergeant Major, and Reg Seekings, Bob Bennett and Johnny Cooper were all promoted to Sergeant. Recruited by Stirling personally, Cooper was the youngest of the SAS originals, a man who'd lied about his age to first sign up. Just nineteen years old, he still looked like something of a boy scout, but his fresh-faced, boyish looks belied a resolute inner toughness.

Cooper, who was slight of frame, with delicate features, neither smoked nor drank. Despite being a teetotaller, due to his promotion he was obliged to be inducted into the sergeant's mess at Kabrit. Pat Riley oversaw things.

'Well, young Cooper, I know you don't drink alcohol, so you'd better have a non-alcoholic drink,' Riley suggested.

'Yes, Sergeant Major,' Cooper agreed, a little overawed by the whole occasion.

'We have a drink here which is definitely non-alcoholic – it's called cherry brandy,' Riley announced, as he ensured Cooper's pint tankard was filled to the top.

Cooper was obliged to neck the entire lot, never taking his lips from the rim. He just managed to get the thick, sickly red liquid down, before bolting from the mess tent and throwing up. For the next forty-eight hours he'd nursed the mother of all hangovers, vowing never to touch a drop of the stuff again. Cooper had served in Jock Lewes's stick on Operation Squatter, but with Lewes dead and buried the young sergeant was mostly to operate alongside Stirling, as he had on the Buerat raid.

Upon Stirling's return to Jalo oasis, en route back from Buerat, there had been shocking news. General Rommel had launched a masterful series of attacks, and the Eighth Army was even then being driven back three hundred miles or more. Jalo itself was about to fall, and the LRDG were preparing to flee, blowing up their supply dumps and evacuating the SAS with them. It was such an unexpected reversal of the Allies' fortunes. Earlier that month General Auchinleck had cabled Churchill, stating: 'Evidence as to enemy weakness and disorganisation is growing daily.' Typically, Rommel's counter-punch had come when the British commander had least expected it, blindsiding him.

Worse still, January 1942 marked an absolute low point for the Allies. As Rommel wrote, on the eve of his offensive, the Japanese were being everywhere victorious. Suffering defeat in East Asia, the British would be even keener for victories in North Africa, 'but they're going to be very disappointed ... I'm full of plans that I daren't say anything about around here. They'd think me crazy. But I'm not; I simply see a bit further than they do.' By 'they' Rommel meant his comrade-commanders, the Italian generals alongside whom he operated. A few days later he wrote to his wife, Lu (Lucie), proclaiming: 'Four days of complete success lie behind us. Our blows struck home. And there's still one to come. Then we'll go all modest again and lie in wait ...'

Reeling from a series of surprise attacks and outflanking thrusts, the Eighth Army had managed to stabilise its lines, but no one was kidding themselves that things were not dire. In advancing little short of four hundred miles, Rommel's forces had overrun a string of British positions. In doing so, and as the German general noted in his diary, they'd seized 'vast quantities of vehicles, arms and material' with which to equip and motorise their own units.

As news of Rommel's victories spread throughout Kabrit, it proved deeply unsettling. No matter how many warplanes or fuel and ammo dumps the SAS were able to destroy, the march of the Afrika Korps just seemed unstoppable. Somehow, it made all the bitter and bloody sacrifices appear in vain. Rommel's victories had truly upped the ante, but equally his lightning advance meant that he had greatly elongated and exposed his supply lines. Maybe this was the opportunity. As Stirling and

Mayne pondered the dark turn of events, they realised that this was Rommel's Achilles heel.

There was only one suitable response. They would need to strike further, harder and with even greater audacity than ever before.

Unsurprisingly, first into action would be the Desert Rat – Mayne.

CHAPTER FIFTEEN

First into Action

The figures moved cat-like through the darkness, creeping along the perimeter of Berca Satellite Airfield, Benghazi, pausing every few feet to shove their Lewes bombs into the dark heaps that were piled before them, and to crush the glass vials of acid that triggered the timer fuses. As ever, their primary objective had been to seek and destroy enemy warplanes, but when Mayne had discovered stores of munitions stashed in the tarpaulin-covered dugouts ranged around the airbase's perimeter, he'd seized the chance.

In a sense it was quite extraordinary, but on another level it absolutely typified the SAS's *esprit de corps*: one of Mayne's four-man attack party tonight was fresh out of weathering the superhuman escape and evasion undertaken by Bill Fraser and his patrol. Undaunted, just a few weeks after returning to Stirling's Rest Camp – back from the dead – Corporal Jack Byrne had decided rest was definitely *not* on the cards. Raiding was.

Splitting his party into two, Mayne left Byrne and his fellow operator, Lance Corporal Johnny Rose, to deal with those bomb dumps, while he, together with his trusted deputy, Bob Bennett, probed further into the heart of darkness, targeting the distant, indistinct forms lined up on the runway. Mayne liked to quietly observe any new man on his team, for there was no telling how an individual might react to full-on, behind-enemy-lines carnage. With Bennett he was on rock-solid ground. Doubtless, with Byrne also.

Graham 'Johnny' Rose, a former manager at a Woolworths department store, and a No. 8 (Guards) Commando veteran, was a somewhat less familiar proposition.

Decidedly youthful-looking, it was Rose's voice that had drawn Mayne's attention mostly. The Irishman loved nothing more than a good sing-song in the bar at Kabrit – invariably rowdy, boisterous affairs, with a dash of mess-rugby thrown in for good measure. But not when Johnny Rose began to sing. Blessed with the finest tones of any man present, the hubbub would die to an enraptured quiet whenever the former Woolworths manager gave voice. There was a hauntingly soft sentiment to his melodies, which, perhaps inevitably, made the minds of even the roughest desert raiders drift to thoughts of home. Mostly because of this striking gift – his singing voice – Mayne would go on to appoint Rose as one of his key deputies.

But tonight, Rose was an unknown as far as Mayne was concerned, and this was to be his testing.

It was well past 0300 hours on the morning of 21 March 1942, and Mayne and his men had to move swiftly, for time was desperately short. This raid was one of several planned to take place this night. All across the Benghazi Plain, deep inside enemy-occupied Libya, small units, three- to six-strong, were targeting key airbases, as the men of the SAS reverted to what they did best. Mayne already had sixty-six warplanes to his name, and Fraser thirty-eight, so together they had tallied up a hundred-plus. Tonight, they sought a whole bag more.

One of tonight's patrols, formally labelled 'OPERATION NUMBER EIGHT (A)', was commanded by none other than Bill Fraser, leading a mixed bag of fellow escapees, and others, in a six-strong party. If Fraser's mission went awry, he would face a second escape and evasion, but this time with twice the distance lying between his target and the nearest friendly positions. Fraser was hitting Berca Aerodrome, the sister airbase to Berca Satellite.

Reports were that the enemy, fearful of such attacks, were shuttling their warplanes between several such landing-strips, in an effort to frustrate any potential raids.

Leaving Kabrit on 8 March 1942, the raiders had crossed hundreds of miles of punishing desert terrain, deploying via their new forward base at Siwa – Jalo having been overrun by Rommel's advancing forces. Siwa, an isolated oasis lying in the far west of Egypt, was ideally placed for mounting such hit-and-run operations. It was also the perfect point of return after a long desert patrol – that was *if* the raiders returned. Steeped in history, shaded by tall palm trees and lush gardens, the SAS had nicknamed it 'Pollywood', reflecting its film-set ambience and walled lagoons.

Magical and evocative, in earlier times Siwa had been graced with another name, 'Jupiter Ammon', and it was revered in the Ancient Egyptian and Roman eras. The oracle in the main temple had been consulted by such luminaries as the Pharaohs, Alexander the Great, Hannibal, Julius Caesar and Cleopatra. Now, the LRDG and SAS had moved in, and the desert-weary warriors could dive from the stone parapets into Cleopatra's Pool, a deep lagoon of bubbling water where the Queen of the Nile herself was once said to have bathed.

The wider importance of tonight's missions was clear to all. If they could blast apart these aerodromes, that in turn would open up Rommel's supply lines to further attacks by the RAF. Deprived of air cover, his truck convoys could be destroyed from the air. To fulfil that aim, Stirling and his raiders had journeyed for weeks across the desert, intent on turning the tide of the war. Likewise, turning tail tonight was never going to be an option, no matter how delayed Mayne and his fellows might find themselves. A series of rendezvous points had been agreed in the open desert, at which the LRDG would collect them, but as Mayne and his party fully appreciated, they were so far behind schedule they had almost no chance of making theirs.

For the raids here on the Benghazi Plain – heavily fortified and crawling with enemy troops – Mayne and Stirling had executed a detailed reconnaissance. This had brought a curious figure – a grandmaster of clandestine intelligence gathering – into their orbit. A veteran of the First World War, Robert Marie Emanuel Melot had been wounded in combat, flying as a pilot in the Belgian Air Force, and being awarded the Croix de Guerre for valour. Twenty-two years later, and well into his late forties, 'Bob' Melot, as all knew him, had volunteered his services again. With his fluent Arabic and intimate knowledge of North Africa – Melot had farmed cotton and raised a family here during the inter-war years – he was seen as being perfect for intelligence gathering, as opposed to combat operations.

The LRDG weren't simply a taxi service for the SAS – they also bussed agents of the euphemistically named Inter-Service Liaison Department (ISLD) back and forth across the desert. The 'ISLD' was a strikingly dull and boring name: deliberately so. It served as a cover for the British Secret Intelligence Service (SIS), other-wise known as MI6. As well as including details of SAS pick-up and drop-off points, LRDG signals stamped 'Most Secret' often included instructions such as: 'I.S.L.D. and A Force parties to be carried and road watch must be maintained as importance now increasing.' Or: 'I.S.L.D. report no new set necessary . . . and patrol can proceed. This message already sent off for you through I.S.L.D. channel.'

The LRDG were charged to ferry SAS, SIS (ISLD) and A Force parties across the desert – A Force was Brigadier Dudley Clarke's brilliant deception unit in North Africa – plus any supplies they might need, such as a 'new set' (radio), while at the same time maintaining the rigours of road watch. It was a tough juggling act. Schedules were tight and the challenges legion, as this message reflects: 'I.S.L.D. party which LRDG dropped in WADI TAMET . . . has only fortnights food and nine days water and none available locally . . . Can any of your patrols assist without prejudicing road watch?' In short, the LRDG were expected to be all things to all people, and they could not afford to wait around at any rendezvous at which a party did not show – SAS included.

Upon volunteering for wartime service, Bob Melot had been snapped up by the I.S.L.D. He'd spent months living among the Bedouin and the Senussi – the local tribes – somehow blending in perfectly, and managing to avoid the numerous enemy search parties sent out to capture him. But in recent weeks he'd offered his services to Stirling and his crew. Hugely cultured, widely read, grandfatherly – his balding pate was somewhat disguised by a shaven-headed look – Melot liked what he saw of the SAS. He was particularly drawn to Mayne, and the two would become close friends. In his letters to Mayne, Melot would address him as 'Dear Paddy,' and would sign off warning him there is 'no question for you to try and go to any operation without me!'

Over the coming months, Melot would prove himself to be an incredibly daring and courageous operator. That was one of the things that drew him and Mayne to each other. But there was also another key factor. Both were outsiders – Mayne an Irishman, Melot Belgian by birth and international by upbringing. They also shared a love of history. At Siwa, Mayne had asked Melot to show him around, strolling through the palm gardens – among the world's largest – and buying up baskets of rich, golden dates, perfect provisions for long sojourns in the desert. At times, they'd stopped to sample the local hooch, an intoxicating brew distilled from the sap of the date tree and known as '*lagmi*'.

But what had won Melot a ticket on the present mission was chiefly his detailed knowledge of the Benghazi Plain. As they'd neared their objective, Stirling, Mayne and party had reached the Jebel, whereupon Melot had begun to work his magic. As if from nowhere, his 'Arab guides' had materialised, Melot the spymaster dispatching them for an up-close recce of the targets.

They'd returned, reporting 'planes in the BENINA hangars, planes dispersed in the western part of BERCA Satellite and also the western part of BERCA Main.'

As Benina aerodrome was Stirling's target, and the latter two Mayne and Fraser's, it looked as if all were set for a series of highly fruitful raids. Melot had gone on to rustle up a further individual who, upon first impressions, resembled a local Arab, but turned out to be an 'Indian soldier cut off during the last retreat' and who had been 'living with the Bedouins ever since'. Some 2.5 million Indian troops served in the Allied cause during the war, many operating in the North African theatre. Knowing the area well, that Indian soldier had promptly offered himself as a guide. He'd joined Mayne's patrol, for in many ways they faced the hardest approach march of all. Even with his help, the route would prove to be tough going – 'littered with rocks and large stones'.

Riding in the LRDG trucks, descending from the Jebel proved perilous. It was a horrendous stop-start affair, as every few dozen yards they had to halt, to clear the way of boulders. The steeper the incline the worse it became, as loose rocks broke free and crashed into the backsides and flanks of the foremost vehicles. Though they'd set out at dusk on 20 March, it was 0130 on the 21st by the time the LRDG were able to drop Mayne and his party. Pushing ahead on foot, it had taken ninety minutes to reach the airbase, which was sandwiched between the main road and the sea.

Already they were over half an hour overdue for their planned rendezvous with the LRDG. If they pressed home their attack, they would be far later still. But Mayne was not to be deterred. Not tonight. Not after all that had gone before. Bob Bennett was hardly surprised. Mayne seemed able to take on anything yet still emerge with his raiding party unscathed, and his men seemed willing to follow him into the jaws of hell itself.

Making careful note of the Italian sentry rotations, they'd slipped through the Berca Satellite perimeter. Splitting into two parties, they'd set about their stealthy work. The first thing that Byrne had spied was a pair of German soldiers on watch. By the glow of their cigarettes, he could see they were standing beside an anti-aircraft (AA) gun. Creeping forward, Rose managed to reach up and prise free the cover protecting the barrel of the gun, as Byrne stuffed a Lewes bomb down it and crushed the fuse. The German sentries still seemed oblivious to their presence. They'd moved on to the first bomb dump, which was sheltered beneath the cover of some low trees. It was pitch dark and silent as the grave, nothing seeming to disturb their quiet, deadly work.

Byrne and Rose were just planting one of the last of their Lewes bombs, when the peace of the night was shattered by a sharp crack, as the charge that they'd jammed down the AA gun barrel detonated. It was followed seconds later by a cataclysmic blast. In a paroxysm of heat and light, the first of the munitions dumps went up 'with spectacular ferocity'. Moments later, Byrne was aware of a 'terrific continuous roar', like a thunderstorm roiling through the heavens, with 'dump after dump belching out flames and smoke as they exploded in rapid succession'.

Byrne and Rose legged it, but even as they made for the exit they stumbled across a massive dump of fuel drums. Unable to resist, they shoved in their final Lewes bombs, before triggering the 'quick-action pull-switches', giving them just fourteen seconds to get away. Making a mad dash for the foothills of the Jebel, all hell broke loose, the heat of the exploding fuel drums hot on their backs. With the burning dumps belching columns of thick, oily fumes, a dark pall spread across the sky, until the enemy's AA guns opened fire, 'knocking lumps out of the smoke'. A series of further blasts echoed out from the centre of the aerodrome, which had to signify that Mayne and Bennett had found their targets. With ranks of warplanes now going up, the airbase's defenders must have decided they were under air attack, hence the gunners blasting off into the skies.

Once they had reached a patch of decent cover, Rose and Byrne paused to catch their breath. They had two options. Either head for the original rendezvous point (RV), where they would arrive several hours late, or make for the fall-back RV, which had been set at a point where the Jebel melted into the open desert, so on the far side of the hills. The more they debated their options, the more the two men just could not seem to agree. Rose was adamant they should make for the first RV. Byrne figured that was a total waste of time, for the LRDG had a ruthlessly pragmatic attitude. Rather like the SAS, they were not above leaving men behind if they had to.

As neither could convince the other, there was only one thing to do. They split up, a decision that would have fateful consequences.

As Rose hurried off in one direction, Byrne set off at a more leisurely pace in the other, for he had far more time to make the secondary RV. He thought little of striking out on his own. Born in Preston in 1921, he'd grown up in a Lancashire orphanage, where he'd had to learn to look after himself, or go under. He'd attended the Army Apprentices College in Chepstow, Wales, where they trained the next generation of soldiers. There he'd learned a mix of practical crafts, plus martial skills like 'adventure training', 'leadership' and 'character development'. In February 1939, Byrne had lied about his age in order to join the Gordon Highlanders. He was only seventeen. As he climbed into the Jebel, he was happy enough in his own company.

Meanwhile, Mayne and Bennett were wrestling with a similar conundrum themselves. They were elated, for, as they would later report, they'd hit the jackpot at Berca Satellite: '15 aircraft destroyed, 15 torpedo bombs destroyed.' The latter were air-launched torpedoes, which were one of the prime means of attacking convoys of ships. If Fraser and Stirling had scored similar successes, Axis air power would have been dealt a significant blow, and the fate of the Allies would shine more brightly in North Africa. But there was no way of knowing, not until they made it back to the rendezvous. And there Mayne and Bennett encountered their first significant problem.

Whether they were too late or had simply missed it, they 'couldn't find the damned place anywhere', Mayne would remark. The surroundings seemed utterly deserted – that was if they were even in the right location. The maps were terrible, and they spent the remainder of the night in a frustrating search for the secondary RV. By dawn, and despite covering some fifty miles on foot, they were none the wiser, fearing they had been 'walking around in circles in the dark'. By now Mayne had pretty much reconciled himself to a trek across the desert the two hundred-plus miles to Tobruk, the port fortress that was then under siege by Rommel, but which still lay in British hands.

The one bonus was their stumbling upon Corporal Rose, but more by luck than by design. Indeed, lady luck was to play more than a passing role in their fortunes over the coming hours. Taking a pragmatic line – they were in dire need of rest, sustenance and shelter – Mayne approached the nearest tribal settlement. At first, those inhabiting the tented camp were highly suspicious. But once they were convinced that Mayne and his men were 'Inglese' – English – everything changed. These were Senussi people, and they had forged an informal alliance with the Allies. As Mayne was starting to appreciate, 'the Italians treat the Senussi very badly,' which meant they would do just about anything to help British forces.

The three fugitives were ushered into a tent. A fire heated the place. Blankets were thrown down as makeshift bedding. First, they were treated to a feast of boiled eggs – 'damned good' – then platters of dates, after which a huge gourd of goat's milk was brought forth. Mayne figured 'they never wash the gourd, and the sourer it gets the better they like it, and I think they must have liked this stuff very well!' Well fed and feeling secure – 'not one of them would go down and tell the Jerries or the "Eyeties" where we are' – Mayne and his fellows settled down to rest. Byrne's fate remained troubling, as did their failure to make contact with the LRDG. But they couldn't imagine the indomitable Byrne falling into enemy hands, or, if he did, not doing his all to escape. Just like Eoin McGonigal, it was inconceivable that he might be kept down for long.

For forty-eight hours Mayne, Bennett and Rose rested up and husbanded their strength, as they deliberated what to do. The decision was about to be made for them. During their stay with the Senussi, Mayne had found the time to pen a letter to his brother Douglas, urging him to 'never disbelieve in luck again or coincidence, or whatever you like to call it.' He went on to explain how the LRDG patrol – their taxi service – had managed to get hold of a chicken, and how they had decided they wanted it properly cooked. With that in mind, they'd dispatched the Indian soldier-cum-guide to one of the Senussi camps.

The SAS operational report would speak of the LRDG executing a 'very successful raid of their own' in which they had 'captured a chicken. But more successful was the Indian guide who cooked the chicken.' Mayne reckoned there were some thirty to forty Senussi camps in the immediate area, but the guide happened to choose theirs to approach with his feathered friend. Once the Indian soldier and Mayne and his men had been reunited, it was a short hop from there to link up with the LRDG. As Mayne explained, rounding off his letter to Douglas, they wouldn't have to have to 'footslog it across the desert,' for the LRDG would be taxiing them back to Kabrit.

In truth, it had been a close-run thing. The LRDG convoy was scheduled to depart the following morning, with or without Mayne and his men. Such a fortuitous rendezvous called for a celebration. Accordingly, as was noted in the SAS War Diary:

On the evening of the 26th the party went into action with Rum and Lime, Rum and Tea, Rum Omelette, and just plain Rum . . . while Captain Mayne went through the weird ritual of demonstrating how one should NOT fire and NOT take to pieces at night, M.G.s, L.M.G.s, Tommy-guns, pistols and God knows what other intricate pieces of mechanism.

Results: !!!!!!!!!!

Casualties: Incredible as it may seem, Nil.

Opposition: Nil.

There was every need to let off steam. Not all the raids had hit home. In fact, only Mayne's had.

At Berca Main a disappointed Fraser had discovered only the one aircraft and 'four mobile repair wagons'. Even worse, Stirling had found only 'derelict planes' and two torpedo bombs at Benina. Deeply frustrated, he'd pushed on into Benghazi itself, an ancient seaport that for two millennia had been fought over by Greeks, Romans, Spartans, Arabs and Turks, and now by the Axis and Allied powers. He'd got as far as the harbour, proving that a small but determined force could reach the wharfs where Rommel mustered his fleets of supply ships. If they could return with folbots and limpet mines, Stirling figured, they could wreak havoc there. The idea was lodged firmly in his mind.

By the time the LRDG convoy set out for home – distant Siwa – there was still no sign of the absent Byrne. For the first time in a series of highly successful missions, Mayne had lost one of his own. Admittedly, he wasn't present when Byrne had decided to strike out solo, so arguably there was little he could have done to prevent it. But it had been his decision to split the raiding party. Maybe that had been a mistake? But time had been so dead set against them. Would he have allowed Byrne to head off on his own, had he been present? Not a bit of it. He'd have kept them together, and Byrne would very likely be with them now.

When you cared for your men as deeply as Mayne did, each loss was a bitter blow. He vowed to himself to do better.

In truth, Byrne's second escape and evasion attempt in as many months would end up being an epic to rival that of his first. As the SAS War Diary would record of his efforts, 'It was later learned that he had fallen in with friendly Arabs and had walked back 100 miles.' Byrne had set a course on his compass for the nearest friendly position. Trudging through the burning sands, he'd cast his mind back to his previous iteration, his long escape with Bill Fraser and Co., in an effort to bolster his spirits and to give him heart.

He'd commenced his death march equipped with two pints of water, a tin of emergency chocolate and a flask of brandy. Adhering to his iron-willed water discipline, he refused to take a sip until the sun set, resolving to keep marching as long as his legs would carry him. At one point he was forced to a halt by a sandstorm. He curled up and slept through it, awaking freezing cold. A swig of brandy served to warm him. With his water exhausted, he stumbled on. On the night of what he figured was day six he collapsed in the desert, utterly finished. He came back to consciousness, only to realise that he was being watched.

By luck he'd been found by some Bedouin. Though he was a revolting sight, 'not having washed or shaved since leaving the oasis of Siwa more than two weeks before,' the Bedouin took Byrne in, and fed and nursed him back to health. They invited him to join them, for they were engaged in a journey east some 170 miles, so edging closer to British lines. But Byrne was adamant that he had to continue alone and quickly. He had to keep going and return to his unit. Pressing food and water into his hands, the Bedouin wished him luck and Byrne set off once more.

For two days he trekked east, feeling stronger with every step. Hope, and the provisions the Bedouin had provided, kept him going. Eventually, even as he figured he had to be nearing British lines, a Chevrolet truck hove into view. Byrne felt a surge of elation. This had to be friendly forces and could very well be an LRDG patrol. He strode ahead, but even as he moved the desert air was cut by fire, 'and the sand came alive as bullets struck all around'. Moments later, a patrol of German troops emerged from hiding and Byrne was surrounded. The Chevy was a captured British vehicle.

Byrne had stumbled into a well-camouflaged position, where Rommel's Afrika Korps were facing off against the Eighth Army. He had come so close to making it, which was the bitterest blow of all. There was worse to come. Bloodied from a gunshot wound, Byrne was led before a German officer. When he refused to reveal any more than his name, rank and serial number, the officer barked out a dismissive laugh. He knew exactly who Byrne was, he crowed. He served with the Special Air Service, whose commanding officer was Major David Stirling DSO, of the Scots Guards. Byrne was flabbergasted. How could he know so much? Someone must have talked. But how? And why?

Byrne was about to find out. Handed over into the custody of the Italians, Byrne was 'invited' for a meal with an English-speaking Italian officer. That man claimed to be a parachutist, and over dinner he tried to get Byrne to talk about the SAS. When he refused, he was taken to a room and locked in. He awoke in the early hours, to discover two fellow prisoners had joined him. One was dressed in the uniform of a sergeant in the Royal Artillery, the other as an officer of the Fleet Air Arm, the aviation branch of the Royal Navy.

At the first available opportunity, the sergeant used the excuse of giving Byrne a cigarette to whisper: 'Be careful. I think this bastard's an informer.'

Shortly, the door opened and the sergeant was called outside. The figure who remained wore a bandage around his head, as if he'd been in recent combat. Byrne too was heavily bandaged, due to his gunshot wounds. Affecting an easy camaraderie, the figure sidled closer to Byrne and 'revealed' that he had a certain means of getting letters to Britain. If Byrne had any he'd liked to send, he would be able to arrange it.

Then, acting as if he'd just noticed Byrne's jump wings, he remarked, 'I see you are a parachutist?'

'That's right,' Byrne confirmed. He was giving nothing away by doing so, for the iconic SAS wings spoke for themselves. Then he added: 'I also know the Italians use informers.' Slipping a tiny hacksaw blade from his uniform – it was part of the specialist escape and evasion kit carried by all SAS troops – he remarked, menacingly, that if he ever met such a man, 'I would like nothing better than to use this on his throat.'

At Byrne's words the suspected stool pigeon – one of the most ancient and nastiest species of traitor and informer – blanched. He hammered on the door and was released by the guards, after which Byrne never saw him again. But he was starting to get a sense of how others taken captive might have been tricked into revealing details about the SAS. The term 'stool pigeon' derives from the habit of hunters tying a pigeon to a stool, to lure other birds in. In military and espionage parlance the stool pigeon was an informer, who inveigled himself into the confidence of captives by acting as if he was one of them. Simply by listening in on the prisoners' chatter, and posing the odd, seemingly innocuous question, he could garner key intelligence.

Byrne's SAS uniform was taken from him, following which an old Italian tunic was tossed into his cell. In the coming days he would be stripped naked by his Italian captors and beaten to within an inch of his life. Their excuse was that they had discovered his hidden fighting knife, plus his escape equipment concealed in his uniform, silk maps included. Still refusing to talk, he was thrown into solitary confinement for days on end. Finally, Byrne was returned to German captivity.

Flown north to Germany, Byrne ended up being taken to Stalag Luft III, a prisoner-of-war camp situated close to the border with occupied Poland. Reaching the camp on 23 April 1942, he was amazed to discover that a Lieutenant Charles Bonington of the SAS was also being held there. Byrne's spirits leapt. As with so many others, he'd feared that Bonington was dead. The two men were reunited, at which point Bonington was able to reveal the fate that had befallen his patrol, during Operation Squatter. After being damaged by flak, their Bombay had been shot up still further and forced to make a crash landing. All aboard had been either captured or killed.

According to the Germans, Stalag Luft III was escape-proof. From the start Byrne was resolved to prove otherwise. During his capture and interrogation, he'd realised just how much the activities of the SAS had discomfited the enemy, and how much effort – via the stool pigeons and other means – they were putting into discovering the desert raiders' secrets. In many ways it was heartening. It meant that their attacks had hit home. It meant that all the sacrifices – his own included – were very possibly not in vain.

No matter what it might take, Byrne resolved to escape, to return to his unit and to the fight.

CHAPTER SIXTEEN

Treachery

For months, a senior Italian intelligence officer had been trying to discover more about the mystery raiders who struck from out of the desert like ghosts. His interest was hardly surprising. By now, SAS patrols had raided 'all the most important German and Italian aerodromes within 300 miles of the forward area', some of them more than once. Lieutenant Colonel Mario Revetria was the North Africa chief of the Servizio Informazioni Militare (SIM), the Italian military intelligence service. He was experienced, wily and quick-witted. He knew that to combat the raiders he needed to winkle out their secrets – the size of the unit, who was in command, its tactics, techniques and procedures, its routes of ingress and means of attack.

The key to discovering all of that lay in finding the right stool pigeon. In a long-standing member of the British armed forces the Italians happened to have the ideal candidate. Theodore John William Schurch was born in 1918 in London, to a British mother and a Swiss father. Schurch felt he'd been ostracised at school and bullied, due to his foreign sounding name. At age sixteen he'd got a job as a trainee accountant, meeting a young office employee called Irene Page, who was a dyed-in-the-wool fascist. At weekends she'd dress in her grey skirt, black shirt, tie and beret, and head off to a rally of the British Union of Fascists. Though initially attracted to her physically, Schurch found himself drawn to her politics as well. In time he was introduced to an Italian who ran a business in Britain, but who doubled as a recruiter for Italian intelligence.

In short order Schurch was signed up as an Italian agent. In 1936 he joined the Royal Army Service Corps (RASC), the logistical wing of the British Army, at his handler's behest. A year later, he was deployed to Palestine, then a British protectorate bordering Egypt. Securing a job as a driver for staff headquarters, Schurch – a man of innate shrewdness and cunning – was able to glean choice snippets of intelligence, including details of troops movements, the delivery of war materiel and the roles of senior commanders, all largely just by keeping his eyes and ears open. Via an Arab contact, he was able to pass what he learned into the hands of Britain's future enemies. He was paid for his services, and paid well. He started to develop a penchant for the good things and the expensive pleasures of life.

With war's outbreak the pace of work quickened. At the urgings of his handlers, Schurch sought a frontline role, one that would allow him to pass from British to Axis lines. Small of stature, with a pinched, weaselly face and bad teeth, Schurch was hardly the most prepossessing of individuals. But by cultivating a pencil-thin moustache and oiled, slicked-back hair, and mimicking an upper-class accent, he could pass himself off as an officer. Schurch would go on to exhibit remarkable tenacity in that he would repeatedly cross and recross the Allied and Axis lines in the course of his treachery. For his efforts, he would be rewarded with cash, fine wine and a plush villa all of his own.

From the start, Revetria made it clear that a key focus of his interest was the SAS. Posing as a British air force officer, Schurch was ordered to garner all possible intelligence regarding the unit's make-up, activities and intentions. He set to it with a vengeance, joining a network of similar agents, foremost among whom was Franco Ricci, a London café owner of Italian descent who spoke with a strong Cockney accent. Like Schurch, Ricci doubled as a 'stool pigeon, getting information from prisoners of war when wearing English uniform'. Then there was Giuseppe Minetti, another Londoner of Italian extraction, who 'usually worked in the front line on newly captured prisoners'.

All reported to Revetria, although Schurch also forged links with the Abwehr, the German foreign intelligence service. Teaming up with Abwehr agent Fritz Reinhardt, a personal friend of Adolf Hitler, Schurch would help ensnare Allied agents, those secretly working for the British or American cause. In one case, an Italian-American was found to possess a secret radio set, and to be gathering intelligence for the Americans. When Schurch and Reinhardt uncovered his clandestine role, they used that to turn him, forcing him to work for them 'sending out bogus messages to the American Forces'.

Such was the measure of those whose attentions were turning towards Stirling's desert raiders. Schurch was appointed the key agent for SAS captives. He was to mix with them while posing as a fellow POW, in an effort to discover the location of their bases, their rendezvous points and their forthcoming missions. In due course, he would extract information that would lead to 'the capture of one of these [SAS] patrols', and very possibly several more.

For the SAS, the net was closing. Increasingly, it would become a race to stay one step ahead of traitors like Schurch, and whatever intelligence they might garner.

Returning to Kabrit in the spring of 1942, Stirling, Mayne et al. were blissfully unaware of the likes of Schurch and their nefarious activities. But thankfully, of the fate of Bonington, and some of the other Operation Squatter missing, there was now definitive news. Their Bombay had been shot up by a German fighter aircraft and it was forced to crash land. In the process, the pilot was wounded, his co-pilot killed and the wireless operator badly hurt. As for the

SAS patrol the aircraft had been carrying, all survived with varying degrees of injury. All were taken captive, although the patrol sergeant would die some weeks later of his wounds. The rest were listed as POWs, held in various camps.

The news that all-bar-one of Bonington's patrol had survived was hugely uplifting. For Mayne, it held out a faint sliver of hope for Eoin McGonigal and his missing men. That May, he exchanged letters with Eoin's mother Margaret. During his time away raiding Berca airfield, she had written, alerting Mayne to the fact that several members of the SAS had been listed as POWs. They included five individuals whom Mayne confirmed were 'all with Eoin' on his Operation Squatter team. Mayne listed them for her, complete with 'their numbers and regiments':

2698040 MacKay R. Scots Gds [Guards]
2756712 Morris W. Black Watch
5672160 Maloney J. Somerset Lt. Inf. [Light Infantry]
30618334 McCormick C. Royal Scots
811911 Robertson J. Scots Gds [Guards]

In due course Mayne wrote to MacKay, who was being held in Campo PG 52, a POW camp in northern Italy, seeking answers. He passed Eoin's mother MacKay's address, so she could also write, for MacKay should be able to shed light on what had happened to her son. Mayne also sent her what photographs he had of Eoin. A keen photographer, he made sure to keep hold of the negatives, so if his letter went astray he could send her a fresh set of prints. He also promised to send her Eoin's 'cap badge and parachute badge [his wings]'. As he explained, the wings were worn 'on the left side of our tunics . . . after completing the training jumps', plus 'an operation by parachute in the enemy country'.

Though their only airborne mission so far had been the disastrous Operation Squatter, Stirling had insisted that all recruits should be put through parachute training regardless. It was a fine test of the mettle of a man. It sorted the wheat from the chaff. Tellingly, Mayne signed off his letter to Eoin's mother by extending his sympathies to the entire McGonigal family, which seemed to suggest he was coming to accept that Eoin may well have lost his life. Even so, no one seemed to know how the young Irishman had died, *if he had died*. Mayne remained determined to find out, and to bring some closure for himself and the entire McGonigal clan.

Further news filtered in from other POW camps. Of Stirling's Operation Squatter patrol, all bar Stirling and Tait had been captured. But at least one man, Private Fred Trenfield, had spent an incredible ten days marching through the desert towards British lines. He'd go on to make six further escape attempts, both in Italy and Germany, and would be recommended for a decoration. Of the two injured men that Mayne and his patrol had been forced to leave behind, both had survived. Lance Corporal Doug Arnold and Private Douglas Keith had managed to drag themselves away from the DZ, intending to surrender to a passing Italian patrol. Their captors apparently believed the story they had spun – that they were British engineers who had simply got lost in the desert.

But sadly, there was a cruel twist of fate in Private Keith's tale. On 8 December 1941 he had been loaded aboard the Italian ship, the SS *Sebastiano Venier*, sailing from Benghazi to Italy. Some 2,000 British and Commonwealth POWs were stuffed into the vessel's battened-down holds. The following afternoon the ship was spotted by the British submarine HMS *Porpoise*. Unaware of her human cargo, the captain fired a torpedo which struck her just aft of the bows. The *Sebastiano Venier*'s commander managed to run her aground before she sank, and some 1,700 of the POWs were saved. Private Keith was not among them. His parents were told he was listed as missing, presumed dead.

That pretty much closed off the mystery of the Operation Squatter missing. All bar Eoin McGonigal.

Recently, Stirling had pulled off a successful raid on an enemy airbase, leading a four-man patrol back into Benina aerodrome, just outside Benghazi. This time, they had had to sneak into the hangars, before finally discovering '2 Stukas, 2 Me 109Fs, and 1 Ju 52', the latter being the large, three-engine aircraft which was the staple air transport for the German armed forces. It was much prized by Rommel, for it enabled supplies to be rushed forward to frontline positions. All five aircraft were destroyed, which meant that at last Stirling had bagged his first warplanes.

Spurred by his ability to get into Benghazi, Stirling had returned there, leading a raiding party that included none other than Randolph Churchill, the son of Britain's wartime prime minister. Assessed by Mayne as being 'not a bad lad, plucky, but very bad manners', Randolph Churchill had enjoyed the mission immensely. Largely unsuccessful – due to a faulty vehicle, broken boats and dodgy intelligence – the attempted raid had yet again shown how a small force of very determined men could penetrate to that city's very waterfront, seemingly undetected. Benghazi harbour was crying out to be properly hit. Stirling drew up a report, outlining the promise and the potential, before being overtaken by other priorities.

Chief among these were the enemy's counter-measures. Axis airstrips were becoming ever more closely patrolled and guarded. Repeated raids, coupled with the intelligence gleaned by the likes of the stool pigeons, meant that increasingly stringent measures were being adopted to bolster airbase security. A Luftwaffe memo outlined the steps to be taken to thwart Stirling's raiders, who were depicted as 'personnel especially suitable by reason of their profession – acrobats, boxers etc – specially equipped and with an extensive and thorough training for sabotage and offensive raids'.

Among the recommendations were that every sentry 'must be equipped with pocket torch and signal pistol [a flare gun]', and that 'watchdogs with trained men' should be deployed 'on all exposed airfields', plus 'bloodhounds [tracking dogs]'.

If such measures were adopted, there was no way that Stirling's raiders, moving on foot, could prevail. They might get into an airbase. They might even plant their bombs. But there was very little chance that they would get out again or make good their getaway. Of course, the SAS knew precious little about such developments. There was little time to pause, reassess and reflect. As the war in the desert became gridlocked, something was needed to break the impasse; some signal breakthrough to give one side or the other the upper hand. At this juncture, the key was seen as being Malta, Britain's island fortress, which remained under a gruelling siege.

The fate of that Mediterranean island hung in the balance, as enemy warplanes pummelled it unrelentingly, while also hitting the convoys that were attempting to ship in desperately needed supplies. Malta constituted a vital base, providing harbours from which Allied warships could attack the enemy's supply lines. If it fell, Rommel would be free to ship in more troops and war materiel. Churchill believed that if Malta were lost, the Axis grip on the Mediterranean would be total. Likewise, Rommel feared that if Malta held out, the Axis would end up losing control of North Africa. He'd sought permission to seize the island fortress using German and Italian airborne troops. But much to Rommel's displeasure, the mission had been cancelled by Hitler.

Even so, in the late spring of 1942 Malta simply could not hold out, without desperately needed supplies of food, arms and ammunition. The island's Governor, General William Dobie, had telegraphed Churchill in the starkest of terms: 'The very worst may happen if we cannot replenish our vital needs, especially flour and ammunition . . . it is a question of survival . . .' Churchill had piled on the pressure, warning General Auchinleck that unless offensive action was taken to stop the enemy's air attacks, Malta would fall, which would be 'a disaster of the first magnitude . . . There is no need for me to stress the vital importance of the safe arrival of our convoys at Malta.'

Thousands of sorties had been flown by Axis forces against Malta. But if the SAS could destroy the enemy's warplanes on the ground, the Malta convoys would have a far greater chance of getting through. Once again, the key enemy airbases were Berca and Benina, plus two adjacent fields, Derna and Martuba. While it mightn't make a great deal of sense to try to hit those same targets again so quickly, that was exactly what Stirling and Mayne were called upon to do. Only the SAS had the daring and reach to throw out a hand and strike so far into enemy territory. It was early June 1942, and this time, two new outfits were added to the mix to spice it up a little, and with deception and trickery to the fore.

In the SAS War Diary, Stirling recorded their orbat – order of battle – as having expanded in unexpected ways. First off, several dozen members of the Free French parachutists had joined them, plus there was also a mysterious force identified only as 'Captain Buck's German Unit'. To secure the services of the former, Stirling had approached General Georges Catroux, one of the deputies of the Free French leader-in-exile, General Charles de Gaulle. Catroux – presently in Cairo – did not like the English and saw no reason why any Frenchman should take orders from an English officer. Stirling had countered that, as a Scot, he was a firm believer in *'l'ancienne alliance entre la France et l'Écosse contre les Anglais'* – the ancient Franco-Scottish alliance against the English.

It must have done the trick, for Catroux agreed that sixty-six of his men – many battle-hardened; most fully jump-trained – could join the SAS. They were commanded by Captain Georges Roger Pierre Bergé, a diminutive but stocky and forceful figure with a quick wit and a sharp tongue. Wounded twice in the summer 1940 defence of France, Bergé had already been decorated with the French Croix de Guerre, plus a British Military Cross. In September 1940, with de Gaulle's blessing, he had founded the *1ère Compagnie de l'Infanterie de l'Air* – the 1st Air Infantry Company – which put French volunteers through RAF Ringway, near Manchester, the British military's parachute training school.

In March 1941 Bergé had parachuted back into France on Operation Savanna, one of the first ever special forces missions into occupied Europe. Its aim was to ambush and kill as many pilots as possible from the Luftwaffe's Pathfinder squadron, those who navigated the night-time bombing formations onto targets in Britain. Due to faulty intelligence the mission had failed, but Bergé had opted to remain in France, to establish one of the earliest Resistance networks. Once that was done, he'd returned to Britain, and gone on to play a key role in setting up a Special Training Station for the SOE, at which to instruct French agents for deployment back into their native France.

In short, Bergé was the real deal, as was his deputy, Lieutenant Augustin Jordan. Jordan, a civil servant by profession, had escaped to Britain when France fell and had volunteered for de Gaulle. Erudite, highly educated and impeccably dressed, Jordan's refined look and manners were somewhat misleading. Behind the façade lurked a ruthless killer, who was not inclined to take prisoners. Bergé, Jordan and all of their men had come to North Africa to fight, but had yet to see much if any action. Upon their recruitment to the SAS, they sensed all that was about to change. Bergé warned his fellows, pointedly: 'We have a terrible challenge to live up to. They have already a hundred planes to their name. We will have to work double time to catch up.'

By now the SAS tally was well in excess of a hundred. The lion's share – some eighty-plus warplanes – had fallen to Mayne. Bergé and Jordan could hardly fail to be impressed. Hearing of Mayne's Tamet mess shoot-'em-up, they were struck by how, in killing those German and Italian pilots, Mayne and his men had succeeded where Bergé and his team had failed on Operation Savanna, which had had entirely similar aims. Bergé and his compatriots' first close encounter with Mayne was to be on the rugby pitch. For ease of convenience they played French v British, and in no time the wild melee was obscured in a thick cloud of dust. The French quickly realised they were not about to win.

Their riposte was to throw down a challenge to a bout of basketball. While their opponents seemed incapable of grasping the rules, and still appeared to think that scrums, rucks and tackles were perfectly permissible, the French won. Honour was satisfied. Witnessing Mayne's sheer physical presence, and the loyalty he commanded, the Frenchmen coined their own nickname for Mayne. Due to his implacable physical presence, he was 'l'armoire' – the wardrobe. As for his record on the field of battle, he was 'le grand tueur' – the Great Killer. Over time, the French SAS would learn to speak of Mayne 'with tender admiration' and 'as a legend . . . He was a lion,' they would declare.

In some senses this was surprising. Mayne, like many of the SAS originals, had cut his teeth fighting *against* the French, in among the Litani Hills. But Mayne appreciated that the Free French recruits had more reasons than most to despise the German enemy. Their country was occupied. Their people – their loved ones – were reeling under the Nazi yoke. Mayne fought for his fallen comrades, and from a sense of right and wrong. When asked why any Irishman would take up arms in the Allied cause, he gave the classic answer – that he was fighting so that all nations, no matter their size or strength, might have the right to determine their own destiny. But as for the Free French, they fought to liberate their homeland. There could be no more telling reasons to wage war.

As for 'Captain Buck's German Unit', that was one of the strangest and most unconventional outfits ever to have been raised by the Allies. In the SAS War Diary, Stirling described it as consisting of 'ex-German [sic] regular soldiers who had got out of

Germany before the war for political and other reasons'. All largely true, but there was a great deal more to Buck's unit that simply that. To one side of Stirling's Rest Camp, screened off and closely guarded, lay a separate sub-camp. Within its confines a small group of very determined men underwent training to break every conceivable rule of war, and damn the consequences. Their cover name was the Special Interrogation Group (SIG), though there was little that would be interrogatory about their ventures.

The SIG was the brainchild of a nimble-minded and somewhat eccentric British Army officer, who just happened to speak such good German so as to be able to pass himself off as a native of that country. While serving in North Africa in January 1942, Captain Herbert Cecil Buck had been captured. In short order he'd managed to escape, having stolen a German officer's uniform and transport. With his fluent German he'd got behind the wheel and bluffed his way back to British lines. That done, he'd reasoned that if he could blag his way out of enemy territory, a suitably equipped and disguised unit could bluff its way back in again. With official blessing he'd gathered volunteers, the majority of whom were German, Czech and Austrian Jews. They burned to strike back against the Nazi enemy, and for wholly understandable reasons. Many of their loved ones had been shipped off to face the horrors of the concentration camps.

Out at their Bitter Lakes redoubt their training began. Wearing full Afrika Korps uniform down to their underwear, and cautioned to speak only German at all times, they were steeped in the soldiering skills, weaponry, culture and ethos of the enemy. They headed to breakfast every morning belting out rousing German marching songs. They adopted the mannerisms, the lingo and the cussing then common to the enemy. Each was given a wholly convincing cover story, complete with forged documents and with fictitious Aryan-looking girlfriends. Just shy of forty strong, the SIG included Karl Kahane, a veteran of the German Army from the First World War; Charlie 'Chunky' Hillman, the son of a Viennese patisserie owner, hence his portly form; plus Maurice 'Tiffen' Tiefenbrunner, who had fled Europe in 1939 on a ship crammed with fellow Jewish refugees.

But there were also two non-Jewish recruits. Arguing that authenticity demanded it – it was 'a necessary risk for training purposes' – Buck had recruited two former Afrika Korps soldiers. Captured, they'd been vetted by British military intelligence and supposedly turned. 'Walter Essner' and 'Herbert Brueckner' – these were cover names provided by their British handlers – were to lend the final flourish to ensure that Buck's SIG personnel could pass muster when mixing with the enemy. The SIG had been taken under the SAS's wing, as Stirling and Mayne had real need. Encountering ever-more stringent airbase security, they had a hunch that bluff and deception might be the only means to get a raiding party onto some of the most closely guarded airstrips.

As a Trojan horse, and equipped as they were with captured Volkswagen and Opel German military vehicles, the SIG were perfect. Almost . . . The one major note of disquiet concerned Brueckner. Mayne first came into contact with Brueckner – a big-boned, brash, blond-haired bully of a man – at the Kabrit bar. While Essner seemed relatively good-natured and genuine in his anti-Nazi sentiments, Brueckner was a far different specimen, and especially when he'd been drinking. Unsurprisingly, when Brueckner met the tall, quietly spoken Irishman, sparks would fly.

Brueckner revelled in bragging and vulgarity. That night, he was regaling all with a particularly lurid account of a close encounter he'd had with a local prostitute, who proffered her services in a battered old tent. Mayne hated gratuitous obscenity and boasting, as much as he despised making fun of the less fortunate. Just as 'compliments embarrassed him', so 'he detested humbug and conceit', but he would equally 'go out of his way to make himself agreeable to very ordinary people – if he thought they were also decent'.

As Mayne listened to Brueckner's foul-mouthed tale and his grand-standing, he realised the German epitomised all that he abhorred.

Mayne settled into a still and cold rage. Finally, he bade the German hold his tongue. Brueckner, who fancied himself as a bit of a brawler, uttered a riposte under his breath. Mayne, whose mood had flipped in an instant, pounced. Before he could get to Brueckner, another figure stepped in. Fearing for the German's safety, Thomas 'Tommy' Corps, a former heavyweight boxer hailing from Newcastle, and another SAS original, delivered the anaesthetic, knocking Brueckner out. He'd done it for the German's own good. It had saved him from a far worse beating, but not from Mayne's ire and his suspicions.

Mayne had an uncanny ability to assess an individual's character in an instant. Often, one appraising look was all it would take. Once his mind was made up he rarely changed it. Shooting a line with Mayne got you nowhere. Some, interpreting his quiet manner as acquiescence or a lack of confidence, would opt to do all the talking when in Mayne's presence. Being a blabbermouth got you nowhere, too. Seemingly out of the blue, Mayne would insert 'the most discomforting questions in the blandest of manners, and he could cut a person short with hardly a word'.

Mayne shared his disquiet about Brueckner with Stirling. His sixth sense told him that the German simply could not be trusted. They were doubly disquieted when Buck confirmed that he intended both Essner and Brueckner to deploy alongside the SIG. It was one thing to use them for training, quite another to send them on operations deep behind the lines. As matters transpired, their disquiet was shared by many among the SIG. They, too, raised it with Buck. But the English captain refused to countenance that either of his German trainers might be anything other than genuine.

A plan was hatched for the forthcoming operations. As Stirling, Mayne, Fraser and company led the SAS on a string of raids, hitting Berca and Benina aerodromes, so the SIG would take their captured German vehicles, pack them full of Bergé's Free French SAS, who would act as if they were prisoners of war, and bluff their way right through the enemy lines. They would target Derna and Martuba airfields, which were so heavily defended that no SAS party had managed to reach them. Doubtless, the SIG's venture was risky, even before Essner and Brueckner were added to the mix. But no sacrifice was deemed to be too great to relieve the siege of Malta.

And so the die was cast.

CHAPTER SEVENTEEN

The Enemy Within

Whether the enemy had had any forewarning or not, no one could tell, but for once the Desert Taxi Company had been forced to stop well short. The skies had been buzzing with enemy warplanes, and if the LRDG convoy had been spotted surprise would have been well and truly blown. On a mission such as this, returning to raid Berca Satellite aerodrome so soon after the previous attack, surprise was essential. Consequently, Mayne and his raiders had been dropped thirty miles short, and had proceeded to move in on foot. That was easier said than done, for each man was laden down with twenty-four Lewes bombs, either slung from his ammo belt or crammed into his Italian Army-issue haversack.

During that first night's march, 11/12 June 1942, the weight of the explosives just seemed to grow heavier and heavier with each step. 'It was hard work and no mistake!' one of Mayne's men, Corporal Bob Lilley, remarked. Another SAS original, Lilley was hardly in his first flush of youth. Pushing forty, with a wife and children to care for back home, that made him something of an anomaly in the unit. With curly black hair and sparkling dark eyes, the fiercely independent Lilley had been drawn to the self-contained nature of the SAS. It suited his character. Solid, capable, unflappable – neither riotously upbeat nor prone to getting down-hearted – Lilley had a cast-iron reliability about him. Homely of nature, he had a stubborn way of puzzling everything out for himself. There was a sense that no matter what it took, Corporal Lilley would get the job done.

Lilley had more than proven his worth when serving as one of the 'Tobruk Four' – together with Jock Lewes, Jim Almonds and Pat Riley. There were two other corporals making up Mayne's present team – Jimmie Storie and Arthur Warburton. Like Lilley, at first glance Storie – who'd left school at fourteen and worked as a roof tiler before the war – was 'an unassuming and ordinary' looking kind of a man. Few would guess he had the makings of a piratical raider of their ilk. But as the American writer and philosopher Henry David Thoreau, had opined, with immense foresight: 'The hero is commonly the simplest and obscurest of men.'

There was also a Free French SAS contingent moving in consort with Mayne's patrol. They would peel off when the time was right, to strike at Berca Main.

At dawn the raiders reached a small Senussi encampment in the Jebel, and took cover among the flocks of goats and the chickens. It smelt to high heaven. Much that they tried to get some rest, the chickens were 'pecking and chirping' incessantly. Dog tired as they were, most managed to nod off. Come sundown, they shared a meal with their tribal hosts, before pushing off into the gathering darkness. Mayne's target lay a good distance below on the coastal plane, and he aimed to reach it by midnight, latest. The last thing he wanted was to miss another rendezvous with the LRDG, and to tempt fate for a further time.

Pointing the French SAS contingent in the direction of their objective, Mayne wished them a quiet farewell. Their commander tonight, Lieutenant André Zirnheld, was tasked with his first ever SAS raid – 'OPERATION NUMBER TEN (C)'; Mayne's was TEN (A), Stirling's strike on Benina (B). Zirnheld typified the spirit of those Free French SAS recruits. An intensely religious man, he was also a poet and a writer, and had won the admiration of both Stirling and Mayne. Described as a 'fine young officer' and a 'beautiful poet', in one set of verse he'd asked God not for wealth, good fortune or success, but for 'torment and battle' as he took the fight to the reviled enemy.

In spite of the challenges of tonight's inaugural mission, Zirnheld would perform magnificently. Perhaps too well, striking too swiftly . . . Even though they pushed on as quickly as they could, Mayne's party reached the perimeter of Berca Satellite well behind schedule. The terrain, as always, had defeated them. But Lieutenant Zirnheld must have made it to Berca Main bang on time, for even as Mayne and his men studied the airbase perimeter, so a series of explosions tore apart the night. One, two, three . . . Mayne and his men counted eleven in total, all from the direction of Berca Main. Presumably, that was eleven enemy warplanes bagged by Zirnheld and his team, none of which were about to take to the skies to tear up the Malta convoys.

But here at Berca Satellite, the results of Zirnheld's handiwork were doubtless going to prove . . . challenging. Alerted by the blasts, the entire guard force seemed to have been stood-to. Much that Mayne and his men might scrutinise their target, there just didn't seem to be a way through. By the light of the distant fires and explosions, they could make out details suggesting that the enemy had adopted further defensive measures. Those few aircraft that they could see were spaced out generously, with wide open gaps lying between: prime killing ground. Here and there they also spied where groups of sentries seemed to have been assigned to guard individual warplanes.

The conflagration at Berca Main spread, further blasts and gunfire erupting in the distance. It seemed as if a pitched battle had broken out between Zirnheld's Free French SAS and the airbase defenders. The chaos and confusion was contagious. Here at Berca Satellite the guards seemed nervous, trigger-happy, spooked. Groups of Italians began firing on their German comrades and vice versa, forcing Mayne and his men to keep their heads well down. From his study of the airbase's defences, all Mayne could imagine doing was 'stalking each plane and then using grenades to disperse the guards', after which they would plant their Lewes bombs. It would be risky, dangerous and time-consuming. But seeing no other option, he issued his orders.

As Corporal Lilley started to crawl towards the first warplane, Mayne readied his grenades. Lilley had got no closer than ten yards, when a challenge rang out. A sentry was poised beneath the wing of their target, and even as Lilley dropped to the ground, the enemy soldier fired. Mayne didn't hesitate. He lobbed a first grenade, and moments later a group of Italian sentries were blown apart. All hell let loose. In an instant, Mayne and his three raiders found themselves caught in the open, being targeted with accurate bursts. As Lilley fully appreciated, they were taking fire from the enemy from all sides. 'The stuff was whistling over our heads . . .'

Just at this moment a squadron of RAF bombers hove into view, the leading aircraft dropping flares to mark their target, which was Benghazi harbour. Their glare 'lit up the drome and made the approach to any plane without being seen impossible', Mayne would report. Often depicted as a figure who revelled in taking crazy and suicidal risks, the truth was far different, and particularly where the lives of his men were concerned. 'Careless for his own safety, he was very jealous for theirs. Risks there had to be, but everyone knew that if Paddy authorised a venture, it must be well worthwhile and worth the risks involved.'

Mayne's secret was his ability to assess the level of danger in an instant, and to make equally rapid decisions as to how to respond. He did that right now. If they tried to press home their attack, they were dead men, of that he was certain, and no warplane was worth dying for. Even as the wail of air-raid sirens echoed across the airstrip, Mayne yelled out orders. They were to scatter and get the hell out of there.

Keeping low, they 'ducked and ran for it'. Slipping through the enemy cordon, the four fugitives dashed from the airstrip, but they stumbled into a built-up area. Headlights appeared, which looked to be coming right for them. This had to be some kind of mobile search patrol. Mayne ordered his men to fling themselves down and to remain perfectly still. If they moved they were dead, for movement attracted the eye. The ground here was bare, flat and hard. It was a horrible feeling, lying in the open as the convoy ground ever closer.

When the headlamps seemed to be almost on top of them, the vehicles came to a grinding halt. Several dozen figures leapt down and began to fan out. Mayne counted four trucks, each equipped with a machinegun. By the glow of lighted cigarettes, he could see that the vehicles and their weapons were still fully manned. For a moment, he considered storming the enemy with grenades, but their sheer numbers and firepower militated against it. It would be suicide. For what felt like well over an hour they lay there, keeping perfectly still, as the soldiers probed the terrain. Then, all of a sudden one of the trucks fired up its engine. Orders were yelled out in German, the search parties doubled back to the vehicles, and the convoy pulled out.

Having not the slightest idea why the enemy had departed, Mayne and his men got moving. They could hear the distant roar of engines, as patrols hurried hither and thither. The hunt was still very much in full swing. As they made a break for it, Mayne's party got split up – Lilley and Warburton heading one way, Mayne and Storie the other. The first two crawled beneath a thick hedge. It was the only vaguely feasible hiding place they could find. Shortly, a column of six Lancia trucks rumbled to a halt. Lilley watched as they unloaded squads of troops, who began probing every inch of terrain.

Warburton whispered that they should make a run for it. Lilley retorted that he was just too damned tired. In any case, they were bound to be spotted. Shattered, Lilley actually dropped off to sleep. He awoke around first light to discover that Warburton was gone. He also realised that a pair of Italian sentries were positioned no more than a few yards away. Abandoning his kit, and moving as silently as he could, Lilley wormed his way under the hedge for a good distance, before getting to his feet, at which point he simply began to saunter away. There was no point in running or trying to hide, for that would only draw attention. It was all about bluff and front now.

Dressed only in his desert shorts and shirt, for mile after mile Lilley wandered through enemy encampments. On all sides soldiers were washing and shaving or having breakfast. Few seemed to notice him, and those who did appeared to take Lilley for either a German or an Italian. Finally, he reached the railway line, which provided a definitive navigational marker. From there he could steer a path into the Jebel. But just at that instant a young Italian soldier came bicycling by. He stopped and stared at Lilley, before crying out a challenge. Lilley sized him up, realising that the Italian was a lot younger than he was, but at least he wasn't armed. In fact, neither of them had a weapon.

A tussle ensued, which soon became a fight to the death. It ended with Lilley strangling the younger man with his bare hands. 'I can still see his white face and dark brown eyes,' Lilley would relate, while recounting this gruesome story. Placing the dead man's cap back on his head, as a mark of respect, Lilley moved off as fast as he could, making for the high ground. Finally, he reached a Senussi camp. There he was taken in and hidden. Tired beyond measure, he dropped off to sleep. A while later he was awoken, to be reunited with Mayne and Storie. They had also been taken in by the same Senussi settlement. But of Warburton there was no sign. He had simply disappeared.

As Mayne would state in his official report, the enemy had instigated a well-organised 'system of motorised patrols'. Even as he and Storie had tried to slip away, they were forced 'continually to take cover from parties which were driven about in trucks, dismounting and searching'. Security at Berca Satellite had been massively strengthened. Once again, Mayne was extremely lucky to have led two of his men to safety. Napoleon is often quoted as saying, 'Give me a lucky general rather than a brave one.' Mayne it seemed was blessed with both qualities. But tonight he had lost another of his own – Warburton, either killed or captured. And for what? They had not even managed to destroy the one warplane, or to kill a single enemy pilot.

Napoleon was also reputed to have said: 'You must not fight too often with the one enemy, or you will teach him all your art of war.' Such sentiments were starting to ring true. At Berca Satellite they'd come up against a very different set of defensive measures than those they had encountered before: widely spaced aircraft, sentries on each airframe and motorised search patrols. Moving on foot, even with surprise on their side, just didn't seem to cut it any more. Either way, at this moment there was nothing for it but to head for the rendezvous with the LRDG, and to see how the others may have fared.

Reunited with the Desert Taxi Company, they learned all. Sure enough, at Berca Main, Zirnheld's unit had been in the fight of their lives. At times, those Free French SAS had been engaged in running skirmishes with the airbase's defenders, exchanging fire at close quarters. Miraculously, only one man in their party had been hit, suffering a light flesh wound. More to the point, their score of warplanes was well into the double figures.

Stirling's party had been similarly successful. It was his third time striking Benina aerodrome, and they'd actually made it in there early. They'd taken cover on the fringes of the airbase, while Stirling gave a hushed lecture to his men – Reg Seekings and Johnny Cooper – on the art and craft of deer stalking. It had helped pass the time and to settle their nerves. Once again, it was in the hangars that they had struck gold. There, they'd discovered 'one Me 110, two Stukas, two Ju 52s' – a twin-engine fighter-bomber, two dive bombers and one of the large transport planes. They'd also stumbled upon three dozen wooden crates, each of which was packed with a brand new aero-engine.

The entire lot was laced with their sixty-odd Lewes bombs. Pulling out, Stirling did something that he would come to regret, although others on his patrol believed it was entirely justified. Coming across a guard hut, he'd booted open the door and lobbed in a first grenade, yelling out: 'Share this among you!' It came to rest beneath the ranks of beds, on which some two dozen sentries were sleeping. Near by, an officer was seated at a desk, penning a report. The blast shattered the building, and by Stirling's own account ended up 'wiping out the guard'. Later, he would describe the attack as being 'a silly show of bravado' and 'close to murder'.

His men did not agree.

As Reg Seekings made clear to Stirling, the average soldier didn't care much about equipment destroyed. There was plenty more where that came from. But a blasted hut full of dead comrades – that was sure to hit home. While Stirling remained conflicted, he would argue to another of the SAS originals, Bob Bennett, that desperate times called for desperate – and at times murderous – measures. The odds were so heavily stacked against the Allies, they had to strike the fear of God into the enemy. 'It's the only way we can win. It's against my nature to kill people, but it's got to be done.'

Needless to say, Stirling's grenading of that guard hut could equally be accused of being an 'over-callous execution in cold blood of the enemy', or of pushing 'ruthlessness to the point of callousness'. Those were the criticisms that would be levelled at Mayne by Stirling, post-war. More to the point, during his inaugural raid at Tamet, Mayne had killed pilots. Stirling had wiped out a guard force – arguably, a far less legitimate target. But Mayne would rarely if ever have a bad word to say about the SAS founder, not until his dying day.

As David Lloyd Owen had surmised, Stirling and Mayne were the perfect combination as commanders. Each complemented the other. But they were also a dangerous mix, especially when the competition between them was at its fiercest. Mayne had scored not a single hit at Berca Satellite. He'd also lost a man. And while Stirling was nowhere near his hundred-plus score of warplanes, he was creeping into double figures. When operating separately, each tended to be shrewd, calculated and cunning. But after six months of back-to-back operations they also had come to think of themselves as almost immortal and untouchable. There would be hints of that in what was to follow.

Once Stirling had finished recounting the story of his raid on Benina, he added: 'It's a bit of a change to see my fires lighting up the sky instead of yours.'

Mayne's eyes glinted. 'How many hangars did you get?'

All of them, Stirling replied. 'Ju 52s make first rate kindling. You wouldn't like to take a look at the debris?'

'Why not?' They should take a vehicle and drive back towards Benghazi, Mayne suggested. That way they could ascertain if Stirling had got all the warplanes he claimed he had. Just to be sure he wasn't exaggerating, Mayne added, with the glimmer of a smile.

Showing fear in front of a man like Mayne was worse that fear itself, as Stirling fully appreciated, agreeing it 'might be a bit of fun' to go and take a look at the carnage he and his men had caused.

This wasn't totally bravado or a schoolboy dare. Subterfuge would also be to the fore. In the aftermath of the kind of raids they had just executed, it would make sense for German officers to be shuttling back and forth, investigating. Fortunately, they had SIG stalwart Karl Kahane on hand to yell out orders in German should the need arise. Stirling's 'Blitz Buggy' would have been ideal for tonight's little jaunt. It was a cut-down Ford truck, with the sides and top removed. Painted field grey, with Afrika Korps recognition flashes stencilled along the sides, it resembled very closely a German staff car. Stirling had brought the Blitz Buggy on the present mission, but it had been damaged by a mine. As a stand-in, the LRDG offered one of their trucks. The enemy used captured Allied vehicles widely, so with Kahane in full flow they should pass muster.

Plan set, they moved out.

In the SAS War Diary, this ad hoc, spur-of-the-moment venture even got its own mission name: 'OPERATION NUMBER ELEVEN.' The participants were listed as: 'Stirling, Major Mayne [sic: he was a captain], Lilley, Storie, Cooper, Seekings and Karl, an Austrian.' As a cast of the daring and the battle-hardened, these six originals – plus Kahane – were about as good as it got. Of course, Kahane was German, not Austrian. He had served with distinction with the Kaiser's forces in the First World War, winning the Imperial German Iron Cross 2nd Class (EKII), so presumably he was no shrinking violet either.

Squat, dark featured and mostly morose, there was a solid implacability about Kahane that was somehow reassuring. Even better was his rich repertoire of obscene German swearwords – just the kind of epithets with which to harangue any troublesome Italian sentries. Kahane was forever berating his SAS comrades, too, demanding to be told what on earth there was to laugh about in this war. On tonight's little jaunt there would in truth be very little excuse for any humour, or perhaps the reverse was true. It all really depended on your way of looking at things.

The first problem was encountered on the main highway, about a mile short of Benina Main itself: a red light swinging back and forth in the middle of the road. As Stirling noted in his post operational report, it really should not have been there. 'This should not be – there should be no roadblock here.' Mayne, who was driving, pulled to a halt, as Kahane unleashed a barrage of invective at the hapless Italian guard. While he seemed inclined to swing open the barrier, to his rear was a group of heavily armed German soldiers, and the burly sergeant who stepped forward seemed distinctly unconvinced.

'We're coming from the front, haven't had a bath in weeks and we're hungry,' Kahane announced, getting his strike in early. 'So cut the formalities and let us through.'

The sergeant's face darkened. Seeing as though they were seven soldiers riding in a British vehicle and wearing British uniforms, his scepticism was perhaps understandable, and especially since the confounded British raiders had just recently grenaded as many as two dozen of his comrades to death, while they were sleeping in their beds.

'Password?' he demanded.

Kahane began to adlib now, swearing like a true German trooper. 'How the hell do we knew what the ------- password is, and don't ask for our ------- identity cards either. They're lost. We've been fighting for the last seventy hours against these ------- Tommies. Our car was destroyed, and we were lucky to capture this British truck and get back at all . . . and then you so and sos, sitting up here on your asses in Benghazi, in a nice safe job, stop us. So hurry up, get that ------- gate open!'

Still the sergeant wasn't satisfied. He stepped forward, until he was about three feet from Mayne's side of the vehicle, scrutinising the occupants. It was silent now, the atmosphere electric.

Then Mayne made his move. He slid out his Colt pistol and cocked it, the noise of a bullet being rammed into the chamber clearly audible on the still air. The angle of the barrel held in Mayne's lap meant that the first shot would nail the inquisitive sergeant. Beside Mayne, Stirling followed suit with his weapon, as others did the same in the vehicle's rear, a series of metallic clicks ringing out. By now, the sergeant had realised perfectly well who they were. But he also knew that if he challenged them, he was a dead man. Deciding discretion was the better part of valour, he cried out an order for the barrier to be raised.

Fingers on their triggers, the seven pretenders rode through, and accelerated into the darkness. 'We passed numerous parties of Germans and Italians, but we took no notice,' Stirling reported, before finally they stopped to 'blow up dumps'. OPERATION NUMBER ELEVEN had somehow morphed from being a dare, into a full-on sabotage sortie, as 'Cooper and Seekings emptied their guns into men and trucks parked outside a roadhouse . . .' It was swift, dramatic and adrenaline-fuelled, as they blasted the hell out of the enemy targets.

Mayne had a reputation for being able to drive hard and fast, but safely. They were going to need to rely on those skills now. It was a good thirty minutes since they'd crossed the checkpoint. With all the havoc they'd been causing, there would be no way back through again. Instead, Mayne pulled off the road. They were going to try to cross the Wadi Qattara, on the far side of which lay a navigable track, which would take them back to the Jebel. But the wadi was deep and treacherous and there was only one crossing point. Stirling would have to guide them to that, while Mayne drove. Even as they thundered over the rough ground, a set of headlamps stabbed through the darkness. The enemy were in pursuit, trying to cut them off.

Mayne flicked his headlamps on, the Chevy's lights lancing through the gloom. He shot ahead, and the race was on. It was far too rough for either party to fire accurately, but still the gunners in the Chevy's rear loosed off bursts of tracer, trying to blast out the chase vehicle's lights. For a time it looked as if the enemy, riding in an armoured car, were gaining ground. Mayne's response was to drive ever faster. They made the lip of the wadi just ahead of their pursuers, at which point Stirling jabbed out an arm and pointed.

'Look, just to the right!' he yelled.

There was the route leading down into the guts of the ravine.

As they edged down that steep incline, the enemy vehicle came to a halt behind them, at the rim. They'd given up the chase, no doubt fearing an ambush if they ventured into the enclosed terrain of the wadi. The climb out of the wadi and up to the heights of the Jebel proved horrendous, with everyone being thrown from side to side, but finally they made it. Stirling pulled out a flask of whisky from his pack and passed it round.

As Mayne took a nip, he remarked: 'By the way, I forgot to look at those fires in Benina. D'you want to go back?'

Stirling laughed. 'I think you'd better take my word for it.'

The drive continued. Up on the high ground the terrain was like a billiard table compared to what had gone before. Some of the men nodded off. All of a sudden there was a yell of alarm.

'Hop it, quick! A fuse is burning!' It was Storie, in the rear, and he'd detected that the punishing drive had broken one of their timer pencils, the acid triggering a fuse.

Figures vaulted free. Mayne dived from the driver's side, without even applying the brakes, as Stirling – who'd been fast asleep – leapt from the other. Moments later the truck rolled to a halt, and there was the mother of all explosions. The Chevy was obliterated. What little remained could have been loaded into 'a haversack', as Lilley described it. The last to spring free, he'd only just managed to get clear of the truck before it blew itself to pieces.

For a few seconds seven very fortunate raiders stared at the smoking wreckage in a stunned silence, before they burst out laughing. Only, there was one exception: Karl Kahane. He eyed the others as if they were completely insane. 'To laugh at things like this!' he exclaimed. 'I am too old!' Then he added that the German military had always had a poor opinion of the British Army, one that he had tended to share. But after what he had just witnessed, he was convinced that the Axis could never win, for they would never be able to laugh like this in the face of death.

*

Stirling had promised to bring that LRDG vehicle back in one piece. Of course, he had failed to do so and in spectacular fashion. Even so, as was their wont, the LRDG spirited him and his raiders back to Siwa, safe and sound. Decent and reliable as ever, they even managed to tow Stirling's damaged Blitz Buggy with them the four hundred or so miles. At Siwa, the true impact and the wider ramifications of the recent raids would become clear.

Of the two relief convoys that had set sail for Malta, both had been intensively bombed. One had been forced to turn back. But a pair of heavily laden merchant ships had successfully run the gauntlet, the supplies they delivered being enough to see Malta through the worst. All told, the SAS and its sister units – the Free French SAS, SIG, LRDG and the SBS – had accounted for well in excess of one hundred warplanes destroyed on the ground. Stirling was convinced that if those aircraft had been able to take to the skies, none of those ships would have made it through.

But the price paid by the raiders had been high – both in lives, and, perhaps more worryingly, in terms of secrets betrayed. Even as the main SAS parties had headed west across the Sahara, so another group of raiders had set sail aboard the submarine, HMS *Triton*, bound for the German-occupied island of Crete, situated in the Mediterranean due east of Malta. There, they had executed a series of daring raids. At Kastelli Airbase, a three-man party led by Captain Duncan – the Litani River raider-cum-poet – had blown to pieces seven German warplanes, hundreds of 60-gallon drums of fuel, six vehicles, plus three bomb dumps. For his 'courage, resourcefulness and good leadership' during that mission, Duncan would be awarded his first MC.

If anything, the sister raid at Heraklion airbase was even more successful. There, a five-strong party – four of whom were Free French SAS – had accounted for as many as seventy German warplanes damaged or destroyed. But during the escape and evasion, all but one of the party were captured or killed. Surrounded by the enemy, they'd fought to the last grenade and the last round. French SAS commander Georges Bergé was among those taken captive. Pierre Leostic, who had taken Johnny Cooper's place as 'The Kid' in the SAS due to his extreme youth, was killed. Like Cooper, Leostic had lied about his age, being just sixteen when he'd joined up.

The Cretan villagers had also paid a terrible price, as the Germans wrought savage reprisals. The one man to escape from the Heraklion raid was Captain George Jellicoe, 2nd Earl Jellicoe, himself only a recent recruit to the SAS. For his role in the mission – 'his cool and resolute leadership, skill and courage' – he would be awarded the DSO. Some sixty-two Cretan villagers would be executed by the Germans, in what can only be described as brutal revenge killings. Jellicoe would never forget, and he would be haunted by their loss for the rest of his days.

But by far the worst in terms of casualties – *and fallout* – were the SIG/Free French SAS raids on Derna and Martuba airfields. Brueckner, the German soldier turned SIG operative, had volunteered to drive the truck carrying the raiders to Derna airfield. On reaching the outskirts of the base, he'd claimed the motor had conked out and that he needed to fetch some tools. Instead, he'd called the German guards. As the truck was surrounded, one of the SIG pulled the pin on a grenade, and the massive load of weaponry and explosives it was carrying was blown to smithereens, along with most of the raiders. Incredibly, one of those injured in the blast still managed to clamber aboard an Me 110, which he blew up with a grenade.

Of the few raiders who got away all were recaptured, bar Augustin Jordan, the dapper deputy to Bergé. At Martuba Airbase, the Germans were likewise waiting, primed by Brueckner. In a series of firefights, all the raiders were likewise captured or killed. By the time Jordan had made it back to Siwa, he looked 'shrunken and disconsolate'. Fourteen Free French SAS were dead or taken captive, and only he had escaped. But there would be precious little time to grieve for his fallen comrades. With Bergé taken prisoner on Heraklion, Jordan would now have to assume command of the Free French who had survived.

The SIG had given themselves a nickname, one replete with dark irony: the *Himmelfarhts* – the Heaven Platoon. Sadly, and for all the wrong reasons – chiefly Brueckner's treachery – for many, that was exactly what had come to pass. Brueckner, meanwhile, was flown to Berlin and feted, being given the War Order of the German Cross in Gold, one of Nazi Germany's highest awards, supposedly given for repeated acts of bravery. Brueckner's record, and what it revealed, was brought to Hitler's personal attention. The very concept of German citizens fighting for the Allies and against the Reich, infuriated the Führer. His reaction was swift and telling.

A 'Most Secret' order was dispatched to General Erwin Rommel. In it, Hitler outlined what he knew of the SIG, ordering that 'the severest measures are to be taken against those concerned. They are therefore to be mercilessly wiped out in battle, and in cases where they escape being killed in battle . . . they are to be shot out of hand.' This was the first of a series of such orders issued by Hitler, of which the SAS and related special forces units were soon to be likewise the beneficiaries.

But worst of all for Stirling, Mayne and all who were gathered at Siwa, was what Brueckner's betrayal had to signify. He was truly the enemy within. For weeks he had trained alongside them, seemingly befriended them, eaten in their canteen and caroused with them at the Kabrit bar. What was there about SAS operations that Brueckner didn't know, and that he wouldn't now tell? He knew their names, their ranks and their roles; their physical descriptions; he knew their modus operandi, their ethos and their *esprit de corps*. He knew their routes, their hideouts and their means of lying low. He knew their strengths, but also he had come to know their weaknesses.

The ramifications were chilling.

The return to Siwa was also a bittersweet moment for another reason entirely. While the grand total of warplanes destroyed in those June raids was just shy of 150, saving Malta seemed to have made not a jot of difference to General Rommel or his fortunes. In another lightning move, codenamed *Unternehmen Sonnenblume* – Operation Sunflower – Rommel's forces had thrust forward once more, throwing the Eighth Army back across the Egyptian border to a new defensive line at El Alamein. Right now his armoured legions were massed barely 150 miles to the west of Cairo, and the LRDG were preparing to do as they had done previously, at Jalo oasis, abandoning Siwa to the enemy.

As even the newspapers in Britain heralded 'Rommel's brilliant generalship, his boldness and resilience, his tactical cunning', panic spread. With the enemy poised to seize Cairo, nervous officials began burning secret documents, the ash from which rained down upon the city. If Cairo fell, the Nile Basin and the Suez Canal would follow. Suez provided a comparatively short sea route for the transport of Middle Eastern oil to fuel Britain's ships, tanks and warplanes. It offered a crucial link to Britain's far-flung colonies – India, Australia, New Zealand and more. If Suez were lost, supplies of men, raw materials and fuel would have to be routed via South Africa and the Atlantic, a far longer route that was vulnerable to U-boat attacks. The Allied line at El Alamein simply had to hold and Rommel's hitherto lightning advances had to be thrown into reverse.

Stirling, Mayne et al. had returned to Siwa in the third week of June 1942. On the 21st of that month there was a further body blow, as Rommel took Tobruk. The news was shattering. Winston Churchill was in Washington, meeting US president Roosevelt to plan for the first major Allied landings of the war. Instead, via a telegram from London, he received the devastating news. 'Tobruk has surrendered, with twenty-five thousand men taken prisoners.' (In fact, some 33,000 Allied troops had been captured.) Churchill refused to believe it. He demanded to speak to London, only to learn it was all true. 'I did not attempt to hide from the President the shock I had received,' he would write. 'It was a bitter moment. Defeat was one thing; disgrace is another.'

By the time the SAS had evacuated Siwa and made it back to Kabrit, the mood was dark indeed. During seventy-two hours of concerted raiding operations, they had destroyed huge amounts of enemy war materiel. In many ways, this was the most successful the SAS – and sister units – had ever been. It was their high point. But at the same time, the Allies had reached their lowest ebb. In seizing Tobruk, Rommel had truly crowned his triumphs.

On the day after Tobruk's fall, he issued the following Order of the Day to his troops: 'Soldiers! The great battle . . . has been crowned by your quick conquest of Tobruk. We have taken in all over 45,000 prisoners and destroyed or captured more than 1,000 fighting vehicles and nearly 400 guns . . . you have, through your incomparable courage and tenacity dealt the enemy blow upon blow . . . We will not rest until we have shattered the last remnants of the British Eighth Army.'

In Parliament, Churchill faced a no-confidence vote. He defeated it, but still it spoke volumes. Here at Kabrit, no one – neither Stirling, Mayne, nor anyone – was about to face the same from their men. But the mood was the blackest it had ever been since the very low point in the unit's fortunes – the terrible aftermath of Operation Squatter. The Royal Navy began to evacuate, and their warships could be seen steaming down the Bitter Lakes, south towards Suez and relative safety. There was something so deeply symbolic in the ranks of cruisers, destroyers and transport ships moving slowly out of sight. From the beach at the Rest Camp, disconsolate figures waved farewell. From the decks of the passing warships, sailors waved back. The roads were likewise clogged with columns of traffic bearing evacuees.

To those few who were left behind if felt as if they were being abandoned. There were reports of airborne operations being mooted by German forces; of a sudden leap forwards that would wrestle Egypt from the British by daring and by front. In truth, Rommel had laid plans for just such a series of manoeuvres. Even as his forces punched hard into the Eighth Army's frontline positions, so he was preparing to catapult forward his airborne legions in a 'lightning attack' on the bridges spanning the Nile, around Cairo and Alexandria. Cannily, his aim was to strike a crushing blow against British morale, once the troops heard that 'the Germans have reached the Nile.'

At Kabrit, and with their backs to the wall, the SAS wondered – what now? Where did the SAS go from here? How were they to strike back against a seemingly omnipotent foe? If North Africa was lost, what role remained for such a unit as theirs? They were desert raiders. The pirates of the open, empty wastes. They had been formed for this theatre, this kind of terrain and this kind of warfare. If North Africa were lost, did that spell an end to their war, or at least to their unique way of waging war?

Yet in truth, the darkest hour was just before the dawn.

CHAPTER EIGHTEEN

Good Killing

Despite his bullish tones, as Rommel knew well, when waging war in North Africa supply lines were all. While sounding triumphant in public, writing in his diary he acknowledged privately what terrible challenges his army faced in terms of supplies. In truth, following his precipitate advance all of his war materiel had to be transported over as much as 1,400 miles of desert. As he acknowledged in a letter to his wife, they faced some 'extremely critical days. But I am hoping to see them through.'

If Auchinleck and the SAS had their way, he would not.

Of anyone, the seasoned British general seemed least discomfited by the German commander's gains. He believed Rommel had over-extended himself. Now was the time for the counter-strike. For every day of operations, the German general required 1,500 tonnes of supplies, including fuel, ammo, food and water rations. It was an impossible burden, and would be made even more so if the SAS could smash his supply convoys and his airbases, striking time after time, remorselessly. That is exactly what Auchinleck charged his desert raiders to do. If successful, it would have the added benefit of shattering the enemy's morale.

Key to Stirling and Mayne's ability to hit far and hard, *and by surprise*, would be mobility and speed. As all appreciated, they needed to change the means and thrust of their attacks. Of recent, Rommel's defences had proven hard to defeat, but not if they could find some means of approach that was wholly unexpected. It was this that brought the Willys 'Bantam' jeep firmly into the SAS fold. With its reputation for toughness, rock-solid reliability, fantastic off-road performance, plus its versatility, the teaming up of the American-made 4x4 with the desert raiders would prove inspired; a marriage made in heaven.

Come the summer of 1942, Stirling and Mayne were determined to go to war on their own terms. Rommel had very long and vulnerable supply lines. The Willys jeep had a very long and durable reach. There was one other key factor at play here. The Desert Taxi Company were growing tired of their ferrying duties. Meeting the demands of the SAS, the ISLD and others had stretched the resources of the LRDG painfully thin. To better enable the SAS to strike out alone, they released Mike Sadler, their ace navigator, so he could join the ranks of Stirling's raiders. Fittingly, the French SAS would nickname Sadler '*le Sinbad du sable*' – Sinbad of the Sand. Over the coming months his navigational skills would prove indispensable.

In the SAS War Diary there were pasted two photos, as if in a scrapbook. One was captioned: 'Willy's Bantams jeep before conversion.' It showed a bog-standard vehicle devoid of any modifications. The other was captioned: 'Willy's Bantams jeep after S.A.S. had finished with it.' It showed an altogether different vehicle – one draped at every conceivable point with jerrycans, baggage, sacking, shovels, camouflage netting, and absolutely bristling with weaponry. Mounted on the driver's side was a single Vickers-K medium machinegun, while on the passenger side sat the far larger bulk of a Browning heavy machinegun, and bolted to the rear was a twin-Vickers-K, with the pan-fed weapons arranged side-by-side on the one pivot.

While the complement of guns and the positioning could differ, the must-have weapon was the Vickers-K. Few SAS jeeps ever went to war without one or more of those welded to their frames.

Designed as a .303-inch weapon for use in aircraft, its extremely rapid rate of fire – up to 1,200 rounds per minute – was deliberate, due to the short-lived periods that warplanes tended to engage in aerial combat. Needing to strike fast, and seeking to cause maximum damage, before melting away again just as quickly, the SAS would find the Vickers-K perfect for their needs, too.

At their Kabrit base, Gentleman Jim Almonds – the SAS's self-confessed 'bogus engineer' – turned his skills to a new challenge, that of arming their jeeps for war. From a bunch of scrapped Gloster Gladiator biplanes Stirling had got hold of a job lot of Vickers-Ks. Over the space of a few days Almonds, plus a team of helpers, beavered away, fitting the weaponry and test-driving and test-firing. Armour plating scavenged from wrecked Hurricanes was added, plus racks to load on kit and gear. The suspension was reinforced, to deal with the extra weight the jeeps would need to carry, and finally a bespoke paint-job was added, one inspired by the LRDG's pastel shades – pinks, yellows and greens. When the first jeep so adapted was driven into the desert, it disappeared almost completely when viewed from afar.

In recent days, Churchill had wired Cairo HQ: 'Everybody in uniform must fight exactly as they would were Kent or Sussex invaded . . . No general evacuation, no playing for safety . . . Egypt must be held at all costs . . .' The SAS were ready to play their part. Their force now stood one hundred-strong: fresh recruits were drawn to the stories they'd heard whispered in Cairo bars of wild panache and derring-do. They had fifteen jeeps kitted out for war, augmented by a fleet of twenty supply trucks. When they left Kabrit, this would be no passing foray. They were heading into the desert loaded to the gunwales and for the duration. Auchinleck had briefed Stirling on exactly which airbases and supply lines he most wanted hit. They aimed to camp in the depths of the wilderness, and to strike repeatedly until all had been thoroughly laid waste.

Thirty-five vehicles formed up in line, groaning under their loads. The convoy set forth, heading almost due east and striking out for a specific point where they hoped to slip through. The fault-line – where the Allied and Axis forces faced each other with blood, guts and steel – was no more than twenty miles across, stretching from the coastline and El Alamein in the north, south to the Qattara Depression, a vast sunken wasteland of salt marshes and treacherous, boggy sands. Stirling and Mayne's aim was to sneak past the southern extremity of the enemy's lines, where Rommel's forces bled into the heat and dust and the flyblown wastes of the Qattara Depression.

There was said to be a path – the Palm Leaf track – that snaked along the very lip of the Qattara Depression, hugging its contours for the best part of 150 miles. Follow that, and they would be well beyond the enemy's frontline positions by the time they swung north, to strike at their targets. They'd first heard about this ancient, little-known route from the LRDG. Sadler – the Sinbad of the Sand – was said to know the way. In fact, many of the means by which they'd modified their jeeps for desert warfare – their extra fuel tanks, the water condenser fitted in front of the radiator grill, to recycle the precious liquid – were based upon their 'experiences with the L.R.D.G.'.

As ever, imitation was the sincerest form of flattery.

They hit the Palm Leaf track just before first light on 5 July 1942. To their right stretched a chequerboard of burned and blackened debris – the mangled and twisted ruins of war. Both sides had tried to gain ground here. Neither had found a means to blast through. To their left, the terrain slumped in a series of knife-cut steps of rock, plunging several hundred feet to hidden depths, which were obscured in a dull, pinkish, sickly haze. They pushed on, moving swiftly, for the deadline for their attacks was but forty-eight hours away. Stirling had promised to strike on the night of 7/8 July, for it was then that Auchinleck planned the first of a series of counter-attacks.

The column of jeeps and trucks became strung out over several miles, obscured within a haze of dust thrown up by their passing. The heat clawed up from the depths of the Depression, rising from its floor and its rock walls in pulsating waves. Men stripped to their shorts. Some tied lengths of cloth around their heads, to try to keep out dust and sand. Others wore LRDG-style *keffiyehs*, a sand-coloured scarf draped over head and shoulders, with a cord wound around the top to keep it secure. It shaded head and neck from the burning sun, while allowing cooling air to circulate. By mid-afternoon, when the heat was at its most stifling, they reached the end of the Palm Leaf track, and swung north. Less than a hundred miles away lay the coastline and their targets.

If all went to plan, there would be several separate strikes. Jellicoe and Zirnheld would be in one party, hitting the main highway around El Daba, which lay just twenty miles short of the frontline. As a bonus, they hoped to find Rommel himself in residence, for rumour had it that was where the German general had made his new headquarters. By sheer luck they hoped that they might 'catch' him. By catch, they didn't so much intend to capture Rommel, as to nail him in a hail of Vickers-K fire. To the far west, another party would hit the Sidi Barani airfield. In between would be several more strikes, with bang in the centre Fuka Aerodrome, the objective of a force led by the redoubtable Bill Fraser.

As for Stirling and Mayne, arguably they had saved the best, or at least the most symbolic and poignant, for themselves. They were teaming up to hit none other than Bagoush Airfield, the very same base from which they had set out nine months earlier on their disastrous first mission, Operation Squatter. The bitter irony was not lost on anyone, least of all Mayne. They would be riding in three jeeps, plus Stirling's Blitz Buggy – fully repaired, after hitting the mine on their previous mission – and stalwarts Johnny Cooper and Jimmie Storie would be among the six making up their party.

The way ahead lay through territory that was crawling with the enemy, and the jeeps' guns were fully armed for war. The Vickers-K drum magazines – each holding about a hundred rounds – were packed with mixed standard, tracer and Buckingham incendiary rounds, a copper-nickel alloy casing packed with phosphorus and aluminium powder. At anything up to 500 yards range, if a vehicle's fuel tank or its munitions were struck by such an incendiary round, that would light it up very nicely.

As they approached their desert rendezvous – the place at which all would muster following the raids – the terrain became punishing, with sharp, switchback ridges interspersed with loose, jagged rocks which ripped and tore at tyres. Progress was down to a crawl – no more than five miles per hour. Upon reaching the RV, just west of Bir Chalder – an ancient water-hole lying some twenty miles inland – they set about their final preparations, cleaning weapons of caked-on dust and dirt, oiling their working parts, repairing punctures, servicing the jeeps and replenishing supplies.

There was an unusual recruit among their number for the present mission. The SAS had got its first ever medic assigned to its ranks, and he'd made up first aid kits for each man. 'This ought to fix us, Doc!' was the typical response, as he handed out his carefully wrapped parcels. Strictly speaking, Dr Malcolm James Pleydell was here to save lives, and not to take them, and in a sense that gave him a unique perspective on things. A natural observer of the human condition, from the very day of his arrival at Kabrit he'd been fascinated by this unit and by those who made up its number.

With Stirling, he noted, there was the subtle power of the arch persuader. Pleydell watched him wander among the men now, dispensing his magic: encouraging, listening, hearing what each had to say, and making every individual feel special. It was a gift. Rarely forceful – he didn't need to be – there was an 'almost magnetic quality' about Stirling's under-spoken charm'. Within a few minutes he could persuade just about anyone that night was actually day, and that what he was about to do was far more important than anything even the most senior ranks in the Army might ever undertake; that they were the chosen few.

Stirling decided to give an address to the men, but he rarely went in for any kind of a stiff, formal pep talk. He knew far better. First he reminded them of the importance of the coming raids, before adding that if they were attacked on the way in, they still had to press on and attack those airfields. 'Remember that! Nobody turns back.' Having made such a dramatic pronounce- ment, Stirling paused, tapped out his pipe on his boot – he was often to be seen with it inserted the wrong way up, unlit, as a kind of a prop – and gave a flash of his quick, shy smile. 'It will be all right,' he added reassuringly.

By now, Pleydell had perceived that there was a core of cold steel that lurked beneath Stirling's quiet, avuncular exterior. When operating with a contingent of Free French SAS, Stirling had been blasting away at a force of Italians, before turning to his French companions and remarking, affably: 'I like shooting these Italians, don't you?' The French were nonplussed. Stirling, they'd decided, was a 'funny one'. They had explained as much to Pleydell. On the one hand he could look so 'gentle and so kind', but equally there was the heart of a killer that lurked within.

Pleydell's prior form made him peculiarly suited to joining the ranks of the SAS, albeit in non-combatant role (well, sort of, as matters would transpire). His parent unit was the Royal Army Medical Corps (RAMC), and as with so many who made up the SAS his first experiences of the war had been in the June 1940 defence of France. In his mid-twenties, Pleydell had been serving as a ship's doctor, even as the makeshift fleet had sought to evacuate some 300,000 Allied troops from the war-torn beaches. Blood, injury, death, defeat – that had been Pleydell's first taste of the conflict that had engulfed Europe.

He'd been serving on a pleasure steamer, and as they'd neared

Dunkirk the beaches were thick with 'ant-like clusters of men', surging to and from the water's edge as they tried to find safe passage to Britain. Even as they'd headed in to help, a flight of four Stuka dive-bombers had pounced from the skies. The steamer, straddled with bombs, was blasted out of the water, her screws 'racing in the air'. They'd made the quay regardless, the first wounded soldier being loaded aboard appearing like a 'rag doll'. He had been blinded, and his head was swaddled in blood-soaked bandages.

Eventually, Pleydell had a thousand injured men crammed 'like sardines' into the ship's dining salon. The air was thick with the 'smell of stale sweat, dried blood and septic wounds'. As Pleyedell stepped between the mass of stretchers trying to decide who to treat first, the steamer, which had turned around and was motoring back towards Dover, suffered a head-on collision with a British destroyer. The impact threw all – wounded men, the dying and the medics – into a 'jumbled heap'. In the chaos and confusion, the two ships resembled black silhouettes like 'monsters locked in combat'. Eventually, the vessels had managed to prise themselves apart to the sound of ripping metal.

Luckily, the steamer had been holed above the waterline, so it was able to limp into port. But Pleydell remained haunted by those memories. For him, Dunkirk had never really ended and the mental scars endured. Months later, he still suffered flashbacks, 'my pulse racing, and my hands slippery with sweat'. Even so, he'd deployed to North Africa with the Coldstream Guards for the early desert campaigns. In the spring of 1942 he'd not only served on frontline operations, but had volunteered for missions designed to puncture through Rommel's defences, putting himself in the thick of the action. He'd kept a diary of his months at war, one entry capturing the essence of the close shaves he'd experienced while under fire.

'Shells flying around the trucks,' he noted. With German forces racing to outflank them, and shells and small-arms fire raining down, Pleydell's column 'zig-zagged away' in a desperate effort to escape the trap. 'Thought my last time of freedom had come . . . position seemed hopeless . . . Dusk came to our rescue . . . Moved through German lines . . . Very frightening day . . . Seemed certain we were going to be put in the bag [captured].' At one stage his medical truck was shot to pieces, with all of his first aid equipment inside it. There was a ragged hole ripped through his jacket from a lump of shrapnel, which was the closest Pleydell had come to 'a direct hit'.

What had triggered Pleydell's June 1942 volunteering for the SAS – a 'hush-hush' unit of which he knew very little – was his mounting sense of frustration. Ordered back from such daring frontline medical service, Pleydell found himself appointed as a General Duties Officer in a local military hospital, by his own account becoming a glorified pen-pusher, form-filler, memo-writer and something of a matron's pet. He'd hated it. Bored, thwarted and dying a slow death from the tedium of it all, he'd decided to volunteer for something 'new and so entirely uncertain'.

There was a certain eccentricity to Pleydell that made him a fine fit for Stirling's raiders. When serving with the Coldstream Guards, he'd transformed his Regimental Aid Post into something of a zoo. Observing how the seemingly empty desert was actually teeming with life, he'd adopted a brood of chameleons. He'd named them after Churchill and his family, for in Pleydell's view the shape-shifting lizards demonstrated the kind of Churchillian traits that typified Britain's wartime leader. 'With lower jaw thrust forward . . . they pursued their prey, and nothing, it seemed, could alter their purpose . . .'

The Churchill family had been joined by various desert insects, plus a wounded tern – a slimmer, more graceful seabird than the common gull. She had been brought to Pleydell's clinic by some soldiers, who'd found her with a broken wing. They'd decided to name her 'Mrs Hazledene', after a well-known London nightclub hostess, for she was neither shy nor backwards, being 'as bold as brass'. Sadly, Mrs Hazledene hadn't survived, no matter what cures Pleydell had attempted. Shortly after her demise, he'd volunteered for special duties and had been dispatched to Kabrit.

Upon reaching Stirling's Rest Camp, Pleydell had been taken to see the man himself. Attempting to whip up some kind of a smart salute, he'd announced: 'Captain Pleydell, reporting for duty!'

Stirling had seemed utterly nonplussed. Eventually, from somewhere he'd dredged forth a sense of a memory; of recognition. 'Ah, *you're* Pleydell.' Apparently, Earl Jellicoe had recommended Pleydell, which as far as Stirling was concerned was as good an imprimatur as any. Exclaiming how 'marvellous' it would be to have a dedicated doctor on the team, and what a 'real luxury' it constituted, he'd invited Pleydell for drinks in the mess and a spot of lunch.

Over the next few days Pleydell had got a sense of just what kind of a unit he had joined. At first he'd refused to believe it: it was like 'something out of one of those absurd thrillers'. Inevitably, inexorably, he'd found himself drawn to one individual – Mayne. On one of his first evenings in the Kabrit mess he'd studied the legendary figure, whose wings and DSO ribbon alone spoke volumes. Seated at the bar, drinking and smoking, Mayne seemed uncannily quiet. There was little of the clever, witty, showy repartee of some of the others. No. Pleydell was most struck by the strangely unsettling peace of the man. His quietude.

Mayne was obviously hugely popular, and he missed not a thing. Nothing escaped his notice. Oddly, there was something about this first encounter of the quiet observer, Pleydell, watching the quiet observer, Mayne. Like two sides of a coin; or glancing in a mirror. Both men were well read, erudite, cultured. Both were drawn to the tough, hard pursuits of boxing and rugby (Pleydell was a dab hand at both). When a bout of mess rugby broke out in the bar,

Pleydell saw Mayne come alive. So did he, for he loved a good dose of rough-housing. In a sense, they were kindred spirits – '*le grand tueur*'; the Great Killer, Mayne, and the Great Healer, Pleydell. In time they would become firm friends, and remain so long after their shared experiences of the war came to an end.

With his eccentricities, Pleydell felt very much at home. This was a unit that rejoiced in them. Stirling, its figurehead, set the benchmark. Earl Jellicoe followed a close second. Then there was Bill Fraser, who liked to attend the bar resplendent in his Scottish kilt and MC ribbon, and with his dog, Withers, a dachshund – a 'sausage dog'; what else? – dressed in a Royal Navy coatee (a ceremonial tunic), following him everywhere, with its 'deep and very soulful eyes'. The convivial, free-flowing atmosphere reminded Pleydell of the classic bar-room notice, 'Abandon rank all ye who enter here.' His observations were prescient. That, of course, was one of the founding principles of the SAS: merit above rank.

In Stirling, Pleydell figured they had the ideal meritocratic, empowering leader. He'd expected to encounter an archetypal tough – a stereotype in fact of a *Boy's Own* commando. As a non-combatant and a doctor with no battle experience, he'd feared getting poo-pooed. Not a bit of it. Not a hint of the 'mind-you-toe-the-line' kind of attitude. No one for one moment stood upon rank or ceremony here. It was all so inspiring – so much so that Pleydell had volunteered for parachute training right away, and against his better nature. How could he not want to join their exalted throng?

Writing home in June 1942, he assured his then sweetheart and future wife – they would marry in 1945 – that she shouldn't be concerned about his parachute training, for it was 'as safe as houses these days, and absolutely fool-proof'. Life at Kabrit sounded 'pretty good fun', Pleydell added, and he looked forward to being 'fitter than I have been for a very long time'.

For a good while Pleydell hadn't gone out on raids. He'd chatted to Mayne before he'd left on one – the mission to break the

Malta siege – wishing him good luck, to which Mayne had replied matter-of-factly that he hoped for some 'good killing'. Pleydell had wandered back to his tent, feeling a tad unwarlike and weak-kneed. Could he ever imagine some 'good killing', he'd wondered? Thinking it over, he'd decided if his job was to kill, then 'I dare say I would have enjoyed it as well as anyone.' Shortly, he would hunger to have that opportunity – to take life, not to save it. There would be moments when he downed his medical kit and went stalking the enemy with a gun.

There was another aspect of Mayne's character that Pleydell would come to value, as they mustered their forces at Bir Chalder; what set him apart from the others. 'This sort of fighting was in his blood: he thrived on it.' For Mayne, in modern warfare there could be no half-measures. When facing the Panzerarmee Afrika, the days of noblesse oblige and the Knights of King Arthur were long gone. No quarter would be asked for, and none would be given. This was war, and war was all about killing.

As Pleydell saw it, Mayne was blessed with an innate, natural cunning in battle, which was life-saving as far as those who served alongside him were concerned. It might well prove fatal to the enemy, but for Mayne and his fellows it invariably got them in and out of an otherwise deadly situation . . . unscathed. Hugely perceptive, Pleydell would pen a compelling memoir of his time with the SAS, *Born of The Desert*. Written prior to war's end when he was hospitalised, he observed of Mayne: 'A friend's death meant [taking] so many enemy lives in a form of personal revenge, a wiping of the debt as it were.'

Pleydell had his own worries, and especially about Stirling. He'd tried to get the SAS commander to start taking his own health just a tad more seriously. He'd noticed that the SAS commander had a broken wrist – a fractured scaphoid; damage to the bone just below the thumb. It had been X-rayed and put in plaster, but finding the arrangement tiresome Stirling had sliced it off with a pair of scissors. Pleydell had told him it needed to go back into a cast, or it wouldn't heal. Stirling had countered that was impossible, for he couldn't do anything with his arm mummified in one of Pleydell's casts. In other words, it would curtail his ability to wage war.

Then there were the desert sores, which were becoming seriously debilitating. Infected, they could render the blood septic – triggering septicaemia, which could kill. There were those among Stirling's raiders who would die of just such complications – desert sores turning septic. Plus there were the painful, inflamed eyes – desert conjunctivitis – about which he refused to do much at all. Pleydell could understand why Stirling was so driven. He appreciated the need for urgent action. But it made precious little sense for the SAS commander and founder to flog himself to death.

Yet Stirling would not be told, and seemed hellbent on being the author of his own demise.

CHAPTER NINETEEN

We Are the Pilgrims

Jellicoe and Zirnheld's patrol was the first to set out from their Bir Chalder redoubt, leaving a funereal pall of dust hanging in their wake. Shortly, Stirling and Mayne's party, plus Fraser's – with Pleydell among his number – set forth. No sooner were they under way than there was the yell of: 'Aircraft!' The raiders dived for cover as a pair of Me 110s flashed across the horizon.

Once they had slipped from view, all emerged from hiding. Pleydell made his way across to Mayne, who was sheltering beside his jeep. 'D'you think they saw us?' he queried, uncertainly.

Mayne gazed at the medic for a second, before shaking his head. 'Och, no, I doubt it.'

Where Mayne hailed from, the 'och' was pronounced less with a Scottish burr in the throat, and more with an Irish roll of the tongue, and not uncommonly 'hammed up' a little, especially if talking to an English officer that one wished to twist a little.

Pleydell was about to leave, figuring Mayne was done talking, when the Irishman launched into a detailed, and surprisingly solicitous explanation of exactly why Pleydell should take cover whenever aircraft were in the air. Ideally, he should get well away from any vehicles and into the shade of a boulder or a bush. Absolutely key was to remain perfectly still. Movement gave you away. The danger of being seen was two-fold. One, the aircraft might attack. Two, they might report the patrol's presence, at

246

which point 'the fat would be in the fire with a vengeance.' The secret was to remain unseen. While they were fighting patrols, the aim – counter-intuitively – was *not* to fight. It was to cause maximum fear, chaos and carnage, but to slip away before battle was joined.

The convoy got under way again. As the day wore on the column had to skirt enemy encampments and dodge a distant patrol, plus they seemed to have picked up a mysterious tail of unidentified vehicles. But with the onset of dusk, all seemed to settle into empty quiet and darkness. They reached the edge of the Jebel, where the rocky ridge plummeted to the coastal plain. This was the parting of the ways – Stirling and Mayne's party in one direction, Fraser's in the other, taking Pleydell with him.

The racket made by the jeeps' descent sounded earth-shattering, and it was inconceivable that the enemy wouldn't detect their presence. With engines whining and gears crunching, even the four-wheel-drive jeeps found themselves losing grip on the loose scree, and careening downslope in an avalanche of rocky debris. As if to confirm that the enemy knew what was coming, guns below barked fire. Oddly, considering that they were descending from on high, the gunners were shooting off in low, looping trajectories, spurts of tracer licking in slow, lazy arcs across the airstrips. Then, for no obvious reason the firing ceased.

With Mayne leading, the Bagoush raiding party bumped its way onto the main coastal highway. According to the mission report for this, 'OPERATION NUMBER TWELVE', their convoy consisted of '1 cut-down Staff Car [the Blitz Buggy], 3 jeeps.' Off-road the going had proved murderous, with their vehicles suffering several punctures and even a burst radiator. They'd made eight miles in three hours, at which rate they'd never have reached the target in time – hence the decision to take to the main road.

They checked their bearings: Bagoush lay ten miles further west. Stirling figured they should divide forces. While Mayne hit the airbase itself, he would set a roadblock and shoot up any passing traffic. Plan set, they motored west with headlamps full on, acting as if they had every right to be there. To either side stretched a void of blackness. Not a glimmer of light showed in any direction, not even a camp fire. They could smell the sea, which lay a half a mile to their right. Otherwise, all was lifeless. After twenty minutes they pulled off the road. The airbase was a mile further on, and those raiding it would push forward from here on foot.

Mayne, plus Jimmie Storie – the former roof-tiler who'd left school at fourteen – plus two others, slipped away into the night. Once they were gone, Stirling got busy setting up his roadblock. With Cooper's help, he manhandled some boulders downslope and on to the road. That done, they settled into the shadows on either side of the highway, guns primed. Stirling had been briefed that on this stretch of road heavy enemy traffic was to be expected. But it was devoid of movement in either direction. Not for the first time, their intelligence seemed to be way off the mark.

An hour passed. It was 0115 on 8 July, and by rights Mayne's fireworks should have started long ago. Twenty minutes crawled by, and still not a single explosion from the direction of Bagoush, or a burst of fire. Nor was there any sign of life on the road. Just as they were wondering what on earth could have happened to Mayne and his party, a jet of flame leapt skywards, followed an instant later by the boom of a powerful detonation.

Those waiting at the roadside practically cheered. 'There they go!' Cooper exclaimed. 'Now we can sit back and count.'

They did just that, noting twenty-one further blasts, by the end of which the entire length and breadth of Bagoush airbase seemed to be awash with flame. Despite the utter carnage Mayne appeared to have wrought, there didn't seem to be a sniff of any answering fire. It was odd. Decidedly odd. Worryingly so, even.

In truth, despite their successes, Mayne and his men were burning up with anger and frustration. Some bright spark had thought of an innovation to 'save time' on tonight's raids. He'd inserted the fuses into their stock of Lewes bombs some twenty-four hours earlier, calculating that this would give the raiders less to do on target, as they went about their deadly work. But in the interim, the cold desert night air had seeped into the charges, and damp had got into the detonators. While Mayne and his men had planted forty bombs around Bagoush, just under half had failed to detonate.

'Had to leave about twenty aircraft sitting there,' Mayne fumed. 'It's tragic.'

It was doubly frustrating, considering the challenges they'd experienced getting in among those warplanes. The first six charges had been laid without too much trouble, but as they pushed across the airstrip towards a distant rank of planes, sentries were visible on all sides. Mayne took one man with him, in an effort to slip through undetected, leaving the others to give cover. But finding the far side of the airbase to be intensively patrolled, the confrontation between target-hungry raiders and sentries had descended into one of bloody combat at close quarters.

Pulling out, Mayne had reckoned they'd left forty warplanes strung with Lewes bombs. It was a fine haul, and so absolutely fitting for Bagoush, the airbase from which Eoin McGonigal and his party had taken flight, never to be seen again. Mayne hungered for vengeance, and his friend's mystery fate was very far from forgotten. Let Bagoush burn . . . But as he and his men had ticked off the detonations, around half their charges seemed to have failed. While the airfield was thick with figures rushing back and forth trying to douse the fires, there were ranks of warplanes that remained unharmed.

By the time he was back with Stirling, Mayne was seething. 'Damn,' he cursed. 'We did forty aircraft. Some of the primers must have been damp.'

They checked one of the unused Lewes bombs. Sure enough,

moisture had got into the fuse. More haste, less speed was the lesson to be learned, but it was a galling one. At Bagoush, those warplanes had been very closely guarded. There had been sentries at every turn. Mayne figured they were fortunate as hell to have got in and out unscathed. No way did he fancy trying their luck, by sneaking back in again. But it was enough to break his heart, Mayne exclaimed – twenty planes left unharmed, and just 'asking for it'.

For a second or so Stirling was silent, as if lost in thought. Then he gave voice to just what was on his mind. They had three jeeps, boasting eight Vickers-K guns between them. Those vehicles should be 'taken onto the drome and driven round it, firing into the planes'. It made perfect sense, for with such speed and firepower they could smash through the cordon, striking by total surprise, and this was exactly what the Vickers-Ks were designed for anyway – shooting up warplanes.

What more was there to discuss?

They spent a few minutes checking that the guns were fully armed, and spare pans of ammo were close to hand. Then, plan set, the attack convoy set off with the men hunched over their weapons. At the approach to the airfield it seemed unbelievably quiet. It was as if the defenders, having been hit so hard, couldn't conceive of a second strike materialising so swiftly. The vehicles pulled to a halt on the darkened roadside, as the raiders surveyed the airstrip, trying to work out where the greatest concentration of intact warplanes were situated.

The targets were mostly CR.42s and Me 109s. They could see where the burned out, smoking hulks from Mayne's earlier handiwork were interspersed with untouched airframes – those upon which the faulty Lewes bombs had failed to detonate. As this kind of jeep-raiding had never been tried before, Stirling issued some ad hoc orders. They'd sweep around the entire perimeter in line astern, so each vehicle could unleash with its weapons on the broadside, firing into the centre of the airbase.

'Remember, shoot low and aim at the petrol tanks,' he urged. 'Right. Off we go.'

Bumping off the road, engines roared as the convoy gathered speed, the drivers changing up through the gears. Moments later they hit the cordon of the airstrip going at speed, and the guns spat flame. As one, eight Vickers-Ks barked, the combined firepower unleashing some 9,600 rounds per minute of incendiary, standard ball and tracer. Spurts of blinding fire lanced out from the jeeps, and within moments the nearest target had burst into flames. By the light of the conflagration, the next and the next target were made all the more visible. Guns swivelled right, and another warplane dissolved into a mass of fiery ruin.

The noise was deafening: howling engines, jeeps bumping and clattering over rough ground, plus the thunder of the guns, and above it all the hollow crumps as yet another fuel tank was hit and incinerated its host – a German or Italian aircraft. Tearing around in a U-shape, Stirling, Mayne and their men kept pumping in the rounds, as above all rose a roaring cacophony of sound – more and more aircraft starting to burn. Caught totally off-guard, the airbase defenders seemed incapable of responding. As the jeeps snarled, and the guns spat fury and death, there was not a hint of any return fire.

Nearing the end of the return leg of the U, the attack convoy accelerated towards the highway. Now to make good their getaway. To their rear, there were the first hints of a response. An AA gun opened up, most likely a Breda 20/65 20mm cannon, the rounds from which were capable of piercing lightly armoured vehicles. More guns joined the fightback, as tracer rounds burned towards the line of jeeps, passing by uncomfortably close. But moments later the attackers had made the main highway and they accelerated away into the enveloping darkness.

Behind them they counted twelve separate fires, and once more Bagoush was awash with flame. From his vantage point high on the Jebel, Dr Pleydell had been treated to a bird's-eye view, seeing the entire skyline lit up as if a storm was unleashing lightning. That was followed by the low rumble of the explosions, each giving the earth 'a little shudder' as it washed over them. Through their binoculars they could count the individual fires, each marking a burning warplane.

That was Stirling and Mayne's handiwork, as one of the seasoned raiders pointed out to Pleydell. It was. And together, they had just forged a new means of waging desert warfare.

Counting the hits, both from Lewes bombs and Vickers-K broadsides, Stirling and Mayne figured they'd accounted for at least thirty-four enemy planes. They always underplayed the numbers they reported by radio to MEHQ, for fear of being accused of overstating matters. That was just the kind of thing their detractors would seize upon. In fact, as air recces flown by the RAF would show, they'd taken out thirty-seven aircraft at Bagoush, one of which was a captured British Hawker Hurricane. That meant that Stirling and Mayne had just equalled Bill Fraser's all time high of thirty-seven warplanes destroyed, during his first ever successful SAS mission at Agedabia airfield.

Unreported, secret, deniable, raids like these went almost unnoticed by the British and wider public. By contrast, when the renowned air ace Wing Commander Douglas Bader and his five RAF squadrons had downed some thirty-six enemy warplanes, on 18 September 1940, such aerial exploits had attracted international headlines. Rightly so. It was the height of the Battle of Britain and such successes were crucial to the nation's survival. But equally, during one night's raiding a handful of SAS warriors had topped that score. Indeed, by now they were losing count of their running total. It was pushing two hundred enemy warplanes, that was for certain.

Raiding was like a binge at the Kabrit bar: riotous and all-consuming while it lasted, yet with a hangover to follow. The escape and evasion from any such attack was fraught with the strife of the hunted. This raid was no exception. As the column of vehicles raced for the open desert and the promise of safety, those riding in them had little idea what first light might bring. Would they find themselves in a patch of desert offering good cover, or a flat, features plain offering little sanctuary at all?

First light on 8 July revealed the latter to be the case. Stirling and Mayne pulled over to discuss options. A tiny pinprick was visible on the horizon: it just might be a rocky outcrop; cover. It looked to be a good hour's drive away. With no other option they set a course for the distant pimple, but before they could reach it the first enemy warplanes hove into view. Mayne, in the lead jeep, gunned his engine and raced for the outcrop. He made the lip of an overhang just before the first plane pounced. Stirling, in the Blitz Buggy, plus the other vehicles were caught in the open.

'Abandon ship!' Stirling yelled. He and his fellows dived clear of the Blitz Buggy, dashing for whatever cover they could find.

Over the next hour, Stirling and his men played a deadly game of hide-and-seek with two CR.42s, and a lone Caproni Ghibli, as they strafed and bombed. By dodging behind a boulder, they managed to avoid getting hit. But one after the other the vehicles were struck and went up in smoke. The last to be targeted was the Blitz Buggy, after which the pair of CR.42s turned tail and headed for home.

Dusting themselves down, Stirling and his men started off on foot for the distant escarpment. Mayne had positioned his jeep so he could fire at the enemy warplanes, in an attempt to draw them away from his comrades. But the Italian pilots had studiously ignored him, as they'd concentrated on their deadly task. He drove out now in the one surviving vehicle, offering Stirling and his men a lift.

Once they were in cover, Stirling suggested a spot of breakfast. 'Everything's gone, sir,' one of his men pointed out. All their food, water, fuel, weaponry and ammo had been torched in the burning vehicles.

'Not everything,' volunteered Mayne. 'We've got some biscuits and some chocolate. And here's a bottle of whisky.' He eyed the others, with a wry smile. 'Och, it could've been worse. It might have been us instead.'

That was a toast they could all drink to.

Having feasted on what little there was, they waited out the heat of the day, and then, with eight men clinging to the one surviving vehicle, they crawled across the desert to the Bir Chalder RV. They reached it, to learn of the fortunes of the other patrols. Bill Fraser, together with Lieutenant Jordan – the new commander of the Free French SAS, in place of Bergé – had managed to bag fourteen warplanes, but it had been tough as hell. They'd spent much of their time crawling beneath heavily wired perimeters and evading hordes of sentries, while yelling out orders in German in an effort to confuse them, and dodging machinegun and Breda cannon fire. To top it all, they'd had to withdraw from the raid through a minefield. Miraculously, they'd suffered only one man lightly injured, and no fatalities.

Hearing reports of Stirling and Mayne's successes at Bagoush, Pleydell sought out the chief author of so much carnage and devastation. He found Mayne lying in the shadow of his jeep, head stuck in a book. It struck the doctor that even when Mayne was seemingly at rest, he still somehow gave the impression of 'massive latent force and power'.

'Hello, doctor,' Mayne greeted him, 'and how did you get on?' He gestured for Pleydell to join him, squatting together in the shade.

'Well, we probably got about twenty planes,' Pleydell replied, excitedly, 'but we only counted fifteen for certain – that's not bad, is it?'

'Och, no,' Mayne replied, as he tried to suppress a yawn. Then, switching tack unexpectedly, he brandished the cover of his novel, and remarked, 'This is a very good book . . . have you read it?'

Pleydell was somewhat nonplussed. Mayne seemed more interested in the novel than their victories against the enemy. He studied the cover. It was *The Spanish Farm*, by R. H. Mottram, the great classic of First World War literature, a story about love, romance and friendship set amid the horrors of war. No, he hadn't read it, Pleydell confessed. Mayne offered to lend it to Pleydell once he was finished with it. Pleydell was presently reading the *Whiteoak Chronicles*, set in the Victorian era, whose awkward and foolish protagonist, Finch Whiteoak, was forever getting into bizarre and hilarious scrapes. Recently, he'd finished Siegfried Sassoon's part-fictionalised First World War book, *Memoirs of an Infantry Officer*. Bearing in mind Mayne's taste in literature, that might be more up the SAS commander's street, so they might usefully swop.

How did Mayne's mission go, Pleydell asked? That was what he really wanted to learn about, more than Mayne's literary tastes.

There had been 'some good shooting' Mayne confirmed.

'Did you get many planes?' Pleydell pressed.

'Och, quite a few.' Mayne was unsure how many exactly. Thirty? That sounded about right.

Pleydell was amazed. 'Thirty!' Even for Mayne and Stirling in action together, that was still an amazing haul. But he wasn't quite sure how to respond. It seemed almost foolish to congratulate a man with Mayne's record of kills – well over a hundred by now.

'Jolly good show,' was all Pleydell could think of to say.

'You only had the one casualty?' Mayne queried.

Pleydell confirmed that they had and that it wasn't anything serious. He realised then that while Mayne might lounge in the shade with his head stuck in a book, nothing escaped him. Little seemed to escape the notice of the enigmatic SAS commander. Before they could chat any more, there was a cry of: 'Aircraft!'

A lone CR.42 had found them. There was a sharp and fierce gun battle. An LRDG patrol was camped up on the far side of the Bir Chalder rendezvous, and they were more than happy to take on the loathed enemy aircraft. Once the biplane had peeled away, all knew they would have to get on the move. They had been found. More warplanes would be coming.

The last patrol to make the RV was Jellicoe and Zirnheld's. They brought with them three prisoners. Sadly, none was the Afrika Korps leader, General Rommel. Instead of discovering his HQ, they'd come upon a convoy of trucks parked at the road-side. As they were placing their Lewes bombs, they'd surprised some enemy soldiers. They'd sprung upon them, guns levelled, but at first the Germans had laughed. They'd presumed their assailants had to be crazy Italians, for it was inconceivable that British raiders might be so far behind the lines. Zirnheld had soon convinced them otherwise. By the time the trucks were blown up, the three prisoners – a Wehrmacht sergeant and two Luftwaffe ground crew – were aboard the SAS jeeps and speeding away.

Their return journey had been more than a little fraught. Set upon by enemy warplanes, their three jeeps had been reduced to one, and even that was shot to hell. Its radiator was holed and the tyres slashed, leaving it resting on its wheel hubs. The miracle was that the engine still ran. Nine-up, they'd attempted to limp back to Bir Chalder. Thinking laterally, they'd managed to bung up the holes in the radiator with 'plastic explosives from our unused bombs', keeping it topped-up in a novel fashion. 'Each man would relieve himself into the radiator in turn. It worked! But it smelled like a chicken coop!'

That night, the SAS prepared to move out. Most were exhausted and had been trying to grab a little sleep. Rest snatched here and there between long desert drives and night raids led to cumulative fatigue. Now, on all sides, figures rolled out of their blankets fully dressed, the lucky ones with thick goatskin coats thrown over all.

The sky above was a brilliant patchwork of stars, as shadowy forms gathered their bed-rolls and loaded up the vehicles. A first engine coughed into life. A match flared, as the first cigarette glowed rhythmically in the dark. Voices drifted on the still night air. So too did the sound of men urinating noisily on the wheel arches of the trucks.

The column of depleted – and decidedly overloaded – vehicles got under way, nosing into the night. Pleydell was struck by a thought. They were 'fugitives from the light, and children of the darkness'. The lot of the desert raider was an alien kind of existence, 'hiding during the day, and emerging from our lairs by night'. All through the night hours they motored on, seeking safety. Come first light, they were lucky. Up ahead, a thin brown line cut the desert – some sort of rock formation. By the time they reached it, they realised just how fortunate they were.

An escarpment dropped away quite suddenly, falling a good sixteen feet or more, and where the desert wind had whipped along its face, it had scoured out crevices and shallow caves. In no time the vehicles had been tucked away into those. There, they were roped over with camo-netting, plus with some torn-up scrub and camel thorn thrown over the top, to better break up the vehicle's outline. By the time the sun was well and truly up, all were equally well hidden. With clinking mess tins, groups of figures made their way towards the cook truck for some breakfast.

As far as anyone could ascertain, this linear rock feature was named Bir El Quseir, after a water source that lay somewhere along its length. That was a bonus, of course, for it meant there might well be potable water near by. The more Stirling and Mayne took stock of their whereabouts, the more they reckoned this was a perfect forward mounting base (an 'FMB' in military parlance), from which to keep harassing the enemy. The escarpment lays some thirty miles inland, and five miles west of the well-used Qara to Mersa Matruh track, which ran north–south for a hundred-odd miles.

It was hidden, unfrequented, unremarked and deserted, apart from those who had adopted it right now.

Further patrols were sent out – two or three jeeps at a time, with specific targets in mind. On one of the first, Mayne was in action again, leading a party of five – including Lilley, Storie and the evocatively named Corporal Ted Badger, another of the originals. At a coastal airfield they blew up fourteen warplanes, with no casualties. Accounts are unclear, but during one or other of these raids, Mayne was forced to resort to using the knife, in order to break through the cordon of sentries.

This was revealed in the memoirs of David Lloyd Owen, who, as the future commander of the LRDG, wrote some of the most authoritative accounts of that iconic unit's war. Lloyd Owen had no need to embellish his tale. The history of that unit is replete with pioneering desert warcraft, and some of the most incredible exploits in terms of sheer adventure and survival. As Lloyd Owen made clear, while the LRDG's 'road watch' duties had priority, 'none of the Patrols could be expected to operate forever on silent and unobserved tasks without giving them some alleviation . . . They must be allowed every so often to have a "beat-up" [to attack the enemy].'

The way the tale of Mayne's knife-work came to Lloyd Owen's attention is in itself instructive about the SAS commander's true character. It is redolent of Mayne's nature and his spirit. Having returned from one or other of these raids – most likely the first; the initial foray onto Bagoush Airbase, on foot – Mayne fell into conversation with Lloyd Owen. The LRDG were camped up at the Bir Chalder rendezvous at the time, and theirs was a chance encounter. The two men were becoming fast friends, in the way the desert has of forging deep camaraderie in adversity, and swiftly.

'How were things tonight?' Lloyd Owen had ventured.

'A bit trickier tonight,' Mayne conceded. 'They had posted a sentry on nearly every bloody plane. I had to knife the sentries before I could place the bombs.'

The reply had been delivered as if it was nothing out of the ordinary; as if Mayne wouldn't have thought to mention it, had the LRDG commander not asked. When Lloyd Owen probed a little further, he learned that Mayne had actually had to knife to death as many enemy guards as warplanes destroyed. Lloyd Owen was convinced that had he not posed the question, Mayne might never have brought it up, the raid being recorded as just another night's work by a small SAS patrol. Were it not for the remark made to Lloyd Owen, nobody but Mayne would ever have been any the wiser.

Certainly, neither of the SAS after-action reports makes the slightest inference to anything like that having happened. One reads: 'went onto the drome and placed bombs on 14 aircraft.' The other speaks of 'going down the lines of planes . . . placing bombs'. No mention is made of anyone having to resort to close-quarters combat, and wielding the knife, to break through. But that was vintage Mayne. Boasting and grandstanding – 'swanking' as the SAS called it – were two of the things he most abhorred.

This was a man who would become famed for carrying a book of poetry – *Other Men's Flowers* – into battle. The anthology happens to include James Elroy Flecker's *The Golden Road To Samarkand*, part of which was to become the SAS's regimental poem, the opening lines of which are: 'We are the pilgrims, master; we shall go / Always a little further . . .' (Hence members of the SAS being informally known as 'Pilgrims'.) This was a man who counted artists, lawyers, doctors, poets and fellow writers as his friends, and who seemed more at home discussing literature than the bloody business of waging war. Yet this was also a man who had been charged to kill and kill and kill again, on behalf of his country, his fellow raiders, and in freedom's cause.

There is no sense that Mayne rested easy with such killing, especially when executed with the knife. Perhaps that was why he had kept it quiet. Other accounts from the war reflect how difficult it was, in fact, to slay a fellow human with a blade, even when one was trained to do so, as were all commandos. There was never any sense that Mayne was proud of what he had done – of the up-close killing – but of course, he was certainly more than capable.

Mayne had honed his hunting instincts as a child, shooting rabbits on the Mount Pleasant estate. Then there are the reports of his having stalked and killed deer in Scotland, leaving professional gamekeepers and others awed by his natural abilities. Plus there was the 1938 springbok-bagging venture, of course – grabbing some 'Fresh Meat' during the Lions tour. Hunting was in his blood. Stalking a deer or stalking a man – both required the same skills and craft, and Mayne had it in spadefuls.

Needs must, and this was war.

CHAPTER TWENTY

Lili Marlene

Bir El Quseir was an 'infinitesimal crease in the vast dead face of the Western Sahara'. Even so, it proved the perfect place at which to rest and recuperate. Repeated back-to-back missions, combined with fragmented, illusory sleep had transformed Stirling's raiders into walking zombies; 'a party of sleepwalkers'. Those not resting tended to be out on missions, and vice versa. But whenever the two parties ran into each other at Bir El Quseir and there was news to impart, the spirits flowed freely. Storytelling was the chief draw, rum and lime the main catalyst, and singing the great panacea.

A raiding party returning from a successful mission triggered a buzz of excitement; it pulsed along the rock walls of Bir El Quseir. Figures tumbled out of their bed-rolls and emerged troll like from caves and crevices, eager for news. The returnees would recount their tales in the odd slang that the unit had adopted, for in their desert isolation a language all of its own had developed. Key points would be underlined by forceful gestures, as the listeners squatted in the shade, faces tanned a deep brown, hair tousled and matted, beards thick, and with none having washed for days on end, for there was precious little water to waste around here.

As an observer – an insider, yet still an outsider, somehow – Pleydell watched these gatherings, wondering: 'Were any men as happy as these?' Was there another unit like it anywhere, wherein each individual had his own specific role to play and was largely the author of his own destiny? Wherein many treasured the little, notched stick they kept, with each nick representing an enemy warplane that they had personally accounted for? Pleydell doubted it. War for these men was such a deeply personal affair, and he rarely if ever heard the slightest complaint. It only ever happened when an individual felt he had been left out of a raid, at which point he might 'tick' a little.

Pleydell's aid post – secreted in a small cave tucked away at the top of the escarpment – was busy. Desert sores were the main gripe. The chief danger here at Bir El Quseir were the swarms of flies, which would get into open wounds, risking infection. They were the bane of any medic's existence. One morning, one of the German prisoners seized by Jellicoe and Zirnheld paid a visit to Pleydell's makeshift clinic. Whereas the two young Luftwaffe officers seemed like typical arrogant Nazi types, the sergeant – an older figure who'd been a postman prior to the war – was doleful and browbeaten. He had chronic earache and was in agony, he explained. Pleydell did his best to help, administering a poultice to ease the pain. He couldn't but feel sorry for the German, who seemed so lonely and so unlike one of Hitler's archetypal super-warriors. The sergeant made it clear to Pleydell exactly what he thought. The war was no good. In his view, the English and Germans were one race, so why fight? There was certainly no goosestepping, Nazi salutes, or tub-thumping with this guy.

Evenings were the perfect time to come together at their Bir El Quseir hideout, and even the German prisoners were drawn to the conviviality. Sunsets were glorious affairs – a red globe sinking below the fiery horizon, as the soft-hued colours began to creep back into the landscape, painting all in pinks, purples and greys, detail and perspective and colour bleeding back with the cool embrace of evening. Under the full desert sun all would melt away into shimmering foregrounds, shifting mirages and burning horizons – chimeras all. But with dusk all solidified and grew still.

Of the sixty-odd men who deployed on Operation Squatter, less than two dozen would return, shown here shortly after rendezvousing in the desert. Amongst the missing were many Commando veterans, including Lt. McGonigal, Mayne's closest friend. Stirling stands central to the photo, the tallest figure, Mayne on his immediate left, looking downcast. Of all of the patrols only his had come close to hitting its target.

To add insult to injury, as they withdrew from the desert the SAS were set upon by an Italian Air Force Savoia SM79 warplane, plus German aircraft, 'bombing and machine gunning' – the very kind of targets that the SAS had set out to destroy. Back at Kabrit, Mayne and his comrades nursed their injuries and vowed vengeance.

The unit charged to retrieve the SAS from Operation Squatter was the Long Range Desert Group (LRDG), the reconnaissance specialists. Jake Easonsmith (*left*) commanded the patrol. They were the true masters of the desert, and all its varied terrain and beasts, as demonstrated by Corporal George Howard astride the LRDG donkey (*right*). Riding in their 1.5 tonne Chevrolet trucks (*below*), the LRDG offered to ferry the SAS to their targets, in a partnership that would revolutionise the raiders' fortunes.

On the night of 14/15 December 1941, Mayne's raiders struck home in spectacular fashion, destroying 24 enemy aircraft at Tamet airbase. Tamet would become known as 'Paddy's Own,' he would raid it so often. While shooting up the officer's mess, Mayne would grab a handful of cutlery (*below*), each stamped with the Luftwaffe's coat of arms – an eagle, wings outstretched, clutching a Nazi swastika. For this and subsequent raids Mayne would win his first DSO, along with David Stirling.

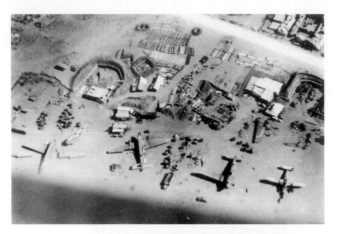

Striking far and wide, during the first months of 1942 the SAS were unrelenting, at this one Cretan airbase (*left*) destroying as many as 70 German warplanes. Fuelled by Benzedrine (*below left*), a powerful amphetamine, they struck time and again. Shortly, all the main German and Italian aerodromes had been raided, some repeatedly. Once the Willys jeep (*below*) was added to the mix, its speed, manoeuvrability, and the sheer firepower of the twin Vickers-K machine guns it carried, made the raiders unstoppable.

"Paddy"

● The four pictures above were taken in the desert by Blair Mayne himself or his batman. Sometimes they used cameras taken from enemy aircraft. Left to right: Italians surrendering; Allied tank on reconnaissance patrol; "brewing up" before a raid; this Jerry plane failed to return.

● A blazing truck, a shattered plane — aftermath of yet another successful desert raid.

● A jeep load of trouble for the Germans. Men like these helped Mayne harass the enemy behind the lines.

● A Special Air Service hideout behind the enemy lines in North Africa. Here the raiders "holed up" immediately before or after an attack. Picture taken by Blair Mayne.

NEXT WEEK

DANGEROUS MEN IN THE DESERT

Blair Mayne becomes "the fighting Irishman" of the S.A.S. . . . and Hitler gets cross.

Despite their standout successes by the autumn 1942 the SAS's detractors had branded them 'raiders of the thug variety,' who should be done away with. But thanks to David Stirling's personal connections to Winston Churchill, their fortunes were transformed. Once Churchill met Stirling, he made sure that stories about these 'Robin Hood raiders' hit the newspapers, bringing the SAS out of the shadows. Mayne, hugely well-read and a keen photographer, took photos capturing key moments.

By the autumn of 1942, Stirling (*left, on one of his last raids*) found the pace of desert raiding, combined with fighting for the SAS's very survival, all too much. With his health suffering, he dispatched Mayne into the Great Sand Sea, charged to harass German General Erwin Rommel's forces relentlessly. With their thick beards and wild hair, with no washing possible, and only open fires to warm the chill desert nights, Mayne's raiders were like 'pirates of the seventeenth century, secure in their palm-fringed' fastness, leaving a litany of 'trains mined, railway stations wrecked, road traffic shot up and aircraft burned.' Forging a unique bond with his men, Mayne (*below, flanked by his youthful raiders*) led from the front, perfecting a new and unique form of warfare.

Rommel – 'The Desert Fox' – knew that 'Stirling's Commandos' were doing incalculable damage to his war machine and the morale of his troops. He formed an elite unit specifically to hunt them down. More damagingly, he deployed 'stool pigeons' – chiefly the standout turncoat Theodore Schurch (*below left*) – plus the only known traitor and future SS/Nazi recruit ever to have served with the SAS, the so-called Honourable Douglas Webster St. Aubyn Berneville-Claye, Lord Charlesworth (*below right*). They would prove highly successful in learning the desert raiders secrets and nailing their patrols.

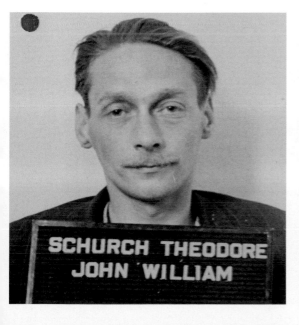

THESE MEN WERE HIS DESERT COMRADES

● Lt.-Col. David Stirling, D.S.O. — the "Phantom" Major. Blair Mayne succeeded him as commander of the S.A.S.

● Maj. J. M. Wiseman. A Cambridge M.A., he served in Syria, Western Desert, Sicily, Italy and N.W. Europe. Major Wiseman was awarded the Military Cross.

● Maj. R. M. E. Melot. First-war pilot in Belgian Air Force. Wounded in both wars. Served Syria, Western Desert, Sicily and Italy. Awards—Croix de Guerre, Croix de Feu, Volont Combattant, Medaille Belge.

In February 1943 Stirling undertook his final, epic mission, which ended in his capture. With the SAS's founder taken prisoner, and the war in North Africa all but won, the SAS's detractors argued they had no further use for the desert raiders. Mayne hit back, fighting tooth and nail to secure a role in the coming battles. Mayne (*front row, centre, below*) gathered his stalwarts – Wiseman, O'Dowd, Bennett, Sadler, Cooper, Seekings, Riley, Melot – for the next challenge, the push into the soft underbelly of Europe; Italy. By war's end the SAS's exploits would be legendary, with Mayne, their longstanding commander, being the most highly decorated soldier in the British Army.

As the first breath of a cool evening breeze caressed the rock face, so the men would refill their water bottles, before digging a hole in a sheltered spot of sand, where it would remain wonderfully fresh and chilled. The next heartbeat of the day was the rum and lime issue. Figures gathered at the cook's truck as the night crept in, a myriad of stars blinking on in a breathtaking, kaleidoscopic display. The air was so clean here, the light pollution so non-existent, that the heavens felt near enough to reach out and touch.

If there was raiding to be done on the morrow, by ten o'clock all would drift off to their chosen patches of sand to sleep. But if there was a rare day of rest to come, an extra rum jar would be broken out and the party mood would grip. Pleydell and Mayne would stretch out together, speaking little, the big Irishman somehow watching over all. Stirling, Jellicoe and a few others would form a group, just a little downslope. The French would gather in a circle, talking volubly, while on all sides groups of shadowy figures sipped their brews. The Germans were drawn inexorably to the throng – the two young Luftwaffe diehards inseparable, the lone sergeant lost in his thoughts.

Laughter and chatter echoed along the rock walls. A match flared, illuminating a craggy, bearded face as a figure bent to light a cigarette, before offering the flame to others. One figure moved from man to man, rum jar in hand, dispensing to each his dram – assuring, quietly: 'The lime'll be round in a minute.'

The ceremony was inviolable.

Darkness descended and a man would begin to sing. If they were lucky, it was Johnny Rose, the former manager of the Woolworths department store turned desert raider, who was blessed with the voice of a god. The words would be picked up by others, a little shyly at first, but with increasing gusto, as a figure on the truck beat out the rhythm with a stick, until eventually the length and breadth of Bir El Quseir was awash with sound. Beyond lay the empty embrace of the desert. But here, within this circle of firelight, only camaraderie and brotherhood held sway. The songs would win no prizes, certainly. Many – Mayne included – were close to tone deaf. But the raw emotion, the dogged defiance and the sheer zest for life was world-beating.

The first songs would be the old classics – Highland ballads with strong martial rhythms and heart, interspersed with a good smattering of Irish rebel songs. The Germans in particular seemed to love all of those fighting tunes. But once those were exhausted, the odd jazz number drifted through the night, to be followed, inevitably, by the lovesick ballads of men far from home. As a giant bearded figure got to his feet, only to belt out a heartrending rendition of 'I'm dancing with tears in my eyes', or 'Don't say it's true', the Germans seemed utterly mystified. Baffled. How could these fearsome raiders be so . . . unwarlike? What was this bizarre outpouring of 'unmanly' emotion and heartache? Maybe the British and the Germans weren't so alike after all?

Wondering how it was that those who inhabited the British Isles could so openly bare their souls before the enemy, Pleydell demanded as much of Mayne. The tough Irishman – the SAS raider without compare – seemed completely at ease with it all.

'Och, Malcolm, there's nothing to worry about,' he reassured. 'They're happy. That's the main thing.'

The French – Jordan, Zirnheld and company – were called upon to sing. They offered up 'La Madelon', a Great War-era tune which tells of a beautiful young waitress flirting with soldiers in a tavern. One falls madly in love with her and asks for her hand in marriage. Madelon's response is the core message of the song, one of brotherhood in adversity:

> But Madelon, not stupid, in short
> Replied to him with a smile:
> 'Why should I take one man
> When I love the whole regiment?'

Uplifting, martial in tone and intensely patriotic, 'La Madelon' was no love-sick lament. Once the last words had drifted away and the escarpment fell silent, the songsters wondered what should come next. Someone took up the cry: 'The Germans! You sing!' The call was repeated by all – *The Germans!* – until the demand for the enemy to offer up a song rebounded off the rock walls like thunder.

The three prisoners looked distinctly nonplussed. They had their heads together, as they wondered what to do. Was this an order from their captors? Could they refuse? If they sang, were they consorting with the enemy? What would Hitler think? Finally, they relented.

They began with a strikingly patriotic martial song – something of which the Führer would no doubt have been proud – faltering at first, but gaining in strength and stridency. It was stirring and evoked heroic deeds, and it was hard not to be impressed. At the song's end there were cries for more. The listeners were rewarded with a rendition of 'Lili Marlene', which all recognised, for this was the marching song of Rommel's Afrika Korps. No SAS raider who had traversed the desert for weeks on end could have escaped hearing it on one evening or another, as he gazed upon an enemy encampment, and those guarding it took up this tune in song.

As the night wore on, Pleydell wondered what the folks back at home would think. Singing and partying with the enemy – 'Would they condemn? Would they be bitter?' He just didn't know. In a sense, it didn't matter, for only those who were here, who had lived this moment, would ever understand. There was something about this place, this time, this life, that made the seemingly impossible possible, not to mention utterly unforgettable. They would never forget this – British, Irish, French, Germans, all. Nothing would ever come close to such intensity of experience. It would live with them, inside of them, indelible. Such was the closeness of these brothers in war.

Capturing that spirit, Mayne would revise the lyrics of 'Lili

Marlene', composing a set of verses that would become the SAS's very own marching song. In doing so, he would co-opt the heart and soul of the Afrika Korps, subverting it. In a sense, this was the ultimate expression of the respect that the desert raiders held for their adversaries. A few of the lines embody that essence and sentiment:

There was a song we always used to hear,
Out in the desert, romantic, soft and clear,
Over the ether, came the strain,
That soft refrain, each night again,
To you, Lili Marlene, to you Lili Marlene.

Check you're in position; see your guns are right,
Wait until the convoy comes creeping through the night,
Now you can pull the trigger, son,
And blow the Hun to Kingdom come,
And Lili Marlene's boyfriend will never see Marlene.

What the combination of their Bir El Quseir hideout and the jeeps gifted to Stirling and Mayne was the ability to hit Rommel's lines in a rolling series of raids. No longer did they have to wait for the moonless period, the once-monthly slot of just a few days when the moon, caught between a waxing and a waning crescent, was all but invisible. Only on such intensely dark nights had raiding-by-foot been possible. But with the jeeps, and with their Bir El Quseir base, they could strike whenever and wherever they chose.

Speed, audacity and surprise – they were even more critical now, as Rommel's legions did their upmost to counter the SAS. His forces were endeavouring to move and to hide their warplanes at night, for the ghost raiders struck from out of the darkness. They were sending out mobile hunter patrols, to try to track the SAS to their lairs. The lesson was clear. If the enemy were upping their game, the SAS would have to do likewise. Right now, Stirling and Mayne's ability to do so rested upon two crucial factors: getting a resupply of stores of all kinds, plus replacement jeeps. There was only one way to organise all of that – to drive back to Egypt and to fetch everything they might need.

It was the second week of July 1942 when Stirling and Mayne prepared to set out on a dash back to friendly lines, leaving a rump of men at Bir El Quseir, Pleydell and Almonds among them. For a while – hopefully only a short while – the fellowship would be broken. Only one route lay open to those executing the resupply run, for the Palm Leaf road had been occupied by the enemy. Instead, they would have to head south for a good hundred miles, before swinging east to slip through the southern lip of the Qattara Depression, and onwards from there to Kabrit. It was a good five hundred miles as the crow flies, far further with all the twists and turns the route entailed. Once again, Mike Sadler, their former LRDG man turned SAS navigator, would be tested to the full.

Those few left at Bir El Quseir felt abandoned. The key figures – Stirling, Mayne, Fraser, Jellicoe – were gone. More worryingly, they were running desperately short of food and water supplies, and had to put themselves on near-starvation rations. Even so, a skeleton raiding operation continued, for Stirling was adamant the pressure on the enemy had to be maintained. The French SAS teamed up with an LRDG patrol for one such raid. It ended in disaster. The aim had been to hit the coastal airstrip situated near Matruh, due north of their hideout. But during the drive the patrol was spotted by a lone CR.42, which swooped low and strafed the vehicles. Several men were wounded.

The worst hit was Lieutenant (the Honourable) Robert Brampton Gurdon, the LRDG patrol commander, who had been shot through the chest and stomach. His fellow LRDG man Corporal Parker had his elbow shattered by a round, plus several of the French SAS had taken flesh wounds. Even so, Gurdon had insisted they press on. Their arrival was met by a searchlight piercing the darkness, which nailed the raiders' vehicles, and a fearsome barrage of fire. All they could do was to turn tail and run, as an armoured-car patrol sped forth, coming right after them. During the getaway Gurdon's condition had worsened. Pleydell was fetched by vehicle from Bir El Quseir, to try to come to the wounded man's aid. By the time he got there, the LRDG commander was dead.

Pleydell was tortured by his failure to save Gurdon. He found himself crying tears of frustration and rage. The two had become friends. Now he was gone. Having dressed Parker's wound – the elbow had been shattered by an 'explosive round' – and dosed him with morphine, the SAS doctor tried to get some sleep. But he was jerked awake in the small hours. There was a roar of aero engines overhead, and the shuddering impact of bombs exploding. Somehow, someone – some hostile warplane – had found them, spying out their Bir El Quseir redoubt. Surely, that meant they would have to move on, but how were they to do so, without Stirling, Mayne et al. on hand?

Pleydell lay awake reflecting on the futility of this war. So much effort and ingenuity and human endeavour concentrated on what – on crossing vast expanses of desert wastes in order to kill each other? But in a sense, this was the best – the ideal – theatre for war, for there were no villages or towns to get caught in the crossfire. Here, it was a 'pure' form of warfare. But likewise, this conflict was millennia-old, as opposing armies had struggled for control of the desert. The Ancient Egyptians, the Romans, the Carthaginians, the Turks – all had waged war here, locking horns in 'pitiless battle'. And then had come the Axis and the Allied powers.

How he missed the others, Pleydell realised.

How he missed the fellowship.

*

It took eight days for Stirling and Mayne to reach Egypt, to replenish and return. By anyone's reckoning it was a record-breaking achievement, especially as they had been forced to steer their way across the treacherous flats of the Qattara Depression, at first trying a track known as the Kaneitra Crossing, but finding that 'completely wrecked', so seeking a route further south. Creeping through a cracked and perilous maze of salt bogs was the only way to avoid the predations of the enemy. The war for North Africa hung in the balance, as Rommel's forces and the Eighth Army locked horns at El Alamein. Not an inch of ground was being conceded by either side.

Stirling and Mayne returned, leading a convoy of twenty jeeps heavily laden with supplies. As the SAS commander made clear, once he was back at Bir El Quseir, now was not the time to falter or to lose heart. But for some the relentless pace of operations had proven too much. Bill Fraser had been left behind at Kabrit, suffering from exhaustion and plagued by desert sores. Seeing the state of Stirling, Pleydell wondered that he hadn't done the same. He could have left Mayne – with Jellicoe, Jordan and Zirnheld as hugely capable deputies – to return to Bir El Quseir and to kickstart raiding. But the SAS commander just seemed driven to distraction to the very end.

One of the first things Pleydell did was drag Stirling into his cave-cum-sickbay. His wrist was playing up. Pleydell insisted the SAS commander allow him to put it into a plaster cast. How long would it take to set, Stirling queried? He had a very special raid in mind. Pleydell told him it needed twenty-four hours. Once he'd applied the cast, they decided to dab it all over with iodine, lending the gleaming whiteness of the plaster a homemade camouflage effect. Otherwise, when out raiding Stirling would be visible from a good few miles away, with his shiny white cast.

Even as the raiders mustered their forces at Bir El Quseir, so Captain George Duncan was in action, undertaking his second seaborne raid in as many months. He would pen no poetry about 'Operation Whynot'. Leading a force of six, they'd sought to strike at a target in Sicily, an airbase boasting some sixty Junkers Ju 88s, the twin-engine *Schnellbomber* (fast bomber). Those flying from this airfield presumably felt reasonably secure, for Italy had escaped the kind of hit-and-run raids of the desert war. Dropped by submarine, Duncan and his men paddled ashore in canoes, only to discover that their target was heavily defended. It looked as if the guards had somehow been forewarned. Even so, they'd managed to place their Lewes bombs among crates of aircraft engines and on communications pylons, before they were spotted and all hell let loose.

Managing to get back to their boats, they'd found that one was damaged. They'd ended up three to each canoe, but the one Duncan was riding in soon became swamped. He could not bear to be a burden on his fellow raiders. So, as Captain Oates had once done, during that ill-fated 1912 Antarctic expedition, Duncan had started to swim out to sea, so that the others might live. They had refused to let him go, and he was dragged back into a canoe. They missed their rendezvous with their submarine and all were captured.

Duncan and his fellows were ill-treated by their captors. Sick from his long immersion in the sea, Duncan almost died. For this second seaborne raid, and for his subsequent escape attempts, he would be awarded a bar to his MC, but he would never write any verses about that ill-fated Sicily mission. The old faithfuls from No. 11 Commando were falling thick and fast.

At Bir El Quseir, Stirling outlined his plan of attack. It was audacious and bold in the extreme. Intelligence reports suggested that Rommel's key staging post for new warplanes – those freshly arrived in theatre – was an airbase called Sidi Haneish, near the small settlement of Fuka (formally known as 'Landing Ground

12' to the British military). All aircraft heading for the front were mustered there. Intelligence reports suggested it was packed with Ju 52s, the transport aircraft that Rommel relied upon to keep supplies flowing to his foremost positions, especially when the land routes became too dangerous or clogged with traffic.

Stirling's plan was fiendishly simple. He intended to use more or less every jeep then available at Bir El Quseir to blanket Sidi Haneish in a whirlwind of fire, ensuring that not an aircraft escaped from the onslaught of some five dozen Vickers-K guns, spitting lead and death. He figured they should launch the attack in less than forty-eight hours' time, when the moon was pretty much full – so when the enemy would least expect it. He outlined the plan to his men, scratching a diagram in the sand as to how the formation of jeeps should execute the raid.

First, making up one column, they would smash their way through the airbase's perimeter, after which they would form into two parallel columns, each with its weapons firing outwards. Like that, they would drive down the central runway, unleashing fire into those warplanes parked on either side. Stirling's jeep would lead, and via a series of colour-coded flares he would signal key manoeuvres – right wheel, left wheel, stop, start ceasefire and so on. As with all great shows, this one required a dress rehearsal. Stirling proposed they should do it in the desert near by, seeing nothing particularly odd about unleashing such a dramatic display of firepower deep behind enemy lines.

The dry run for this, one of the SAS's greatest 'gangster-style' attacks, went ahead that night. Pleydell wasn't going on the mission – he reckoned he would be of more use waiting for any injured at his cave sickbay. Even so, he rode in Mayne's jeep for the dress rehearsal, which he wouldn't have missed for the world. The doctor found himself perched between the big Irishman at the wheel and his front gunner, while in the rear a figure crouched over the twin Vickers. As they bumped across the rough terrain trying to keep in formation, Stirling gave the signal. Every gun opened up in a deafening crescendo, their jeep juddering with each burst of fire, the tracer ricocheting off the desert in an awe-inspiring display of pyrotechnics.

Stirling had them execute the manoeuvres time after time, until they had them down to a T, changing position and wheeling about as one, turning and accelerating through the dark desert terrain. It was crucial to keep strictly in position, for obvious reasons: if the discipline slipped the raiders would end up blasting each other apart. When all seemed to have grasped it, they turned for home. Once the raid was done, they were to split into parties of two or three vehicles, making their own way back to Bir El Quseir. They were only to approach the hideout under cover of darkness, for fear of revealing its location.

As they rattled their way back towards the escarpment, Mayne leaned across Pleydell and threw a query at his gunner in the passenger-seat. 'What direction are we driving in?'

The gunner gazed up at the heavens, searchingly. 'North-east I should say, sir.'

Mayne laughed. The man was completely mistaken. If he found himself abandoned in the desert, he needed to do better than that, or he was a goner.

They set out at dusk the following day, a long column of jeeps bristling with weaponry. Pleydell felt sorry that he was not going with them, but he knew in his heart that he'd made the right decision, at least as a man of medicine. Should all go well, seven or more separate groups of jeeps would steer their way back to Bir El Quseir. Any one of those could be ferrying wounded. Pleydell needed to be where all could find him, if he was to serve his purpose, which was to cure ills, treat wounds and save lives.

In any case, there was work to be done. If the raid on Sidi Haneish went as planned, no one doubted the enemy would come hunting with a vengeance. Pleydell and a handful of other stay-behinds were charged to sanitise Bir El Quseir – brushing away tyre tracks, camouflaging all remaining vehicles and kit, burying any rubbish and generally tidying up the escarpment, so from the air it would look utterly devoid of life.

The jeep convoy pushed north into the gathering darkness. At first there was light enough to see, so they kept to no particular formation, each driver choosing his own route, while trying to avoid the worst of the dust thrown up by the vehicles in front. Moving over flat shingle-like terrain, the convoy maintained a good 20 mph, gun mountings rattling and ammo tins clinking in the rear. An hour after dusk the moon rose, full and bright. They stopped while Johnny Cooper – sharing the navigation with Sadler – set up a theodolite on its tripod to take a reading from the stars. He double-checked it with Sadler, as they crouched over maps and charts, torch-beams playing across the detail.

They moved off, the terrain to all sides awash in an unearthly glimmer of silver. Of all lights, that of the moon was the most confounding. A black line up ahead could be a spine of mountains twenty miles distant, or a small ridge twenty yards away. Clouds blew across the moon, killing much of the light. The pace slowed. They reached a cliff. It reared from the desert, seemingly presenting an impassable barrier. Stirling dispatched jeeps to the left and right. One found a possible way up, a narrow wadi that cut through in a sharp cleft. The first jeep climbed halfway, hit a boulder, and slid back down again. Another made a run at it and reached the top, blazing a trail. One by one, the rest of the vehicles followed.

They moved into terrain inhabited by the most dangerous animal in the world – man. The first signs were subtle, but unmistakable to the desert veterans – a jeep suddenly bumping over unseen ridges, like a ploughed field. That meant they had crossed a well-worn, rutted track. Ghostly silhouettes – a wrecked truck; piles of discarded war debris – reared to either side. Then, floating over the distant horizon like an alien apparition, a brightly coloured light, hanging in the heavens for what seemed like an age. It was a Very light – a flare round, fired skywards to illuminate the terrain as it floated to earth beneath a parachute.

Light by which to see and to kill.

Stirling called a halt. Cooper and Sadler exchanged notes. They reckoned they were four miles short of the target. Five minutes, Stirling warned, for final preparations. There was a sweet-sickly smell to the air here. All knew it. Rotting flesh. A few dozen yards away lay the hulk of a burned-out vehicle. British. Beside it, two barely recognisable forms. Bodies. They pushed on, skirting past the dead. Moments later, the skyline ahead dissolved into a grey opaqueness, a void that signified they'd reached the far side of the Jebel, where it plunged to the coastal plane. A few minutes of slip, slide and scrape, and the convoy was safely down, speeding into the 'grey uncertainty beyond'.

Two flares rose far to the left of the jeeps, hanging for an instant in the sky, then they dipped below the horizon. The engines growled, as Sadler and Cooper steered for the target. There was a sense in the air now of imminent action. Of danger. More lights appeared, but these had the appearance of vehicle headlamps moving on the main highway. Stirling signalled the convoy to halt. He got down, pipe jammed in his mouth, upside-down as usual. Last minute preparations, he announced – then all jeeps should close up into attack formation.

Sidi Haneish lay just a couple of miles inland from Bagoush, the airfield that Stirling and Mayne had torn to pieces in the SAS's inaugural jeep raid, less than three weeks earlier. Would the enemy be ready? Primed? Waiting? Here and there figures popped Benzedrine, a powerful amphetamine colloquially known as 'bennies'. It promised wakefulness. Focus. Euphoria. A massive booster, for whatever surprises might lie in store.

'We'll go in now,' Stirling announced, as he turned back to his vehicle, 'form up on my jeep . . . and for God's sake keep in formation. Don't waste ammunition.' For once the SAS commander sounded tense, nervous even, his orders terse and clipped.

Here and there vehicles shunted back and forth, getting into the line of march. The dust thickened. The convoy moved off, proceeding at a dead slow to keep the formation intact. The moon slipped from behind the cloud, so the entire column was stark and clear again as it crawled across a land bathed in silver. Gunners gripped the Vickers-K handles, thumbs on safety catches, barrels levelled to front and sides. The ground was cratered and uneven. Wheels crashed into potholes, as the overloaded jeeps, weighed down with pans of ammo, kangarooed across the terrain. If the jeeps hadn't been seen, surely the enemy had to hear them coming. But not a light showed anywhere. There wasn't the slightest indication they were anywhere near an enemy airbase even.

Suddenly, a louder roar cut through the night, drowning out the noise of their progress. An aircraft soared overhead, low, its under-carriage down. It had the unmistakable silhouette of a Heinkel He 111, the twin-engine bomber with the distinctive all-glass nose cone. Before the raiders knew what was happening the terrain to their front was thrown into blinding relief, as if the illuminations of a giant Christmas tree had suddenly been switched on. Rows of lights stretched ahead, like the streetlamps lining a dual carriageway. The hidden airstrip's landing-lights had been flicked on, to guide the incoming warplane down.

The timing was uncanny; impeccable even.

The jeep column adjusted its line of march, swinging around and straightening up, heading down the throat of the runway. Flares looped above the airbase – the recognition signal for the Heinkel pilot, clearing him in. The pace quickened, as Stirling pressed home their advantage – the airstrip lay right ahead, revealed for all to see. A rifle barked a solitary challenge. The muzzle flashed once, before there was an answering belch of flame from the lead jeeps, as a solid stream of red and white tracer sliced through the darkness, engulfing that lone sentry in fire.

More figures broke cover and ran. Stabs of burning tracer chased after them, like a dragon's avenging breath, as incendiary rounds tore into the earth and vegetation, which caught flame. Moments later the tip of the spear had broken through the outer guard, even as that lone enemy aircraft came in to land. There was a brief pause, as figures leapt from the jeeps and went to work on the fencing, slicing through the wire. Then Stirling's jeep took point, as the remainder fell into a double column behind.

As one, the attack convoy accelerated through the broken fencing and powered onto the airfield.

CHAPTER TWENTY-ONE

Gangster Style

Some sixty-odd Vickers-Ks breathed fire.

First, the trigger guns of the lead vehicle opened up – Stirling's charger. Then began the 'whole shattering belching medley', as jeep after jeep let rip down the entire line, the column of vehicles blasting out a murderous barrage of rounds from all sides. The first target was the lone Heinkel that had come into land. As it taxied across the runway it was 'blown to pieces before it had drawn to a halt'. Moments later, concentrated bursts ripped into further airframes, at no more than fifty feet range. As fuel tanks were torn apart by incendiary rounds, the first warplanes began to burn fiercely.

A pilot was spotted lying on the ground beneath one of the aircraft, sandwiched between its wheels and too scared to move. Rounds tore into the warplane, flames licking over the fuselage. They flashed lower, found the bomb bay, and moments later there was an almighty blast. Those riding in the jeeps felt their hair and eyebrows singeing in the heat. The ramrod of jeeps thrust onwards, as fires lit up either side of the airstrip in a burning orange, further targets being silhouetted in the glare. The Vickers kept barking, unleashing in one uninterrupted paroxysm of fire, the only break occurring when a gunner reached down to change ammo pans.

The noise was like nothing else on earth. Exploding warplanes added to the din. As more and more rounds were fired off, smoking hot cartridge casings spewed out of breeches and cascaded down at the driver's feet. The air was thick with the smell of burned powder, leaking aviation fuel, scorched rubber and raw fear. In a matter of seconds, an airbase that had been the archetype of German order and efficiency had been transformed into utter confusion, chaos and bloody mayhem. For those manning Sidi Haneish the speed and surprise of the attack, coupled with its sheer potency, must have been terrifying.

A series of huge silhouettes loomed on the column's right: a rank of Junkers Ju 52s, their giant forms fronted by a sharply raked nose, which ended in the ring of the cylindrical engine cowling and the two-bladed propeller sat out front. It gave each of the distinctive transport aircraft an oddly pig-snouted look. Unmistakable. A whirlwind of rounds tore into the nearest Junkers, the individual volleys making an odd 'swishing sound' as they cut through its corrugated aluminium fuselages. For a brief moment the hold of the closest aircraft seemed to glow an angry red, before there was the dull crump of an explosion and the entire airframe burst into flames.

The explosion rocked the nearest jeeps on their springs. Clouds of angry sparks spiralled above the burning aircraft. The sound of aviation fuel pouring out of ruptured tanks was clearly audible above the roar of battle, as fire fought gravity for the spoils. Fire won, catching the fuel trails, flashing along them, hungrily seeking the source. A second Junkers burned furiously, while beneath it a pair of figures were spotted, lying flat on their stomachs a dozen yards from the aircraft's wheels, frozen in fear. Their heads were raised slightly, as they watched the phalanx of jeeps, seemingly unable to tear their eyes away.

'They're Jerrys,' someone shouted.

'Well, shoot at them,' came back the yelled reply.

Up front Stirling began to wheel left, the entire column

mirroring his move. More aircraft hove into view. Stukas, the hated, reviled dive bomber. Several dozen Vickers swung to meet them, unleashing hell. Spurts of tracer groped for their targets, found them, and moments later the airframes glowed red, before fire ripped through the fuselage, a dragon's breath of hot air belching over the nearest vehicles. Many of the warplanes seemed to be 'bombed-up' – loaded with munitions in readiness to fly sorties. A Dornier Do 17 – known as the 'flying pencil' – was spotted and raked with fire. Seconds later the twin-engine bomber was engulfed in a massive explosion, after which the entire aircraft sagged to the ground in flaming ruin.

As scores of fires licked skywards, they threw all into stark relief, but also served to silhouette the column of raiders. A row of tents was swept with murderous bursts, figures dashing in and out still in their pyjamas. Above the roar of the Vickers-Ks, a new sound cut the night – the shriek of an incoming round. A mortar exploded, rapidly followed by more, as the enemy gunners tracked the progress of the attack column. A Breda 20/65 opened up, its signature slow, throaty tattoo cutting through the night. It was firing from a gun pit set a few hundred yards to the front of the column, its 20mm rounds ripping past the raider's heads. Luckily, the Breda gunner was shooting high. For now.

A mortar tore into the ground, dangerously close. The lead vehicles halted, those behind following suit, like a crocodile. The jeeps were bunched close. Dangerously so. Why had they stopped? From the front came yells, cries, confused shouts. A Stuka burned fiercely, just a few dozen yards away. The light of the leaping flames illuminated the entire line of jeeps in its stark glare. A second Breda opened fire, twin lines of tracer groping for targets. The jeeps' gunners answered fire with fire, as Bredas and Vickers-Ks duelled for supremacy; for kills.

At the column's head the lead vehicle had taken a direct hit in its engine, the 20mm round missing Stirling's legs by inches.

With their jeep knocked out, he, Johnny Cooper and Reg Seekings made a dash for one of the vehicles to their rear, clambering aboard. They discovered a corpse slumped over the vehicle's rear guns, head and shoulders resting upon the weapon. The jeep's gunner had been shot in the head and killed instantly. Easing him out of the way, Cooper took over his weapon, as the jeep moved into pole position, and the column prepared to get under way once more.

Momentarily, a cry echoed down the line. 'Anybody hurt? Any ammunition left?'

Reports were shouted in: Two drums! One drum! Only half! Everyone seemed to be burning through ammo.

'Any ammunition? Any ammunition?' the cry went back and forth, as those running low tried to scavenge spare drums.

Stirling gave the word to move off. Even as the column got going again, a Breda gunner found his mark, a round ploughing into the guts of a jeep. The driver, Lieutenant Stephen Hastings, a recent recruit to the SAS, found himself momentarily blinded, as was his front gunner, a jet of hot oil spurting into their faces. The jeep careered off course, before Hastings somehow managed to wipe his eyes clear and wrench the vehicle back into line. Miraculously, it still seemed drivable, but for how much longer no one could tell.

The column ground forwards, wheeling right, as all around them airframes crackled and burned. A distant plane, about 200 yards away, was saturated with rounds. It stubbornly refused to burn. Instead, the sheer concentration of firepower just seemed to cause it to collapse in on itself. Nearer, a Me 109 hove into view. A few squirts of tracer and incendiary bullets, and it burst into flames. Turning again, the piston of jeeps drew level with a final row of Junkers, the prized transport aircraft. Within seconds those jeeps with ammo remaining had hammered in a storm of rounds, tearing into the rank of warplanes and ripping apart their innards, as one by one they started to smoke and burn.

Stirling signalled to make a break for the exit – back out the way they had come. As drivers gunned their engines and bumped off the tarmac runway onto the rough ground beyond, one vehicle broke from the line of march. It pulled aside and halted. A figured vaulted out and ran. As he dashed across the open space, he seemed remarkably swift and athletic for such a large-limbed individual. Jinking between debris, he made for a last Junkers, one that somehow all had missed. Reaching it, he reached up high and lobbed a Lewes bomb onto one of the wings.

He must have triggered the bomb's quick-action pull-switch, for even as he made a dash back towards his jeep, it detonated, one wing seeming to detach itself completely from the warplane, after which it collapsed into a heap of fiery ruin. With that, Mayne leapt back behind the wheel of his jeep, and gunned the vehicle into motion so as to catch up. Seconds later the column of vehicles thundered through the perimeter wire, racing into the beckoning embrace of the night. Behind them, they left a scene of chaos and mayhem, as a dark pall of smoke spread high over Sidi Haneish.

A mile or so beyond the airbase Stirling called a halt. In hurried tones he explained what was what. In the two-and-a-half hours remaining before daylight they had to try to find cover. A quick refuel and they should split into smaller groups, and get going. There was a good deal of reassigning of vehicles, for several had taken hits, Stirling's and one other being abandoned. Lieutenant Hastings' jeep was not the only one on life-support right now. Many were damaged, and an effort was made to team up intact jeeps with those worst hit. Amazingly, there had been just the one fatality – the rear gunner who was killed on what was now Stirling's vehicle.

The convoy split up, each group taking a separate path in an effort to escape what they knew was coming. Stirling's group of four vehicles edged into the darkness, camel thorn scraping along the jeeps' sides. To their rear the airbase was still clearly visible, as it crackled and burned. They reached a ridge, scaled it and the conflagration was finally lost from view. A few minutes later Hastings' jeep gave up the ghost completely. A Lewes bomb was shoved inside it with a short fuse. They were down to three jeeps now, heavily loaded with men.

For two hours they crawled south, fourteen figures clinging onto three vehicles, with the body of the dead gunner lain in the rear of one of the jeeps. First light revealed their predicament. The terrain was flat, rocky and hard as nails. Not a hope of any place to hide. But by a twist of good fortune, a low ground mist clung to the desert. It should conceal their progress, for now. No one doubted that the enemy would get every available warplane into the skies once it was light enough to see and to hunt.

The fog began to lift. Still the terrain looked hopeless. Bracing themselves for the first roar of an aircraft, they pressed on, in hope. Luck was with them. They reached a sharp drop in the landscape. Beyond lay a large bowl-shaped depression, cut here and there by wadis and thick with scrub. It was perfect. Nosing in among the densest vegetation, the vehicles pulled to a halt. Within minutes they were draped in camouflage nets and thorn bushes torn from the ground. Like that they were invisible at anything beyond a few dozen yards.

Stirling and his party breathed a collective sigh of relief. They gazed at each other, catching each other's look. Bearded, caked in dust and grime, hair matted, and draped in shapeless overcoats to ward off the night chill, eyes red-rimmed with strain, they were a piratical looking bunch. Desperadoes. There was a foul taste in the mouth, a burning sensation behind the eyes. One figure, Captain Sandy Scratchley, another recent recruit, was trying to scrape the dried blood of the dead gunner off his trousers. All craved rest.

It was 0530. Stirling ordered tea: 'Brew up.'

They needed to be quick about it. Just enough mist clung to this depression to hide a cooking fire. Two battered tins were readied, one filled with petrol soaked scrub, the other brimful of water perched on top. As the fire was kindled, another party were tasked to dig a grave. The tea was served hot, black and with a hint of sugar. It was life-giving. The grave was declared ready. The body of the dead man was carried to the shallow scratch in the desert, to be laid to rest.

Hailing from Gateshead, in the north-east of England, John Robson was aged just twenty-one and had been a factory worker prior to the war. This was his second mission with the SAS. His body was lowered and sand and rocks heaped on top. The survivors gathered around the grave, bareheaded. There were two minutes' silence, during which all were lost in thought. Most had hardly known Robson, but somewhere they knew that parents and siblings, and very likely a sweetheart, would be heartbroken when finally they learned of his passing. Buried here, the body would very likely never be found. They'd taken a map reference, but with their headlong flight no one would bank upon its accuracy.

They wandered back to the jeeps. All knew the drill. A long day under a blistering sun lay before them. Not before dusk could they get on the move again. Barely had they crawled into cover and shade when there was the cry of: 'Aircraft!' A fleet of enemy warplanes flashed into view. Across the aerodromes that neighboured Sidi Haneish search parties had been mustered, charged to seek out the murderous British raiders who had struck from out of the night. That first air patrol passed them by, but there would be more.

They remained hidden all that day, roasting, fly-ridden, sleepless. Several times they heard the drone of aircraft, but nothing came too close. Once, there was the distant rattle of machinegun fire and the crump of bombs. Someone, it seemed, 'was catching it'. Come dusk they set out once again. Two of the jeep had damaged engines. They were knocking horribly, making a hell of a racket. They crawled south until a tyre burst. The innertube was in ribbons. Irreparable. They were all out of spares. Hard to cram fourteen men onto two jeeps. The crippled vehicle would need to keep going, driving on its flat tyre and rims. Progress dropped to a dead slow, and as the night wore on the party became convinced they had lost their way.

Luckily, with unerring skill Johnny Cooper managed to guide them, finally, to their hideout. The news there was mixed. For the race back to Bir El Quseir, Mayne had teamed up with some of the French. There had been four jeeps in their convoy, but two had gradually fallen behind. One, carrying Andre Zirnheld, blew first one tyre and then another. They'd managed to get it into a camouflaged position just as the dawn mist was clearing. Shortly, a convoy of thirty German vehicles thundered to a halt, no more than two kilometres away. A pair of Fiesler-Storch light aircraft flew over – the distinctive looking German spotter planes, named the 'Stork' due to its gangly, long-legged, spindly look. In their wake came a squadron of Stukas, with Me 109s in support.

The German warplanes made nine separate attacking runs, the machinegun fire sounding like 'a summer hailstorm'. Zirnheld was hit first in the shoulder. He tried to brush it off. *'Je suis touché au bras. Ce n'est rien'* – I've been shot in the arm, but it's nothing. But on the penultimate pass he was hit again, this time in the guts. Zirnheld told his comrades: *'Je suis foutu. Laisse-moi ici et pars avec les hommes'* – I'm finished. Leave me here and get away with the men. Still they refused to abandon him. Instead, one party set out to fetch Pleydell, while the rest stayed with their injured comrade. But by the time they'd fetched the doctor, Zirnheld had passed away.

They buried him where he'd died, piling rocks on the grave to protect it from scavengers. On a small cross cobbled together from old ammo crates, they wrote the following: *'Mort au champ d'honneur'* – died on the field of honour. Before setting out for the mission, Zirnheld had had a premonition of his own death. He'd told one of his fellow French SAS, 'I'm going to die. But I am at rest.' Upon returning to Bir El Quseir, his comrades gathered up their dead commander's possessions, among which they discovered a poem entitled '*La Prière du Para*' – The Paratrooper's Prayer.

A few of the lines from it give the measure of the man:

> I ask not for riches,
> Nor success, nor even health.
> My Lord, you are asked for such things so much
> That you cannot have any more.
> Give me, my God, what you have left.
> Give me what others don't want.
> I want uncertainty and doubt.
> I want torment and battle.
> And give them to me absolutely, O Lord,
> So that I can be sure of having them always.

Inevitably, the runaway success of the Sidi Haneish raid was tempered with loss. At Bir El Quseir they counted the cost. Six jeeps damaged – three of which had had to be abandoned – and two fatalities: Robson and Zirnheld. By comparison, they reckoned that as many as forty warplanes had been destroyed, though they would report just thirty, lest MEHQ accuse them of grandstanding. But still the ghosts of the dead haunted the escarpment, and no one doubted that the hunt was still very much on. After such an audacious attack, the enemy were bound to keep coming after them every which way they could.

Their Bir El Quseir hideout seemed in danger of discovery. Mayne had been among the first to make it back to the escarpment. Knowing nothing of Zirnheld's fate, he'd been sought out by Pleydell, who was yet to be asked to go to the wounded Frenchman's aid. Pleydell and the other stay-behinds had been eager for news. They'd found Mayne in one of the caves, looking as unconcerned as ever, head stuck in a Penguin. His fingers were bandaged, as he was suffering from desert sores.

'Hello, Paddy, how did things go?'

'Och, it was quite a good craic.'

That was typical Paddy Mayne, Pleydell mused. They probed some more, pestering him with queries, asking how many planes he'd destroyed and if anyone was injured.

'How many planes?' Mayne wondered out loud. 'It's hard to say. Forty maybe. I doubt we'll be claiming more than thirty . . .'

Mayne told them that Robson had been killed, plus there were a few minor injuries. Other than that, nothing too serious. He'd glanced at his hands, asking Pleydell if he might be able to redo the bandages. The flies were getting into them. As they walked to the doctor's cave, Pleydell tried to extract more details from Mayne about the raid, but not for the first time he seemed reticent to talk about it. It was to others that Pleydell would have to turn, to hear the full details of what had transpired.

He had just finished bandaging Mayne's hands, when there were three sharp blasts on a whistle – the agreed warning that aircraft had been sighted. This time, it was no distant drone. Instead, the roar of warplanes filled the caves, as they tore down the guts of the rockface. It was a flight of Stukas flying low, with fighter planes as escorts. They buzzed the SAS positions, but finding the escarpment seemingly deserted, they rerouted and pounced upon Zirnheld's convoy of jeeps instead. No one doubted they would be back.

A report in from MEHQ, based upon enemy signals intercepts, indicated the level of anger and rage the Sidi Haneish raid had provoked. Enemy commanders were apoplectic. Further search patrols were being dispatched, both by land and air. All told, some 500 enemy soldiers and airmen had been tasked with hunting down the desert raiders. Stirling discussed the ramifications with Mayne. Inevitably, such long and heavy use had left tell-tale signs here at Bir El Quseir. Tyre tracks hewn across the desert converged on the one point – their escarpment hideout. They would need to move and move quickly. They resolved to leapfrog some thirty miles west, to a similar-looking desert feature that they had discovered.

The move was completed that night, but with the relentless pace of operations and the lack of rest, figures were literally falling asleep at the wheel. Luckily, there were no accidents or fatalities. With water and food running low, they also needed to arrange an urgent resupply. They planned to do so by air. Two rough landing grounds had been checked out, in the desert near by, ones that the RAF had used earlier in the war. The plan was to get a fleet of Bombays to fly in laden with supplies. Stirling and Mayne were determined to keep the pressure on Rommel's forces, so the pace of raiding could not let up.

They also had prisoners to whisk back to MEHQ. The newest were a German doctor and his pilot, a curious and intriguing pair. They'd been captured in the most surprising of ways, when a Storch light aircraft had touched down in the open desert, ostensibly for a spot of spur-of-the-moment sightseeing. A combined LRDG/SAS patrol happened to be passing. They shot up the aircraft and seized both pilot and doctor as prisoners. The latter, Surgeon Captain Baron Markus von Luterroti, was something of a nobleman, while the former, a Luftwaffe officer, was Rommel's personal pilot. They were bound to have useful intelligence to offer MEHQ, and they were due to be dispatched aboard a Bombay once the supplies had been offloaded.

At least, that was the plan. But when Stirling made radio contact with Cairo, there was unexpected news. The entire SAS, lock, stock and barrel, was ordered to return to Egypt. Those vehicles that were serviceable were to be driven back, while any excess personnel were to be picked up by Bombays. Stirling, in particular, was needed in Cairo. Few details were provided as to why exactly, other than that a major operation was in the offing. Stirling objected vociferously. It made zero sense to recall his unit. They were here in the desert, with jeep-borne-raiding a proven winner, and with Sidi Haneish under their belt. They needed to be left to get on with the job at hand.

Stirling told MEHQ as much. They could achieve a great deal, 'if supported, not thwarted' by headquarters. They could paralyse Rommel's supply lines and shut down his key airbases. What could be more important? Sticking his neck out, he threatened to refuse the order, even if he faced a court-martial. But it was something of a hollow gesture. Without a resupply, they were finished here anyhow. Without bombs and bullets – and the means to sustain life – they were impotent. Typically, MEHQ would not be swayed. Orders were orders – they were to return or face the consequences.

Stirling stewed and seethed. He told Mayne that their best option was to execute a raid on MEHQ itself. The Irishman had trouble calming the Scotsman's rage. Of course, Mayne fully appreciated Stirling's anger. Just as they'd found their groove, they were being pulled back. Unless there was something they didn't know or understand, the order was senseless. But equally, there was no point fighting it. They would just have to rearrange their schedule. Stirling would have to go in the vanguard, flying out, while Mayne would bring up the rear, driving the convoy of battered, battle-worn vehicles.

That night they prepared to move. Repeated desert crossings had taxed nerves and alertness to the limit. In all the rush and confusion, it was discovered that the two newest prisoners had escaped. Search parties were sent out to track down the Surgeon Captain Baron and his pilot. Pleydell, who felt he had befriended the German doctor and won his confidences, felt particularly aggrieved, writing of their 'long chats' together. 'The German doctor reckoned another two years at least to the war, and the news is so bad I fear he is correct.' He had fine memories of a recent sing-along, the Germans belting out '*Marlene*; the good night of the Afrika Corps is very catchy and pleasant.'

The German doctor's escape felt like a personal betrayal to Pleydell. More to the point, it 'made things dangerous for us, as we work behind their lines,' he wrote in a letter home. 'We do our damage and get our results; in a few hours we do what it takes the Air-Force several weeks to do!' But that was all now thrown into jeopardy by the escape of those two captives.

Grabbing his pistol, Pleydell joined those heading into the night, hunting. Putting himself in the Baron's shoes he tried to imagine what direction the two fugitives would have taken. He'd follow the north star, of that Pleydell was certain. It was a sure-fire way to get to the coast. He set off in that direction, 'peering this way and that and clutching tightly at my revolver'. But the Baron and his pilot had slipped away. No amount of searching would find them.

Come dawn the hunt was abandoned. As Mayne pointed out to Stirling, the two escapees only had sixty miles to cover, after which they'd be reunited with their comrades, and there wasn't a great deal about the SAS that those two didn't know.

'Cheer up, David,' he added. 'The Jerries will have a full description of us by noon tomorrow. It's just as well we're leaving.'

Stirling's response was a disgruntled harumph. That was the last thing any of them needed right now.

CHAPTER TWENTY-TWO

The Fighting Irish

The SAS's 2/3 August 1942 pull-out from their Bir El Quseir hide-outs had been just in the nick of time. Over-flights by the RAF shortly thereafter revealed that an entire German armoured-car regiment had scoured the length and breadth of the rockface. Sure enough, the Surgeon Captain Baron and his Luftwaffe pilot had made good their escape, reporting to German high command that David Stirling and his British, Free French and 'Free German troops' – the SIG – were encamped there. A massive seek and destroy mission had followed, and the desert raiders had only just managed to slip away.

Once back in Egypt, Stirling's men felt alienated. Pleydell's experiences were typical. They'd spent so many long weeks either 'sand-happy or bomb-happy', only to return with shaggy hair and thick beards, to face the tedium and opprobrium of offi-cialdom. Charged to replenish the SAS's medical supplies, Pleydell found himself frustrated at every turn. The 'torpid' desk jockeys at MEHQ viewed the desert raiders with thinly disguised dis-dain. They were an outfit of 'hooligans' who wouldn't know how to use proper medical equipment. RAF crews were seen as being educated and intelligent, and were permitted to carry their own morphine phials and injecting kits. By contrast, the SAS were 'too ignorant' to be allowed any, so one morphia tablet per man would have to do.

After the pure kill-or-be-killed of desert warfare, Pleydell hated all of this, and especially the Cairo game-playing. Very quickly, he found himself longing to be back in the open wastes of the Sahara, stalking the enemy. Or rather, saving lives, as that was strictly his role. After their long Bir El Quseir sojourn, he was like a fish out of water. He couldn't wait to return to where he felt most at home. Very few of the raiders felt differently, Stirling first and foremost, as he was forced to confront the worst of the Cairo intrigues, which threatened all that he and Mayne held dear.

The SAS had been recalled from Bir El Quseir to undertake a mission that sinned against every cardinal rule of their existence. Taking Stirling's early pronouncements about how easy it had been for him and a small group of men to penetrate Benghazi harbour, planners at MEHQ had dreamt up a series of grandiose ventures, supposedly designed to strike a chain of killer blows against Rommel, even as his forces and those of the Eighth Army battled for supremacy. With deep irony, the mission had been codenamed Operation Agreement – Stirling, Mayne et al. were certainly *not* in agreement with any of it – while the SAS's own role was given the sub-name Operation Bigamy.

A slew of near-impossible targets were to be hit: Benghazi, Tobruk, the Jalo oasis, plus enemy communications and aerodromes. Every conceivable force was to be thrown into the fray: SAS, SIG, SBS, LRDG, ISLD, the commandos and more. The SAS alone was to be doubled in size, with the addition of a hundred 'commandos', who, while being excellent troops, were far from being versed in the ways of deep-desert raiding. Their target, Benghazi harbour, was to be occupied and laid waste. In order to do that, their two-hundred-strong force was supposed to cross over a thousand miles of desert, unseen and undetected, with a pair of M3 Stuart 'Honey' light tanks in tow, and keeping to a rigid schedule – for all the raids were slated to strike on the night 13/14 September 1942.

Operation Agreement was so blatantly ill-conceived, it held out all the promise of a badly scripted Hollywood disaster movie. But Stirling felt he could do little to resist. He was under orders, but more importantly the backroom manoeuvring to scupper the SAS was at its zenith. Despite their Sidi Haneish success and other recent victories, the Cairo mandarins – many of whom had grown up in the Victorian era – were determined to put the kybosh on the desert raiders, whose activities were really not the sort of the thing that British soldiers should be engaged upon, and certainly not British officers, and especially since they barely answered to any kind of orders or higher authority.

The previous month a closely typed memo, marked 'Secret', had been circulated by 'GHQ MEF' – Middle East Headquarters – 'considering the future of 1 S.S. Regiment'. Oddly, bearing in mind the obviously distasteful connotations of calling British special forces units 'S.S.' (an abbreviation of Special Service), some persisted in doing so, MEHQ being at the front of the queue. In the memo, Stirling's raiders were described as being 'raiding parties of the thug variety'. *Of the thug variety*; deeply insulting, not to mention mendacious and just plain wrong.

On the second page of the convoluted and perplexing document, it was mooted that: '1 S.S. Regt. as such to be disbanded.' The SAS was to be retained in some capacity, but it was to be incorporated into a 'Base Depot Special Forces', to be commanded by 'a Lieut.-Col. to be called "O.C. Base Depot and Commander Special Forces"'. Beneath the mind-numbing mumbo jumbo and gibberish, the memo dripped double-speak and the heavy hand of the 'layers of fossilised shit' at play. Boiling it all down, it amounted to a power grab, usurping Stirling and Mayne, and dragging the raiders firmly into line.

While Stirling should have been concentrating on the preparations for Operation Bigamy, and very possibly trying to argue against its sheer, blatant insanity, he was having to fight for the very survival of the SAS itself. Fortunately, in that endeavour he had a secret ally: Winston Churchill. During one of the SAS's previous forays into Benghazi, Churchill's son, Randolph, had formed part of Stirling's raiding party, of course. In time he'd written to his father, praising Stirling – 'a very great friend of mine' – and expounding upon the exploits of the SAS. Winston Churchill had never heard of these daring desert buccaneers or their exploits. His eyes and ears were duly opened.

Describing Stirling, Randolph Churchill had gushed: 'He is only 25 and recently got the DSO for his attacks on enemy airfields. At the moment the unit has 121 enemy aircraft to their credit . . . Not being a regular soldier he is more interested in war than in the army. He is one of the few people who think of the war in three dimensional terms.'

Despite the somewhat breathless tones, the letter was largely accurate and surprisingly perceptive. By the time of Randolph's involvement with the SAS, their tally of warplanes did stand at around '121'. More to the point, Stirling, aided by Mayne and Fraser, did have the ability to perceive the desert war, at least, from multiple perspectives, and especially from those least considered by other, more conventional mindsets. Randolph's words hit home. Churchill asked privately if a briefing might be given to the British newspapers, so that the desert raiders might get a little press coverage – and the British public a much-needed lift.

In early August 1942, Churchill happened to pay a visit to Cairo. His schedule was unbelievably hectic. Recently in Washington for his meetings with Roosevelt, he was en route to Moscow to see Stalin, and bearing something of a poisoned chalice. His mission was to sell to the Soviet leader the plans for Operation Torch, the first major amphibious operation by joint US–British forces in the war. Stalin had pushed for an assault on Europe. Operation Torch wasn't quite that, for the landing forces intended to hit the beaches of north-west Africa – chiefly Morocco and Algeria. Consequently,

Churchill felt as if he was 'taking a large lump of ice to the North Pole'.

Unsurprisingly, his Cairo stopover was short and frenetic. Somehow, he managed to find time to meet with Stirling, the commander of a unit in which his son had served, and which seemed to hold out such great promise for daredevil exploits, martial spirit and elan. Churchill was reportedly bowled over by the SAS commander. He borrowed a quote from Byron's *Don Juan* to sum up his impressions: 'He was the mildest-mannered man / That ever scuttled ship or cut a throat.' The result of their meeting was a short note, addressed to Stirling and asking him to outline what 'should be done to concentrate and coordinate the work you are doing'.

In the SAS War Diary, that 'Most Secret' missive was given pride of place. It was captioned: 'Note from Churchill's private secretary written the morning after David Stirling had dinner with the Prime Minister.' Dated 9 August 1942, the note, penned by Sir Leslie Rowan, then serving Churchill in that role, asked for Stirling's written response that very day. In other words, Churchill wanted to read it, and to take action on its contents, before he caught a flight onwards towards Moscow. Stirling's – of necessity, hurried – response began: 'PRIME MINISTER, I venture to submit the following proposals . . .' So rushed was it, that it included several spelling errors and even missing words. Nevertheless, the meaning and import were clear.

Stirling's two-page proposal effectively cemented his role as commander of the SAS, plus related special forces units, to run operations entirely independently and as he saw fit. In a sense it was a power grab, one designed to insulate him and his men from the layers of fossilised shit. But Stirling also made some telling points, one of which read: 'The planning of Operations by those who are to carry them out obviates the delay and misunderstanding apt to be caused by intermediary stages and makes for speed of execution which/in any Operations of this kind is an incalculable asset.' (The 'in' had been left out of the first draft, so was inserted afterward by means of a slash, and left sitting above the line.)

Despite the sloppy typing and grammar, Stirling's point was well made. Speed, aggression, surprise – none of that was possible if the SAS had to answer to a cumbersome and outmoded chain of command. Planning of operations should be vested with the SAS, Stirling averred, while the unit remained at the disposal of the Eighth Army and related forces, for specific missions. Solidifying command and control would prevent any clashes, 'of which there has already been more than one'. Training would be boosted, which, with the number of recruits flocking to Kabrit, was an absolute priority.

Churchill appreciated how winning wars was as much about the message as the means. In his view, the SAS commander possessed just the right combination of daring, panache and charm. As he had captured Churchill's imagination, so Stirling and his unit of daring buccaneers would capture the hearts and minds of the British people. It was exactly what the moribund war effort in North Africa needed. Churchill coined the name 'the Scarlet Pimpernel' for Stirling, the hero of the novel of the same name, which features a wealthy, foppish protagonist who is in reality a master swordsman, plus a doyenne of trickery, deception and disguise.

Articles began appearing in the British newspapers, trumpeting the exploits of 'The Phantom Major'. A 3 September story in the London *Evening Standard* recounted the tale of the SAS's raid on Benina Airbase, which had ended with Stirling attacking the hut full of sleeping guards, describing how he 'lobbed the grenade and slammed the door'. The press took up the hue and cry, lauding the 'newest terror of the desert', a 'Robin Hood in battledress' who quartered enemy lands with his band of 'merry men' behind enemy lines. 'Over the far-flung wastes of the great Western Desert no name strikes more fear in the heart of the enemy than that of the Phantom Major.'

Though somewhat lurid and sensationalised, the press coverage served its purpose. The SAS had crept out of the shadows. It would be much harder to kill off the Phantom Major and his band of raiders, now that their exploits – or at least, a little of the basic detail – were public. The British people were in dire need of such tales – of success, of striking back, of taking the fight to the enemy. Stirling and his men had delivered.

Had Churchill not happened to be transiting through Cairo in the late summer of 1942, the SAS might well have been eviscerated; killed off; disbanded. Certainly, if dragged into the remit of MEHQ's 'Base Depot Special Forces', key figures – Stirling, Mayne, Fraser – would have lost heart. As it was, Churchill had ridden to the rescue. In a little over a week's time he would be back through Cairo, his work in Moscow done, by which time the future of the SAS would have been decided. Instead of being hamstrung, it was to be expanded into a full Regiment, with promotions in rank for the key players. Stirling had aimed for the stars. With Churchill's backing, he'd pretty much got there.

The very same 'GHQ MEF' luminary who had composed the July memo – depicting the SAS as raiders 'of the thug variety' – ate a large dollop of humble pie. Executing a rapid volte-face, this was now a unit worthy of high praise – 'a body organised essentially as a raiding force behind the enemy's lines . . . It has had conspicuous success in the past and its morale is high.' Using phrases apparently borrowed from Stirling's own memo to Churchill – 'avoidance of some of the overlapping which might lead to disaster' – the author declared that 'the personality of the present commander . . . is such that he could be given command of the whole force with the appropriate rank.'

In short, Stirling was to be promoted to lieutenant colonel,

Mayne to major, and the SAS was to be hugely expanded and let off the leash. As Mayne would express it, pithily: 'The buggers in Cairo were at last beginning to show a titter of wit.'

The SAS was truly back in business.

Only, it very nearly wasn't. In the interim, Operation Agreement had gone ahead, the SAS riding into an unmitigated disaster.

By the time the massive convoy of vehicles had executed their 1,200-mile infiltration into the Jebel, the two Honey tanks had given up the ghost, and the greatest fear was that the enemy knew the SAS were coming. Bob Melot – ISLD aficionado turned desert raider – had his spies out in force. Their warnings were stark: the Benghazi garrisons knew all about the coming raid. The enemy had drafted in hundreds of extra troops and were ready and waiting. Fearful of what lay ahead, Stirling radioed Cairo, seeking guidance. The response was that they were to ignore all such warnings – dismissed as 'bazaar gossip' – and to proceed as planned.

Accordingly, on the night of 13 September 1942 a vast column of jeeps trundled toward the port city, with tension and angst at fever pitch. They drove straight into a trap, as mortars and machine-guns opened up from all sides. The first vehicle, Gentleman Jim Almonds' jeep, was packed with explosives intended for blowing up enemy shipping in the harbour. As Almonds revved his engine and gunned his jeep through a first roadblock, so they were hit, petrol and explosives igniting in a cataclysmic blast. Mayne's vehicle and one other took up pole position, and it was largely due to the fearsome work by their Vickers-Ks gunners that many would escape alive.

As Mayne held firm, a relatively fresh recruit, Chris O'Dowd, was on the twin-Vickers in the rear, hammering out the fire. O'Dowd, a southern Irishman, had been hand-picked by Mayne for this mission, as had Bob Bennett and one or two others. Though O'Dowd and Mayne hailed from different sides of the border, there had been an instant bond between them. 'Mayne was proud to be Irish, and liked nothing more after a few jars than to belt out "The Mountains of Mourne" or "Come Back, Paddy Reilly" at the top of his somewhat unmelodic voice,' wrote Gearoid O'Dowd, Chris O'Dowd's nephew. Lance Corporal O'Dowd had been tested in battle already, and had not been found wanting. On the outskirts of Benghazi, ensnared in that murderous ambush, he would truly come into his own.

O'Dowd found himself 'in the thick of it, coaxing the twin Vickers-K to its optimum performance'. The concerted firepower of the lead jeeps brought the rest of the column precious time, allowing Stirling to signal an immediate withdrawal. That was easier said than done. The enemy had mined either side of the road to ensure the SAS were trapped. Chaos ensued, 'amid the din of machinegun fire, explosions and revving engines'. Mayne's jeep and its sister vehicle kept hammering out the fire, unleashing 'a devastating attack', burning through pan after pan of ammo. Once the rest of the convoy had finally made an about-turn, Mayne gave the word for the last two vehicles to pull out. With one last, devastating salvo they turned tail and ran.

At age eighteen O'Dowd had run away from home, in his native Galway on the west coast of Ireland, to join the British Army. One of eleven siblings from farming stock, when attending the local Gortjordan School, O'Dowd had been obliged to bring a daily sod of peat for the classroom fire, or they'd freeze in winter. Hunting and fishing were his earliest pursuits and he was a crack shot, but he was also blessed with a strong sense of right and wrong. His parents, who had Irish folk music and singing in their blood, impressed upon him the need to stand up to bullies. He'd done just that at Gortjordan, learning to be good with his fists. Witnessing the rise of Hitler – a bully and despot without equal – he'd hungered to fight back, but how?

Finally, he'd taken the plunge, eloped to England, and signed up with the Irish Guards. Fortunately, his parents had forgiven his running off to war. He'd deployed first to Norway before being recalled for the defence of France. In August 1940 he'd volunteered for Special Service, joining No. 8 Commando and deploying to the last-ditch defence of Crete. Fully three-quarters of the commandos were killed or wounded, and 'Cristy', as he was universally known, was lucky to have made it out of there alive. With Middle East Commando being disbanded, O'Dowd had volunteered for the SAS, but due to various delays had only made it into the ranks that spring.

O'Dowd shared with Mayne a certain penchant for fisticuffs. In a Cairo bar, a 'loud-mouthed' Australian soldier had taken a dislike to him. They'd set upon a way to decide their differences. They'd have a punching competition, the prize being a crate of beer. The Aussie went first, cracking O'Dowd on the chin so hard, he expected the Irishman's head to come off, or at least to knock him senseless. Instead, O'Dowd just stood there and readied his counter-punch. Apprised of his adversary's composure, not to mention his grit, the Australian pulled out a wad of cash, paid for the beer, and left.

With O'Dowd, as with Mayne, fighting ran deep in the blood. As a man of Reg Seekings' calibre would conclude, O'Dowd was a very fine soldier, none better. This wasn't the first mission on which the Irishman had served as one of Mayne's party, but it was to be the first upon which O'Dowd would witness just what made Mayne so special, forging him into an unsurpassed leader of men. Running from that Benghazi ambush, they'd raced for the comparative safety of the hills. Even as they had done so, the sky began to lighten and there were the first distant growls of enemy aircraft.

A deadly game of cat and mouse ensued, as Mayne tried to dodge the avenging warplanes. At one point, a particularly determined pilot stuck doggedly on their tail. In an effort to lose him, Mayne had floored the accelerator and thrown the vehicle this way and that, as the aircraft kept squirting out bursts of fire. On a particularly testing turn, one of Mayne's men was hit and tumbled off the rear of the speeding vehicle. Mayne sought cover in a deep chasm that cut through the Jebel. Once they'd made it in there, without a word to the others Mayne hurried off on foot, heading back the way they'd come.

A while later he reappeared, their wounded comrade slung over his shoulders. Laying him down, Mayne made the injured man as comfortable as he could, while Bob Bennett forced a drop of rum through his parched lips. He came around, mumbling incoherently, but at least he was alive. All that day they'd remained hidden in the shadows of that deep ravine, listening to the bark of machineguns and the crump of bombs.

Some 'poor sods' were taking a real pounding, Mayne growled, as each successive air attack reached its crescendo.

At one point a particularly fearsome explosion erupted on an overhanging cliff, an avalanche of blasted rocks tumbling down.

Mayne fixed his comrades with a look. 'What the blazes ... am I doing here in this bloody war?' he demanded. Back home in Ireland he could be 'fishing and shooting and drinking to my heart's content'.

Bob Bennett shrugged. By now he was getting accustomed to his commander's somewhat unorthodox mindset, and how to deal with it. 'I really don't know, sir. Unless, sir, it's because you just love a scrap.'

Whatever was the truth of the matter, Mayne made it clear how fed up he was with 'this bloody fly-infested desert'. He wasn't the only one who was brassed off right then. As O'Dowd fully appreciated, he was 'one of the lucky ones'. As yet he was uninjured, and he put his incredible good fortune down to being part of Mayne's party, for the SAS commander's good fortune seemed to follow him everywhere. But one of O'Dowd's close friends, Corporal Anthony Drongin, had been far less fortunate. Riding in a different jeep, he'd been hit during the ambush, suffering horrific wounds. A former Company Sergeant Major (CSM), Drongin had proved to be a hard, hard man and something of a loner, but equally he was utterly selfless – Stirling's ideal recruit.

During the Benghazi ambush an armour-piercing round had smashed through Drongin's hip, while a second man in their jeep had had his arm blown apart. So serious was Drongin's injury that he'd asked Reg Seekings to shoot him. Instead, they'd left him by the side of a track, promising that they'd come back with the medics, and 'pick him up and take him in'. Whether Drongin would make it was anyone's guess, especially as they faced a gruelling journey across hundreds of miles of desert, just to reach friendly lines.

As they sheltered in that ravine, what really flummoxed Mayne was just why the enemy had failed to close the trap at Benghazi. They'd had ample forewarning, so how had they let that massive column of jeeps slip away? Air attacks were all well and good, but they should have finished the raiders when they had the chance. If Mayne were commanding the city's defences, he'd have sent out motorised columns on one front, while dropping airborne troops on the other, boxing in their prey. The lack of initiative shown by the enemy was confounding. How on earth had they bungled it at Benghazi?

Come to think of it, Mayne mused, why didn't they hit the SAS training base at Kabrit? That was exactly what he would have done. Drop airborne troops over Kabrit and cut the head off the SAS snake. The Germans had the capability. They'd proved as much when attacking Crete, unleashing thousands of paratroopers. If they struck at Kabrit with overwhelming force they could seize the base and get re-supplied by air, becoming a real thorn in the backside for British forces. The lack of such initiative from the German high command was mystifying.

In fact, Rommel had been struck by the breadth and reach of the

Operation Agreement raiders. Though all the assaults had largely failed – barring one, against Barce Aerodrome – they'd caused him a great deal of alarm with this concerted attack deep behind his own lines. Rommel had grown used to such operations being executed by 'the Commandos under the command of Colonel Stirling', which had caused 'considerable havoc'. But the scale and barefaced daring of the Agreement raids was something new, forcing Rommel to double and triple his defences.

Come nightfall, Mayne and his men loaded up their jeeps and headed back to the rendezvous point, a deep wadi that cut through the Jebel. There, Pleydell had established his aid station. They reached it, only to discover the worst. Bob Melot was severely wounded, having been shot in the stomach and legs. Drongin was there, and the prognosis for him was bleak. There were dozens more wounded, some severely. The situation had been made infinitely worse in that a greenhorn raider – one of the Operation Bigamy recruits – had driven his jeep into the RV point in broad daylight, so alerting the enemy to its location.

Carnage had ensued. Enemy warplanes had pounced, and soon the length and breadth of the wadi was full of burning vehicles and dead and wounded. Pleydell would be awarded a Military Cross for his heroics that day. The citation would praise his attending to 'the wounded without any thought of his own safety . . . paying no attention to the bombs and bullets . . . He undoubtedly saved many lives by his bravery and skill.' At one stage he'd headed out in a jeep to fetch one of the injured, despite the fact that movement drew the enemy. That was how Corporal Drongin had been brought in.

With nightfall, the survivors of that nightmarish day took stock. One thing was for certain: to remain there any longer would spell death or capture. Mayne offered to take a first convoy, blazing a trail back towards friendly lines. As all were running low on fuel, food and water, he would have to pioneer a route that would offer the chance of resupply for those who followed. Stirling, tortured by their losses, opted to remain in the Jebel, in an effort to round up stragglers. Then there would be a third escape party orchestrated by Pleydell, and laden with the wounded. But now came the crunch moment. Some were simply too badly injured to survive such a long drive. It would be the death of them. Of that Pleydell had no doubt, and he had good reason for such certitude.

During the journey out two men had been injured, when their jeep had hit a mine. Pleydell had done all he could to save them. By a herculean effort he'd got them to the Jebel alive. At that point, Mayne had wandered over, offering each of the wounded a cup of hot sweet tea. The SAS commander had supported each man, as he'd sipped at the brew. It was typical Mayne, Pleydell observed, 'always ready to help' while being careful not to get in the way. Mayne told the doctor that his evening meal was ready at the cook's lorry. Pleydell went to eat, Mayne keeping an eye on the wounded. Later that night one of the injured men passed away. Pleydell was forced to amputate the other's leg, in a desperate effort to save him, 'with an officer to help me, and the dust blowing'.

Those experiences had been harrowing. Now, Pleydell had dozens of injured, and some were never going to survive the coming journey. 'It was the devil,' Pleydell would write, in a letter home. 'Again, I was alone . . . damn difficult to see what you are doing. I did not dare risk any bleeding . . .' To make matters worse, with the number of vehicles that they had lost there was precious little space for any stretcher cases. Bob Melot refused to be left behind. No matter what, he vowed he would survive the rigours of any journey. But with four of the worst injured – Corporal Drongin, plus Captain Chris Bailey, Sergeant James Webster and Eustace Arthur Sque, a logistics officer attached to the SAS – there was no other option.

Pleydell volunteered to remain with the wounded, but that

was vetoed by Stirling and Mayne. He was far too valuable to lose. The SAS doctor had two medical assistants, recent recruits, attached to his team. They were obliged to toss a coin, to decide who would stay behind. 'It was a strange scene that night, by the fitful light of the burning lorries,' wrote Pleydell, 'tossing a one piastre piece and the two medical orderlies solemnly calling heads or tails.' It was Johnson, one of Pleydell's assistants, who made the losing call.

The plan for the wounded was simple, but it relied upon the enemy showing the kind of clemency and due process that should be extended to bona fide prisoners of war. They would be loaded aboard one of the surviving trucks, which would be driven back towards Benghazi, flying a Red Cross flag. There, Johnson would give them up to the mercy of the enemy. That decided, Pleydell's convoy of injured left in one direction, heading east towards safety, while Johnson and the worst wounded set off in the lone vehicle, heading in the other. None of those five men, not even Johnson, would survive, though their actual fate at the hands of the enemy remains shrouded in mystery.

Like Mayne, Pleydell had a firm belief in luck and fate. He'd write home about how the number thirteen had proved cursed here in the desert. 'I have been in two attacks launched on the thirteenth, and they were both such utter washouts . . . we only just got away . . .' The second of those two missions was the Operation Bigamy raid, and the long and fraught escape and evasion that followed would tax all to the limit, and beyond.

The herculean exploits executed by the survivors of Operation Bigamy, as they pressed east into the open desert, seeking sanctuary – running desperately short of food, water and fuel – would turn into an epic to rival that of Bill Fraser's escape and evasion from Marble Arch, some nine months earlier. Indicative of this, on 21 September 1942 MEHQ sent a message to the LRDG, demanding of them 'What is the last known location of FORCE Z [code for the SAS]? For over a week during their escape from Benghazi the SAS had simply fallen off the radar.

After innumerable trials and tribulations, Mayne's convoy finally made it to friendly lines. It was the first to do so. They'd headed for Kufra, a born-again version of Jalo or Siwa, and perhaps the most isolated and remote oasis in the entire Sahara. Lying over five hundred miles south of the Mediterranean coastline, and a hundred this side of the Egyptian border, Kufra was as far from the clutches of Rommel's Afrika Korps as one could possibly hope to venture. It was also the only option left open to the Operation Bigamy fugitives – the first viable port of call that might offer sanctuary.

That first evening at Kufra, Mayne was haunted by the memories of those they had been forced to leave behind. Those final, tortured hours would live with him for ever. The previous evening, as they'd camped in the desert, he'd wandered into the open seeking a few moments of solitude. Alone in the darkness, he'd heard the voices of those left behind, 'in the orchestra of the sand, that weird and macabre singing and wailing that haunts the wilderness'. He'd felt the spirits of his abandoned comrades, those they'd abandoned on the Jebel, the 'dying and dead in that accursed wadi'.

Shortly after reaching Kufra, Mayne and his party were made aware of a German radio report that claimed that the daring Colonel David Stirling was a prisoner-of-war of the Germans. The news spread fast. Churchill himself intervened. He cabled Cairo: 'Personal from Prime Minister to Commander-in-Chief, Middle East. Have you heard any rumours that David Stirling is missing? Can you give me any news?' It was a massive relief when Stirling and his party finally made it to Kufra, safe and sound. They'd lingered for as long as they could, trying to round up some of the dozens of missing men.

*

Against all odds, the SAS had survived – badly mauled, but far from down and out. In Mayne's mind the unit's longevity was down to one man – David Stirling. Though many might try to shift the credit onto Mayne, he shrugged it off. He nurtured a deep respect and friendship with Stirling, things he did not offer lightly to any man. He'd write of Stirling, when on operations without him later in the war: 'I only wish that D.S. was around.' This was in a note to Bill Stirling, who had played a behind-the-scenes role guiding his younger brother, David, in shaping the SAS, so it was a heartfelt admission. Likewise, Stirling valued Mayne's friendship enormously. He would make the enigmatic comment; 'I loved Paddy. I was far more fond of Paddy than he was of me.'

Mayne had once remarked to Bob Bennett, with whom he had a habit of sharing some of his most revealing insights, that, 'True riches cannot be bought.' You simply couldn't buy the doing of brave deeds or the camaraderie of close companions, to whom you were 'bound forever by ordeals suffered in common'. In short, friendship was an 'emerald beyond price'. Sage words, and so very fitting for the long months that they had spent in the desert at war.

Writing in the SAS War Diary, Stirling would conclude of their abortive Benghazi mission: 'I lost about 50 three-tonners [trucks] and about 40 jeeps on this raid but fortunately not very many personnel . . . It was a sharp lesson that confirmed my previous views . . .'

In truth, Operation Bigamy was a disaster on a scale eclipsing even that of Operation Squatter, the SAS's inaugural mission. At least with Squatter, the intentions and theory had been sound, and the motives wholly admirable. It was only the weather that had defeated them, and they had learned so much of such inestimable value. By contrast, all had known from the very outset that Bigamy was woefully ill-conceived. Imposed on the SAS and related units from on high, many fine men had lost their lives, or suffered horrendous injuries – and for what?

For a set of unrealistic, misguided priorities, but more to flatter egos, and due to the hubris of a few back in Cairo.

Moments before their jeep had been blown to pieces at the outset of the Benghazi ambush, Jim Almonds and an Irish Guardsman called Fletcher had fortunately leapt free. They were captured and subjected to a horrific humiliation, being dragged through the streets of Benghazi and abused, beaten and spat at, before suffering mock executions. Later, Almonds was joined in his cell by what was apparently a British officer and a fellow POW. That figure introduced himself as a Captain John Richards, explaining that he'd been on an intelligence-gathering mission, and was trekking back to friendly lines when he was captured.

Appearing almost obsequiously friendly, there was something that struck Almonds as being not right about 'Captain Richards'. For a start, he claimed to have crossed eighty miles of desert on foot, but his boots appeared squeaky clean, and he didn't seem the slightest bit fatigued by his ordeal. He also asked a great deal of questions. Captain Richards was in reality Theodore Schurch, and he was there at the behest of Lieutenant Colonel Mario Revetria, the regional head of the Servizio Informazioni Militare (SIM). Of course, Schurch was seeking yet more detail on the bête noire of the Axis powers in North Africa – the SAS.

Thankfully, Almonds, suspicious from the outset, wasn't inclined to talk. Yet there would be other captives who would not prove quite so perceptive or so sharp. More to the point, other traitors were waiting in the wings, and one would penetrate right to the heart of the SAS itself. That man would take the form of The Honourable Douglas Webster St Aubyn Berneville-Claye, Lord Charlesworth, or at least that was the title he claimed to exult in, when he volunteered for Special Service in the autumn of 1942. To expand to Regimental status – some 600-strong – required massively boosting the ranks of the SAS, but even so for a recruit of Berneville-Claye's calibre and background to be accepted was shocking.

In truth, D. W. St Aubyn Berneville-Claye was really plain Douglas Clay, son of a sergeant in the British Army hailing from a working-class East London family. Clay had an incredibly scurrilous and chequered past. At age seventeen he'd enrolled at the Army Technical School, Chepstow, but had quickly resigned, so as to marry his then girlfriend. That union had lasted a matter of weeks, after which Clay signed up to the RAF, but went AWOL to marry a second young lady – bigamously. From both marriages there was a child. Clay began wearing his father's old uniform, onto which he sewed a set of RAF's pilot's wings. He stole a chequebook and started writing false cheques, which landed him in court.

He was charged not just with fraud, but with impersonating an officer in the Armed Forces. Undaunted, he adopted his 'Honourable' title and the convoluted and entirely fictitious name and, armed with that, he blagged his way into Officer Training at Sandhurst. He claimed to be an alumnus of Charterhouse, a top public school, and of both Magdalen College, Oxford and Emmanuel College, Cambridge. In October 1941 he'd been commissioned as a second lieutenant. He was again charged with cheque fraud and was court-martialled, but claiming to be a qualified barrister he'd represented himself and somehow got off. In June 1941 he'd been posted to Egypt, and three months later he volunteered for the SAS, arriving for training at Kabrit shortly thereafter.

In short, Clay was a choice cad and a bounder. More to the point, he was a dangerously deluded fantasist. But with his dark wavy hair, clipped moustache and his boyish 'film star looks', he could be highly convincing. He had the gift of the gab and could pull the wool over most people's eyes. It seems that Stirling, in his hunger for new recruits, was likewise duped. More worryingly, Clay had a knack for pretending to 'be one of us', while holding quite contrary views and values. From the outset, Clay – or Berneville-Claye as he now called himself – proved a deeply unpopular recruit at Kabrit. Nicknamed 'Lord Chuff' – chuff being slang for the backside – he was shunned like the plague.

Stirling would claim that Lord Chuff was only ever allocated to a quartermaster or stores role, and to 'transport convoy' duties. It would have been wholly advisable to restrict the only traitor ever recruited to the SAS to far less than that, if not to clap him in chains. Unfortunately, 'Clay', as official SAS documents referred to him, did far more than simply muster the stores or drive trucks. By early October 1942 he was firmly ensconced at Kufra, the SAS's new forward base, and had talked his way into overseeing signals traffic from there to Kabrit. His clear lack of experience was reflected in the flurry of messages, and the schoolboy errors they contained.

One, to 'SAS BDE KABRIT' from 'BERNEVILLE CLAYE', complained that he was 'unable to send roll of personnel holding squadron appointments until they are known'. It attracted a more or less instant rebuke from Stirling, who told him, 'In future you will cut out all but the last of your names from signals i.e. CLAY.' Stirling further warned that he was 'too busy to cope with domestic administrative difficulties', which should in any case be raised by 'letter', restricting wireless signals to 'matters of operational' importance.

On that note, Stirling went on to demand of Claye: 'State how many 3 tonners required to lift stores to RV and by what date they are expected by Mayne.' By now, Stirling was shuttling between Kabrit and Cairo, busy overseeing the training of hundreds of fresh recruits, when he wasn't hospitalised with desert sores and various other ailments. Mayne had returned to what he did best – he was out in the desert, raiding.

And Claye, a future member of the SS (*Schutzstaffel*) who would vow to fight in the Nazi cause, was serving as some kind of go-between.

CHAPTER TWENTY-THREE

Raiders of The Great Sand Sea

Rarely had war been waged like this before. Finally, Mayne was in his element. Isolated in this great sea of sand, the worries of the outside world were so distant, so hard to bleed through, that they could not impinge. Here, it was finally possible to distil all of life – all human existence – into waging war. Here, they could deliver butcher-and-bolt raiding at its purest – just as Churchill had called for. Here, Mayne could forget all about his woes – the dead, the missing; Eoin McGonigal even – and concentrate one hundred per cent on battle. It was perfect. No distractions. No tiresome orders being dispatched from on high. No interference from the pointy-headed mandarins at MEHQ.

Nothing to get in the way of the business at hand: that of kill or be killed.

Cradled in the deep desert, more or less totally immune to air attack, insulated from any interference from any senior command, this was where Mayne truly came into his own. Keeping true to a lesson first learned in his No. 11 Commando days, he was determined to look after his Jocks, while at the same time waging total, incessant war on the enemy. His radio signals from the time, though few and far between, reflect that very essence: *give me the tools to look after my men, and to do the job.* Nothing more. Nothing less.

'TO S.A.S. KABRIT. MOST IMMEDIATE. 150 ignitors

percussion. Sealing compound 1 pint. 24 one and a quarter lb incendiary bombs. 1 bale K.D. [khaki drill] shorts. 1 bale towels. 1 bale socks. Sun compass needles and fix screws and brackets and azimuth cds (cards) to me . . . Rations sent are battle rations and have no Potatoes, Bacon etc. Who is responsible for this. Send the rations . . . straight away. Ack [Acknowledge].'

As with their commander, so it was with his men.

Mayne had become their talisman – his means of waging war their means. There were no intricate plans drawn up. No agonising over whether a painstakingly calculated mission should or should not proceed – the kind of thing that time and again had stymied No. 11 Commando. No. Here, basically, there was very little planning required. This was an entirely different way of soldiering. This was all about instinct, intuition, grabbing the moment, spying opportunity, seizing the element of surprise and striking without warning or deliberation or a moment's hesitation, because you knew in your gut that this was right; that at this moment, in this place, with this target, you would win through and strike the fear of God – or more likely, the devil, bearing in mind the raiders' very appearances – into the hearts of the enemy.

No amount of planning could achieve that. In fact, overly detailed planning very likely ran contrary to the philosophy and the ethos that underpinned the present means of operation – which was all about audacity, flexibility, swift movement, instant decision making and the delivery of death and destruction when and where it was least expected. Elaborate planning tended to frustrate all of that. It slowed down the flash to bang; the transition from realisation of opportunity to action; to the strike; to pulling the trigger or planting the bomb and delivering the knockout blow.

Plans got in the way.

It was far better, as Mayne would show time and time again, to sally forth with all of your senses on maximum alert, hunting for your prey. They were out there. Unsuspecting. Unwilling to believe

311

that this far behind their own lines the British enemy might be present, and predatory, and very much seeking to attack. And that was why when they struck – when Mayne and his men thundered out of the empty desert, appearing like an impossible apparition, guns blazing – they delivered such a terrifying, crushing blow.

In this, Mayne led by example. He taught by example. He expected his men to follow. To adopt his form of warfare and to make of it their own. As Mayne knew fully well, this means of waging war – akin to that of the ancient Irish chieftains, or the berserkers of old – could not be taught in any kind of a staff college or classroom. It could only be learned out here, in the burning maw of the desert, deep inside the enemy's backyard, as small columns of heavily armed jeeps headed out time and again into battle.

They had travelled here via Kufra, pushing north from there to this deep-desert hideout. This was Bir El Quseir reborn, only in arguably the most beautiful and captivating, yet harshest, of all parts of the Sahara – the Great Sand Sea. Immured in this end-less ocean of giant, sweeping, awe-inspiring dunes, they'd made their home in a part of the desert that the enemy believed it was impossible to navigate, let alone inhabit. Four hundred miles long by two hundred wide, no German or Italian columns ventured into the Great Sand Sea. No enemy aircraft patrolled its vast expanse, for fear of bailing out over such a landscape, wherein their bones would get bleached white among terrain that offered not the slightest scrap of shade or shelter, or of moisture to sustain life.

It was the autumn of 1942, and in the interim the SAS had very nearly been wiped out – literally on their ill-fated mission to Benghazi, and figuratively through the plotting and scheming of their detractors in Cairo. Stirling wasn't here with them. He'd remained in Egypt, tasked with his two-fold mission: one, to recover his health, for Operation Bigamy had truly taken it out of him; two, to train the flood of new recruits.

Not only had the SAS secured Churchill's crucial backing, they'd also received support from another key quarter. Recently, Lieutenant General Bernard Law Montgomery had taken over command of the Eighth Army, as General Auchinleck was replaced, part of Churchill's desire to ring the changes. In his field office 'Monty', as he was known to all, had pinned a photograph of General Erwin Rommel to the wall, and his pet spaniel, lying beneath his desk was also named ... 'Rommel'. Monty believed in knowing one's enemy; his rivalry with the Afrika Korps commander was fierce and distinctly personal.

From the outset he'd communicated his intentions to his troops most powerfully, signalling that the tide of battle was about to turn, the string of defeats transformed into victory. As he prepared to launch a massive counter-attack, he exhorted his men to 'destroy ROMMEL and his Army ... We are ready NOW. The battle which is now about to begin will be one of the decisive battles in history. It will be the turning point of the war. The eyes of the world will be on us, watching anxiously which way the battle will swing. We can give them their answer at once, "It will swing our way." ... LET NO MAN SURRENDER SO LONG AS HE IS UNWOUNDED AND CAN FIGHT.'

No fan of irregular warfare, at his first meeting with Stirling the sparks had flown, Montgomery expressing himself 'not inclined to associate myself with failure' – in other words, Operation Bigamy. It was a bluntly spoken and stinging rebuke. But privately, he acknowledged Stirling's unique, albeit mercurial, strengths. 'The boy Stirling is mad. Quite, quite mad. However, in war there is often a place for mad people!' In light of this, Monty charged the 'quite mad' Stirling with a specific set of tasks. The SAS was to strike at Rommel's supply lines relentlessly and without let-up, to add impetus to the coming offensive. Montgomery was convinced that the work of the desert raiders would have a 'really decisive effect on my forthcoming offensive'.

With backing from those two, hugely influential figures – Churchill and Montgomery – the SAS was beyond reproach or censure . . . for now, at least. It was broken down into four separate units: A Squadron, commanded by Mayne; B Squadron, presently being trained by Stirling et al. at Kabrit; C Squadron, consisting of the Free French contingent, and D Squadron, made up of what had once been the Special Boat Section, to concentrate on waterborne raiding operations and commanded by Jellicoe.

With his A Squadron, Mayne made sure to secure his A-team. Bill Fraser, now a captain, served as his second-in-command. Mike Sadler, promoted to lieutenant, was his steadfast navigator, Pleydell his stalwart medic. Proven hands included O'Dowd, promoted to corporal after his Benghazi heroics, Bennett, Rose, Lilley and more. To his eternal regret Seekings wasn't there, as he'd been retained for training duties at Kabrit. New faces included demolitions expert Lieutenant Bill Cumper, who like Fraser, was far from being typical 'officer class', and was renowned for his blunt-spoken ways and for being an irrepressible practical joker.

Mayne's policy was to take anyone, as long as they had the right mental attitude, were up to scratch physically, and would fight. At the other end of the social spectrum there was Lieutenant Harry Wall Poat, who had farmed tomatoes in Guernsey before the war. Poat spoke with a cut-glass accent and endeavoured to keep a neatly trimmed moustache and immaculate dress, even after weeks sojourning in the desert.

Lieutenant Johnny Wiseman, another fresh recruit, was a veteran of fighting the Vichy French in Syria. He'd volunteered for the SAS the September just gone. Over time Wiseman would grow close to Mayne, learning to respect and fear him, as they fought side-by-side. 'He was an exceptional man, particularly in action; the calmest, quietest man you ever saw . . . He could be quite frightening. Not a man to get on the wrong side of.'

The appearance of Mayne's Great Sand Sea raiders was likewise sure to instil fear. All supplies had to be driven out from Kufra, water included – so there was none to spare for washing or shaving. As a result, hair and beards grew wild. Unsurprisingly, the raiders appeared as a 'terrifying bunch' to any enemy forces they set upon. Mayne had a list of the types of targets to hit: rail-lines, locomotives, supply convoys, airbases, communications. But it was entirely up to him how, when and where he attacked. While he was absolutely in his element, there were those in MEHQ who shuddered to think of these 'raiders of the thug variety' running riot deep in the desert, where no one could exert an iota of order or control.

The base camp for A Squadron's was carefully 'tucked away in a deep hollow' with towering dunes rising on all sides. It was clean, quiet and isolated in the extreme, and at times it proved strikingly beautiful and captivating. At dawn and dusk the shadows were intensified, accentuating the 'symmetrical curves and sinuous out-lines' of the dunes, furnishing an 'artistry one could not easily forget'. At sunset, an ocean of sandy peaks and troughs rolled onwards, suffused in a thousand soft hues of purples and pinks. Come nightfall, the heavens stretched from horizon to horizon, presenting a vista 'of unfathomable depth enhanced by the deep blue sky, the brilliancy of the stars', which soothed away all 'cares and anxieties'.

Situated some 200 miles from the coastline, it was a three-day drive from there to reach the killing fields – Rommel's costal road and rail links. From the Great Sand Sea to the battle grounds seemed a whole world away, both physically, in terms of terrain, and mentally, in terms of peace and solitude. The dunes were packed hard on the windward face, with a softer, more friable leeward side. From time to time an overhanging drift would form on the crest of a dune, eventually collapsing in an avalanche of sand, making a distinctive, eerie noise – what the raiders termed the 'singing sands' or the 'booming sands'. As the sand sea was always moving, the tracks left by a patrol one week might be wiped out the next.

The dunes were generally orientated north-to-south, which was most fortunate. Many ran for dozens of miles, the trough between dunes offering terrain upon which it was possible to motor at 30–40 mph, north, towards enemy lines. Cross dunes were caused by wind eddies. When reaching one, it generally presented a smooth slope on one side rising to a knife-cut crest, with a precipitous face on the other, known as the *glacis*. The best way to cross was to charge up the gentler face, top the ridge, and ease over the drop on the far side.

By trial and error, Mayne and his men had mastered navigating the Great Sand Sea. They'd even managed to get Pleydell's new pride and joy there, an Indian-pattern ambulance – basically the same kind of Chevrolet as the LRDG used, but with a bulky ambulance-style back bolted onto it, emblazoned with giant red-cross symbols. Pleydell wanted it for dealing with any casualties, and to furnish 'solace and shade' in the furnace-like heat of Mayne's deep-desert raiding camp.

Riding in Pleydell's ambulance had come his new best friend, a coal-black dog that he'd acquired back at Kabrit. He'd christened her 'HMS Saunders', after the military camp of her origin. Intended to be a faithful companion, remaining at his side as he tended to the wounded, it was not to be. Shortly after HMS Saunders reached the Great Sand Sea, she became every man's dog. She upped sticks and set up camp at the cook house. In time it wasn't just the food that drew her.

An 'Italian' dog had been seized on an early raid, and she became HMS Saunders' running mate and best friend. Mayne, of course, fully approved. No military camp was complete without a dog or two. On one patrol they would realise that HMS Saunders had gone missing, intent on some doggy business or other. Mayne ordered an about turn, as they raced back many miles and duly retrieved her. As Pleydell himself conceded, of his four-legged friend: 'She was no longer my dog; she had become "A" Squadron's mascot.'

Ensconced within the Great Sand Sea, Mayne found time to read. Isolated in the desert he felt renewed, and peculiarly at home, considering that he hailed from the rain-lashed Emerald Isle. There was something of the Bedouin about Mayne, and he thrilled to the wild, open, uninhabited, timeless sweep of the terrain. Here, he rediscovered his love of poetry, and especially that of Omar Khayyam. Here, it spoke to him most powerfully. For Mayne, Khayyam, a Persian polymath, astronomer, philosopher and poet who lived almost a millennium ago, captured the sense of this place and this time admirably.

> One moment in Annihilation's Waste,
> One moment, of the Well of Life to taste –
> The Stars are settling and the Caravan
> Starts for the dawn of nothing – Oh, make haste!

Mayne had brought with him the Irish poems that were etched into his memory. Of an evening he would recite one or two, 'becoming so enrapt with their spirit that . . . his brogue became marked enough . . . to find the verses hard to follow'. Here, he was free to shape and to brand his Squadron as he saw fit. It took on a distinctly Celtic hue, as the Irishmen in his unit painted lucky shamrocks on their jeeps, and Mayne's deputies were wheeled out to croon their range of rebel songs.

'Paddy was Irish all right,' Pleydell would remark, 'Irish from top to toe; from the lazy eyes that could light into anger so quickly, to the quiet voice and its intonation.'

Mayne drew the Irish to his Squadron, just as naturally as the desert soaks up a rare burst of rainfall. There was O'Dowd, of course, but also the tall, fair-haired southern Irishman, Lieutenant

317

Bill McDermott. When he and O'Dowd teamed up together, they would wreak havoc and chaos almost without compare. Mayne never tired of quoting the oft-given refrain, whenever one of his fellow Irishmen was asked why they were fighting in this war: 'Of course, it's for the independence of the small countries.'

For Pleydell, there was something of the Spartans – the 300 at Thermopylae - about Mayne's A Squadron. After the Operation Bigamy debacle, he and Paddy Mayne had taken a weekend's leave together in Cairo, and their bonds had deepened. 'He is now my squadron leader and a Major,' Pleydell would write home, proudly, 'and I'm damn glad I'm with him. You can rely on him 100% to get you out of anywhere if things look a bit sticky.' Pleydell shared that sentiment with many in the Squadron, and for sure they were ready to wage war.

Mayne led one of the first missions. A fleet of jeeps motored to a point just a few miles short of the northern fringes of the Great Sand Sea, where a small dump was made, consisting of spare ammo, water and fuel. Those jeeps carrying the extra supplies turned for home, while Mayne's and three others headed into enemy lands. Pushing on, they quartered the desert. At one point they hid out in a deep wadi which had been used by a previous patrol. O'Dowd was with Mayne, and his jeep had developed mechanical problems. Leaving him and his party to repair it, Mayne pressed on, but ran into an area thick with enemy, coming under heavy machinegun and 20mm cannon fire. Turning back, he collected O'Dowd and his jeep, now fixed, and as a foursome they went hunting.

It was an hour before dusk when they came upon the perfect target: a convoy of trucks, heading along the track that led from the coast south to the Siwa oasis. Mayne ordered two of his jeeps to speed to the front and two to the rear, to box the enemy in. As the jeeps thundered across the open desert, a race began between the hunters and the hunted, the trucks charging ahead, throwing up a massive cloud of dust. By the time Mayne and his men were in range, the leading vehicles had got away, but the rest were raked with broadsides of Vickers-K fire. Realising that to continue spelled certain death, the drivers brought their bullet-torn vehicles to a grinding halt. The trucks were searched and planted with Lewes bombs, before the raiders withdrew to a safe distance.

They had some twenty Italian and German prisoners in tow. As they watched their trucks blown to pieces, they were visibly distraught. Chiefly, they feared being left in the desert to die. Mayne made it clear that he only had room to take a few. The rest would have to wait to be rescued. Some of the would-be POWs began to cry, begging to be taken, but there was no room. Leaving the group of wannabe captives with what little food and water they could spare, the jeeps powered away. Mayne and his men didn't doubt that those left behind would get picked up, for the Siwa track was well used. Indeed, in a sense they *needed* them to be. Only by hearing reports from such terrified survivors could the fear be multiplied and spread. Such eyewitness accounts were vital to undermining enemy morale.

As Mayne would write to his brother Douglas of the attack: 'We were like a lot of pirates – 10 days' beard – the poor wee Jerries and Eyeties, driving along as happy as you like . . . We whipped up from behind and the first they knew was our bullets, smacking through their three-tonners . . . Funniest thing were the prisoners – we can never afford to take many as they eat too much of our rations, so I only intended to take the one . . . the others looked so pitiable at being left that I took a couple more – they are useful at washing dishes and keeping my equipment clean.'

But for now, Mayne had a different use in mind for one of his Italian prisoners. 'Can you sing?' he demanded.

The captive confirmed that he could.

'Then sing!' said Mayne.

And so, 'through the desert night the S.A.S. men drove . . .

with the Italian singing all he knew from Verdi or Rossini . . .'
Getting into the spirit of things, Mayne threw in the odd Percy
French number, 'perhaps not strictly tuneful, but lively!' Finally,
a good while after leaving that shattered, burning convoy, Mayne
signalled that the choral party was over. He ordered his patrol to
split up. His and one other jeep would head south to pick up a
much-needed fuel and water resupply, while O'Dowd and three
other raiders would press north to hit the main coastal railway.

At 0200 hours the following morning, that four-man party crept
up to a stretch of track just a short distance inland from the port of
Mersa Matruh. Of course, thanks to their Kabrit training, O'Dowd
and his three fellows knew exactly how to cause maximum damage
to the track, and they set their explosives accordingly. 'Charges
were fixed four on rails and two on telegraph poles,' related the
official report. 'No sign of any life anywhere. Time pencils were
fired and party left area heading due South . . .'

So far, so good, but it was then they hit trouble. They'd only
made it a mile from the railway when O'Dowd's jeep suffered a
puncture. With the fuses running down to detonation hour, they
hurried to fix it, but all four spares proved unusable. They were
still struggling with it, when the first blasts tore apart the still of
the desert night.

The delay in fixing that puncture meant that come daybreak,
they were moving through open desert when an enemy warplane
was sighted. It was flying low, and there was zero cover anywhere.
Fearing they had been 'caught with trousers down', O'Dowd and
his team did the only thing they could think of. With bluff and
front to the fore, they pulled to a halt, hoping the aircrew would
mistake their vehicles for another group of wrecks, as the desert
thereabouts was littered with the detritus from recent fighting. It
must have worked, for no bombs or bullets were unleashed their
way.

A day's driving later they reached the borders of the Great Sand

Sea, having managed to shoot a gazelle en route. 'Made very good eating.' As they pushed on towards the SAS camp – known to all as 'Howard's Cairn', due to a distinctive pile of rocks erected not so far away, as a navigational marker – they came upon Mayne's party. They had also been in action, and had suffered their fair share of problems. Mayne had been forced to drive for twenty-four hours with both of his front tyres flat, for their only pump was in O'Dowd's vehicle. Fortunately, he'd run into Bill Fraser and his gang of raiders who were setting out on their own mission, and so had begged the use of a pump.

Under way once more, Mayne and his party had stumbled upon the most amazing sight imaginable. A Heinkel He 111 warplane had made a forced landing in the open desert. The aircrew were madly tapping out a message in Morse code, seeking assistance, when Mayne's convoy appeared. They got assistance of a kind, but certainly not what they had been hoping for. Shortly, the five airmen were forced to watch as their Heinkel erupted into a violent burst of flame.

There was an added bonus to coming upon that aircraft, for as Mayne explained to his brother Douglas, the 'loot question has looked up very well in the last few days'. Before wrecking that warplane, they retrieved 'automatics, a shotgun and a roller flex [sic] camera . . . with the reflex view-finder'. Mayne was an avid photographer, and he was forever taking souvenir snaps of his men in the field. No wonder he was happy at their haul of 'loot'.

This time, the German aircrew *had* to be loaded aboard the jeeps, for to have left them would have amounted to a death sentence. Privately, Mayne had a degree of sympathy for the enemy, and especially when they were vanquished and fearful. At heart, he appreciated that most of humanity – British, German, Italian, whatever – lived with the same hopes and fears and were burdened by similar troubles, and inspired by common goals. It was the machinations of the megalomaniacs like Hitler and his cronies that had brought them all to this point, and set them at each other's throats.

For O'Dowd, even as their convoy of jeeps neared the SAS base camp, the story of their raiding was far from over. It was 26 October 1942, and another patrol, commanded by the Irishman Bill McDermott, was heading out for war. During the drive through the dune sea, one of McDermott's seven-man party had been injured. So, O'Dowd – though he was 'no doubt looking forward to a rest' – volunteered to take the wounded man's place, which meant that he turned right around to head into the fray once more.

The official report on O'Dowd's second raiding mission in as many weeks reads as a terse, sparse, rigorously factual account, pared-down to the bare bones. 'Captured 4 M.G. [machinegun] posts on [railway] line south of Barrani-Bir Rim. Blew line and sidings. Trucks, food and water dumps and Jerry signals wagon destroyed. Strafed road and got two Lancias. Losses, one jeep and one to be recovered. Returned 3rd November.'

In truth, under McDermott's leadership and with O'Dowd to the fore – plus with Mayne's spirit and example driving them forward – they had, among many other wild exploits, captured an entire enemy railway station, taken all the staff prisoner, and thoroughly laid waste to it. Their exploits were driven partly by frustration, partly by an overexuberant enthusiasm to cry havoc and let slip the dogs of war.

Having set a pressure-activated charge on a section of rail track, they'd watched, aghast, as a locomotive had passed over it, unharmed. For some reason the explosives had failed to detonate. An enraged McDermott had ordered his men to seize the nearby railway station at Mersa Matruh instead. Shortly, the guards had been torn from their sleep at gunpoint. Mostly they were Italian, but a pair of Germans were also discovered high on a telegraph pole, having made an early start in an effort to mend the telephone line. At gunpoint, they were persuaded to come down.

With dawn fast approaching, the raiders got to work, lacing the station from end to end with bombs. O'Dowd set a charge with a 14-second fuse, having ordered one of the drivers to position a jeep near by, and to be ready to step on the gas. Triggering the fuse, O'Dowd made a dash for the vehicle and vaulted aboard. The driver, in his eagerness to get away, floored the accelerator, and O'Dowd promptly tumbled off the rear. The German and Italian prisoners were watching, the former dissolving into fits of laughter. Despite their predicament, they couldn't help but see the funny side of it, especially as O'Dowd had emerged unharmed. The Italians, by contrast, were 'cowering in sheer terror', and were unable to see the humour at all.

For his many raiding operations, and particularly for wrecking the Matruh train station, O'Dowd would be awarded the MM, his citation stressing his 'consistent bravery and steadiness'. It also made special mention of O'Dowd's actions on Operation Bigamy – '[he] was in the last vehicle to leave covering the withdrawal with accurate and sustained machinegun fire.' Regarding his Matruh railway station exploits, it stressed their 'capturing eighteen prisoners, blowing up the railway line and destroying wireless equipment'.

The LRDG's intelligence officer, Bill Kennedy Shaw, was one of the many who gazed upon A Squadron's exploits at this time with something close to awe. Mayne and his men reminded him of 'pirates of the seventeenth century, secure in the palm-fringed creek of some West Indian island, thrusting forth to raid the fleets of Spain'. There were tales of 'trains mined, railway stations wrecked, road traffic shot up and aircraft burned on their landing grounds'. Mayne's raiders would blow up the coastal rail line at least a dozen times.

Recognising the frenetic pace of operations, towards the end of October 1942 Stirling sent a 'secret cipher message' to Mayne:

'This station on continuous watch and can take or send messages at time most convenient for patrols.' In other words, Stirling's signals team were on permanent standby to respond to Mayne and his raiders' messages, whether regarding supplies, injuries or fatalities, or intelligence needs. Despite the massive distances involved, key radio signals did get through. One, from Stirling, on 27 October, proved invaluable. 'ITALIAN password from 22 (22) Oct until 5 (5) Nov is EUROPA (EUROPA) answer VESUVIO (VESUVIO).'

Most useful, and for all the obvious reasons.

Mayne's outgoing messages from the Great Sand Sea were all about securing the means to keep on keeping on. The tempo of raiding meant upping the frequency of supply convoys dispatched from Kufra, not to mention the in-bound flights from Kabrit laden with stores. Mayne's signals from the time reflected the punishment his jeeps, in particular, were taking: 'Ref tyres and tube size 6.15/16 also need rubber solution temperature gauge torch batteries ... Require also now GASKETS CYLINDER HEAD for Jeeps soonest possible.'

Stirling, overseeing all, was engaged in a tough and unrelenting juggling act. Towards the end of October he messaged Kufra: 'Reference requirements HOWARDS CAIRN convoy unable to dispatch by plane until Monday (.) Can you delay convoy until Tuesday.' The man orchestrating the bulk of the radio traffic at Kufra, and sorting out the convoys to be dispatched to A Squadron, was of course none other than Berneville-Claye. Gaff-prone, deluded, attention-seeking, he was about to make his biggest mess-up yet.

A new recruit, Corporal John 'Jack' Sillito, had joined Mayne's Squadron. In late October Mayne had sent a radio report - 'SILLETO [sic] missing since 18th Oct.' In the same 'secret cipher message' he recorded their one fatality so far during the weeks of intensive operations. '[s]HORTON [sic] killed in sand sea when his JEEP overturned he was buried by me.' Lieutenant Raymond

Shorten was both a former commando and a veteran of the mass jeep raid on Sidi Haneish airbase and of the ill-fated Operation Bigamy. It hit the Great Sand Sea raiders hard that a man of Shorten's calibre could have been killed, as his jeep plunged over a dune-crest, rolling down the far-side – the *glacis*. 'It's bloody awful,' Pleydell would write. 'I have lost a lot of friends.'

Not content with burying Shorten, Mayne messaged SAS headquarters: 'Can you send me his father's address?' He was scrupulous about writing to the nearest kin of those he lost, or went missing, in action. As for Corporal Sillito, he was even then engaged upon one of the most awe-inspiring trans-Saharan escapes ever. He would reach the fringes of the Great Sand Sea looking like a wraith, with 'blistered feet' and covered in 'desert sores', only to be discovered by an out-going patrol. His had been an eight-day survival marathon, during which he'd resorted to drinking his own urine to survive. Once back at the SAS's desert camp he was handed into Pleydell's solicitous care. As the SAS doctor noted of Sillito's epic sojourn, the 'dazed vacant look in his eyes told their own story of the harrowing experience'.

Even so, Sillito was very much alive, being dispatched to Kufra to properly recuperate. But for whatever reason, Berneville-Claye decided the truth was otherwise. On 31 October he sent a message to 'SAS KABRIT (R) STIRLING,' marked 'MOST IMMEDIATE' in bold red. Clearly, Claye felt he had something of real import to report. 'Regret parachutist SILLETTO [sic] 5672680 died in hospital in KUFRA today. He was brought in from HC [Howard's Cairn base] by LRDG suffering from diphtheria.' Diphtheria, a nose, throat and skin disease, is rarely fatal to adults. Sillito had certainly not succumbed. Scrawled in red pen across Claye's message were the words: 'Not so.'

Three days later Sillito was flown to a Cairo hospital, still very much alive. He would make a full recovery and return to raiding operations. As Claye was based at Kufra, the mistake was confounding. Perplexing. Inexplicable – unless viewed from the wider context of the deluded and fantastical alternative universe that 'The Honourable Douglas Webster St Aubyn Berneville-Claye, Lord Charlesworth,' inhabited. The fantasist received a stinging rebuke: 'SILLETTO [sic] arrived CAIRO today by air (.) Do not understand your message of 31/10 reporting his death . . . Signal name and number of parachutist who died in hospital at KUFRA.'

There is no record of any reply from the accused. Presently, Berneville-Claye was a troubling liability; a loose cannon. But before long he would cross the line to being the enemy within.

Amazingly, considering where they had based themselves, Mayne was sending at least some of his reports to Stirling by carrier pigeon. It was via a tiny canister attached to a winged-messenger's legs that the SAS founder was learning of the successes of his desert raiders. Stirling in turn was radioing Mayne specific target requests: 'Send earliest small party to blow line again between TOBRUK and FRONTIER also STRAFE road . . . After arrival convoy from KUFRA . . . prepare to attack MT [motor transport] staging point at SIDI BARHANI . . . Say whether you can undertake all tasks.'

By pigeon flights, among other means, he was getting confirmation of such missions. 'Am reassured by your . . . pigeon and aircraft Sitrep,' Stirling confirmed to Mayne. But at the same time the SAS founder was flagging. By the start of November 1942 he'd developed 'severe desert sores which are being converted into bed sores by treatment'. Hospitalised, he was forced to message Mayne that he was hors de combat, and that from now on, 'Actual choice of targets . . . and method of attack up to you (.) Congratulate all ranks on good performances especially STILLETO.'

Even as Stirling's own command, B Squadron, was being prepared for action at Kabrit, so he had fallen victim to the desert-raiding burn. The freshly trained recruits of Stirling's unit were slated to roll through Mayne's area of operations, so as to hit Rommel's supply lines beyond the Great Sand Sea, pushing further west than they had ever gone before.

Long before then, the Phantom Major needed to get well and be ready.

CHAPTER TWENTY-FOUR

This Is Not the End

Despite the churn of back-to-back raiding, Mayne found time to write. To his mother he sent assurances, fretting that after the growing press coverage she might be concerned for his safety. 'I hope you weren't worrying . . . after all the nonsense they were talking on the wireless . . . I am perfectly fit & contented & spend most of the time eating dates.' In fabulous Mayne fashion, he dropped in the following remark: 'Incidentally I am a Major now, I must develop a red nose and a pompous manner.' His letter is redolent of the pressing need to see home and family; 'there is an off chance that after things settle down a bit . . . I might get back home to see you, don't bank on it but it could happen.'

After asking if the cheque he'd sent 'Daddy' had arrived safely, to cover some of his home expenses, he turned to the question of the lost, for Mayne did not forget friends easily. He mentioned how 'George Duncan whom Babs knows about is missing.' Captain Duncan, the soldier-poet captured during Operation Whynot, the Sicilian airbase raid, was someone about whom Mayne had written to his sister Barbara before. Then he turned to Eoin McGonigal, for the Irishman was never far from his thoughts. 'I had a letter from Mrs McGonigal. I am awfully sorry for her but she is very plucky – [it will] soon be a year now since Eoin was killed.'

Eoin was killed: finally, Mayne appeared to have reconciled himself to the loss of his young friend. But the search for answers as to how, where and when he had died would be ongoing. Mayne would doggedly follow that trail, as he sought to learn of his friend's fate, and so he could tell those who cared something of the truth about what had transpired. Eoin McGonigal's mother Margaret was equally in need of answers and some form of closure. Via the Red Cross, she'd managed to track down those of Eoin's stick who had survived Operation Squatter, and she was determined to send them food parcels and discover more about his fate.

Margaret McGonigal had a prayer card printed for her missing son. It reflected the angst she felt at his loss and the nature of his dying; the dark mystery; the lack of knowing. On it she'd written: 'So when they told me you'd been left for dead I wouldn't believe them, feeling it to be true. Next week the bloody Roll of Honour said "Wounded and missing . . ."' Increasingly accepting that Eoin was gone, she would speak of his loss quoting John Maxwell Edmonds' 1919 epitaph, *Inscriptions Suggested for War Memorials*, 'When you go home, tell them of us and say, / For your tomorrow these gave their today.'

Mayne's closeness to his family was reflected in the strong relations he forged with his new family – his A Squadron SAS, the raiders of the Great Sand Sea. Utterly isolated as they were, he and his men had little sense of the war's bigger picture. In truth, the fortunes of the battle were turning. Privately, Rommel had recognised how dire things were looking, with stocks and supplies on all fronts being so low that his men were plagued by 'shortages of every kind', with debilitating effects.

At the end of October 1942 Rommel had written to his wife Lu, admitting that the situation was 'very grave'. By the time she was reading his letter, 'it will no doubt have been decided whether we can hold on or not. I haven't much hope left. At night I lie with my eyes open, unable to sleep . . .' Following a fearsome and intensive artillery barrage, Montgomery's forces finally broke through Rommel's lines. Mayne was ordered to stop blowing up the coastal railway, for it provided a useful supply route for the advancing British troops.

An early November 1942 message from MEHQ to 'All Patrols' reflected how Rommel had been thrown onto the back foot: 'Signs enemy withdrawal may be general. Much M.T. [motor transport] Rpt. M.T. reported along Coast Road . . .' How the tables looked to have turned. Regardless, Mayne did not appear inclined to let up the tempo one jot. A day after that 4 November message from MEHQ, Bill Fraser radioed SAS headquarters: 'Urgent message from MAYNE (.) Jeep tyres and tubes must be flown to KUFRA immediately otherwise unable to operate . . .' Mayne himself followed up the same day, with this: 'Also send here any good JEEPS.'

From the perspective of the Great Sand Sea raiders, the Eighth Army's breakthrough didn't change matters a great deal, if at all. There was still fighting to be done, and Rommel's fractured lines, riven by confusion and falling into disarray, were bound to offer rich pickings.

In fact, Montgomery's 200,000-strong army, with a thousand tanks in the vanguard, had punched through the German general's best-set defences in dramatic fashion. Days after scoring that historic breakthrough, Operation Torch went ahead. On 8 November 1942, a massive Anglo-American amphibious force landed on the beaches of Morocco and Algeria. From there they would push east, as the Eighth Army advanced west, catching Rommel's Afrika Korps and their Italian allies in a crushing, vice-like grip.

This marked a real turning point in the war. It was the first major Allied triumph since 1939. In London, Winston Churchill would celebrate this 'remarkable and definite victory' by ordering church bells to be rung the length and breadth of Britain. On 10 November 1942 he delivered his iconic speech, heralding how this pivot in the war in North Africa marked the change all had been waiting for: 'Now this is not the end. It is not even the beginning of the end. But it is perhaps the end of the beginning.'

But in the Great Sand Sea, life – and death – went on pretty much undisturbed. There was a tad more attention paid by Mayne and his men to the BBC news bulletins. Momentous events were clearly afoot. But as that arch-observer Pleydell noted, all felt 'a curious sense of detachment in listening to . . . these wireless programmes; it was like tuning into life in a different world; something that we had known in the past but dared not recall too closely . . .'

There is a marked sense of alienation in those words. As Pleydell would write to his sweetheart, he would have been horrified if anyone had told him before the war that he would be involved behind-the-lines raiding work, 'but now it seems as normal as crossing a street . . . I am afraid you will find I have changed.' Life in the Great Sand Sea with Mayne's raiders felt so intense and real, Pleydell wondered what the point of the 'dull routine life' had been that they had all led before. 'I wonder if I shall ever get back to it? . . . I do hope I don't find the post-war life too boring for words.'

One evening the wireless was tuned to a station playing the tunes of a London dance band. Pleydell watched, in bemusement, as two figures rose from the sand and mimicked the devil-may-care moves of the jazz-age dance craze, the Big Apple – 'swinging it hot!' More of Mayne's raiders got to their feet, and to the tunes of Bing Crosby, Vera Lynn and Jimmy O'Dea they grabbed an invisible, make-believe dance partner and began to strut their stuff in the sand. 'We laughed until our sides ached,' remarked Pleydell, at these 'weird antics in the vast and vacant setting'.

All danced, from the senior ranks to the lowest. There was no class or rank distinction in Mayne's Squadron. As the melodic strains of the dancehall numbers drifted over the night-dark desert, all were united in their isolation; their otherness; their killer mission. This was something that truly set them apart. Normal life

331

as they had once known it 'was now something that belonged to a different world', Pleydell observed. 'It . . . no longer belonged to us; it was unreal.'

Did that make these wild-haired, unwashed, bearded raiders bitter? Was there envy at the warmth and laughter and light spilling out of England's dancehalls, not to mention the smart and beautiful gowns of the girls twirling on the stage? Perhaps, yes, there was, for all things emanating from England appeared 'so smug and so superbly self-satisfied'. By contrast, here there was only sand and flies and heat and dust . . . and bloody killing to be done.

Mayne exhorted Pleydell to dance and sing with the rest of them. Pointing to those who gyrated and crooned amid the dunes, he tried to reassure the doctor, who was inclined to look askance at such wild excess, that they weren't totally losing it. 'He's singing his heart out. Don't you see, he's happy as a skylark. Och, never you mind, Malcolm, we'll have you singing "Macnamarra's Band" [sic] yet!' 'MacNamara's Band' was a turn-of-the century Irish song popularised by Bing Crosby and an old favourite of St Patrick's Day celebrations. It tells of various foreigners coming to Ireland to perform with the band of the song's title, one verse pretty much giving a flavour of the whole:

Oh, I wear a bunch of shamrocks and a uniform of green,
Hey, I'm the funniest lookin' Swede that you have ever seen!
There's Ryans, O'Brians, Sheehans and Meehans – they
    come from Ireland,
But, by yimminy, I'm the only Swede in MacNamara's Band.

As Pleydell watched and listened and Mayne exhorted him to join in, he was struck by one, overriding thought: how were any of these men ever going to return to 'normal' life, after this? Surely, many – possibly most – would experience real difficulties in settling back into a humdrum peacetime existence. There was something about the raw, animal, adrenaline-etched, kill-or-be-killed, almost tribal existence here in the Great Sand Sea that fulfilled a deep longing within the hearts and the instincts of young men. 'Could that longing, once allowed free rein, be curbed and suppressed again?'

Well, right then they were not about curbing or supressing any of it. Quite the reverse. Right then, that spirit needed to flow and to rage and to burn. They were about to head west once more. As the battlefront migrated, so did Mayne's raiders . . . Abandoning the magical setting of the Great Sand Sea, with regret, by late November 1942 they had motored west to Bir Zelten, a rendezvous set some 200 miles beyond the Jalo Oasis. There, they met up with Stirling and B Squadron, fresh out from Kabrit.

There were many new faces. Most had precious little raiding experience. In time, it would show.

From Bir Zelten, Mayne's men would keep doing what they did best, hit-and-run jeep-borne operations, harassing Rommel's beleaguered forces along 200 miles of their supply lines. As for B Squadron, they were to leapfrog ahead of Mayne's area of operations, thrusting into new and uncharted territory. It would prove murderously hard to navigate and it turned out to be crawling with enemy forces, not to mention less-than-welcoming locals. Badly mauled, firmly on the back foot, the enemy hungered for vengeance, and nowhere more so than against Stirling's desert raiders.

Shortly after B Squadron began their raiding operations, entire patrols started to disappear – killed or captured, no one seemed quite sure. Some of Stirling's men had been forced to surrender: with their supply lines being so impossibly elongated and fraught, they were all out of fuel, ammo and water. Unbeknown to the SAS, Rommel had charged his troops to hunt down 'Stirling's commandos' remorselessly. Not only that, he had formed a specialist unit to do so, which had even trained with captured Willys jeeps, to better assess their capabilities. That unit came complete with local trackers who could follow a mouse through the desert if charged to do so.

By late December 1942, B Squadron had lost over a dozen of its men and fully one-third of the officers commanding patrols. Reg Seekings, who had deployed alongside the B Squadron recruits, narrowly escaped death or capture himself, after his patrol was cornered by the enemy. He was not alone in attributing the high attrition rate to sending the least experienced men into the toughest of areas. As Pleydell would remark, the experience of the veteran raider was far more vital to this kind of work than 'zeal and valour'.

But of course, the losses were also down to the predations of the stool pigeons, like Schurch, those who had diligently worked to winkle out the SAS's inner secrets.

Shortly there would be worse.

Around mid-November 1942, Berneville-Claye had fallen off the logs of the SAS's signals traffic. Perhaps after reporting Sillito's death in error, he had finally got the boot. By 18 November, a 'Barlow' had taken over Claye's role, liaising between Stirling at Kabrit and Mayne in the field. But somehow, even after all that had transpired, Claye had gone on to deploy into the desert, at the very least taking 'charge of a transport convoy'. Giving such a man such a role was a fateful and inexplicable error, especially since it would lead, in turn, to Claye falling into enemy hands.

On 26 December 1942 – Boxing Day, no less – Eighth Army headquarters would send a radio message to the SAS in the field, with the alert: 'still no news CLAYE.' Whatever mishap had befallen Claye and his party, by 28 December, Eighth Army confirmed: 'CLAYE . . . NOT yet returned.' Berneville-Claye never would return to British lines, or at least not of his own free will. Indeed, for the enemy he would prove to be a very accommodating and obliging captive. Once his treachery was suspected,

Berneville-Claye would be assessed by British Intelligence as an 'intelligent and vain man who always brags that he has titled relatives and endeavours to live expensively and generally make himself conspicuous'. He was perfect stool pigeon material, of course.

He was also a veritable gold mine of information. As he would later confess, he was questioned for days on end about his time with the SAS and his knowledge of their activities, 'with special regard to the operative systems of our Special Service units'. No doubt he spoke volubly on the subject, revelling in the limelight. In due course, at various POW camps Claye would get slated and accused of betraying his fellow prisoners – Brits, Americans, Australians and more – to their captors. When finally he was forced to make his way towards Allied lines, Claye would do so dressed in the uniform of a SS *Hauptsturmführer* serving in the III (Germanic) SS Panzer Corps. In the interim he had volunteered to fight *against* Allied forces in the Führer's cause.

Since its formation over a year earlier, the SAS had weathered some of the harshest conditions known to man in the trackless wastes of the Sahara, and fought against, and bested, units of Rommel's highly respected Afrika Korps. But there was a chink in the armour of Stirling's raiders: the greatest threat to the unit came from within. It came from those trusting individuals who fell victim to the false bonhomie of the stool pigeons, and ultimately from a fantasist who acted and spoke like a high-born British officer, but who was in truth the lowest form of life – a standout traitor.

Perhaps unwisely, Stirling – driven, undaunted, tireless, but equally plagued by sickness and exhaustion – had set himself the single greatest challenge of all, that winter of 1942. He was to take a patrol of jeeps hundreds of miles beyond any of his own – or Montgomery's – forces, pushing west across the lines of the enemy, in an effort to link up with American forces that had spearheaded Operation Torch, the landings in North West Africa. It was a daunting undertaking by anyone's reckoning. Stirling and his party would have to navigate hundreds of miles of uncharted territory – terra incognita to the SAS – find a route around a vast and treacherous salt marsh, avoid the mass of Axis troops that were being driven into an ever-shrinking area, and approach the American lines without falling victim to a case of mistaken identity or friendly fire.

Avowedly, the mission had a compelling intelligence objective – to establish if Allied forces could circumvent the Mareth Line, which was effectively Rommel's final bulwark of defence. If the Allies could sweep south via the desert and outflank the enemy, that would spur final victory in North Africa. But Stirling's grand venture was also a deliberate stunt; if successful, it would put the SAS indelibly 'on the map' and beyond any risk of being stamped out by their detractors. To be the first to meet the advancing American forces was an irresistible proposition, hence Stirling's five-jeep convoy packed with fourteen men setting forth, as he once again aimed for the stars.

Stirling had Mike Sadler with him, for his superlative navigational skills would prove invaluable. He had Johnny Cooper, a man who'd served alongside Stirling since January of that year on many key missions. They took Free French veteran Freddie Taxis, who spoke good Arabic, for where they were heading being able to communicate with the locals, whoever they might be, was sure to prove vital. Stirling had also persuaded Mayne to lend him his southern Irish warrior Bill McDermott, fresh out of laying waste to Matruh railway station. There was also a phalanx of jeeps riding in the van, as a party of French SAS, under the command of Augustin Jordan, blazed the trail.

As Stirling's convoy pushed west, the terrain proved the worst ever. Their route lay across the Great Sea Erg, an area of dunes less extensive than Mayne's former desert redoubt, but far more difficult to cross. Whereas the Great Sand Sea's towering ocean swells had proved regular and navigable, here the choppy, saw-back breakers offered only a rough, bone-breaking ride. Progress was often reduced to little more than walking pace. Emerging from that sandy hell, if anything things got worse. Boggy, treacherous patches of salt marsh alternated with knife-cut ravines, plus stretches of thick, clogging sand.

Gradually, inexorably, Stirling's patrol were channelled towards the Gabes Gap, a narrow neck of land sandwiched between the coast and the vast, impassable salt-marshes to the south. Ahead of them, Jordan's patrol had suffered exactly the same fate, being compelled to brave that tiny, intensively patrolled five-mile-wide speck of land. It had not gone well. They'd passed through the Gap seemingly undetected, but in truth they had been trailed, tracked and hunted. In an intensive series of firefights almost all of them would be captured or killed. Stirling knew none of this, of course, even as his own patrol prepared to edge its way through the Gabes Gap under cover of darkness.

It was 22 January 1943, and at dusk a pair of German spotter planes buzzed Stirling's convoy. Regardless, they pressed on. Hours later, in the still hours of 23 January they slipped through the Gap, their nerves on edge. A mile further on a German armoured unit was camped by the roadside. Stirling and his men kept driving and, with a nod and a wave, they seemed to bluff their way through. With dawn fast approaching, they needed somewhere to hide and double quick. A nearby ravine cut through the Jebel. It offered the chance of cover, the shadowed guts of the place being thick with thorny bush.

Pulling in, the jeeps were camouflaged as swiftly as possible, before the men bedded down to rest. Stirling and his party had just completed a thirty-six-hour non-stop epic, with barely a break and with little food or water, and all of it fraught with tension and fear.

337

They were utterly shattered. Doubtless, sentries should have been set. None were. Sometime later, the sleeping men were jerked awake by the crunch of boots on rock, and cries of 'Raus! Raus!' – Out! Out! – as gun-barrels were thrust into startled faces. A force of some 500 German troops had tracked Stirling's patrol to its hideout. Sure enough, this was the *Fallschirmjäger* z.b.V. 250 battalion – elite paratroopers formed into a hunter-force at Rommel's behest, and specifically trained to track down Stirling's men.

Stirling and most of his party were captured without a fight. Three figures managed to slip way. Woken by all the kerfuffle, Sadler, Cooper and Taxis made a dash for the ridge above them, even as gunfire erupted from behind. As the three desperate fugitives burrowed into the densest thickets of undergrowth they could find, the rest of the patrol were rounded up and herded towards their captor's trucks, before being driven away in triumph. Sadler, Cooper and Taxis remained utterly still and silent, as German troops combed the ravine. Only come nightfall did the enemy withdraw.

Emerging from their place of hiding, the three SAS veterans took stock. East lay only the deathly salt marshes and the enemy. Somewhere to the west lay the Allied frontline. There was only one way to go. Theirs would end up being one of the finest escape and evasion stories of the entire desert war. In time, they would achieve Stirling's original goal, being the first Eighth Army troops to link up with the advancing American forces. More to the point, Sadler, blessed with his newfound knowledge of the terrain, would end up guiding Allied forces around the southern flank of Rommel's defensive line, just as they had originally hoped. That outflanking manoeuvre would contribute hugely to the collapse of the Axis, and to Rommel's final defeat in North Africa.

As for the rest of the patrol, they had been spirited away into captivity, despite an early escape attempt by Stirling and McDermott. Both were recaptured, Stirling, being seized by a burning rage, beating up the local Arab who had betrayed him, 'bashing him into the ground'. Stirling was duly paraded before none other than Colonel Mario Revetria, of Italian military intelligence – the man who had been orchestrating the hunt for the Phantom Major for many months. Even the Axis press were referring to Stirling by that name by now.

Revetria was so overjoyed to have caught Stirling that he couldn't help but boast. He spouted off regarding all that he had learned about the SAS and their means of operations. Stirling was amazed. Revetria seemed to know as much about the unit as did its founder. Shortly, he was placed aboard a Junkers 52 – one of the three-engine transport aircraft he had so long hunted, and with such tenacity – and spirited across the Mediterranean to Italy. There, he was incarcerated in a Rome prison camp, in an effort to prevent any further escape attempts.

Rommel was informed that his nemesis had been caught. He was overjoyed, noting how his forces had 'captured the commander of 1st S.A.S. Regiment, Lieut.-Col David Stirling'. His diary entry reflected the detailed state of the German general's knowledge. There were indeed two SAS Regiments in the offing then: Stirling's original, 1 SAS, plus a second, 2 SAS, which was being raised under the command of his elder brother, Bill. That Rommel knew all of this so quickly spoke volumes about just who had talked and with what depth of insider knowledge.

Rommel went on to describe Stirling's escape attempt, and how 'the Arabs, with their usual eye to business, offered him to us for 11 pounds of tea – a bargain which we soon clinched. Thus the British lost the very able and adaptable commander of the desert group which had caused us more damage than any other British unit of equal strength.' In truth, in terms of enemy warplanes destroyed, the SAS had caused the Axis in North Africa far greater harm than many units of greater strength. Arguably, more than the entire Royal Air Force over the same period, for the SAS had accounted for 367 confirmed aircraft 'kills', and very possibly as many as 400.

Two days before Christmas 1942, Rommel had got a sniff of the hunt for himself. He'd headed out into the desert for a festive treat – a spot of gazelle hunting. Instead, he'd ended up searching for what he suspected was Stirling's raiders. Pushing into the desert, they'd stumbled upon tracks made by British vehicles, 'Stirling and some of his people . . . harassing our supply traffic.' The tracks looked fresh and Rommel and his party maintained a 'sharp lookout to see if we could catch a "Tommy"'. They did indeed spot a lone vehicle speeding through the desert and gave chase. It turned out to be one of Rommel's own patrols, who were themselves on the trail of the 'Commandos'.

But either way, they'd finally got their man. Stirling, the Phantom Major, had been well and truly nailed.

CHAPTER TWENTY-FIVE

Rise of The Phoenix

Mayne knew nothing of the calamity that had befallen Stirling and his patrol. Their last known whereabouts had been signalled on 17 January 1943: 'Stirling at QZ 9090.' (QZ were Cassini Grid coordinates, a system of mapping then in use by the British military.) After that, nothing. Then, a week later, a hint of something. A radio message was sent from Eighth Army HQ, regarding a group of Italian POWs. Under questioning, the prisoners had reported 'one Captain one Lieut five ORs [other ranks] ES [estimate] five Jeeps captured.'

The ranks were wrong, but that was an easy enough mistake for enemy troops to have made. Could this be Stirling's party? They'd been riding in a five-jeep convoy, for sure. There was simply no way of knowing.

In any case, Mayne was busy, as he and his Squadron executed dozens of strikes against Rommel's crumbling supply lines. Their casualties were few, their successes many; luck was with them all the way. At one point, Mayne's patrol had stumbled across a trio of Bristol Blenheim bombers that had force-landed in the desert. All but one of the aircrew had perished. In the cockpit of the aircraft, they'd discovered the poignant flight logs. A small, seemingly trivial navigational error had resulted in the crew dying a terrible death of thirst.

The experience reminded all of the transient nature of human life in such an unforgiving theatre of war. In a letter to his sister Barbara, Mayne had written of his longing for some leave, and to see home and family again, but at the same time he'd confessed that he really couldn't take any until 'we clean up the Jerries out here'. His reluctance to be parted from his men until the job was done spoke volumes.

In late January 1943, Mayne's area of operations was overrun by the victorious Eighth Army, signifying that their mission was done. After months of unforgiving and unrelenting desert raiding, Mayne and his men were finally granted leave in Egypt. Most headed for Cairo, via Kabrit. There, Mayne discovered some wholly unexpected and deeply unsettling news. On 10 January 1943 his father, William, had passed away, aged sixty-five. Mayne asked for compassionate leave, so he could travel home to be with his family at this difficult time. Unbelievably, after all that he had given and all that he had achieved, his request was point-blank refused.

'Poor old Paddy had the news that his father had suddenly died,' Pleydell would write home. 'What a rotten time to get the news – he can't get home either.'

Mayne's relatives wrote of 'Willie Mayne ... the head of our clan' being a true gentleman, who was 'so good-hearted nothing would annoy him'. One added, poignantly, 'if he had lived to see his Boys come home victorious it would have been a glorious meeting ...' Doubtless it would have been, but it was not to be. More to the point, due to the mealy mouthed naysayers at MEHQ, Mayne was denied the chance to be at the funeral. With Stirling missing, there was no one left to fight his corner. No champion. Though Stirling was seen as being 'quite, quite mad', he had powerful connections. Mayne, the arch-raider, did not.

None had given more than Mayne. His sacrifices were legion, as were his triumphs. Yet he had been denied the chance to say a proper farewell to his father. To make matters worse, Douglas, Mayne's younger brother, was sick at the time of the funeral, so

'Bill was the only one there.' (Bill was the oldest surviving brother.) Resentful, hurting, blazing with anger, Mayne went on an epic bender, Cairo taking the brunt of his frustration and his rage. Bars were trashed; fights sought . . . The stories are no doubt exaggerated, but six Military Policemen (MPs) were said to have borne the brunt of his drink-fuelled ire.

David Lloyd Owen, the LRDG commander and one of Mayne's greatest admirers, was present at the time. He claimed to have seen Mayne hurl three MPs, one of whom was senior, down the steps of Shepheard's, then Cairo's leading hotel and a celebrated watering hole. The bar was known as the 'long bar', for it took an age to get served among the crowds. Mayne ended up being thrown into a Cairo cell. It took a powerful intervention to set him free. 'Release this man,' came the order from on high. Mayne was far more useful out leading raids than locked up and facing disciplinary charges.

Mayne was not alone in losing it in Cairo. Bill Fraser would return to their Kabrit base sporting a pair of spectacular black eyes. They lingered for an age, the darkness around his eye-sockets lending him an even more 'doleful look' than usual. As Pleydell had so sagely observed, the desert raiders would find it tough trying to return to normal life and readapting to 'civilised behaviour', even for a short while. This had been but a brief sojourn: imagine attempting anything like a permanent reintegration.

Fisticuffs apart, Mayne and his men had serious matters to deal with, as January bled into February 1943. The French contingent of the SAS were leaving. De Gaulle, the leader of the Free French, was setting up headquarters in newly liberated North Africa, and he'd ordered what remained of the French SAS firmly back under French command. Earl Jellicoe was scheduled to take D Squadron east to Beirut, to prepare for waterborne raiding missions, as Allied attentions turned towards the 'soft underbelly of Europe' – Italy.

More importantly, on 14 February 1943 Stirling and his patrol were formally listed as taken captive. The handwritten entry in the SAS War Diary for that day reads: 'Lt. Col. A.D. Stirling DSO (Scots Gds), the Commanding Officer of this unit, was officially reported as missing, believed prisoner of war.' If the legendary commander of the SAS was indeed 'in the bag', what now for the iconic unit that he had founded, and fought to keep alive so tenaciously? 'He ran the unit,' as Pleydell noted, 'so now the ship is without a rudder.'

It was only when Mike Sadler and Johnny Cooper returned to Kabrit, after their stupendous escape, that the full story of the fate of Stirling's patrol finally became clear. As those at Kabrit listened, the mysterious silence that had surrounded the fate of Stirling and his party was lifted at last. No one was in the slightest doubt any more: Stirling had been captured, which begged the question – who now would take over his mantle? Much that Stirling had striven to lead things at the hard end of operations – out raiding in the deep desert – he'd been equally tenacious in fighting the SAS's bigger battles: for recruits, for supplies, and not to mention arguing for the unit's sheer survival. Very often he'd provided the top cover, so that his key deputies – Mayne first and foremost – could concentrate on what they did best, raising merry hell.

Now he was gone, and it left a gaping void.

Even as the Phantom Major had been captured and installed at that Rome prison camp – Castro Pretorio Barracks – his desert heroics and inspirational command had attracted high praise. In early March 1943 General De Gaulle had put him forward to receive the Croix de Guerre with Bronze Palm, a high-valour French decoration. The citation, written in French, described Stirling as a 'remarkable organiser and great trainer of men', who led 'English commandos' and 'French paratroopers on several operations', which were distinguished by the 'magnificent results obtained'. Jellicoe, and one other SAS veteran, were also recommended for the award, and both would receive it. But Stirling's nomination was shelved, for 'Lt. Col. Stirling is now a prisoner of war.' London decreed that de Gaulle's nomination could be revisited 'at the end of hostilities, unless he [Stirling] escapes'. Stirling never did, and neither did he ever receive the French decoration.

Shortly after Stirling's arrival at the Castro Pretorio Barracks, the stool pigeons were shipped in, charged to get to work. Schurch was in the vanguard. Established in a cell next to Stirling's, he introduced himself using his long-standing alias 'Captain John Richards', claiming to have been captured in Tobruk the previous November. Bizarrely, Schurch had felt something close to a surge of pride upon being told that the SAS founder had been caught. 'At last he was going to meet the commanding officer of the men and officers with whom he had spent all his time obtaining information.'

Schurch's primary mission was to discover who would take over command of the unit, now Stirling was in captivity. He spent two weeks working his charm and weaving his web of deceit, the results of which are somewhat contested. Stirling would maintain that he'd been warned by a fellow inmate of 'Captain Richards'' treachery, and that, 'Such information as I passed was untrue and designed to deceive him.' Schurch's account of their time together differs markedly. As all the intelligence they had sought regarding the SAS had 'already been obtained', Schurch would boast, he needed only to discover the name of Stirling's successor. 'This I found out to be a Captain Paddy Mayne.'

Mayne was, of course, a Major at the time, but it seems likely that Schurch's account is accurate. Which meant that in a truly bizarre twist of events, enemy intelligence knew who would be taking over command of the SAS before the man himself was aware of it. In Cairo, and at Kabrit, following the confirmation of Stirling's demise, all was in disarray. As the SAS War Diary noted, 'David Stirling was captured March '43 [sic]. Chaos resulted. A split in S.A.S. . . .' Strife, division, disorder and confusion reigned.

In due course Stirling would run into Berneville-Claye at one of the POW camps he was moved to. Ostensibly, Claye came seeking preferential treatment, demanding to be put at the front of the queue for those 'awaiting assistance for escape'. Sensibly, Stirling told him that he would have to 'join the queue', and not a great deal more. There were grave suspicions among Allied POWs surrounding Claye's true allegiances. Accusations abounded regarding his nefarious activities, which had led to other escape attempts being thwarted, not to mention the arraignment and punishment of those involved.

In time, Stirling managed to get word out that only one man was fit and proper to take over command of the SAS – Major R. B. Mayne. 'Paddy was hugely brave,' he would later remark of this moment. 'I do not think he could ever have commanded an ordinary regular regiment, but he was exactly the man I wanted to succeed me in command of 1 SAS.' Needless to say, it was not a popular choice on high.

To the fossilised shits, the 'quite mad' Stirling had been a tough enough pill to swallow, but he was at least 'one of their own'. The idea of Mayne taking over as leader of this band of piratical raiders was sacrilege. He was not of the 'gentleman class'. He was certainly not to the manner born, having been educated at a grammar school of all things. He wasn't a true Englishman even. One minute of his faltering, under-spoken, thick Irish brogue, and you knew that much. In fact, as the war in North Africa was all-but over, why shouldn't these 'raiders of the thug variety' be disbanded? Surely, the SAS had 'outlived its usefulness'. The war was moving on. They may have done the business in the wide open desert – distasteful though it might have been – but Europe was an entirely different proposition. This was the chance to kill off the 'thug raiders' for good.

Unsurprisingly, Mayne's first and biggest battle right then was for the very survival of the SAS itself. On 8 March 1943 a 'consultative document' was circulated to Mayne, Jellicoe and others, inviting comment. It sought feedback on the proposition that the SAS would be subsumed back into where it had come from – the commandos. The possibility was raised to disband the SAS completely. With their being no further need of their unique talents in the desert, weren't they a busted flush? Unsurprisingly, Mayne fought tooth and nail against all such suggestions, knowing this would be the kiss of death for the iconic unit that Stirling had founded, and which they had shaped and nurtured together.

Confounding the naysayers – those who argued that the fiery Irishman might well be a sterling berserker, but was far from suited for higher command – Mayne was surprisingly successful. As the SAS War Diary put it, pithily: 'In response to a summons, Major Mayne – as he was then – went to GHQ Cairo to discuss the future of the Unit.' Finding himself in the lion's den – or, more accurately, the pit of intrigue – Mayne discovered his inner purpose. Come hell or high water, he was going to champion this unit, and those who had served it so faithfully, not to mention those who had made the ultimate sacrifice. When the 'suggestion was made that it had outlived its usefulness', Mayne struck back. The war in Europe was coming, he argued, and he and his men would have a key role to play.

The result of his dogged tenacity was not all that he had hoped for, as he'd 'fought hard for the preservation' of the SAS and all it stood for, but it sure came close, for 'the Regiment lived on'. On 19 March the decision was made to split 1 SAS. The first unit, under Jellicoe, would consist of some 235 men, and would be renamed the Special Boat Squadron (SBS), which was charged with amphibious raiding operations, aiming to pioneer the sabotage of shipping, as well as enemy airbases. The second unit, under Mayne, was renamed the Special Raiding Squadron (SRS), and consisted of some 280 men. Crucially, within the ranks of this new outfit were the majority of Mayne's A Squadron veterans – his tried and tested and much-loved raiding family. Their challenge now was to train for a new theatre, and for a new form of war fighting entirely.

Within the ranks of the SRS, Mayne, thankfully, had retained his trusted crew. Bill Fraser was there, as his second-in-command. Sadler, Cooper and Pat Riley were there, though all three were shortly to be ordered back to Britain, for some formal officer training. Bob Melot was there, somehow having overcome the terrible injuries he had suffered during Operation Bigamy, and keen as mustard to return to the fight. O'Dowd, Lilley, Bennett, Rose and Johnny Wiseman were there, chafing at the bit to get busy on European shores.

They'd lost their iconic identity, of course. Strictly speaking, they were 'SRS' now, not SAS. But Mayne was determined that the tried and trusted brand under which so many had soldiered so bravely for so long would rise, phoenix like, from the ashes of Stirling's capture, and the predations of Cairo headquarters. All things in time. First, they would need to prove themselves all over again and in a new theatre of war. They'd need to show they weren't simply a *desert* raiding force; that Stirling's original precept of small-scale units of courageous men operating by speed and surprise deep behind the lines could yield exceptional results in Europe, just as it had in North Africa.

Having mustered his new force, two things were foremost in Mayne's mind. The first was training. With what all knew were coming – the landings in southern Italy – they would need to be ready to execute very different kinds of missions in a very different kind of terrain. Along the North African shoreline, among rocky gullies and plunging cliffs, Mayne envisaged a training regime that echoed that of his earliest No. 11 Commando days, and the rigours demanded by the late, great Colonel Pedder. But first, there was some leave to be had. It came way too late for his father's funeral, but not to address another signal loss, one that Mayne felt deep in his soul.

Sometime in late April 1943, Mayne set out alone to travel to Gazala, long liberated by the Eighth Army. His aim was to discover the fate of one of the first of the fallen, and the one he regretted and missed most – Eoin McGonigal. It was a year and a half since Operation Squatter, the SAS's inaugural mission on which his great friend had been lost. Requisitioning a truck, Mayne set out on his lonely journey; a pilgrimage almost. As he pressed on into the open desert, he must have known in his heart that 'after so much time it was most probably a hopeless cause.' But he would soon be leaving North Africa, and he felt he couldn't simply abandon his brother in arms.

There had been any number of conflicting rumours as to what had happened to McGonigal, but the reports were so contradictory as to leave no one much the wiser. One of the survivors from McGonigal's patrol would report from a POW camp that 'Lt. MacGoneagle [sic], who was badly injured, died the same day,' – i.e. early on 17 November 1941. Another account would have McGonigal perishing the evening before, 'with his body up against a wrecked Messerschmitt 109. He'd landed, but had been dragged by the storm and killed.' Still other accounts had McGonigal being taken captive, but dying at some stage thereafter from injuries suffered during the parachute drop.

Stirling himself had seemed convinced that McGonigal and his party had made it through to one of the targets, at least – Tmimi Airbase. He'd describe how some eighteen aircraft on Tmimi landing ground had ended up with 'holes in them and the petrol systems buggered up', which he put down to McGonigal and his patrol's handiwork. Stirling had seen those wrecked warplanes with his own eyes, when his own raiding party had paid a visit to that airbase. They'd been convinced that McGonigal and his men had set upon some novel means to wreck those aircraft – 'to put them out of operation' – after their charges were ruined by the torrential rains.

Stirling's theory was lent weight by an official investigation, carried out after British forces overran Tmimi. They discovered two dozen warplanes 'damaged in a makeshift fashion' and scattered around the airstrip. Whatever was the truth of the matter, practically speaking Mayne's April '43 mission of detective work was abortive, but not emotionally so. He'd done his duty to his fallen comrade, and that was especially important to a man such as himself. He'd quartered the area where Eoin McGonigal most probably had lost his life, but no further evidence, nor any remains, were to be found. If nothing else, it allowed him to send news to Eoin's mother Margaret, in response to which she dispatched a heartfelt reply:

My Dear Blair

I have just got your very kind letter & really feel I cannot thank you enough for all your great kindness. It was terribly good of you to have gone to Gazala & taken so much trouble to try to find Eoin's grave. I know he did not have an identity disk, I think he just wanted to be an unknown soldier, but I had hoped he had been found and buried as I meant to go to Gazala after the war . . . I miss him so much – more in fact every day, but I know he is safe & happy & terribly interested in what you are all doing. I am sure he has been with you in your operations since he died . . . Thank you very much for all your goodness – it has made such a difference.

As with so many mothers during the war, Margaret McGonigal was struggling to come to terms with her loss. All that remained of her son from his war years were those few mementoes that Mayne had managed to send to her – his SAS badges (never worn), the photos that Mayne had taken, but not Eoin's dagger, which seemed to have gone missing in the post. Even so, while her boy was an 'unknown soldier' lost in the North African desert, at least she had the comfort that Eoin 'still had a friend out there looking for him'.

Having searched for his missing comrade, Mayne returned to the chief task in hand: training and shaping his new command. In the second week of May 1943, Axis forces had finally surrendered in North Africa, some 250,000 German and Italian troops being taken captive. Almost a month earlier, Rommel had been ordered back to Europe, for he was physically unwell and exhausted, not to mention frustrated and disheartened at the reversal of his fortunes. North Africa would serve as the base for the next stage of the war – the Allied landings in Italy, spearheading the liberation of occupied Europe.

In all that was coming, the SAS would have a key role to play, and there was much to prepare for. Apart from Eoin McGonigal, and the other fallen and captured, one other figure was missing from Mayne's new command – the redoubtable Malcolm Pleydell. Struck by the 'cafard' – a bout of melancholia – and with all the uncertainty and changes afoot, the SAS medic had decided it was time for him to 'bid my farewell'. It was all the more surprising, in that Pleydell had only recently been paid the ultimate compliment, when one of the injured had averred 'the lads would go anywhere with me behind them!'

Mostly, it was the 'mental strain' of being the sole hope for the wounded that had exhausted Pleydell, striking him down with the cafard. In his place he'd recruited Philip Gunn, one of the finest doctors Pleydell had ever come across in the desert war. He was leaving Mayne and his men in good care. More to the point, Pleydell was certain he was departing from a unit that was stronger than ever, especially under Mayne's stewardship, for the Irishman was even then laying the 'firm foundations of the new S.A.S.'.

Pleydell was right, of course. Mayne's squadron would go on to achieve great things: many triumphs and battle honours and decorations would follow. Even so, not for one moment would the naysayers and the disparagers be silenced. Much that Mayne would fight the enemy without – the forces of the Axis powers – he would be obliged to combat the enemy within, as he battled for the survival of the unit that he had helped pioneer and was now to lead.

As their victories grew, and as they thrust deep into occupied Europe, so too would the Nazi enemy quicken the hunt for these daring and audacious Special Service raiders. Falling away from Rommel's attention, they were soon to become the chief enemy of Hitler himself, as the Führer turned his gimlet eye on those who dared to defy him so blatantly, and so far beyond his own front-lines. But all of that lay a way in the future. For now there was training to be done, and a new round of missions to prepare for.

They were heading for Europe, and Mayne and his raiders had better be ready.

The sequel to *SAS Brothers in Arms* will tell the story of Blair 'Paddy' Mayne and his band of raiders as they spearhead the advance into Europe, and of the daring and bloody battles to liberate the continent from Nazi tyranny.

It will be forthcoming in Autumn 2023.

Acknowledgements

First and foremost, thank you to my esteemed readers. You go out and buy my books, in the hope that each will deliver an enjoyable, rewarding, illuminating read; another work that brings a story to life in vivid detail. I am most grateful and I hope I have managed to deliver that kind of reading experience in this book. Without you, there could be no author such as myself. You enable individuals like me to make a living from writing. You deserve the very first mention.

The second massive thank you is extended to Fiona Ferguson (née Mayne) and her husband Norman, for inviting me into your family home, repeatedly, so that I might delve into Lt Col Robert Blair Mayne's war chest and the plethora of other wartime memorabilia, and discuss at length with you his wartime and post-war story, gaining enormous and invaluable insight in the process. Your unconditional welcome and your openness was, and is, hugely appreciated, as is all the correspondence we have shared over the long years that it has taken for this book to come to fruition. I am most grateful.

I owe another debt of gratitude to Peter Forbes and his wife Sally, and their children, who hosted me in their home in Northern Ireland and who, in Peter's case, first alerted me to the wealth of private family archive held by Lt Col Mayne's family. Peter, you are in your own right acquiring the reputation of being an expert and an authority on the life and soldiering of this great war hero, and I have been privileged to have been given access to your own extensive personal archive and to your wisdom and advice. You are a scholar and a gentleman and you have been enormously generous with your hospitality, not to mention your time and expertise.

I extend my enormous thanks to John O'Neill, great nephew of Lt Col Robert Blair Mayne DSO and author of *Legendary Warrior of The SAS*, for entrusting me with your extraordinary private family archive concerning your great uncle's war years, and also for offering such personal and incisive insight into your great uncle's wider character and what troubled him post-war. John – you remind me so much of your great-uncle – physically, of course, but also in your soft-spoken tones, your quiet wit and with your off-beat humour and your laughing eyes. I am hugely grateful for all your help and support.

I extend my heartfelt thanks to Patric McGonigal, who corresponded with me widely about his late great-uncle, No. 11 Commando and SAS man, Lieutenant Eoin McGonigal, and who shared with me aspects of the McGonigal family archive and also the early draft of his as then unpublished book, *Special Forces Brothers in Arms* (published by Pen and Sword in 2022). This was and is hugely appreciated. I extend also my thanks to Patric's father, Eoin McGonigal, the nephew of the SAS man of the same name, who likewise corresponded with me at length about the wider McGonigal family's wartime story and history.

Thank you, as ever, to my long-standing friend and reader of early manuscripts, and commentator thereon – Second World War veteran of the LRDG, SAS and SBS, Jack Mann. As you knew Lt Col Mayne personally, your comments and remarks on an early draft of this book are treasured, as always.

Thank you also to Alec Borrie, SAS veteran of the Second World War, who served alongside Lt Col Mayne and many others of those portrayed in this book, for speaking with me about your wartime experiences and memories. Again, such contributions from one who was there have been invaluable and I am hugely privileged and grateful for all your help and contributions.

Huge thanks to Gary Hull, the son of wartime SAS operator Billy Hull, for inviting me into your home and for sharing with me your stories and recollections about both your father's wartime exploits, and those of his commander and close friend, Lt Col Robert Blair Mayne. Thank you also for giving me access to your father's wartime letters, records, photos, memorabilia and other materials, which proved so useful in the research for this book.

Very great thanks to Margaret Duncan, the daughter of Captain George Duncan MC, for reaching out to me about your father's wartime story and for sharing with me your father's wonderful poetry from that time. For that I am very grateful.

Thank you to Christine Gordon, the daughter of Ireland and British Lions rugby international George Ernest Cromey, for helping me relate the story of the springbok hunting episode that happened during the 1938 Lions tour of South Africa. Thanks to David Robson, for sharing with me the stories of how Lt Col Mayne helped guide him as a young man in his life choices. Thanks also to Barbara Coffey, whose father, Dr Cole, was a close friend of Lt Col Mayne's, and who shared with me stories of childhood memories. Thanks to Harold Hetherington for sharing with me the stories of how Lt Col Mayne was in the habit of rounding him and his brothers up as young and somewhat wayward boys, and ensuring they did attend the local school.

Thank you to Eric Lecomte and Arnaud Blond, for all the correspondence, help and kind assistance you were able to furnish concerning my research into the operations of the Free French SAS, and also for your kind invitations to France, to look into more of the same. This was invaluable and I am hugely grateful.

Thank you to Nicholas Jellicoe, the son of Brigadier Earl George Jellicoe DSO MC, for sharing with me the early draft manuscript of the book telling your father's wartime story, *George Jellicoe SAS and SBS Commander* (published by Pen and Sword in 2021), and for our conversations and correspondence over all things SAS and SBS in the Second World War. I am most grateful.

My gratitude is also extended to Alison Smartt, for the very kind permission to quote from the private papers of Captain M. J. Pleydell MC, including his letters and diaries. Captain Pleydell was an astute, incisive, sympathetic and hugely eloquent observer of the early days of the SAS, and his writing captures the spirit and essence of their desert operations most admirably.

Thank you to Ros Townsend, a specialist working with the fantastic charity PTSD Resolution, for sharing with me your expert perspective on the history of diagnosis and recognition of post-traumatic stress disorder and your personal feedback and observations on the trauma suffered by Second World War veterans in particular. This was invaluable. Thank you also to Colonel A. de P. Gauvain (Retired) FHGI, Chairman and CEO of PTSD Resolution, for all the help, support and advice you kindly extended to me in connection with the writing of this book.

Thanks as ever to Julie Davies, ace researcher and translator, for sharing with me the journey of discovery embodied in this book, and for your astute and pertinent observations, assessment and guidance, as always; but most of all for your heartfelt enthusiasm that the full story of Lt Col Mayne's wartime exploits, and that of his comrades, should be told. With this book it is begun.

Thanks are also extended to the following individuals, who are all experts in their own right on various aspects of Second World War history, and helped me in my research: Jonathan Woodhead, Michael Caldwell, Tom Hunter, Thomas Harder, Jimmy Russell Norman and Andrew Glenfield.

I also extend my warm thanks to my early readers: Paul and Anne Sherratt, as always, at the top the list of 'thank yous'. Long may you keep providing me with such pertinent and telling feedback and comment. Sandy and Erica Moriarty, as our wonderful neighbours just across the track – again, your detailed remarks, and your enthusiasm for this story, proved invaluable.

Thank you, again, to Nina Staehle for your excellent research in Germany concerning this story and for your translations from German to English. As ever, with remarkable tenacity you unearthed some true gems concerning this story, and for that I am hugely grateful.

Huge thanks as always to Simon Fowler, my researcher in the UK – your hard work and insight was invaluable, as ever, and your perseverance during the long hangover from the Covid lockdown was admirable. Your work winkling out the files from where they were hardest to find, as always, was remarkable. Bravo!

Thanks again to my mother, Christine Major, for her refreshing thoughts, enthusiasm and input into an early draft of this book. I hope it helped ease you through the trials and tribulations of what would seem to be 'long-Covid', at least getting your mind off of the angst and worries of same.

Thanks also to Paul Hazzard, long-standing reader and friend, for perusing an early draft and for your deeply perceptive comments. Thanks to John R. McKay, a fellow author and Second World War historian of great talent, for reading an early iteration of this book and for all your invaluable comments. It was great to have that support, as ever, my friend. Thank you also to Richard Domoney-Saunders for reading an early version of the manuscript and for your comments and suggestions.

Thanks especially to SAS veteran Des Powell (with whom I co-authored *SAS Bravo Three Zero*), for it was immensely refreshing to have the thoughts and feedback of a more modern generation 'pilgrim' – an SAS veteran – on this Second World War story of the SAS in its founding years. Well done, my friend, and massively appreciated. The legacy lives on in individuals such as yourself.

Thank you also to the Churchill Fellowship, for backing me

with a Fellowship many years ago, which ignited the spark in a young man to be curious about all things Winston Churchill, and especially the legacy of this extraordinary wartime leader.

I have benefited greatly in the research for this book from the resources that the British, German and other governments, and related institutions, have invested into preserving for posterity the archives from the Second World War era. The preservation and cataloguing of a mountain of papers – official reports, personal correspondence, telegrams, etc. – plus photographic, film and sound archives is vital to authors such as myself, without which books of this nature could not be written. Devoting resources to the preservation of this historical record, and to making it accessible to the public, is something for which these governments and other institutions deserve high praise.

All at my publishers deserve the very best of praise for their committed, enthusiastic and visionary support of this project from the get-go. In the UK, Richard Milner, my long-standing editor and good friend, provided seminal guidance and feedback, as always. The wider Quercus team also deserve the highest praise, especially Charlotte Fry, Hannah Robinson, Bethan Ferguson, Ben Brock, Dave Murphy, and Jon Butler. In the USA the publishing team at Kensington Books were superlative, as always. Thank you to all of you, but especially to Wendy McCurdy, Ann Pryor, Rebecca Cremonese, Barbara Brown, John Son, Elizabeth Trout, Lynn Cully, Jackie Dinas, Steven Zacharius and Adam Zacharius.

Special mention must also be made of Kensington Books, for their excellent fundraising to support freedom and justice in Ukraine, on which note Marisa Young deserves special praise, for her generous support for the same – in the memory of her father, Paul R. Young, and those who served alongside him on the USS *Chenango* (CVE-28), a Second World War escort carrier.

*

My gratitude as always is extended to my literary agent at Curtis Brown, Gordon Wise, to my US literary agent, George Lucas at Inkwell Management Literary Agency, and to my film agent at Curtis Brown, Luke Speed. Thank you also to Sophie Ransom, of Ransom PR, for your huge enthusiasm for this story from the very outset, and for working your special magic, as always.

Finally, of course, I need to extend my deep thanks and heartfelt gratitude to my family – Eva, David, Damien Jr and Sianna – who once again had to put up with 'Pappa' spending far too long locked in his study trying to do justice to this story. That I have – if I have – I owe to you all; to your forbearance, your love and support and kindness, and for putting up with me through it all.

This, of course, is a very special story for the Lewis family, if for no other reason than because of our deep links to Ireland, and because my wife has played a very hands-on, indispensable role in the research, writing and the revisions of this book. This book has been a labour of love, and you stayed the course over the long years that it has taken to come to fruition, for which I am hugely grateful.

Acknowledgements on Sources

I am indebted to the following authors, who have covered some of the aspects of the story I have dealt with in *SAS Brothers in Arms* in their own writing. As detailed in the Author's Note, I extend my deep gratitude to those who granted me kind permission to quote from their material. For those readers whose interest has been piqued by this book, these authors and their titles would reward further reading.

Patric McGonigal, whose book *Special Forces Brothers in Arms: Eoin & Ambrose McGonigal: War in the SAS & SBS*, tells the McGonigal brothers' wartime story in great depth, Patric having enjoyed access to the McGonigal family archive and war memorabilia, among other such troves of resources.

John O'Neill, the great nephew of Lt Col Robert Blair Mayne DSO, and the author of *Legendary Warrior of The SAS: Robert Blair Mayne DSO, The Original who kept the SAS alive*, whose biography of his great-uncle benefited greatly from the O'Neill (Mayne) family archive, and is rich in biographical detail.

Nicholas Jellicoe, whose biography about his father, entitled *George Jellicoe SAS and SBS Commander*, is a sterling tour de force and rich in intensively researched detail, not to mention being a detailed chronicle of the life of an extraordinary warrior.

I am also grateful to the following publishers, authors and estates for granting me permission to quote from their works (full details in Bibliography):

Lorna Almonds-Windmill, *Gentleman Jim*, 2011 – all rights reserved.

Roy Close, *In Action With the SAS*, 2005 – all rights reserved.

Virginia Cowles, *The Phantom Major: The Story of David Stirling and the SAS Regiment*, 2010 – all rights reserved.

Malcolm James, *Born of The Desert: With the SAS in North Africa*, 2015 – all rights reserved.

W. B. Kennedy Shaw, *Long Range Desert Group*, 2015 – all rights reserved.

David Lloyd Owen, *The Long Range Desert Group 1940–1945: Providence Their Guide*, 2001 – all rights reserved.

Gearoid O'Dowd, *He Who Dared and Died: The Life and Death of an SAS Original, Sergeant Chris O'Dowd, MM*, 2011 – all rights reserved.

Ian Wellsted, *With the SAS Across the Rhine: Into the Heart of Hitler's Third Reich*, 2020 – all rights reserved.

Selected Bibliography

Anon, *The SAS War Diary*, Extraordinary Editions, 2011

Lorna Almonds Windmill, *Gentleman Jim*, Pen & Sword, 2011

Michael Asher, *Get Rommel*, Weidenfeld and Nicolson, 2004

——, *The Regiment*, Viking, 2007

Roy Bradford and Martin Dillon, *Rogue Warrior of The SAS*, Mainstream Publishing, 2012

Daniel Allen Butler, *Field Marshal*, Casemate Publishers, 2017

J. V. Byrne, *The General Salutes a Soldier*, Robert Hale, 1986

Roy Close, *In Action With the SAS*, Pen & Sword, 2005

Johnny Cooper, *One of The Originals*, Pan Books, 1991

Virginia Cowles, *The Phantom Major*, Pen & Sword, 2010

Margaret Duncan and Sue Knight, *Behind Barbed Wire*, privately published by Solway Print, 2021

Raymond Forgeat, *Remember: Les Parachutistes de la France Libre*, Service Historique de l'Armée de Terre, 1990

Stephen Hastings, *The Drums of Memory*, Pen & Sword, 1994

Robin Hunter, *True Stories of The SAS*, Weidenfeld & Nicolson, 1986

Malcolm James, *Born of The Desert*, Frontline Books, 2015

Nicholas Jellicoe, *George Jellicoe*, Pen & Sword, 2021

W. B. Kennedy Shaw, *Long Range Desert Group*, Frontline Books, 2015

Damien Lewis, *Churchill's Secret Warriors*, Quercus, 2014

——, *SAS Ghost Patrol*, Quercus, 2018

——, *SAS Band of Brothers*, Quercus, 2020

——, *SAS Great Escapes*, Quercus, 2020

——, *The Flame of Resistance*, Quercus, 2022

B. H. Liddell Hart, *The Rommel Papers*, Harcourt Brace and Company, 1953

David Lloyd Owen, *The Desert My Dwelling Place*, Cassell & Company, 1957

——, *The Long Range Desert Group*, Leo Cooper, 1980, rev. ed. 2001

Patrick Marrinan, *Colonel Paddy*, Ulster Press, 1983

Carol Mather, *When the Grass Stops Growing*, Leo Cooper, 1997

Stewart McClean, *SAS: The History of the Special Raiding Squadron 'Paddy's Men'*, Spellmount, 2005

Eoin McGonigal, *Special Forces Brothers in Arms*, Pen & Sword, 2022

Ian McHarg, *Litani River*, www.litaniriver.com, 2011

Ben McIntyre, *SAS Rogue Heroes*, Viking, 2016

J. Frazer McLuskey, *Parachute Padre*, Spa Books, 1985

Charles Messenger, *The Commandos 1940–1946*, William Kimber, 1985

Gavin Mortimer, *David Stirling*, Constable, 2022

Robin Neillands, *The Raiders: Army Commandos 1940–46*, Fontana, 1989

Gearoid O'Dowd, *He Who Dared and Died*, Pen & Sword, 2011

John O'Neill, *Legendary Warrior of the SAS*, Menin House, 2015

Hamish Ross, *Paddy Mayne*, Sutton Publishing, 2003

Gordon Stevens, *The Originals: The Secret History of the Birth of the SAS in Their Own Words*, Ebury Press, 2005

A. P. Wavell, *Other Men's Flowers*, Jonathan Cape, 1978

Adrian Weale, *Renegades: Hitler's Englishmen*, Pimlico, 2002

Ian Wellsted, *With the SAS Across the Rhine*, Frontline Books, 2020

References to Sources

Imperial War Museum

Documents

Private Papers of Captain M L Pleydell MC, IWM Documents 337
Private Papers of Sir Carol Mather MC, IWM Documents 17403
Private Papers of Mrs. A M Street, IWM Documents 6433
Private Papers of Winston Churchill, *Speech at Mansion House, 10 November 1942*, IWM Documents 24715

Audio Archives

Bob Bennet interview, IWM Sound Archive 18145
Earl George Jellicoe interview, IWM Sound Archive 13039
Reg Seekings DCM MM, IWM Sound Archive 18177

Liddell Hart Centre for Military Archives

Street, Major-General Vivian Wakefield (1912-1970), GB 0099 KCLMA Street

Churchill Archives Centre, Churchill College, Cambridge

CHAR 1/369/3-4
CHAR 20/65/106-145
CHAR 20/205/49
CHAR 20/65/146-148

CAB 106/389 – Litani River

PREM 3/330/9 – Combined Ops

WO 222/1568 – Locations of British General Hospitals during WWII

WO 373/26 – Pleydell's MC Citation

WO 373-185-19 – French Awards Stirling/Jellicoe

WO 373-185 – French and American awards for Stirling etc.

WO 201/727 – Raiding Forces – Personal File of Lt Col J. E. Haselden

WO 201/748 – Agreement, Bigamy, Nicety: reports

WO 201/765 – Raiding Forces: signals in

WO 201/763 – OUT messages Jul–Nov 42

WO 201/764 – OUT messages Dec 42–Mar 43

WO 218/91 – Special Service War Diaries: Long Range Desert Group

WO 218/119 – HQ SAS Troops Norway

WO 171/766 – Raiding Forces In Signals Dec 42–March 43

WO 201/765 – Raiding Forces In Signals Jul–Nov 42

WO 373/46/23 – Raiding Forces

WO 218/119 – Operation Archway

WO 218/91 – War Diary 1 SAS 1943

WO 218/97 – Special Service War Diary 1940 onwards

WO 218/98 – Special Service War Diary 1940 onwards

WO 218/99 – War Diary Raiding Sqn 1943

KV 2/626-1 – Douglas Webster Dt. Aubyn Berneville-Claye

KV 2/626-2 – Douglas Webster Dt. Aubyn Berneville-Claye

KV 2/627-1 – Douglas Webster Dt. Aubyn Berneville-Claye

KV 2/627-2 – Douglas Webster Dt. Aubyn Berneville-Claye

KV 2/77-1 – Theodore John William SCHURCH: deserted to the Italians and collaborated with them and . . .

KV 2/77-2 – Theodore John William SCHURCH: deserted to the Italians and collaborated with them and . . .

OTHER PUBLISHED SOURCES

Max Arthur, 'Obituary: Reg Seekings', Independent, 3 May 1999

Ron Gittings, 'Tarnished Hero of the SAS', *Medal News*, April 2007

Jack Loudan, 'The Man Who Dared', *TV Post*, 23 August 1962

Jack Loudan, 'Braves bullets to save his wounded men', *TV Post*, 27 September 1962

Alastair McQueen, 'How the spirit of bravest SAS hero will live on', *Express*, 1 March 1997

Margaret Metcalf, 'My father the war traitor', BBC News, 29 March 2002

UNPUBLISHED SOURCES & MISCELLANEOUS

Anon, 'Major William (Bill) Fraser MC, 1917–1975', undated paper

Anon, 'Unveiling of the Memorial to Lt Col Robert Blair Mayne DSO', Ards Borough Council, 2 May 1997

Anon, 'Robert Blair Mayne of Newtownards: A Commemorative Booklet', Rotary Club Of Newtownards, undated paper

'Report for Term Ending 18th December 1925', Newtonards Academy, John Rodgers, BA, Principal

Anon, 'Blair "Paddy" Mayne', World Rugby Museum, 2013

Rev. J. Fraser McLuskey, 'Between You and Me', eulogy for Lt Col R. B. Mayne, undated

Anon, 'The Second World War: All RAF aircrew were volunteers', Royal Airforce Museum, undated

Anon, 'Olympians Sports Gossip – Some Stories of Blair Mayne', *Johannesburg Star* draft article, 26 February 1942

'Churchill's Government defeats a No Confidence motion in the House', International Churchill Society, 12 March 2015

Anon, .303 inch Incendiary, British Military Small Arms Ammo, undated

Omar Khayyam, 'One Moment in Annihilation's Waste', *The Rubaiyat of Omar Khayyam*, First Edition, The Lieder New Archive

James Bruce, 'When you go home . . .', GCHQ official history, undated

'The End of the Beginning', The International Churchill Society

Index

PTSD Resolution, Charity No. 1133188, provides therapy for the mental welfare of Forces' Veterans, Reservists and their families. Treatment is free, effective and delivered promptly and locally through a network of 200 therapists nationwide, and also by phone and internet during the pandemic. Contact www.PTSDresolution.org.

Founded in 2009, and with over 3,500 referrals to date, the charity delivers therapy in an average of six sessions, with 78% of cases seeing an improvement in reported symptoms to where the client and therapist agree that no further therapy is required.

The charity is one of the only organisations to provide therapy to veterans suffering with addiction issues or who are in prison - as well as to family members, including partners and children, who may experience the symptoms of trauma from living with a traumatised veteran.

PTSD Resolution has a unique 'lean' operation, with no salaried staff or assets - funds are used to deliver therapy and for essential research and public information.

Key features of PTSD Resolution's service:-

Free, local, prompt and effective help for Veterans, Reservists & families suffering from mental health issues
Confidential, no GP referral is needed
Local help through a UK network of 200 therapists
Fast treatment, issues usually resolved in an average of six sessions
Easy to access – first session booked often in days

Compassionate: clients do not have to talk about events in their
  past
Cost-effective, £750 per programme – free to the people we help
Transparent, results are monitored and reported
No one is turned away: including HM prisoners and those with
  addiction issues
Cobseo members, working with other Forces' charities (Cobseo,
  the Confederation of Service Charities, provides a single point
  of contact for interaction with Government, the Private Sector;
  and with other members of the Armed Forces Community)
'Lean' charity management: we own no assets, have no salaried
  staff: donations are used for essential treatment, research and
  communications.

Veterans In Action is an armed forces charity that helps veterans and their families who have suffered the effects of war or who have found the transition to civilian life difficult, focusing on the emotional and physical well-being of those involved to help them grow as an individual or family.

The charity was founded in 2009 by Billy MacLeod MBE, who had served in the Royal Engineers who after looking at what was on offer for veterans in the UK looked further afield to the United States and Australia for inspiration.

The aim was to set an up an organisation based on the experiences and the camaraderie of serving in the Army and particularly the Royal Engineers and the tasks they carried out around the world, with the aim of helping ourselves by helping others.

A study in Australia was found called Wilderness and Adventure Therapy which became the basis of Veterans In Action's own unique ALIVE programme designed by the charity founder, that takes a non-therapy long term approach to veteran's mental health, to help veterans and their families grow at their own pace working alongside their peers on the projects run at the ALIVE Centre or off site in the surrounding area or on long-distance expeditions.

Veterans In Action projects are based on the decades old study of Post-Traumatic Growth. Veterans In Action's ALIVE Centre is the charity HQ and is ideally set on a beautiful private estate seven miles from Andover on the Hampshire/Wiltshire border with beautiful walks through woodlands and the scenic Hampshire countryside. This environment helps veterans to de-stress as soon as they enter the estate and veterans feel 'safe' and relaxed in the quiet of the countryside.

From 2009 until 2016 Veterans In Action carried out a series of long-distance walks across the UK called the Union Flag Walks with each walk forming a separate part of the Union Flag covering a distance of 13,500 miles with over 500 veterans suffering from PTSD taking part.

In 2017 the charity started a new project called Veterans Expeditions Overland where veterans strip and rebuild Land Rovers and prepare them to expedition standard which are then used to undertake long distance overland expeditions.

Due to the success of this project, it has now become the basis of all other projects that complement each other. All work on the vehicles and on expeditions are filmed by veterans on a project called Veterans In Focus where veterans learn to film and edit the footage for a YouTube Channel called Veterans Expeditions Overland.

We know that veterans can achieve remarkable accomplishments and they possess a myriad of unique skills that when harnessed can be used on many different projects here at home, becoming valuable members of their community.

Veterans In Action is committed to helping veterans unlock the potential they have to make a difference throughout their lives not only for themselves and their family but also their standing in the local community where they can develop projects to help others. This is the true definition of Post-Traumatic Growth.

War Years Remembered War Museum (WYR, Charity NIC101112) is a cross community war museum and charity with the objective of protecting, preserving and presenting heritage material relating to the First and Second World Wars. It strives to advance public education in Irish military & social history, and promote better community relations through the teaching of the shared wartime experiences in Ireland and afar.

WYR houses a collection of tens of thousands of items, including uniforms, vehicles, weapons, documents, pictures, badges, homeware and more. It was established in 1994 by its Founder, David McCallion, who has collected wartime memorabilia since the age of 8. Many of the artefacts were also donated by families who sought a home for their relatives' wartime belongings and histories. WYR is privileged to showcase the memorabilia of Lt. Col Robert Blair Mayne among other extraordinary exhibits associated with wartime servicemen and women. Visitors can experience a fully replicated 1940's house, the trenches of the First World War, see what it was like to sit in a Willy's Jeep, Ford Armoured Car or a Morris Gun Tractor from the D-Day landings. It has thousands of unique artefacts that can't be found in any other museum and prides itself on showcasing original items and not replicas. The collection also extends beyond the island of Ireland, containing items and stories relating to people from Great Britain, Poland, Belgium, Germany, America and more.

The museum is staffed by a team of volunteers who give up their time to host and engage with other charities and groups. These can range from primary and secondary schools, Scouts, Guides and Boy's Brigades to disability groups like the Disabled Police Officer's

Association, veterans groups such as BLESMA and various special needs charities. Its visitors include historical societies, pensioner groups, churches and different vintage clubs. Educating all, young and old, creates a lasting legacy for our veterans, whose artefacts and stories are central to the very fabric of War Years Remembered.

The museum has also helped many families over the years in their own family research, as many are elderly and do not have access to computers etc. WYR has also helped researchers and authors through its archive "History shared is history preserved" and has been involved in film and TV productions, from advising wardrobe, to loaning props, etc.

Over the years WYR has survived mainly on the generous donations of its visitors. However, it was hit hard during the Covid-19 pandemic and now seeks to find permanent premises and accredited museum status to provide a genuine and much needed war museum in Ireland. Funds are actively being sought to enable this.

If you are interested in learning more please contact us via our email admin@waryearsremembered.co.uk.

You can also find us on Facebook, TripAdvisor and www.waryearsremembered.co.uk